JAZZ

A Regional Exploration

GREENWOOD GUIDES TO
AMERICAN ROOTS MUSIC

JAZZ

A Regional Exploration

Scott Yanow

Norm Cohen
Series Editor

GREENWOOD PRESS
Westport, Connecticut • London

Library of Congress Cataloging-in-Publication Data

Yanow, Scott.
    Jazz : a regional exploration / Scott Yanow.
      p. cm. – (Greenwood guides to American roots music, ISSN 1551-0271)
    Includes bibliographical references and index.
    Discography: p.
    ISBN 0-313-32871-4 (alk. paper)
    1. Jazz—History and criticism. I. Title. II. Series.
ML3508.Y39 2005
781.65'0973—dc22   2004018158

British Library Cataloguing in Publication Data is available.

Library of Congress Catalog Card Number: 2004018158
ISBN: 0-313-32871-4
ISSN: 1551-0271

First published in 2005

Greenwood Press, 88 Post Road West, Westport, CT 06881
An imprint of Greenwood Publishing Group, Inc.
www.greenwood.com

Printed in the United States of America

The paper used in this book complies with the
Permanent Paper Standard issued by the National
Information Standards Organization (Z39.48-1984).

10 9 8 7 6 5 4 3 2 1

Contents

Series Foreword

If present trends are any indication, soon anyone with access to the Internet will be able to tune in to music from any part of the world. When that happens, listeners may well find Kentucky bluegrass bands playing Tex-Mex music along with banjo tunes and gospel favorites, while musicians in India may intersperse elements of American rap music with their own native raga traditions.

It's difficult to predict right now, but even to understand the significance of this revolution requires an appreciation for the fact that until recently all musical genres, like every aspect of human activity, were associated with relatively compact geographic regions, bounded not only by national boundaries but also by the more limiting barriers of language, religion, geography, and cultural heritage. In the United States, regional boundaries might enclose an area as large as the vast Southwest or as small as the immediate environs of Galax, Virginia.

This series of musical studies seeks to describe American musical traditions that are, or once were, associated with geographic regions smaller than the nation as a whole. These musical varieties include jazz, blues, country music, Hispanic American music, Irish American music, polka music, Franco-American music (including Cajun and Zydeco), Native American music, and traditional folk music. Jazz music originated in New Orleans and other cities along the lower Mississippi River in the early 1900s, but by midcentury it was equally at home in New York and San Francisco as in New Orleans or Memphis. Jazz was in turn heavily influenced by blues music, an African American creation born in the broader regions of the Deep South.

Country music of recent decades is a merger of two regional Anglo-American musical traditions, one from the Appalachians and other southeastern states, and the other from the southwestern plains. Its earlier name of country-western music reflects more clearly that parentage. Irish American music, brought to these shores mainly in the 1840s and later by emigrants from the Ireland, flourished best in the big cities where the Irish made their new homes: Boston, New York, Philadelphia, and Chicago.

Hispanic (Latino, Tex Mex) music migrated north from Mexico and other Latin American countries. In the early 1900s it could be heard only in Texas, New Mexico, and California; a century later, Spanish language radio stations reach almost everywhere in the lower forty-eight. Polka music was brought to the New World by musicians from Central Europe—Germany, Switzerland, and what used to be Czechoslovakia. It was fruitfully transplanted to the Midwestern states from Texas north to Nebraska and the Dakotas.

The music of First Nations (Native Americans) was spread across the continent in varieties associated with particular groups of peoples, but as a result of ethnocentric federal policies that forced their relocation to "Indian Reservations," was subsequently located in regions that were often at great distances from the original homelands. Traditional folk music, the product of evolved music of European American and African American immigrants, had developed distinct regional characteristics in the New World by the eighteenth and nineteenth centuries, but as a result of internal, primarily western migrations, had changed considerably by the early twentieth century.

Four of these musical styles—jazz, blues, country, and traditional folk—are treated in separate volumes; the other "ethnic" traditions (Hispanic, Cajun/Zydeco, Polka, Irish, and Native American) are presented together in a fifth volume.

American music continues to evolve. Readers of these volumes can doubtless think of changes in music that have taken place in their own lifetimes. The many musical heritages of the nineteenth and twentieth centuries laid the foundations for today's music. The advent and growth of national media—radio, television, digital recordings, Internet—exert powerful forces on the nature of musical genres that were once regional. Ironically, national media permit two contradictory phenomena. At first, they introduce listeners to the regional musical forms that a wider audience otherwise might never have known about. Eventually, though, they provide the mechanism for the scrambling and cross-pollination of what were once distinct styles.

This does not mean that American musical regionalism is gone forever, doomed to a homogeneous culture that is the same in Key West, Florida, as in the San Juan Islands of Washington. If the past is any guide, new regional styles will continually emerge, gradually to become part of the national mix. As long as immigration to these shores continues, the influx of new musical styles will contribute to and invigorate the old. It is an exciting prospect.

Norm Cohen
Portland Community College, Oregon
Series Editor

Preface

Jazz enters people's lives many different ways. A lot of new listeners have come from rock and fusion, perhaps excited by the guitar playing of John McLaughlin or Al Di Meola, and wondered about the roots of their styles. Some have discovered jazz because they enjoyed the singing of Diana Krall, or maybe they arrived at jazz after starting out with the Latin music of Tito Puente or the r&b-oriented rhythm and jazz of David Sanborn. Because jazz is to a large extent underground music, it is not played on many radio stations, nor are its stars featured on *Entertainment Tonight*; one often has to go out of one's way to find it. Jazz is a very viable music, quite healthy artistically, constantly full of surprises, and well worth discovering, exploring, and savoring.

I first became interested in jazz when I was fifteen in 1970. In the previous year I had been listening to the rock hits of the era, but I was ready for something else. I noticed in the *Los Angeles Times* that there was a Dixieland jazz radio program on KRHM from 5 to 6 p.m. Monday through Friday, and since Dixieland is a very happy style, I thought I would see what it was about. Benson Curtis, the deejay, did a very good job presenting the music in an open and informative manner. Soon I was hooked, taping songs from the radio with my little cheap tape recorder. After a few months I discovered the syndicated radio series *Chuck Cecil's Swinging Years*, and I became interested in swing too.

At college I was considered a bit of an oddity because of my love for Dixieland, 1920s jazz, and swing. I heard the names of Charlie Parker and Dizzy Gillespie, but knew nothing about their music except that it seemed quite radical compared to swing. One day in a used record store, I saw a Charlie Parker LP on sale for $1.99. I did not recognize most of the tunes ("Groovin' High," "A Night in Tunisia," and "Cool Blues" among them) but did know one song, "White Christmas." I listened to the album two or three times a day for a week, not caring for it much at first but determined to understand and appreciate it. About the fifth day, the doors opened, and I was able to enter the world of bebop. Within a short time I moved into all eras of jazz including the avant-garde (late period John Coltrane) and fusion such as Miles Davis' *Live/Evil* album. Now I was considered odd among my fellow students because my music was too radical.

I have not been bored since, except during the rare moments when I have been away from jazz. Jazz is a vast world, but one often missed by Americans. This book introduces the rich, democratic, and exciting music in all of its styles to open-minded listeners. One warning though: Jazz is very addictive!

There are many eras and styles of jazz, and although it is often portrayed as an art form, listeners should never let that statement scare them away. A person does not need a music degree to appreciate the music, and because of its many overlapping styles, chances are that most listeners who are exposed to the music will find some artists that they enjoy. Although usually performed at concerts or sit-down clubs, much of the music is actually quite danceable. Some fans emphasize its intellectual qualities, but the music is also often emotional, soulful, and catchy. What could be more exciting than listening to a musician or singer creating new music? Jazz can seem a bit forbidding to new listeners because there is an endless number of musicians, styles, and pieces; sometimes it is very difficult to know where to start. This book focuses on the music's development that resulted in different styles and approaches to jazz improvisation being created in different cities and areas of the country. While all of the major innovators are mentioned, keep in mind that there have been literally thousands of talented musicians who have their own identities in jazz and are well worth hearing. It is an endless world of music, one that every listener should experience.

I wish to thank the leading jazz journalists who in their articles, essays, reviews, and interviews have helped to educate me through the years. These include Leonard Feather, Nat Hentoff, Ralph Gleason, Stanley Dance, Ira Gitler, Dan Morgenstern, Phil Ellwood, Gary Giddins, and the masterful Whitney Balliett. Also deserving thanks from all of us are the countless musicians who chose (or felt they were chosen) to play jazz as opposed to more potentially lucrative styles of music. I wish to dedicate this book to my wife Kathy and daughter Melody for their love, patience, and understanding.

Chronology

1895	Buddy Bolden forms his first band, an event that serves as the symbolic beginning of jazz.
1897	William Krell's "Mississippi Rag" and Tom Turpin's "Harlem Rag" are the first ragtime pieces to be published.
1899	Scott Joplin's "Maple Leaf Rag" is published. Duke Ellington is born.
1900	"Maple Leaf Rag" becomes a major hit, sparking the ragtime craze.
1901	Louis Armstrong is born.
1902	Scott Joplin composes "The Entertainer," "The Ragtime Dance," and "Elite Syncopations."
1903	W. C. Handy hears a street performer singing the blues for the first time.
1906	Freddie Keppard forms the Olympia Orchestra.
1907	Buddy Bolden is committed to Jackson Mental Institution.
1909	Bassist Bill Johnson takes New Orleans jazz to California.
1910	Oscar Celestin forms the Tuxedo Band.
1911	Scott Joplin composes *Treemonisha*.
1912	W. C. Handy publishes the "Memphis Blues."

1913   James Reese Europe's Society Orchestra makes its first recordings.

1914   W. C. Handy composes "St. Louis Blues."

1915   Jelly Roll Morton plays jazz in San Francisco.

1916   Freddie Keppard turns down a chance to be the first jazzman to record, feeling that other musicians would steal his stuff. Jazz catches on in Chicago due to the success of Johnny Stein's Jazz Band and its successor, the Original Dixieland Jazz Band (ODJB).

1917   The Original Dixieland Jazz Band is the first jazz group to record, causing a sensation with their recording of "Livery Stable Blues" and their nightly performances in New York. Scott Joplin dies, and Dizzy Gillespie is born.

1918   Paul Whiteman forms his orchestra.

1919   The ODJB is a big hit in Europe, as is Will Marion Cook's Southern Syncopated Orchestra with Sidney Bechet.

1920   Mamie Smith's recording of "Crazy Blues" starts a blues craze. Paul Whiteman's band catches on in New York. Charlie Parker is born.

1921   Alberta Hunter, James P. Johnson, Fletcher Henderson, Ethel Waters, and Clarence Williams all make their first recordings.

1922   The New Orleans Rhythm Kings' recordings set the pace for jazz.

1923   King Oliver's Creole Jazz Band becomes the most important band in jazz, playing in Chicago and documenting classic performances. Oliver, Jelly Roll Morton, Louis Armstrong, Johnny Dodds, Bessie Smith, and Sidney Bechet are among those appearing on record for the first time. James P. Johnson writes "The Charleston."

1924   Louis Armstrong moves to New York and joins Fletcher Henderson's orchestra. Bix Beiderbecke records with the Wolverines, and George Gershwin debuts *Rhapsody in Blue* with the Paul Whiteman Orchestra. Duke Ellington's Washingtonians make their first recordings.

1925   Louis Armstrong returns to Chicago where he begins his famous string of Hot Five recordings.

1926   Coleman Hawkins records "The Stampede," the first important tenor-sax solo. Jelly Roll Morton's Red Hot Peppers record for Victor. Miles Davis and John Coltrane are born. Louis Armstrong's "Heebie Jeebies" popularizes scat-singing.

1927   Louis Armstrong's Hot Five and Hot Seven recordings include "Struttin' with Some Barbecue" and "Potato Head Blues." Bix Beiderbecke records with Frank Trumbauer (including "Singin' the Blues") and joins Paul Whiteman. The McKenzie-Condon Chicagoans introduce Chicago jazz. Duke Ellington's orchestra becomes the house band at the Cotton Club.

1928   Louis Armstrong and Earl Hines create musical magic, especially on "West End Blues" and "Weather Bird." Johnny Hodges joins Duke Ellington's orchestra.

1929   Bix Beiderbecke leaves Paul Whiteman. Louis Armstrong moves to New York and begins recording with big bands. Bessie Smith records "Nobody Knows You When You're Down and Out."

1930   The Boswell Sisters and Cab Calloway make their first recordings. "The Peanut Vendor" becomes a hit years before Latin jazz catches on.

1931   The Depression results in King Oliver and Jelly Roll Morton losing their recording contracts as the record industry shrinks. Bix Beiderbecke and Buddy Bolden die. Cab Calloway's "Minnie the Moocher" is a big hit.

1932   Louis Armstrong is a big attraction in Europe. Duke Ellington records "It Don't Mean a Thing If It Ain't Got That Swing" three years before the swing era starts.

1933   Duke Ellington visits Europe. Bessie Smith makes her last recordings, while Billie Holiday makes her first ones. Django Reinhardt and Stephane Grappelli form the Quintet of the Hot Club of France.

1934   Fats Waller, Louis Prima, and Wingy Manone all start recording a series of popular small-group swing sessions. Benny Goodman's big band appears regularly on the *Let's Dance* radio series. *Downbeat* publishes its first issues.

1935   Benny Goodman's band makes it big playing at the Palomar Ballroom in Los Angeles, starting the swing era. Ella Fitzgerald joins Chick Webb. Fifty-second Street in New York begins to develop into Swing Street.

1936   Count Basie's orchestra is discovered and travels east. Many new big bands are formed due to the success of Benny Goodman.

1937   Lester Young and Buck Clayton start recording with Billie Holiday. Tommy Dorsey and Bunny Berigan have hit records, and Harry James joins Benny Goodman's band.

1938   Benny Goodman's Carnegie Hall concert is a highpoint for the swing era. Artie Shaw records "Begin the Beguine," and his orchestra becomes world famous. John Hammond's From Spirituals to Swing concert makes boogie-woogie popular.

1939   Glenn Miller's orchestra starts its string of major hits, becoming the most beloved big band of the swing era. Charlie Christian, while with Benny Goodman, helps to popularize the electric guitar.

1940   Duke Ellington's band, with new members Ben Webster, Jimmy Blanton, and Billy Strayhorn, records one classic after another. The

King Cole Trio has its first hit with "Sweet Lorraine." Charlie Parker plays in New York with Jay McShann's orchestra.

1941   Harry James' band competes with Glenn Miller's for popularity. The swing era is at its height, shortly before the attack on Pearl Harbor.

1942   World War II results in several bandleaders, including Glenn Miller, Bob Crosby, and Claude Thornhill, breaking up their bands to enlist in the military. Lionel Hampton's "Flying Home" (with Illinois Jacquet) leads to rhythm and blues. The Musicians Union recording strike stops all recordings by August 1.

1943   Duke Ellington performs at Carnegie Hall, debuting "Black, Brown and Beige." Earl Hines' big band features Charlie Parker, Dizzy Gillespie, and Sarah Vaughan, but the recording strike means that the band is completely undocumented.

1944   The recording strike comes to an end. Coleman Hawkins leads the first bebop record date, and the Billy Eckstine Orchestra helps to introduce bop. Glenn Miller dies. The first Jazz at the Philharmonic concert takes place and is recorded.

1945   The recordings of Charlie Parker and Dizzy Gillespie first shock then change the jazz world. Harry James has a hit with "It's Been a Long Long Time," but the swing era begins to end as bebop takes over jazz.

1946   Dizzy Gillespie forms his big band, while the orchestras of Benny Goodman, Harry James, Jack Teagarden, and Woody Herman (the First Herd) break up. Gil Evans contributes boppish arrangements to Claude Thornhill's orchestra.

1947   Charlie Parker's quintet features Miles Davis. Chano Pozo becomes a member of the Dizzy Gillespie big band. Thelonious Monk leads his first record dates. Louis Armstrong breaks up his big band and forms the Louis Armstrong All-Stars with Jack Teagarden and Barney Bigard.

Woody Herman's Second Herd records "Four Brothers."

1948   A second Musicians Union recording strike lasts for much of the year, but Charlie Parker records "Parker's Mood" anyway. The Miles Davis Nonet works at the Royal Roost.

1949   Charlie Parker records with strings, the Miles Davis Nonet makes some of its famous "Birth of the Cool" recordings, and the Lennie Tristano Sextet records its most influential selections including two free improvisations. Many former swing big bands turn temporarily to bebop. Count Basie breaks up his orchestra. The George Shearing Quintet is formed.

1950   Stan Kenton leads his Innovations Orchestra. Sonny Stitt and Gene Ammons co-lead a quintet. Horace Silver joins Stan Getz's quartet. Dizzy Gillespie breaks up his big band.

1951   The Dave Brubeck Quartet with Paul Desmond is formed. Sidney Bechet moves to France where he becomes nationally famous.

1952   Cool jazz catches on, especially the Gerry Mulligan Quartet with Chet Baker. The Oscar Peterson Trio starts to tour, Howard Rumsey's Lighthouse All-Stars become popular, and King Pleasure records "Moody's Mood for Love." Count Basie forms a new big band.

1953   Chet Baker leads a quartet featuring pianist Russ Freeman. Laurindo Almeida and Bud Shank record "Brazilliance." Buck Clayton begins his series of recorded mainstream jam sessions.

1954   Hard bop has its first great band in the Clifford Brown/Max Roach Quintet. George Wein founds the Newport Jazz Festival. Miles Davis records "Walkin'."

1955   Art Blakey's Jazz Messengers and the Chico Hamilton Quintet are formed. Miles Davis puts together his first classic quintet with John Coltrane, Red Garland, Paul Chambers, and Philly Joe Jones. Gunther Schuller and John Lewis found the Jazz and Classical Music Society. Charlie Parker dies.

1956   Horace Silver puts together his quintet. Dizzy Gillespie leads a new big band. Clifford Brown dies in a car accident. Duke Ellington becomes the hit of the Newport Jazz Festival thanks to Paul Gonsalves' lengthy solo on "Diminuendo and Crescendo in Blue."

1957   Miles Davis records "Miles Ahead" with the Gil Evans Orchestra. John Coltrane is part of the Thelonious Monk Quartet. Lambert, Hendricks, and Ross debut.

1958   Miles Davis leads a remarkable sextet that includes John Coltrane, Cannonball Adderley, and Bill Evans. Ornette Coleman makes his first recordings. Bossa nova is introduced in Brazil. Lee Morgan joins Art Blakey's Jazz Messengers.

1959   The Ornette Coleman Quartet moves to New York and plays at the Five Spot. Miles Davis' "Kind of Blue" and John Coltrane's "Giant Steps" are historic recordings, as are Dave Brubeck's "Take Five" and Cannonball Adderley's "This Here." Billie Holiday and Lester Young die.

1960   John Coltrane forms his own quartet. Archie Shepp records with Cecil Taylor. The Ornette Coleman Double Quartet records Free Jazz. The Jazztet features Art Farmer and Benny Golson.

1961   Freddie Hubbard joins the Jazz Messengers. Preservation Hall opens in New Orleans. Eric Dolphy plays with the John Coltrane Quintet.

1962   Stan Getz and Charlie Byrd cut a hit recording of "Desafinado" on their bossa nova album *Jazz Samba*. Benny Goodman tours the Soviet Union with a big band. John Coltrane and Duke Ellington record together.

1963   Miles Davis forms a new quintet with George Coleman, Herbie Hancock, Ron Carter, and Tony Williams. Stan Getz, Antonio Carlos Jobim, and Joao and Astrud Gilberto record "The Girl from Ipanema."

1964   The John Coltrane Quartet records A *Love Supreme*, and Lee Morgan has a hit with "The Sidewinder." Wayne Shorter joins the Miles Davis Quintet in Coleman's place. Louis Armstrong records "Hello Dolly."

1965   John Coltrane and his expanded group record "Ascension." Ornette Coleman leads a trio with David Izenzon and Charles Moffett. The Association for the Advancement of Creative Musicians (AACM) is formed in Chicago.

1966   Cannonball Adderley records "Mercy, Mercy, Mercy." John Coltrane leads a quintet with Pharoah Sanders. The Art Ensemble of Chicago (originally known as just The Art Ensemble) plays its first concerts.

1967   John Coltrane dies. Chucho Valdes, Paquito D'Rivera, and Arturo Sandoval help form the Orquesta Cubana de Musica Moderna in Cuba. The Dave Brubeck Quartet breaks up.

1968   Eubie Blake, the last link to the ragtime era, is rediscovered. Dave Brubeck leads a new quartet with Gerry Mulligan. Anthony Braxton makes his first recordings.

1969   Miles Davis' recordings of "In a Silent Way" and "Bitches Brew" help start the fusion years. Tony Williams puts together Lifetime. Les McCann and Eddie Harris are the hit of the Montreux Jazz Festival.

1970   Weather Report is formed by Joe Zawinul and Wayne Shorter. Freddie Hubbard records *Red Clay* and *Straight Life* for CTI. Radio Free Jazz is founded by Ira Sabin; it would later be renamed Jazz Times.

1971   Chick Corea teams up with Stanley Clarke, Joe Farrell, Airto and Flora Purim in Return to Forever. John McLaughlin forms the Mahavishnu Orchestra. Louis Armstrong dies.

1972   The Newport Jazz Festival moves successfully to New York City. Sonny Rollins ends a six-year retirement.

1973   The second version of Return to Forever is comprised of Chick Corea, Stanley Clarke, Lenny White, and Bill Connors. Herbie Hancock leads the Headhunters and has a hit with "Chameleon." Irakere is formed in Cuba. Joe Pass records "Virtuoso."

1974   Scott Joplin's "The Entertainer" becomes a pop hit. The Sacramento Jazz Jubilee, the top trad and Dixieland festival, debuts. Duke Ellington dies. Al DiMeola becomes a member of Return to Forever. Chet Baker begins his successful comeback.

1975   Ornette Coleman forms Prime Time. Miles Davis retires. John Klemmer has a pop/jazz hit with "Touch." Pat Metheny records *Bright Size Life* with Jaco Pastorius and drummer Bob Moses.

1976   Jaco Pastorius joins Weather Report. The World Saxophone Quartet is formed. Spyro Gyra has its recording debut. Return to Forever breaks up. George Benson has a big hit with "This Masquerade" that leads to him emphasizing his vocals over his guitar in the future. The jazz magazine *Cadence* starts up. Dexter Gordon returns to the United States.

1977   The third version of Return to Forever only lasts a few months. Avant-gardist Vinny Golia starts the Nine Winds label. Scott Hamilton makes his recording debut. Eighty-two-year-old Alberta Hunter makes a comeback. Keith Jarrett and Jan Garbarek record *My Song.* Chuck Mangione's "Feels So Good" is on the pop charts.

1978   Benny Goodman is featured at his fortieth anniversary Carnegie Hall concert. Marian McPartland's *Piano Jazz* radio series first airs. The Pat Metheny Group (with keyboardist Lyle Mays) makes its initial recording.

1979   Jack DeJohnette's Special Edition features David Murray. Jerry Bergonzi is a member of the Dave Brubeck Quartet.

1980   Wynton Marsalis joins Art Blakey's Jazz Messengers. Paquito D'Rivera defects to the United States from Cuba. Teenage guitarist Bireli Lagrene debuts, sounding like Django Reinhardt. Grover Washington Jr. records *Winelight.*

1981   After six years off the scene, Miles Davis begins his comeback. Banu Gibson forms her hot jazz band in New Orleans. Wynton Marsalis signs with Columbia and quickly becomes the leader of the Young Lions movement.

1982   Terence Blanchard succeeds Wynton Marsalis with the Jazz Messengers. Poncho Sanchez forms his Latin jazz band. An appearance on a television jazz special leads to Diane Schuur becoming a star.

1983   Eubie Blake dies five days after his one hundredth birthday. Keith Jarrett forms a "standards" trio with bassist Gary Peacock and drummer Jack DeJohnette. Mel Torme begins recording for Concord, resulting in the finest work of his career.

1984   Count Basie dies. Guitarist Stanley Jordan signs with Blue Note and displays his remarkable tapping technique. Bobby McFerrin records *The Voice.*

1985   The M-Base movement spearheaded by Steve Coleman begins to be documented on records. Dexter Gordon stars in the film *Round Midnight.* Wynton and Branford Marsalis record *Black Codes from the*

Underground. Pat Metheny records with Ornette Coleman. Weather Report breaks up.

1986   Chick Corea forms the Elektric Band. Eddie Daniels records "Breakthrough." Kenny G's *Duotones* is a giant hit in the contemporary jazz world. Woody Herman celebrates his fiftieth year as a bandleader, one year before his death.

1987   After years in the studios and with the Brecker Brothers, Michael Brecker begins his solo career. Harry Connick Jr. begins to be noticed. The Rippingtons become a strong attraction in the pop/jazz world. The Knitting Factory opens in New York.

1988   Chet Baker falls or is pushed out of a second-story window to his death. The fiery saxophonist Charles Gayle makes his first records. The Harper Brothers is formed. *Carmen Sings Monk* is one of Carmen McRae's finest recordings.

1989   With his recording debut, Joey DeFrancesco's rise to prominence helps the organ make a comeback. The formation of the Royal Crown Revue leads to the retro swing movement in the 1990s. Bela Fleck, the world's only fusion banjoist, forms the Flecktones.

1990   Art Blakey dies. Teenage altoist Chris Potter is a member of the Red Rodney Quintet. Arturo Sandoval defects from Cuba, settling in the United States.

1991   Jane Bunnett records *Spirits of Havana.* Miles Davis dies. Joe Henderson records a Billy Strayhorn tribute album, *Lush Life*, that gets a great deal of attention. An all-star group of Young Lions called Jazz Futures tours and records. The Mingus Big Band is formed.

1992   Tenor-saxophonist Eric Alexander has his recording debut. Bill Frisell records *Have a Little Faith.* Medeski, Martin & Wood is formed, predating the jam band movement by several years.

1993   Dave Douglas, James Carter, Joshua Redman, and Diana Krall all have their recording debuts as leaders. Dizzy Gillespie dies. Cassandra Wilson records *Blue Light Till Dawn.*

1994   Trumpeters Nicholas Payton and Ingrid Jensen are the newest young trumpet stars, making their first recordings as leaders. Joe Lovano's *Rush Hour* is one of the year's best CDs.

1995   Kurt Elling records his first album for Blue Note and becomes the leading voice among younger male jazz singers. Brad Mehldau also makes his debut as a leader.

1996   At the age of ninety-one, Doc Cheatham holds his own with twenty-three-year-old Nicholas Payton on a swing-oriented record date. Chick Corea tours with his "Tribute to Bud Powell" band, a short-lived group also featuring Wallace Roney, Kenny Garrett, and Joshua Redman.

1997   Benny Carter, still in his musical prime, retires at the age of ninety. Wynton Marsalis' *Blood on the Fields* wins a Pulitzer Prize. Jason Moran works with Greg Osby's quartet. John Scofield records with Medeski, Martin & Wood.

1998   The Dave Holland Quintet with Chris Potter and trombonist Robin Eubanks records *Prime Directive*.

1999   Wynton Marsalis releases a remarkable number of CDs on Sony/Columbia, including a superb seven-CD set *Live at the Village Vanguard*. Chick Corea leads a new sextet, Origin.

2000   The Roy Hargrove Quintet features altoist Sherman Irby. Jane Monheit records her first CD.

2001   Dave Douglas records *Witness*. The definitive Latin jazz film *Calle 54* is released.

2002   Herbie Hancock, Michael Brecker, and Roy Hargrove tour together in a quintet. Wayne Shorter leads a quartet also featuring Danilo Perez, John Patitucci, and drummer Brian Blade. Diana Krall records *Live in Paris*.

2003   Kurt Elling forms Four Brothers, a vocal group with Jon Hendricks, Mark Murphy, and Kevin Mahogany. After missing from jazz and presumed dead since 1967, bassist Henry Grimes is discovered living in Los Angeles; he soon makes a comeback. The Pete Jolly Trio (with bassist Chuck Berghofer and drummer Nick Martinis) marks its fortieth year together.

2004   The Newport Jazz Festival celebrates its fiftieth anniversary. Jazz is alive and well 109 years after Buddy Bolden's debut.

Introduction

Jazz is one of the most exciting genres of music ever created. It is a music that emphasizes self-expression without overlooking teamwork, creativity and chance taking, and breaking the rules once the rules have been mastered. Unlike classical music which is written out, or pop music whose goal is often to recreate recordings at concerts, jazz is about spontaneity and improvisation; making up ideas on the spot.

Jazz has been in its golden age since 1920, and it shows no sign of decline. Many jazz books make the mistake of glorifying the music's past while overlooking jazz of the present. It is true that jazz evolved very quickly during the period from 1920 to 1975, and its evolution has become more complex since then, going in many different directions simultaneously, rather than following one dominant path. It is always moving forward, however, with fresh, new ideas and colorful voices.

This book differs from other jazz history books in its emphasis on the regional aspects that were so important in the evolution of jazz. Before mass communication made events in one part of the world known immediately to listeners everywhere, a musical style was often created in a specific geographical area that then became its home base and main breeding ground before spreading elsewhere. The West Coast cool jazz versus East Coast hard bop debates of the 1950s are a very good example of regionalism, not to mention the styles that developed in New Orleans and Kansas City.

WHAT IS JAZZ?

In the early days of jazz history, because there were only one or two styles, it was easier to define and make general statements about rhythm, harmony, melody, the type of instruments used, and the music's feel. Now jazz has been in existence for over a hundred years and has evolved steadily in many different directions, so it is much more difficult to specify the qualities of music that make up jazz. As soon as someone comes up with a list of restrictions and rules, innovative players will find a way to reinvent the music, making the definition obsolete.

Perhaps the best way to answer the question, What is jazz? is by asking a different question: What do the many styles of jazz, from New Orleans jazz and swing to bebop, free improvisations, fusion, and today's many idioms, have in common? In other words, what makes these types of music jazz?

There are only two qualities common to all styles of jazz that make jazz stand apart from other types of music. It is not rhythm, for rock, county, and pop all use rhythms; and some styles of jazz (particularly free improvisations) are occasionally played without rhythms at all. It is not superb musicianship or even being in tune, nor is it the repertoire or instrumentation. For music to be jazz, it should emphasize improvisation and always have the feeling of the blues. Improvisation can be thought of as making things up as the music goes along. Jazz continually changes, and many times a group's live performance of a particular song will differ drastically from its recording. Even musicians who utilize tight arrangements will make subtle changes in their phrasing and solos, for the goal is to be constantly creative. In the early days of jazz, the improvising was generally done by a full group, shifting during the 1920s toward soloists. Improvisation, one of the most exciting aspects of any jazz style, allows listeners to hear artists create in public, and even the musicians do not always know what the results will be.

Improvisation alone is not enough to make music jazz, for early classical music, Indian ragas, bluegrass, and rock all use improvisation. The second quality that appears in jazz performances is the feeling of the blues, even when it is very subtle or abstract. "The feeling of the blues" does not refer to the technical blues structure, but the idea of communicating by bending notes (never done in classical music) and developing an individual speechlike style. When someone speaks through his or her instrument or voice in a creative and spontaneous fashion, chances are it is jazz.

There have always been many performances that straddle the boundaries between jazz and other styles of music, and it's possible to get a bit carried away debating whether something is jazz or not. Jazz is always borrowing from other idioms, transforming the music and expanding it in unpredictable ways, while some pop music groups use a little bit of jazz as a flavor. When trying to decide whether a certain recording or performance is jazz, it is best to look at the overall picture.

Ultimately what matters much less than whether or not something is jazz is whether it is enjoyable, well played, and memorable. That evaluation is up to each listener.

THE PREHISTORY OF JAZZ

Although it is often said that jazz originally came from Africa, drummer Art Blakey visited Africa in 1949 and was disappointed that he could not find much that he considered jazz there. What was brought rather reluctantly from Africa to North America by captured slaves were rhythms and the idea of improvisation. Playing homemade drums and percussion was a major part of African musical culture. The polyrhythms (layering of multiple rhythms) created by Africans were unprecedented in Western music.

Starting in the 1500s Africans were imprisoned by Europeans and brought to North America to provide very inexpensive labor, and there were over 400,000 slaves imported by the early 1800s. The slaves were usually forbidden to play drums that had been used as a means of tribal communication, but the legacy of the drums lived on, particularly since new generations of slaves were brought to the United States as late as the 1850s and thus retained the traditional forms after emancipation. Although slaves were not allowed to play instruments, they were permitted to sing while engaged in fieldwork, particularly when it was realized that the expression of emotions increased their productivity. Their singing was considered strange and exotic, but relatively harmless. These "field hollers" had the two ingredients that would become vital to jazz: improvisation (as new lyrics were constantly being invented) and the feeling of the blues. The slaves bent and sang between notes, adding to the emotional intensity of the music. Field hollers were a major form of work songs, vocal music performed by oppressed people while at work.

In the 1700s and 1800s, white Americans were constantly trying to come up with ways to tame the black African slaves so they would be calm and productive, mainly by converting them to Christianity. While the whites were affecting the blacks' feelings about God, the slaves gradually formed their own brand of church music. By utilizing call and response (with the congregation answering the preacher rather than just singing in unison) and bending notes to express emotions and ad-libbing, the music became much more powerful and infectious. Whites could not really complain since the blacks were dedicating themselves to God, but they were often quite bewildered by how the simplest little hymn was turned into a very passionate religious work. Over time, blacks developed their own religious songs that were called spirituals. They were similar to field hollers except that the message always dealt with God. Spirituals were the predecessor to gospel music, just as field hollers preceded blues.

During the late nineteenth century, an era when radio did not exist and the recording industry was just starting, the popular music of the day comprised traditional hymns, themes from classical music that could be played by local bands, and sentimental ballads and novelties that were published as sheet music. In the 1840s minstrel shows began to proliferate in the South. These low-budget productions originally featured whites performing both music and comedy inspired by black slaves, often in crude and satirical ways with the performers wearing blackface. After the Civil War freed the slaves, African American minstrel shows became popular, with black performers essentially satirizing whites satirizing blacks. The music tended to be more creative in the black shows than the white ones. The clichéd humor, rampant racism, and use of outrageous stereotypes would be barely watchable by today's standards, but at the time, for those performers who could survive the crude working conditions, the minstrel show offered travel, a bit of excitement, and an opportunity to grow musically. It brought entertainment to small rural towns in the South, helped build the popularity of new songs (including those of songwriter Stephen Foster), and gave singers, dancers, and musicians a chance to have a more exciting life than working in the field. By the early 1900s some jazz musicians were employed in minstrel shows along with pioneering blues singers. Competition from vaudeville, jazz, and movies (along with some gradually enlightened views on racism) doomed the minstrel show, although it still survived on a lower level into the 1950s.

The blues, an important element of jazz, has an origin buried in legend. It was a natural outgrowth of the work song and field hollers but performed on street corners, at parties, and at functions rather than at work. Unlike the field hollers that were sung a capella, bluesmen (few women were involved in the early days) generally accompanied themselves with a guitar or banjo. Although the blues, a common form of music throughout the South, was largely unrecorded until 1920 (other than some slightly earlier jazz band instrumentals and a few rarities from vaudevillians), it was an early influence on jazz, particularly in its use of bent notes and sliding between notes.

The irony of the blues is that the word means both a sad feeling (having the blues); and a style of music that is meant to dispel the blues and make listeners happy, even when the subject matter deals with the singer's bad luck. The chord changes of the standard twelve-bar blues, which in the key of C could be simplified to be four bars of C, two of F, two of C, two of G, and the final two in C, are used frequently in jazz at every possible tempo, and the blues have been part of jazz since its beginning. Early country blues performers, who differ from the city blues singers, often varied the length of their choruses unpredictably, depending on how it fit the song and their mood. This method works best when playing unaccompanied rather than in groups.

Although Mamie Smith's "Crazy Blues" in 1920 was the first lowdown vocal blues recording, Ma Rainey was singing blues songs at least as early as 1902. W. C. Handy, who worked for years as a teacher and as a cornetist with minstrel shows, later wrote that in 1903 at a train station he observed a guitarist playing his instrument with a knife and singing the blues, something he had never heard before. Handy was inspired to search out street performers and write down some of the melodies and lyrics that he heard. Their ideas became the inspiration for his own pieces including his 1909 "Mr. Crump," which later became "Memphis Blues," his 1914 "St. Louis Blues," and his 1916 "Beale Street Blues," "The Yellow Dog Blues," "Ole Miss," "Loveless (or Careless) Love," and "Atlanta Blues," also known as "Make Me a Pallet on the Floor."

Other influences on early jazz included concert bands, 1890s' popular melodies, waltzes, marches, and music used in vaudeville, Broadway shows, and theaters.

THE PROBLEMS WITH TRACING PRE-1917 JAZZ

One of the most basic questions about jazz is, How and when did it start? The first jazz recordings were made in 1917, but the music existed at least twenty years earlier. Virtually nothing was written about jazz during that shadowy period, and the influence of jazz was nearly nonexistent on early popular recordings. Significant interviews were not conducted with the surviving pioneers of jazz until the 1930s at the earliest, and by then their memories of events from the previous thirty to forty years were understandably foggy, contradictory, and incomplete.

Because jazz in its earliest days was primarily played by blacks in New Orleans and a few rural areas in the southern part of the United States, it received virtually no publicity in the white press and was thought of as a small part of the entertainment world, when it was thought of at all. In fact, the name "jazz" was not even used prior to 1916.

A few things are clear about jazz during the period prior to its documentation. Like the United States (a country founded and constantly invigorated by immigrants), jazz was a melting pot, combining aspects from very different musical forms, which means that it probably could not have been formed anywhere but in the United States. In its earliest days the unnamed jazz music was part of everyday life in selected areas of the South (particularly New Orleans) rather than being thought of as concert music or an art form. From its start, jazz was less about following rules and maintaining the status quo than it was about finding a unique voice and adding new ideas to its legacy.

Cornetist Buddy Bolden's first band in 1895 is the symbolic start of jazz, but the lack of recordings means that there really is no way to know how his group sounded or if there were earlier jazz groups. Nevertheless, this book begins with a discussion of some of the many different areas of music that contributed to the beginnings of jazz.

1

Sedalia and St. Louis: Ragtime

WHAT IS RAGTIME?

Ragtime was the first African American music to catch on, and it could be considered America's first nationwide musical craze. During its prime from 1899 to 1915, ragtime's popularity was measured not in record sales (the recording industry was still in its infancy), but in sheet music sales. During an era that was long before radio, the main form of family musical entertainment centered on the piano. As Ted Gioia notes in his book, *The History of Jazz*, the number of pianos built annually in the United States grew from 100,000 in 1890 to 350,000 in 1909. Even households that did not have a pianist in the family often had a piano in case friends dropped by, or perhaps they invested in a new invention called a player piano (first widely available in 1897) that made it possible for rags and popular songs to be heard at home.

Although some jazz history books claim that ragtime preceded and directly evolved into jazz, it was actually a contemporary of early jazz, and stands apart as a different style of music altogether, despite its influence. Classic ragtime is written out like classical music and generally utilizes the structure A-A-B-B-A-C-C-D-D, with each of the letters representing a melodic theme. There is no blues feeling in ragtime, and improvisation was frowned upon, at least at band concerts and straight renditions of rags. Influenced by both marching band and classical music, even in its early days the form had its own catchy syncopations and "ragged" rhythms, leading to the term ragtime. Its greatest composers considered ragtime to be an art form in the years before the as yet unnamed jazz music was known beyond the South, and it was seen by some of its main supporters as the American alternative to European classical music.

SEDALIA AND ST. LOUIS: THE RAGTIME YEARS

The genesis of ragtime was in the unrecorded and undocumented playing of working pianists during the mid- to late 1800s. These musicians operated as one-man bands, performing at bars, establishments, and parties, often "ragging" popular melodies by using syncopated rhythms. By the time the music solidified in 1897, the centers of ragtime were Sedalia, Missouri, where Scott Joplin lived, and St. Louis, the home of such ragtime composers as Tom Turpin, Louis Chauvin, and Artie Matthews. In addition, nearby Carthage was where the up-and-coming composer James Scott resided, so for the first time in its history Missouri was the home for a major musical style.

Of all the ragtime composers, Scott Joplin towered over the rest. He was born in Texarkana, Texas, where his father played violin and his mother was a banjoist. Joplin learned the piano early and was a professional pianist as a teenager. In time he became a teacher and sang with a quintet, but it was as a composer that Joplin made his mark. In the mid-1880s he moved to St. Louis, working as a soloist in bars and with bands. At the 1893 World's Fair in Chicago, early ragtime was performed, and Joplin was quite impressed. He settled in Sedalia the following year, studied harmony and composition, and began to compose seriously. Within two years his works were published by John Stark, who became one of his major champions.

Joplin wrote regular songs, marches, and waltzes, but his rags were most popular. During the late 1890s he often worked at the Maple Leaf Club in Sedalia, and the establishment lent its name to his 1897 composition "Maple Leaf Rag," which was destined to become the most famous of all the rags. Published in 1899, it only sold 400 copies of sheet music the first year but then became a giant hit in 1900, essentially launching the ragtime era; in time it sold over a million copies of sheet music.

Joplin became known as "The King of Ragtime" due to the high quality of his compositions, his productivity, the fact that his pieces solidified and defined what classic rags were, and because of "Maple Leaf Rag." He was not the first ragtime composer, since he had been preceded in 1897 by the publication of William Krell's "Mississippi Rag" and Tom Turpin's "Harlem Rag," but he was its biggest success story and most famous celebrity. Ragtime caught on fast in the late 1890s: twenty rags were published in 1897, two years later 120 came out, and Joplin was a large part of the reason.

Sedalia, a small Midwestern town, may seem an odd place to be the center of a major music style; but ragtime, unlike jazz, is as much a composer's art form as a forum for performers. Joplin enjoyed the quiet city and found the time to write many of his most famous rags there. In 1901, however, after John Stark had moved to St. Louis, Joplin also relocated, becoming part of that city's ragtime community. During his St. Louis period, Joplin evolved, writing such rags as "The Ragtime Dance," "The Entertainer," "The Easy Winners," "Elite Syncopations," and "Solace," using a tango rhythm on the last. He was the main inspiration for most of the younger ragtime composers, including James Scott and Joseph Lamb, the latter a talented white composer from New Jersey.

A serious and distinguished man, Joplin wanted his rags to be played as written and not at flashy tempos. He considered ragtime to be art music, and he sought to uplift ragtime from being thought of as bordello and bar music into an art form comparable to Western classical music. In 1903 he wrote the first ragtime opera, *A Guest of Honor*, about Booker T. Washington's 1901 dinner at the White House with President Theodore Roosevelt. Joplin formed an opera company and went on a tour of the Midwest, but it was somewhat disastrous. Someone stole the box office receipts at one point, the show was largely ignored by the press, and after a few weeks Joplin was unable to pay the performers. All of his possessions were confiscated, most notably the music from the opera, which was lost forever. Joplin had better luck with his more conventional pieces, writing "Cascades" for the 1904 St. Louis World's Fair, an event that frequently featured performances by ragtime pianists.

An establishment owned by Tom Turpin called the Rosebud Bar became a major hangout for ragtime pianists and composers in St. Louis during the prime years. Turpin only wrote five rags in his life, but he was an important force in the music, encouraging pianists and hosting jam sessions that gave up-and-coming musicians such as Joe Jordan, Louis Chauvin, and Charlie Warfield an opportunity to show their stuff.

While it lasted, ragtime attracted many composers. In addition to the big three (Joplin, Scott, and Lamb), the major ragtime composers of the classic era included Artie Matthews, Eubie Blake, Charles Hunter, Tony Jackson, Arthur Marshall, and Euday Bowman who wrote "Twelfth Street Rag." Other than Blake, few of the composers ever recorded. There are no recordings of Scott Joplin (though he did cut a few player-piano rolls), or of the man considered the number two ragtime composer, James Scott. Very few solo pianists recorded before 1917, although banjoists Fred Van Eps and Vess Ossman cut some rags, as did some military bands.

For a period ragtime seemed to be everywhere, spreading beyond Missouri to the rest of the nation. Rags were added to the repertoire of the orchestras of John Philip Sousa and Arthur Pryor and of local ensembles that played band concerts. As with all styles of music that suddenly and unexpectedly catch on, however, businessmen who cared little about art and music managed to turn it into a fad. By 1910 many popular songs were being called rags even though they had no real relation to ragtime. Irving Berlin's early hit "Alexander's Ragtime Band" was a major example of a pop song being mistakenly called a rag, and it seemed to symbolize the decline of ragtime. With so many inferior songs being called ragtime, by 1915 the general public had become tired of the fake rags and the ragtime fad, and its attention went elsewhere. Few musical styles have faded as quickly or as thoroughly as ragtime did between 1915 and 1920. Replaced in the public mind by the popular songs of Irving Berlin and Jerome Kern and the boisterous jazz music, ragtime was virtually forgotten except as nostalgia, and the ragtime composers either switched to other styles of music or retired altogether.

In 1911 Scott Joplin moved from St. Louis to New York, symbolically ending St. Louis' reign as the center of the music. Joplin would not last much longer, worn down both by syphilis and frustration at not succeeding with his second ragtime opera *Treemonisha*, which had only a single performance during his lifetime. He passed away in 1917, by which time ragtime was considered a thing of the past.

THE RECORDING INDUSTRY PRIOR TO 1917

In 1877 Thomas Edison invented the phonograph, a machine that used a brass cylinder and could duplicate the human voice, a pioneering tape recorder. After some initial excitement, Edison worked on other projects (including the light bulb) and did not return to the phonograph until 1887. By 1889 it was apparent that the best use for the machine was to record music, using wax cylinders. The first instrumental recordings date from that year, and Edison's company would continue to record and issue cylinders until 1929.

Unfortunately, cylinders were fragile and were soon overshadowed and in time replaced by 78 records. Emile Berliner in 1887 patented the gramophone, a machine that played flat discs that held about three minutes of music. By the late 1890s, 78s were more popular than cylinders, and they would be the main recording form until the late 1940s. Victor and Columbia emerged early on as the leading record labels.

The original recordings of 1889 to 1916 are often difficult to listen to, partly because of the very primitive recording quality, but also because of the content. Best are the concert band recordings and the works featuring classical-oriented virtuosi such as trombonist Arthur Pryor and cornetist Herbert L. Clarke. More difficult to sit through are the so-called comedy records (most of which were quite racist) and many of the vocal records (usually featuring singers more notable for their volume than their talents), with a few exceptions. It is due to these early records, however, that listeners today can hear Enrico Caruso, Al Jolson at the beginning of his career, ragtime banjoists Fred Van Eps and Vess Ossman, some early vaudevillians, and the orchestra of James Reese Europe.

Because the record labels were based in New York rather than Sedalia, St. Louis, or New Orleans, many of the early twentieth-century jazz performers missed being documented. It is a major disappointment that Scott Joplin and the other early ragtime composers and pianists never had an opportunity to record.

ST. LOUIS IN THE 1920s

St. Louis was not finished as a music city when the ragtime years ended. Because of its location as a main stop for the steamboats traveling on the Mississippi River, it was important as an entertainment and tourist city, particularly through the 1920s. Like New Orleans, St. Louis had a large red-light district and many cafes and bars, so there was plenty of employment for musicians. Of the bands coming up the river from New Orleans, pianist Fate Marable's was one of the most impressive. Before these musicians settled in Chicago, Marable's group featured such top players as cornetists Louis Armstrong and Tommy Ladnier, clarinetist Johnny Dodds, bassists Pops Foster and (in the 1930s) Jimmy Blanton, and drummers Baby Dodds and Zutty Singleton.

The influx of musicians in the early 1920s made St. Louis one of the more important Midwestern cities for jazz, although the lack of local record companies led to insufficient documentation of local bands and the dominance of Chicago and Kansas City overshadowed St. Louis' role. In the 1920s the most significant jazz groups were led by trumpeters Charlie Creath, who led the Jazz-O-Maniacs, and Dewey Jackson, who headed the Peacock Orchestra. Creath's band recorded just a dozen selections from 1924 to 1927 for the Okeh label, when the company took a mobile recording unit on field trips, while Jackson just led one four-song session. Other recording groups included the Arcadia Peacock Orchestra of St. Louis and the unrelated Arcadian Serenaders, with either Sterling Bose or Wingy Manone on cornets; the latter played music similar to that of the New Orleans Rhythm Kings.

In truth there was not much difference between the music that was recorded in St. Louis and that being played at the same time in Chicago. Although St. Louis developed a tradition of great trumpeters, from Dewey Jackson and Harold "Shorty" Baker in the 1930s to Clark Terry and Miles Davis in the 1940s, and had a worthy avant-garde movement during the 1960s and 1970s that resulted in the Black Artists Group (BAG), the city's musicians had to move elsewhere to gain much recognition. After the Depression hit in the early 1930s and the music played on the Mississippi River riverboats declined in popularity, St. Louis became a minor league jazz city, a situation that has not changed to the present day. St. Louis does have a glorious past, however.

RECOMMENDED RECORDINGS

Although some of the performances on these CDs and those cited in other chapters were not necessarily recorded in the same cities as the theme of each chapter, they offer strong examples of the regional styles.

Jazz in St. Louis. Timeless, 1036.
Ragtime to Jazz 1. Timeless, 1-035.
Ragtime to Jazz 3. Timeless, 1-070.
Real Ragtime. Archeophone, 1001.

2

New Orleans Jazz

NEW ORLEANS: A MUSICAL MELTING POT

New Orleans was always one of the most international of all American cities. Founded in 1718 it was ruled by France until 1774, by Spain from 1774 to 1800, and by France again from 1800 to 1803 before finally became part of the United States with the Louisiana Purchase of 1803. In addition to a large black population, by the 1800s the city had many citizens of French or Spanish heritage, plus there were many immigrants from England, Ireland, Germany, Italy, Cuba, and Haiti, all contributing to the city's culture. The many different nationalities each had their own music that over time blended together. It has often been said that jazz is a combination of West African rhythms with European harmonies and instruments. Due to the mixture of many cultures, New Orleans was one of the few places in the world where jazz could have been born.

In New Orleans as early as 1817, slaves were allowed to congregate in Congo Square on Sundays to sing, play percussion and string instruments, and dance wildly in circles later named a "ring shout." This rare bit of freedom, which continued as a tradition for years after the Civil War, uplifted the spirit of the slaves and was one of the few opportunities for them to be creative and to experience music with others. It also showed that their African culture and the legacy of their rhythms both managed to survive, despite the attempts by slave owners to destroy them. While New Orleans would be segregated deep into the twentieth century, it had a slightly more liberal attitude toward race relations in the 1800s than most of the South, with whites listening to the "barbaric" music of the blacks, and vice versa.

Military bands were a popular form of entertainment throughout the 1800s, and due to the very musical nature of New Orleans day-to-day life, brass bands became plentiful throughout the Crescent City. By the 1880s white, black, and Creole brass bands were a constant in New Orleans, playing for parades, parties, weddings, funerals, and a variety of social functions.

Creoles were mixed-race citizens who were part French and part black, having their own French-oriented culture separate from darker-skinned blacks, and even their own language. For a time they had greater opportunities in New Orleans than blacks, and that included classical music training. With the passage of the Louisiana Legislative Code in 1894, Creoles were classified as blacks, and their former privileges were taken away. Suddenly the only way Creoles could make a living in music was to play with the blacks, who did not have the technical musical training but had something much different and special: the ability to improvise. Creoles could teach black musicians conventional technique and musicianship, and African Americans showed Creoles how to put their own personalities into the music and be creative.

Most black musicians of the 1890s in New Orleans did not read music, having learned to play by ear. Although it is not known precisely when jazz was first played, it is not too much of a stretch to imagine it occurring when brass band musicians in the 1890s began to improvise on marches, adding blue notes and speechlike phrases. The early jazz musicians were very aware of ragtime, often using similar musical structures with multiple themes and syncopated rhythms, but jazz headed in a different direction.

The music in New Orleans was primarily ensemble oriented, with the improvising sticking close to the melody and the chord changes being fairly basic. Musicians were rated high if they had a pretty tone, knew how to infuse the music with blue notes, were expressive, never lost sight of the melody, and could get audiences dancing.

The typical jazz band, the ones playing at parties and social functions rather than parades, developed a set instrumentation with each instrument having its function. The cornet played the melody and the lead, the trombone offered percussive harmonies, and the clarinet created a second lead and a counter-melody. Usually there was also a banjo or guitar, a tuba or bass, and drums operating as a colorful percussion, with some bands also including a violin or a saxophone. Only on rare occasions did a jazz group include a piano at this early stage. Brass bands that performed at parades and funerals had many more horns and separate musicians playing snare bass and bass drums.

The earliest known jazz musician was cornetist Buddy Bolden, who formed his first band in 1895. He became famous locally for his powerful sound and his ability to play the blues, but his reign as the first king of jazz was tragically brief, and he never recorded. Bolden was plagued by bouts of insanity in 1906 and the following year was committed to Jackson Mental Institute, where he spent his last twenty-four years, completely forgotten.

Many of the early jazz history books center on Storyville, the New Orleans legal red-light district from 1897 to 1917, where prostitution and large, fancy bordellos were plentiful. Storyville did offer steady employment for a variety of pianists, including the jazz pioneer Jelly Roll Morton, who were not part of the marching brass bands. These pianists sought to be one-man bands, often adapting the music of jazz groups to their instrument and developing a separate but complementary tradition. It is inaccurate, however, to state that jazz was born in Storyville or that the closing of the district in 1917 directly led to an exodus of musicians from the city. After all, large jazz bands, if they had been hired for Storyville, would have shattered the mood of bordellos.

New Orleans was unique in American history in that music was a major part of everyday life. Not only were there brass bands for all occasions (parades, parties, celebrations, and funerals), but most corners had street musicians and singers, willing to entertain for pennies. No day went by without live music being heard, and it spawned an atmosphere where many talented players learned their craft. Among the key stars of the period were cornetists Freddie Keppard and King Oliver, trombonist Kid Ory, clarinetists Sidney Bechet and Johnny Dodds, bassist Bill Johnson, and drummer Baby Dodds, all of whom would get to record in the 1920s. There were also dozens of now-forgotten but once-popular early jazz players whose accomplishments are lost to history.

By 1910 the New Orleans brass bands, the most famous of which were the Excelsior, Eureka, Onward, and Imperial, had a repertoire dominated by jazz originals, blues, and

Sidney Bechet was the master of the soprano saxophone. *Photo courtesy of the Wayne Knight Collection, Star Line Productions.*

traditional melodies. The parade rhythms generated by these bands would have a major impact on virtually all of the music to come out of the city in future generations, though they would not be captured on record very well until the 1940s.

Most New Orleans musicians of the era were part-time players who had day jobs. There was plenty of work in music, although it did not pay much. Music was everywhere in the Crescent City.

THE EXODUS, THE 1920s, AND THE COMEBACK OF NEW ORLEANS JAZZ

From 1910 to 1930 there was a mass exodus of African Americans from the South to northern cities. Although racism was a part of day-to-day life in the

North, it was subtler than in the South, and there was more potential up North for blacks to have a decent life. The exodus affected New Orleans and the local music scene because many of the top jazz musicians chose to leave town. Some joined minstrel shows, went on the black vaudeville circuit, or became part of traveling shows; while others simply moved up North or West, without any clear job prospects, for the adventure of it all.

Bassist Bill Johnson was among the first to leave New Orleans, introducing jazz to California as early as 1909. Most of the top jazz musicians who departed ended up relocating to Chicago, including cornetists King Oliver, Freddie Keppard, and the young Louis Armstrong, trombonist Kid Ory (after a stay in Los Angeles), clarinetists Johnny Dodds and Jimmie Noone, and pianist Jelly Roll Morton.

For those who chose to stay in New Orleans, work remained plentiful throughout the 1920s. The unfortunate part was that recordings were fairly scarce, being dependent on occasional field trips from northern record labels, and none took place in New Orleans until 1924. Although some musicians, particularly cornetists Manuel Perez, Chris Kelly, and Buddy Petit, never did make a recording, others fared better.

While pre-1920 New Orleans jazz rarely featured any solos, with the lead passed between instruments and all of the musicians playing on nearly every chorus, by the mid-1920s the local music scene was affected by recordings from Chicago and New York. Groups such as Johnny De Droit's New Orleans Jazz Orchestra, Oscar Celestin's Original Tuxedo Orchestra, Johnny Bayersdorffer's Jazzola Novelty Orchestra, the Halfway House Orchestra, the New Orleans Owls, and Sam Morgan's Jazz Band alternated ensembles with occasional solos. Many of the local bands also utilized saxophones and were larger than the standard six or seven pieces that had been popular earlier.

During the 1920s and 1930s, rather than setting trends, most jazz in New Orleans followed the evolution of the music that took place in Chicago and New York. The onset of the Depression hit the music scene hard, and most clubs closed. While there were still parade bands, there was less to celebrate during this era, and musically New Orleans was in decline. Very few recordings were made in the city during the 1930s.

By the late 1930s a growing number of record collectors became interested in the roots of swing and wanted to hear more of the earlier styles of jazz. Some of the more enterprising fans ventured to New Orleans to check out the local scene and to search for the legendary musicians who had chosen to stay home rather than venture up North. Could they be lost links to the past who could give newer listeners an idea of what jazz sounded like before it was recorded, during the Buddy Bolden era?

The publication of the book *Jazzmen* resulted in a great deal of interest being invested in the legendary trumpeter Bunk Johnson. After a bit of a search, Johnson was discovered working outside of music. He claimed to have played with Bolden, saying that he was born in 1879; chances are he was really ten years younger and may have been an early mentor to Louis Armstrong, who later denied being taught by Bunk. Johnson had been a major local player in New Orleans from around 1910 until the early 1930s before bad economic times forced him into retirement. After he was found alive, money was raised to buy Johnson a new set of teeth and a trumpet. He was privately recorded in 1942, played in San Francisco the following year, and was soon making records and appearing in New York. Some fans of New Orleans jazz who considered swing to be rather commercial, celebrated Bunk Johnson as a major figure and a new messiah; while others, hearing Johnson slip out of tune and miss notes, considered him a hack. The truth was somewhere in between. He was capable of playing with great beauty, but he sometimes sounded rusty and erratic, a condition not helped by his alcoholism. In 1945 Sidney Bechet, wanting to form an old-time New Orleans band, hired Johnson, but the trumpeter quickly drank himself out of the group. On and off from 1944 to 1946, Johnson used a band that included clarinetist George Lewis and trombonist Jim Robinson, but personality conflicts caused its breakup. In 1947 Johnson led his final band, utilizing fine swing-era musicians, and recorded one of his best albums. The following year he returned permanently to Louisiana and retired, passing away in 1949 as a controversial legend.

George Lewis, who recorded with Johnson and also as a leader in the mid-1940s, returned to New Orleans in 1946. Like Johnson, he had played extensively in New Orleans in his early days but had been out of action for a decade when he was discovered in 1942. Unlike Johnson, Lewis in time became a world traveler. He worked locally with his band until a 1950 article in *Look* magazine gave him nationwide exposure. By 1952 the clarinetist was playing up North, and many tours of Europe and Japan followed. Lewis, who was far from a virtuoso, had a distinctive sound on clarinet that was quite expressive and beautiful. He was very affected by his sidemen, however, so if his

The veteran New Orleans cornetist Bunk Johnson was rediscovered in the early 1940s and made a historic comeback.
Photo courtesy of the Wayne Knight Collection, Star Line Productions.

trumpeter, who during the 1950s was often the erratic Kid Howard, was having a bad day, Lewis tended to sound subpar too. There were some occasions when trombonist Jim Robinson, a superior ensemble player, was the actual star of the evening; but under the right circumstances, Lewis could be inspired to play extremely well. He became a symbol of New Orleans jazz, being active until his death in 1969.

Although they did not sound exactly like musicians from Buddy Bolden's day since they were familiar with swing music, Bunk Johnson and George Lewis served as links to the early days. The music they and other veterans played in New Orleans differed from Dixieland in that the emphasis was much more on ensembles, though there were solos too. The musicianship in classic New Orleans jazz is often not as high quality as in the usual Dixieland groups, with some of the players being occasionally out of tune. The musicians' expressive qualities are considered more significant than their intonation. If musicians have the spirit and an appealing sound and can play ensembles well, then they will be valued more than a less-emotional virtuoso.

With the rediscovery of Bunk Johnson and George Lewis, and a greater interest in general for New Orleans jazz in the 1940s, a large industry developed. Tourists came to New Orleans hoping to hear fun music, so many clubs opened, often featuring flashy Dixieland that delighted audiences who wanted to hear loud and fast versions of familiar tunes. The aficionados and record collectors who loved the original music were distressed to see a commercial and rather obvious version of Dixieland being considered representative of New Orleans jazz.

Of the newer musicians from the era, clarinetist Pete Fountain and trumpeter Al Hirt became famous. Both were based in New Orleans, with Fountain gaining national exposure while he was featured with the *Lawrence Welk Show*. The clarinetist, still active into the twenty-first century, could be quite predictable, often sticking to a small repertoire, but always played with enthusiasm and joy. Hirt, whose virtuosity made him a bit overqualified to play Dixieland, had two pop hits in the 1960s but mostly stuck to Dixieland warhorses. Both Fountain and Hirt owned clubs in New Orleans for many years.

The Dukes of Dixieland, featuring trumpeter Fred Assunto and trombonist Frank Assunto, caught on in the 1950s due to a steady stream of records for the Audio Fidelity label. When they signed with Columbia in the 1960s, the Dukes were at their prime, featuring clarinetist Jerry Fuller and a relatively modern rhythm section. Tragically, both of the Assuntos died prematurely from cancer, but they did leave behind many recordings. The current version of the Dukes of Dixieland has no real relation to the original group.

While such white stars as Fountain, Hirt, and the Dukes of Dixieland became famous, it did not seem right that the veteran black musicians did not have a regular place to play. In 1961 that problem was fixed when Preservation Hall opened in New Orleans' French Quarter. The young tuba player Allan Jaffe ran the hall, and he organized tours by the musicians, who were grouped together as the Preservation Hall Jazz Band. Such players as trumpeters Kid Thomas Valentine, Punch Miller, De De Pierce, and Percy Humphrey; trombonists Jim Robinson, Louis Nelson, and Frank Demond; clarinetists George Lewis, Albert Burbank, and Willie Humphrey; and pianists Billie Pierce, Sweet Emma

Barrett, and Joseph Robichaux were among the musicians who had the opportunity to spread the joy of New Orleans music around the world. Their playing was far from flawless, but their spirit helped keep the tradition of New Orleans jazz alive. In the twenty-first century after a great deal of turnover, the Preservation Hall Jazz Band still tours regularly, keeping traditional New Orleans jazz alive.

RECOMMENDED RECORDINGS

Al Hirt/Pete Fountain. *Pete Fountain Presents the Best of Dixieland*. Polygram, 549362.
Bunk Johnson. *Last Testament*. Delmark, 225.
Dukes of Dixieland. *At Disneyland*. Columbia, 1966.
George Lewis. *Doctor Jazz*. Good Time Jazz, 12062.
New Orleans in the '20s. Timeless, 1-014.
Sweet Emma Barrett. *New Orleans: The Living Legends*. Original Jazz Classics, 1832.

3

Chicago: Classic Jazz

THE CLASSIC JAZZ ERA

In 1915 jazz was virtually unknown outside of the southern United States, and it did not even have a name. By 1930 jazz was famous all over the globe, it was influencing most types of popular music, and a few of its top stars were household names.

Four events made it possible for jazz to enter its golden age: (1) the exodus of thousands of African Americans from the South to Chicago and other northern cities; (2) the documentation of jazz on records; (3) the rise of the jazz soloist; and (4) the gradual improvement of recording quality, culminating in the switch from acoustic to electric recordings by 1926.

The United States was completely segregated in 1915, and racism was an accepted institution, the way of life. In the South not much had changed from 1870, and the day-to-day existence of African Americans was only slightly improved from the days of slavery; they simply had no legal rights and at best were treated as unskilled labor. The North was somewhat more liberal in that, although blacks were considered second-class citizens, there was less chance of physical violence, and there were some geographical areas, generally in pockets of big cities like New York's Harlem, where blacks were able to live relatively peacefully and have their own culture, even while struggling to make ends meet with their menial jobs.

To the African Americans in the South, the North looked like a comparative paradise. From 1915 to 1930 a countless number of African Americans moved out of the North and into such cities as New York, Detroit, Philadelphia, and most importantly for jazz, Chicago. Many of the major New Orleans jazz musicians spent time performing and recording in Chicago from 1922 to 1927 before New York started becoming the center of jazz in 1928.

Jazz would have been destined to remain a regional folk music without the increasing influence of recordings. While the music evolved very slowly between 1900 and 1915, once it was documented on records starting in 1917, the music was no longer only heard in the southern United States. Jazz became a worldwide phenomenon, and the music went anywhere that records traveled, influencing musicians everywhere. Because jazz is an innovative music full of creative individuals, once the music could be heard and studied, it moved forward rapidly as musicians came up with new ideas and approaches. Music that sounded fresh and new in 1921 was considered hopelessly old-fashioned by 1927. Jazz's evolution would proceed at a rapid pace for quite a few decades.

Jazz in New Orleans in 1915 was almost entirely performed by ensembles. One of the horns, the trumpet or clarinet, might take the lead, but the other musicians continually played in at least supportive roles. The new idea of group improvisation resulted in many exciting performances. It was only a matter of time before individual soloists would become stars, for some players were more technically skilled and creative than others. Although he was not jazz's first soloist, Louis Armstrong's rise to fame permanently changed jazz from a music that featured ensembles to a medium that starred virtuoso soloists. Why should a player such as Armstrong be continually buried in a group when he was obviously a star? The switch from ensembles to solos led to jazz being accepted more quickly because, rather than dealing with anonymous groups, the media, dancers, and fans could now focus on their favorite individuals.

When the Original Dixieland Jazz Band (ODJB) made its first recordings in 1917, the group sounded like it was being recorded in a wind tunnel. The recording quality of the era was quite primitive, and only certain instruments could be recorded decently. Drums were out of the question except for cymbals and woodblocks. Bass instruments were discouraged since they did not pick up well. The same was true of guitars that, because they were nearly inaudible, usually had their spots taken by banjos. Although the recordings made between 1917 and 1924 are extremely valuable in saving for posterity many of the top players of the period, they are far from lifelike and need a lot of tolerance on the part of today's listeners.

Starting in 1925 with the development of electrical recordings that used a microphone instead of a large horn, the quality of reproduction quickly improved. Most labels switched to electrical recording by 1927, and records began to sound truer to life. Some labels, particularly Victor and Okeh, were much better at reproducing clearer sounds than others, most notably the blues-oriented Paramount label, which became infamous for its distracting surface noise.

There were other factors that led to jazz increasing in popularity throughout the 1920s. The rise of the thirty-two-bar popular song—as composed by Irving Berlin, Jerome Kern, George Gershwin, and others—gave musicians a steady stream of new and interesting songs to play. There was a demand for a new type of dance music that was more uninhibited and hotter than the relatively sedate music of 1915; jazz fit the bill quite well. With the development of arrangers who learned how to infuse their arrangements with jazz rhythms, phrasing, and solos, larger orchestras and dance bands became more jazz oriented by 1925, following the lead of the freewheeling, smaller combos. Jazz also became identified as the ideal party music, a new style for the youth of America and eventually the world to enjoy while their elders listened to classical music and the quieter dance bands.

The biggest city in the United States after New York, Chicago had a rapidly growing African American population between 1915 and 1925. Working-class blacks from the South struggled to carve out lives for themselves, and so did musicians, including many of the top players from New Orleans. In theaters, dance clubs, and nightclubs, there was a great demand for entertainment, and black musicians, escaping from the South, had opportunities to play together and exchange ideas.

Because the United States was segregated, there were separate black and white jazz scenes in Chicago. By 1920 Chicago was the center of jazz, and many of the top musicians spent time in the Windy City, including the Original Dixieland Jazz Band, the New Orleans Rhythm Kings, King Oliver, Jelly Roll Morton, and Louis Armstrong. Their innovations while in Chicago permanently changed jazz.

THE ODJB AND THE NORK

Being the first recorded jazz group, the Original Dixieland Jazz Band (ODJB) made a major impact and officially launched the jazz age. While the band made it big in New York, the site of most of its recordings, the ODJB first came together in Chicago. In 1916 cornetist Nick LaRocca, clarinetist Alcide "Yellow" Nunez, trombonist Eddie Edwards, and pianist Henry Ragas left New Orleans to join drummer Johnny Stein's Dixie Jass Band in Chicago. The word "jass," which earlier had a sexual meaning, was for a brief time associated with the new music before it was changed to jazz. Stein's band was a big hit at Schiller's Café, delighting the dancers and gaining a great deal of attention. After three months LaRocca and the other players wanted to break the contract and take a higher paying job in another club. When Stein refused, the sidemen mutinied and broke away, forming the Original Dixieland Jazz Band. LaRocca became its leader, and Tony Sbarbaro was hired on drums. After a period, a personality conflict resulted in Yellow Nunez's departure, being succeeded by Larry Shields.

The ODJB was an instant success in Chicago. Although jazz had been available to northern audiences to a small degree for a few years as southern black musicians traveled on the vaudeville and theater circuit, none had the exposure of the ODJB. The Original Dixieland Jazz Band relocated to New York in January 1917, made its debut recordings, and was the pacesetter, at least on records, from 1917 to 1921, with many other groups emulating its all-ensemble style and repertoire.

The New Orleans Rhythm Kings (NORK) was one of the first jazz groups to break away from the ODJB model and move jazz forward. Although its period in the spotlight was brief, the NORK became influential, mixing together ensembles with short solos. Cornetist Paul Mares, trombonist George Brunies, and clarinetist Leon Roppolo knew each other growing up in New Orleans. In 1919 Mares moved to Chicago to play with drummer Gababy Stevens' band; Brunies joined a year later. When Mares organized a group to perform with singer Bee Palmer at Chicago's Friar's Inn in August 1921, he sent to New Orleans for Roppolo and hired Brunies. A few weeks later Palmer departed, and Mares became the leader of the Friar's Society Orchestra, soon renamed the New Orleans Rhythm Kings.

The NORK had six recording dates in 1922 and 1923. Other than the three main horns, their personnel differed constantly, ranging from a quintet to a ten-piece group and introducing such future Dixieland standards as "Tin Roof Blues," "Farewell Blues," "Panama," "That's a Plenty," and "Weary Blues." Mares's mellow lead was more flexible than Nick LaRocca's. Brunies proved to be particularly skilled in ensembles, and Roppolo emerged as one of the first significant horn soloists on record. The band only lasted as long as the Friar's Inn engagement, concluding in the spring of 1923. Two reunion dates in July 1923 were significant for having Jelly Roll Morton guest on piano on most of the songs, making this one of the first integrated jazz record sessions and showing how highly regarded the NORK was by the black jazz musicians.

Unfortunately the reunion was brief, and Brunies became a long-term member of Ted Lewis' band. Back in New Orleans, in January 1925 Mares tried to revive the NORK, using Ropollo, trombonist Santo Pecora, and Charlie Cordilla on tenor for a record session. Roppolo's mental health was shaky, however, and he soon suffered a mental breakdown, spending his last twenty-seven years in an institution. For NORK's final record date, on March 26, Roppolo was absent, and Cordilla switched to clarinet.

Although Paul Mares was still just twenty-five, he chose to retire from music and work at his family's fur business. During 1934 and 1935 he made a brief comeback, playing cornet part-time in Chicago while running a barbecue restaurant and recording four songs with his Friar's Society Orchestra. Otherwise Mares felt that he had already made his mark on music with the NORK, and he did not feel the desire to make a comeback.

KING OLIVER AND HIS CREOLE JAZZ BAND

The breakthrough year for jazz was 1923. Although it had been six years since the Original Dixieland Jazz Band had first appeared on records, very few

African American jazz musicians had recorded. Other than records of the musicians who backed the classic blues singers, there were not more than a handful of documented performances by black jazz musicians. These earlier recordings were of James Reese Europe's orchestra before his untimely death in 1919, two obscure performances cut in Los Angeles in 1922 by a group called Spikes' Seven Pods of Pepper Orchestra that was actually led by New Orleans trombonist Kid Ory, and a few isolated piano solos, including the earliest sessions of James P. Johnson and Fats Waller. A large part of the reason was racism, but some record company executives also felt that there was no market for black recordings. The success of the classic blues singers in New York starting in 1920 led to a complete change in that way of thinking.

King Oliver, Johnny Dodds, Louis Armstrong, and Jelly Roll Morton, all Chicago-based at the time, appeared on records for the first time in 1923. Joe "King" Oliver was the third major cornet king from New Orleans, after Buddy Bolden, who reigned until 1906, and Freddie Keppard, whom Oliver had largely bested by 1915. Oliver gained his early experience playing at parades, parties, funerals, and social functions with many top local groups including the Melrose Brass Band, the Olympia Band, the Onward Brass Band, the Magnolia Band, the Eagle Band, The Original Superior Band, Allen's Brass Band, Richard M. Jones' Four Hot Hounds, and Kid Ory's unit. Oliver was part of the huge exodus of New Orleans jazz musicians to Chicago, moving up North in March 1919 to join bands led by clarinetist Lawrence Duhe and the pioneering bassist Bill Johnson. His attractive sound, ensemble playing, and expertise using mutes to distort his tone made him such a big attraction that by 1920 he was leading his own group, the Creole Jazz Band, at Chicago's Dreamland Café.

Oliver's Creole Jazz Band featured such major players as trombonist Honore Dutrey, pianist Lil Harden, drummer Baby Dodds, and his brother, clarinetist Johnny Dodds, who developed into arguably the top clarinet soloist of the 1920s. The band had long residencies in San Francisco and Los Angeles in 1921, helping to popularize jazz on the West Coast, before it returned to Chicago in 1922 and settled into the Lincoln Gardens. Oliver, feeling prosperous and wanting a second cornetist to harmonize with, sent to New Orleans for his protégé, the twenty-one-year-old Louis Armstrong. Armstrong was thrilled to play with his hero, and although he quickly developed into the more powerful player, he was happy to play behind his new boss and seemed to anticipate his every musical move.

Even with the inclusion of occasional short solos, the Creole Jazz Band mostly played ensembles. Oliver's outfit is considered by many to be the last great classic New Orleans jazz group and one of the most influential bands to record. In 1923 Oliver and his group made thirty-seven recordings, and despite some erratic recording quality, the excitement of the band comes through. Oliver and Armstrong's harmonized two-bar breaks, Dutrey's distinctive sound, Johnny Dodds' cutting tone, and the solid rhythm section's emphasis on every beat gave

The top band of 1923, King Oliver's Creole Jazz Band consisted of Baby Dodds, Honore Dutrey, King Oliver, Louis Armstrong, Bill Johnson, Johnny Dodds, and Lil Harden.
Photo courtesy of the Wayne Knight Collection, Star Line Productions.

this group its own sound. In addition the occasional solos, such as Oliver's famous three choruses on "Dippermouth Blues," pointed toward the future.

Due to money disputes, the Creole Jazz Band did not last. By early 1924 the Dodds brothers had departed, and midway through the year Armstrong accepted Fletcher Henderson's offer to join his big band in New York, at the urging of his new wife Lil Harden Armstrong. Even with replacements, by the fall Oliver was reluctantly forced to break up his group.

Although he would never be quite as prominent again, King Oliver was quite adaptable to the changes in jazz during the remainder of the 1920s. In February 1925 he formed the Dixie Syncopators, a group that featured both arranged passages and a greater emphasis on solos, played regularly at the Plantation Café, and recording frequently during the next two years. In 1927 Oliver moved to New York where he would struggle to gain the fame that he had achieved in Chicago.

JELLY ROLL MORTON

Throughout his career, Jelly Roll Morton often proved to be his own worst enemy. He was a braggart who talked about himself excessively and made few friends. In the late 1930s when he was angered at W. C. Handy being introduced on a radio show as "the father of the blues and jazz," Morton wrote a letter to *Downbeat* claiming that he had invented jazz in 1902; never mind that he was only seventeen years old that year and that Buddy Bolden had been active in 1895. His bragging was ironic, because in reality it was not an overstatement to call Morton the first giant of jazz and a major pioneer and innovator as a pianist, composer, arranger, and bandleader. He was also an important transitional figure between ragtime and classic jazz.

The pioneering pianist, composer, arranger, and bandleader Jelly Roll Morton was one of jazz's first true giants.
Photo courtesy of the Wayne Knight Collection, Star Line Productions.

Born Ferdinand Joseph La Menthe in 1885, Morton began playing piano when he was ten after short periods on guitar and trombone. Morton worked in Storyville, the legendary red-light district of New Orleans, for several years and began to travel throughout the South around 1910. During the next dozen years, playing piano and writing songs was only a small part of his life. He also worked as a comedian in traveling shows, a pool hustler, a boxing promoter, the manager of a gambling house, a tailor, a hotel manager, and a pimp. Life was a constant hustle for Morton, who renamed himself Jelly Roll when he began working as a pianist, and he spent time living in Chicago in 1914, San Francisco in 1915, Los Angeles between 1917 and 1922, Alaska, Wyoming, Tijuana, Denver, and parts of Canada.

Morton began to dedicate more of his time to music by 1920, settling in Chicago in 1923. By then he had already developed a distinctive style on piano, becoming one of the first major jazz stylists. Morton played his instrument as if it were a miniature orchestra, and many of his later band arrangements found their birth as a piano showcase. He used two- and four-bar breaks in his music to generate suspense and made each chorus count by utilizing multiple themes and building up his performances to their climax.

Shortly after moving to Chicago, Morton recorded a set of brilliant piano solos, introducing such original pieces as "King Porter Stomp," "Grandpa's Spells," "Wolverine Blues," "Shreveport Stomp," "Jelly Roll Blues," and "The Pearls." While his earliest band performances were poorly recorded and very primitive, starting in 1926 he created a couple of dozen classic combo records. Fortunately Morton by then was recording for Victor, the label with the most advanced recording equipment, so his performances are easy to enjoy today. Using such players as cornetist George Mitchell, trombonist Kid Ory, clarinetist Omer Simeon in his bands, and other top young musicians based in Chicago, Morton proved to be one of jazz's first great arrangers. He mixed together arranged and jammed ensembles and featured logical horn solos. In fact, there are times when the solos are such a close part of the arrangement that it is difficult to tell whether the soloist is making up his chorus or playing the notes as they were written. Such titles as "Black Bottom Stomp," "The Chant," "Dead Man Blues," and the band recording of "Grandpa's Spells" and "Doctor Jazz," featuring Morton's only vocal of the 1920s, are three-minute masterpieces full of constant surprises.

Like Oliver, Morton moved to New York when he felt that the center of jazz was shifting toward the Big Apple, leaving Chicago in February 1928.

LOUIS ARMSTRONG: THE CHICAGO YEARS

Decades after his death, Louis Armstrong is still the most famous of all jazz musicians. A large part of his popularity during the later part of his career was due to his distinctive singing and joyful personality that were always impossible to resist. Armstrong's musical innovations early in his life are so enormous that he permanently changed jazz and was arguably the most significant of all musicians to play jazz.

Although he believed, and it was widely reported, that he was born on July 4, 1900, after his death a birth certificate was found that showed his birthdate as August 4, 1901. He grew up in a very poor, fatherless family, first performing music by singing in a kid's vocal group on the streets. In New Orleans Armstrong was always surrounded by music, and he was inspired to start playing cornet when he was eleven, hoping someday to play in the city's parades. The turning point of his life occurred on New Year's Eve of 1912 when Armstrong found a pistol and shot it off in the air in celebration. He was quickly arrested, and when it was deemed that he was not being brought up properly, he was sent to live in a waifs' home.

Although being confined could have permanently damaged his life, Armstrong enjoyed the disciplined setting and the home's student bands. He began to work earnestly on his cornet playing, and by the time he was released two years later, he was an up-and-coming player with a growing reputation. Back in the streets of New Orleans, he began to be hired by local groups while retaining a day job for a few years. He befriended King Oliver, who became his mentor and role model. In 1919 when Oliver moved to Chicago, Armstrong took his spot with trombonist Kid Ory's band. Armstrong also began working on the riverboats with Fate Marable's highly rated group. While with Marable, he learned to read music very well and developed quickly as a technician. In 1922 when King Oliver offered him a job with his Creole Jazz Band in Chicago, Armstrong was ready.

While with Oliver's band, where his nickname was "Satchelmouth," Armstrong amazed listeners by spontaneously harmonizing two-bar breaks with the other cornetist. He was mostly restricted to playing second cornet behind Oliver in the ensemble-oriented band, but when he took occasional short solos, it was obvious that he was surpassing his inspiration. He made his recording debut with the Creole Jazz Band in 1923, and on his very first solo, "Chimes Blues," the notes may have been worked out in advance, but his sound, phrasing, and personality were already in evidence. Armstrong married Oliver's pianist, Lil Harden, who urged her new husband to leave Oliver, feeling that he would never be a star if he had to play second cornet. Armstrong was reluctant and stayed with Oliver until mid-1924 when he accepted an offer to join Fletcher Henderson's big band in New York.

A year and a half later, Armstrong moved back to Chicago. On November 12, 1925, he recorded the first three numbers with his Hot Five. Although he was featured nightly during the next couple of years with big bands in Chicago theaters, including Erskine Tate's Vendome Orchestra and the Carroll Dickerson Orchestra, his recordings with his Hot Five and Hot Seven from 1925 through 1928 were Armstrong's greatest contributions to music. In 1927 he switched permanently to trumpet. The original Hot Five, which recorded through 1927, teamed the cornetist with clarinetist Johnny Dodds, trombonist Kid Ory, pianist Lil Harden Armstrong, and Johnny St. Cyr on banjo and guitar. The band was on the surface a conventional New Orleans jazz group; Ory played percussion while Dodds offered countermelodies, and the pianist and banjoist emphasized every beat. It was also a giant step ahead due to the leader. While there were plenty of ensembles, particularly in the earlier recordings, it was Armstrong's solo flights and his joyful virtuosity that made these recordings so special.

On "Gutbucket Blues," for only the second time on record, Armstrong's voice is heard as he introduces his sidemen. He took vocal choruses on a fair number of these combo recordings. While nearly all singers up to that point sang pretty straight, sticking to both the words and the melody of the sheet music, Armstrong was constantly improvising, phrasing in an unpredictable

Louis Armstrong revolutionized jazz with his trumpet solos and vocals, while his personality helped to popularize the music.
Photo courtesy of the Wayne Knight Collection, Star Line Productions.

but logical manner, and altering notes that often made songs seem more rewarding and certainly more swinging than they had previously. In addition, he was a master at making up nonsense syllables called scat-singing and soloing in his vocals like a horn. Although a 1908 record by Gene Greene "The Ragtime

King" is the earliest known scat-singing to be documented, Armstrong popularized it with his instantly recognizable gravelly voice. By the late 1920s many vocalists were scatting, even quite a few who did not realize that their ideas were copies of Armstrong's.

Oddly enough, the Hot Five only appeared in public once, at a special concert held by their record label, Okeh. Although the band sounded like an organized group, with spots for each musician, Armstrong was the dominant force. The original Hot Five made thirty-three recordings including such classics as "Heebie Jeebies" that featured Armstrong's influential scatting, the initial version of Ory's "Muskrat Ramble" that became a Dixieland standard, "Big Butter and Egg Man," the eerie "Skid-Dat-De-Dat," a spectacular showcase for Armstrong on "Cornet Chop Suey," a perfect trumpet solo on "Struttin' with Some Barbecue," and a tradeoff between Armstrong and guest guitarist Lonnie Johnson on "Hotter Than That."

In 1927 for eleven selections, the group expanded with drummer Baby Dodds, Pete Briggs on tuba, and John Thomas substituting on trombone for Ory to become the Hot Seven. Armstrong's outstanding playing on "Willie the Weeper," "Wild Man Blues," and particularly "Potato Head Blues," with him playing over a stop-time rhythm on which the rhythm section accents the first beat of a bar together, but otherwise drops out, sounded way ahead of his time. No jazz trumpeter was on his level during this era, and he continued to progress.

Inspired by the piano playing of Earl Hines, Armstrong made a set of 1928 recordings with his Savoy Ballroom Five, which was actually six or seven pieces. Like Armstrong, Hines enjoyed playing with time, breaking up the rhythm, and taking adventurous breaks that found him stretching the boundaries of classic jazz. Third in importance with the group was drummer Zutty Singleton who made the most of the least, playing almost as a percussionist with cowbells and cymbals. The other musicians, trombonist Fred Robinson, Jimmy Strong on clarinet and tenor, banjoist Mancy Cara, and sometimes altoist Don Redman, had relatively minor roles because the music had moved beyond the democracy of New Orleans jazz.

Armstrong's creative ideas and Hines' innovative piano playing are very evident during such numbers as "Fireworks," "A Monday Date," "Basin Street Blues," "St. James Infirmary," and particularly in their time-defying trumpet-piano duet on "Weatherbird." "West End Blues" was Armstrong's favorite personal recording and the musical highpoint of his career. It has a remarkable opening trumpet cadenza, inspired scatting by Armstrong, and a very dramatic closing instrumental statement. It is one of the great moments of recorded history, showing that jazz had already evolved at that early stage from a regional folk music into an art form.

While Louis Armstrong was now famous among musicians and in Chicago, it was time for him to stretch out even more. He relocated to New York in 1929.

EARL HINES

Stride piano was the dominant style in the late 1920s, but Earl Hines was the first major pianist to move beyond it. Rather than continuously keeping the beat with a steady stride, he often suspended time with his left hand, taking unexpected breaks yet always coming back without missing a beat. His right often played ringing octaves that emulated a horn, allowing him to be heard over a band, and was dubbed "trumpet style."

The pianist first emerged in the early 1920s playing with singer Lois Deppe's group in Pittsburgh. After moving to Chicago, Hines played with local orchestras and met Louis Armstrong; they worked together in a big band throughout 1927. The next year was one of Hines' greatest: he played and recorded regularly with Jimmie Noone's Apex Club Orchestra, recorded some stunning piano solos, was featured with Louis Armstrong's Savoy Ballroom Five, and on his twenty-fifth birthday in December debuted his big band at Chicago's Grand Terrace Ballroom. Although he played more conventionally with his big band until the mid-1940s, whenever Hines took a piano solo or performed unaccompanied, he always proved that he was one of the most exciting of all jazz pianists.

THREE MAJOR CLARINETISTS

Johnny Dodds did not start playing clarinet until he was seventeen in 1909, but soon he was one of the best in New Orleans. He seemed to be everywhere in Chicago during the 1920s, a key member of King Oliver's Creole Jazz Band in 1923 and 1924, Louis Armstrong's Hot Five and Seven, Jelly Roll Morton's Red Hot Peppers, and with his own groups. His cutting tone was unmistakable, his sound in the lower register was haunting, and he was masterful at playing blues. Unfortunately Dodds' decision to stay in Chicago rather than relocate to New York hurt his career, as did the Depression. He played on a part-time basis throughout the 1930s and only recorded twice, in 1938 and 1940. Johnny Dodds died in 1940 from heart disease at age forty-eight.

Although Jimmie Noone's career was similar to Dodds', his smooth tone was much easier to copy and could be found in the playing of many other clarinetists, most notably Benny Goodman. Noone worked in New Orleans during the teens, played with Freddie Keppard in Chicago as early as 1917, worked with Doc Cook's Gingersnaps between 1920 and 1926, and led his own groups, usually known as the Apex Club Orchestra, from 1927 to 1943. His 1928 band featured Earl Hines. Noone, who made the song "Sweet Lorraine" famous and loved to play solos while an alto sax stated the melody, stayed active throughout his life and was poised to make a comeback with Kid Ory's band in 1944 when he suddenly died, also at age forty-eight.

Born in Chicago, Benny Goodman started playing clarinet when he was ten, and he developed very quickly. In 1921 when he was twelve, Goodman won a talent contest by imitating Ted Lewis. He joined the Musicians Union the following year and was considered an unofficial member of the Austin High Gang, although he was easily the youngest of the teenagers. Goodman worked with local bands, met Bix Beiderbecke in 1923, and performed with Art Kassel in 1924 and 1925. By the time he joined Ben Pollack's orchestra in 1925 when he was sixteen, he was already an accomplished musician.

The Ben Pollack big band was one of the very best white orchestras to emerge from the Chicago jazz scene of the 1920s. Pollack, who was one of the better drummers of the 1920s, sought to balance his jazz instincts with commercialism but never quite gained the fame that he hoped for. He performed early on with the New Orleans Rhythm Kings in 1923. After freelancing in Los Angeles, Chicago, and New York, Pollack settled back in Chicago in the spring of 1926. By then his orchestra featured as its main soloists Goodman, Jimmy McPartland, and trombonist Glenn Miller. The Pollack band was so successful in Chicago, however, that in 1927 it had become part of the musicians' exodus to New York.

CHICAGO JAZZ

In the early 1920s, a group of teenagers from suburban Chicago's Austin High School got together regularly after school at the Spoon and Straw malt shop, to play 78s on the store's Victrola. They could usually only listen to top pop/dance bands, but one day a new release by the New Orleans Rhythm Kings was in the pile. The music had such an impact that the youths decided spontaneously to become professional musicians. Some, like Jimmy McPartland, his brother guitarist Dick McPartland, banjoist Eddie Condon, clarinetist Frank Teschemacher, and pianist Joe Sullivan, were already playing music, although Dick McPartland and Teschemacher were actually learning violin at the time. The others in the loose aggregation, including tenor-saxophonist Bud Freeman, drummer Dave Tough, bassist Jim Lannigan, and drummer Gene Krupa, were just starting. The Austin High Gang began to see the NORK and King Oliver's Creole Jazz Band perform as often as possible, getting ideas and inspiration. At first their own jam sessions featured more enthusiasm than obvious talent, but within a few years, each of these youths was revitalizing the Chicago jazz scene.

The freewheeling music that the Austin High Gang developed would be called Chicago jazz and, after it was formalized in the 1930s, Dixieland. Essentially it was New Orleans jazz but with much more room set aside for solos. In its more stereotyped format, it features a seven-piece band consisting of trumpet, trombone, clarinet, piano, banjo or guitar, bass or tuba, and drums. Its typical framework has a couple of ensembles at the beginning, solos from clarinet, trombone, trumpet, piano and sometimes banjo, a couple of ensembles, a four-bar drum break, and a four-bar tag by the full group. There are many variations to both the format and the instrumentation. Eddie Condon's bands often employed tenor-saxophonist Bud Freeman, some groups did not use banjo or guitar at all, and occasionally the solo order was shuffled. Although Chicago jazz has been used as a term by some of the musicians playing this freewheeling music, there is virtually no difference between Chicago jazz and Dixieland.

Eddie Condon started off on ukulele, worked as a banjoist including with Hollis Peavey's Jazz Bandits in 1922, and by the mid- to late 1920s was playing rhythm guitar. Though never a soloist, Condon worked steadily and proved masterful at organizing bands. On December 8 and 16, 1927, he led the McKenzie-Condon Chicagoans, a group sponsored by singer and comb player Red McKenzie, on two recording sessions that resulted in four numbers: "Sugar," "China Boy," "Nobody's Sweetheart," and "Liza." These exuberant performances were the recording debuts of Condon, Frank Teschemacher, Bud Freeman, Joe Sullivan, Jim Lannigan, and Gene Krupa, with Jimmy McPartland (who had recorded in 1924) leading the ensembles.

In 1928 Condon and most of the other musicians moved to New York, although they returned to Chicago through the years. Their music continued to be called Chicago jazz, no matter where they were performing, letting listeners know where their brand of musical excitement originated.

Chicago lost many of its greatest musicians to New York between 1927 and 1929 as Harlem blossomed and jazz grew in popularity nationwide. Because it could not compete in the long run with New York's theaters, radio stations, studio work, and record labels, Chicago was less significant in the 1930s and 1940s, but still, like New Orleans, it had its top players including Johnny Dodds, Jimmie Noone, and the Earl Hines Orchestra (which was based at the Grand Terrace Café) along with many blues artists.

Chicago's next major contribution to music was in the 1950s when it became arguably the most significant city for electric blues. And as far as jazz goes, Chicago continued having a strong local scene, but would no longer set trends, at least not until the Association for the Advancement of Creative Musicians (AACM) was formed in the mid-1960s. That development is discussed in chapter ten.

Chicago's legacy as the center of jazz from 1920 to 1927 is an important part of jazz history, resulting in classic music and setting the stage for New York's rise to prominence in jazz.

RECOMMENDED RECORDINGS

Earl Hines. *1928–1932*. Classics, 545.
Eddie Condon. *Dixieland All Stars*. GRP/Decca, 637.
Jelly Roll Morton. Retrieval, 79002.
Jelly Roll Morton. *Centennial: His Complete Victor Recordings*. Bluebird, 2361, 5 CDs.
Jimmie Noone Collection, Vol. 1. Collector's Classics, 6.
Johnny Dodds. *1927–1928*. Classics, 617.
King Oliver's Creole Jazzband 1923–1924. Retrieval, 79007, 2 CDs.
King Oliver: Vol. 1—Sugar Foot Stomp. Frog, 34.
Louis Armstrong. *The Complete Hot Five and Hot Seven Recordings*. Columbia/Legacy, 63527, 4 CDs.
New Orleans Rhythm Kings and Jelly Roll Morton. Milestone, 47020.

4

New York: The Classic Jazz and Swing Eras

A DOMINANT FORCE

Today it seems inevitable that nearly all styles of American music are based in New York City. Certainly by the 1930s, New York's dominant influence was as the home for the major record labels, the most famous radio stations, the nationally famous theaters and clubs, Broadway shows, and the recording studios. By 1920 the most technically skilled musicians worked in New York where their technique, precision, and accuracy were greatly prized.

Jazz did not actually originate in New York, and during the first half of the 1920s, the New York musicians mostly lagged behind the New Orleans transplants who were working in Chicago. Listening to the typical New York band from 1923, it sounds several years behind King Oliver's Creole Jazz Band when it comes to spontaneity, swing, and phrasing, often emphasizing staccato rather than legato lines. The New York players, even when they were improvising, sounded as if they were reading the notes rather than being creative, and few knew how to utilize bluish and bent notes in their solos.

One of Louis Armstrong's greatest contributions to music was the impact that he made during 1924 and 1925 when, as a member of the Fletcher Henderson Orchestra, he altered the New York jazz scene nearly overnight. Even before his arrival, however, there was some notable music performed in the Big Apple.

THE ODJB IN NEW YORK

When Nick LaRocca brought his band to New York in January 1917 and they performed at Reisenweber's, they caught on even bigger than they had in Chicago. On February 26, the Original Dixieland Jazz Band (ODJB) became the first jazz band to ever record, cutting "Livery Stable Blues" and "Dixie Jazz Band One Step" for the Victor label. "Livery Stable Blues" has the novelty of three horns imitating barnyard animals, and when Victor rushed the music out for release, it became a surprise hit. Although the music sounds quite primitive today, being all ensembles except for some two-bar breaks, these pioneering recordings were very radical for their time, particularly in their display of raw emotions. Between 1917 and 1921 nearly every jazz group that recorded did their best to imitate the ODJB.

World War I ended in 1918, and in early 1919 the Original Dixieland Jazz Band became the first American jazz group to visit Europe. Having conquered Chicago and New York, the ODJB became a big hit in London, playing for nine months at the Hammersmith Palais and launching a jazz craze on the Continent. Returning to New York in 1920, the ODJB had a strong seller with their recording of "Margie," but otherwise they began to struggle due to competition from other groups. In addition, personality conflicts resulting from Nick LaRocca's prickly manner were hurting the band's progress. Henry Ragas had died in 1918 during the influenza epidemic, and J. Russell Robinson replaced him without a loss in quality. In 1921, however, when both Robinson and Shields departed, the band's sound was weakened. After January 1921 the group only recorded eight more numbers before its breakup in 1925. By then the ODJB was considered a ghost of the past, merely a historic, rather than a pacesetting, band.

Eleven years passed during which LaRocca ran a contracting business, Edwards occasionally played in society orchestras, Shields was working outside of music, Robinson became a successful songwriter, and Sbarbaro was the only ODJB alumnus still playing jazz fulltime. In 1936 LaRocca, who was still just forty-seven, was persuaded to get the band back together. All five musicians practiced until they were playing at a high level again, and soon they were appearing on the radio and making a few new recordings in New York. Their music was largely unchanged from 1920, even though it was now the swing era, and the musicians still stuck to ensembles without featuring any solos. Unfortunately, more personality conflicts arose, and the novelty of the historic group ran out. The Original Dixieland Jazz Band permanently broke up on February 1, 1938.

THE SINGERS THAT BROUGHT THE BLUES TO JAZZ

When the ODJB caught on big in 1917, many imitators appeared, and quite a few songs were written that used the word "jazz," treating it as if it were a fad.

The same thing happened during the blues craze from 1920 to 1923. It all started innocently enough. A veteran thirty-six-year-old singer, Mamie Smith, was appearing in the show *Maid of Harlem* at New York's Lincoln Theatre. When Sophie Tucker, the production's star, decided not to attend a record session, Smith was enlisted in her place. On February 14, 1920, Smith made her recording debut with "That Thing Called Love" and "You Can't Keep a Good Man Down," becoming the first non-gospel black singer, other than actor-comedian Bert Williams, to record. The sales of the record were solid, so on August 10 Smith was back in the studios, cutting "Crazy Blues" and "It's Right Here for You." Within six months the latter recording sold over a million copies, and the blues craze was on. Earlier recordings included "Memphis Blues" in 1914, the ODJB's "Livery Stable Blues," and even a few rare blues vocals by vaudevillians. Although "Crazy Blues" was not the first blues ever recorded, it was the first documentation of a black vocalist singing blues.

The surprise success of "Crazy Blues" showed record company executives that there was a market for recordings by black singers and musicians and that African Americans were potential consumers. Soon dozens of black female singers were recording blues in hopes of duplicating the success of "Crazy Blues." Many of those performers were vaudevillians who were not necessarily blues singers, although some ended up showing a great deal of talent. Nearly all had experience at performing a variety of material in theaters, generally in the South. Quite frequently their recordings were released on special "race record" labels aimed at the black market. Among the more talented classic blues singers were Ma Rainey, whose pioneering work earned her the title of "Mother of the Blues", Ida Cox, Lucille Hegamin, Trixie Smith, Lizzie Miles, Clara Smith, Sippie Wallace, Rosa Henderson, Bertha "Chippie" Hill, and Victoria Spivey, each of whom had significant careers.

Of the scores of singers who were rushed into recording studios from 1920 to 1924 before the blues craze subsided, most only recorded a handful of titles. In addition to Bessie Smith, the Empress of the Blues, three other New York–based singers deserve special mention: Mamie Smith, Alberta Hunter, and Ethel Waters, who is covered later in the chapter.

Mamie Smith and Alberta Hunter

Mamie Smith had the distinction of being the first recorded classic blues singer, the one who set the standard. She initially worked as a dancer, became a respected singer of a variety of material, and worked with revues and in Harlem clubs. Smith recorded ninety-one numbers during her career, with all but eighteen being cut between 1920 and 1923. She was wise enough to use the top musicians of the time, so despite the primitive recording quality, most of her records are still quite listenable. Her best sidemen had opportunities to take short solos on many of her records, and the young tenor-saxophonist Coleman Hawkins made his recording debut with Smith in 1921. Although her voice grew in strength as the 1920s progressed and her backup bands became more jazz-oriented and swinging, with the passing of the blues craze Smith, whose "Goin' Crazy with the Blues" is a classic, stopped recording after 1926, other than a few titles in 1929 and 1931. She remained active in the 1930s and appeared in a few obscure films before her death in 1946.

Alberta Hunter had the longest career of all the classic blues singers. She started performing in 1906 as an eleven-year-old runaway. After working in Chicago, adapting her style from early popular songs to the blues, she began to record in 1921. Hunter, like Mamie Smith, always used the best musicians she could find and never worried about being overshadowed by such notables as Louis Armstrong, Sidney Bechet, Fats Waller, King Oliver, Duke Ellington, and Eubie Blake. Among her best recordings in the 1920s were "Someday Sweetheart," her composition "Downhearted Blues," "I'm Going Away Just to Wear You Off My Mind," "Old Fashioned Love," and "Nobody Knows the Way I Feel This Morning."

Unlike most of the classic blues singers, Hunter spent years away from the blues. After moving to London in 1928 to co-star with Paul Robeson for a year in *Showboat*, she worked in Paris singing cabaret music and sentimental ballads with John Jackson's Orchestra, and spent most of the 1930s in Europe largely free of being stereotyped either racially or musically. In 1939 with World War II looming, she returned to New York and recorded some jazz and blues using swing musicians that looked back towards her early days. Hunter spent much of the next few years touring for the U.S.O., singing for American servicemen.

Although not having many opportunities to record, Hunter remained active as a singer until 1956. Then, at the age of sixty-one, she decided to become a nurse, claiming that she was forty-four. Other than a couple of nostalgic record dates in 1961, she was away from the music scene, working as a nurse until 1977, when it was thought that she had reached the mandatory retirement age of sixty-five; she was actually eighty-two!

Initially a bit depressed about being put out to pasture, Hunter was soon contacted by Barney Josephson, the owner of the Cookery in New York, asking if she would like to sing there. Having nothing better to do, Hunter made a major comeback, becoming one of the last living links to the 1920s. She still sang with plenty of spirit, interpreted vintage double-entendre blues with sass, recorded several albums, and made history during the seven years before her death in 1984 at the age of eighty-nine.

Bessie Smith: The Empress of the Blues

Of all of the classic blues singers of the 1920s, none had the power and authority of Bessie Smith. She began her career singing with the Moses Stock Company as a teenager, inspired by the revue's star, Ma Rainey. Smith worked throughout the South in a variety of productions and by 1919 was leading her own *Liberty Belles Show*. The hypnotic quality of her most intense blues performances and the joy that she expressed at singing made her a major name among black audiences in the South before she ever recorded.

Visiting New York in February 1923, Smith made her recording debut, and it was a big hit. Her version of Alberta Hunter's "Downhearted Blues" was a major seller and resulted in her recording frequently through 1931. Although the quality of her early records is primitive and the accompaniment of some of her musicians is indifferent, Bessie's voice is so powerful that she overcomes and overwhelms everything. In fact, no vocalist on record in 1923 comes across as fresh and relevant today as the Empress.

The many classics recorded by Bessie Smith included "Tain't Nobody's Bizness if I Do" (more than a decade before Billie Holiday sang it), "Cake Walkin' Babies from Home," "St. Louis Blues" (one of nine numbers that teamed her with Louis Armstrong), "Careless Love," "I Ain't Goin' to Play Second Fiddle," "Back Water Blues" (from Smith's first session with her perfect accompanist, pianist James P. Johnson), "After You've Gone," "Muddy Water," "There'll Be a Hot Time in the Old Town Tonight," "Trombone Cholly" (featuring trombonist Charlie Green), the two-part "Empty Bed Blues," and the immortal

Bessie Smith, the Empress of the Blues, was the most powerful singer of the 1920s.
Photo courtesy of the Wayne Knight Collection, Star Line Productions.

"Nobody Knows You When You're Down and Out."

With her talents and ability to sing popular songs in addition to blues, Bessie Smith continued to prosper after most other classic blues singers were fading. Unfortunately, the collapse of the recording industry after the Depression resulted in her recordings stopping after 1931, other than one final session in 1933.

Still just forty in 1934, Smith gradually reinvented herself as a standards singer and worked fairly steadily, if at a lower profile, as the swing era began. She was poised to make a major comeback, but on September 26, 1937, she died after having a car accident. At the time some claimed that she had been initially taken to a white hospital and refused treatment, causing her demise, but those stories were false. Unfortunately it was an undeniable fact that the voice of the Empress of the Blues was permanently stilled.

LOUIS ARMSTRONG AND THE FLETCHER HENDERSON ORCHESTRA

Fletcher Henderson led one of the top jazz orchestras in 1924. He had started on piano at six, but after earning degrees in chemistry and mathematics, he moved to New York in 1920 with hopes of becoming a chemist. Because racism, even in the comparatively liberal North, made that impossible, Henderson turned to music. Just an average pianist, Henderson had a distinguished air that made him an ideal frontman. He worked for the Black Swan label, led Ethel Water's backup band in 1921 and 1922, and the next year formed a ten-piece orchestra.

The Fletcher Henderson Orchestra, which by the summer of 1924 was based at the Roseland Ballroom, was at first a jazzy dance band featuring futuristic arrangements from clarinetist-altoist Don Redman with some solos from the young tenor Coleman Hawkins. The big band had players who were proud of their ability to read and play anything. At the time, however, there was a major difference between jazz in Chicago and in New York. The latter musicians tended to be superior technically and better sight-readers, but they did not know how to "tell a story" with their solos, often relying on silly effects. Henderson's orchestra used staccato phrasing, Don Redman's arrangements were both futuristic and rhythmically awkward, and the soloists rarely played anything memorable. When Louis Armstrong showed up for his first rehearsal with Henderson, the other musicians, thinking they were so sophisticated, had doubts due to Armstrong's out-of-date clothes and rural manners. When the cornetist blew his horn, however, it changed everything.

Armstrong's beautiful tone and wide range were impressive, but it was his ability to dramatically use space and silence and to build up his improvisations melodically while using a swinging legato phrasing that was most revolutionary. He infused the music with bent and sliding notes, essentially putting the blues in popular music. The effect was electrifying. His recordings with Henderson from October 1924 to November 1925, particularly in the earlier months, find the band sounding stodgy until Armstrong soloed. His moments in the spotlight sound as if they were from a different decade; he was so far ahead of his contemporaries, and it was obvious to every listener that he was leading the way.

Don Redman noticed, and he modernized his arrangements, emphasizing a swinging feel and less cluttered ensembles. Coleman Hawkins also noticed, and he soon dropped his reliance on slap-tonguing and staccato effects. And the other New York musicians, who gathered on a nightly basis to see Armstrong's exciting solos, became very influenced by his playing. By the time Armstrong in late 1925 decided to return to Chicago, jazz in New York had come a long way toward catching up with Chicago.

Big band swing originated with Henderson and Redman thanks to the inspiration of Louis Armstrong. Although Fletcher Henderson was not a great pianist or even much of an arranger prior to the early 1930s, he proved to be a masterful talent scout. Among his superb musicians from 1925 to 1934 were cornetists/trumpeters Joe Smith, Tommy Ladnier, Rex Stewart, Bobby Stark, Cootie Williams, and Henry "Red" Allen; trombonists Charlie Green, Benny Morton, Jimmy Harrison, Sandy Williams, and J. C. Higginbotham; clarinetist Buster Bailey; tenor-saxophonists Coleman Hawkins and Ben Webster; altoists Benny Carter and Russell Procope; bassist John Kirby; and drummers Kaiser Marshall and Walter Johnson. After bad business decisions resulted in his orchestra breaking up, Henderson, whose writing for Benny Goodman helped launch the swing era, made a comeback in 1936 as the bandleader of a fine, new, big band for three years. For a time it featured trumpeter Roy Eldridge and tenor-saxophonist Chu Berry.

As for Louis Armstrong, after his timeless Hot Five and Hot Seven recordings in Chicago, he returned to New York in 1929. At first he appeared in the show *Hot Chocolates* and played nightly in Harlem clubs with a big band. His recordings changed, with his combo replaced by an orchestra that mostly served as a backdrop for his trumpet solos and singing. And instead of mostly playing jazz originals, Armstrong was featured performing the top pop hits from such writers as Hoagy Carmichael, George Gershwin, and Jimmy McHugh. Rather than leaving jazz, he successfully turned every song he interpreted into jazz, including "When You're Smiling," "I Can't Give You Anything But Love," "I'm Confessin' That I Love You," "Body and Soul," "Star Dust," "Memories of You," "Sweethearts on Parade," and Fats Waller's pioneering antiracism song "Black and Blue," adopting "Sleepy Time Down South" as his permanent theme song. He made "Ain't Misbehavin'" into a hit and was outstanding on his recording of "I'm a Ding Dong Daddy," scatting up a storm and building up his trumpet choruses to a high note.

Louis Armstrong, a household name in the United States by 1931, visited Europe for the first time the following year where he was an immediate hit. When an English writer fumbled on his Satchelmouth nickname and called him Satchmo, the formerly impoverished youth from New Orleans gained a new lifelong nickname. Based in New York after 1935 but spending much of his life traveling the world, Armstrong had a decent big band from 1935 to 1947 before forming the Louis Armstrong All-Stars, a Dixieland-oriented sextet that had tremendous commercial success. Although Louis Armstrong's trumpet solos could be predictable in his later years, he remained an exciting, infectious, lovable, and, in his own subtle way, creative performer throughout his career. Satchmo passed away on July 6, 1971, but is still the most famous and beloved of all jazz musicians.

KING OLIVER AND JELLY ROLL MORTON IN NEW YORK

King Oliver and Jelly Roll Morton had similar careers after they left Chicago to try to make it even bigger in New York. Oliver's Dixie Syncopators relocated in 1927, often performing at the Savoy Ballroom. The cornetist made a major mistake when he turned down a contract with the Cotton Club because he felt that the money offered was not sufficient. Duke Ellington took the job instead and became famous due to the regular radio broadcasts. In contrast, Oliver's job with the Savoy soon ended, and he broke up his band. After freelancing in 1928, he emerged the following year with an excellent ten-piece orchestra that recorded for Victor and hinted strongly at swing. Unfortunately, by this time Oliver was having problems with his teeth, which he had neglected for years. As a child Oliver had often consumed "sugar sandwiches," and years later his dental woes were making it painful for him to play cornet. His recorded solos became briefer, and some of his records did not even have a note by the leader, instead featuring his nephew trumpeter Dave Nelson or a guest soloist.

By the time of his final recordings in April 1931, Oliver was largely forgotten in the jazz world, whereas Louis Armstrong was becoming an international star. The former king of the cornet left New York with a band in 1932, performing at low-paying jobs during disastrous tours filled with buses breaking down, racism, money problems, and complete obscurity. The Depression alone would have made things difficult, but since Oliver could barely play anyway, there was little hope for a real comeback. His pride kept him from accepting money from Armstrong or his other friends, and in 1937 he took a job as a poolroom attendant in Savannah, Georgia. By then his health was bad, and he passed away in 1938 at the age of fifty-two, alone and forgotten. Ironically the music of his Creole Jazz Band from fifteen years earlier would become the inspiration for the Dixieland revival of the 1940s, but King Oliver did not live long enough to reap the benefits.

Jelly Roll Morton moved from Chicago to New York in February 1928, and his first few record dates there are similar to his Chicago classics. Unfortunately, by 1929 Morton was finding life more difficult. His bragging caused many New York musicians to ridicule him and underrate his abilities, he found it difficult to gather players for jobs, and his 1929 and 1930 recordings were sometimes erratic and overcrowded, although an occasional gem emerged.

As with King Oliver, the onset of the Depression ended Morton's string of Victor recordings. After 1930 he only made one record date during the next eight years, as a sideman on a 1934 session led by trumpeter Wingy Manone. His jobs were low profile and paid very little. When the swing era began, some of Morton's tunes were constantly being played on the radio in newer big band arrangements, but Morton received little or no pay, having been swindled by his publishers. While Benny Goodman became world famous, the composer of Goodman's first hit, "King Porter Stomp," was completely unknown to a newer generation of jazz fans, running a low-level bar in Washington, DC.

In 1938 it looked as if Morton were going to have a big break. Alan Lomax contacted him to talk about the early days in New Orleans for the Library of Congress. Morton was interviewed extensively, telling stories, playing songs, and singing. There was enough material to later fill eight LPs, but none of the music was released until after Jelly Roll's death, and he was never paid for any of this work. Still, the renewed interest lifted his spirits, and he planned a comeback. In early 1939 Morton returned to New York and began writing new songs that he hoped would generate hits. In September 1939 he recorded his first sets as a leader since 1930, and there were further recordings through the next January. Included were some brilliant piano solos, with vocals on "I Thought I Heard Buddy Bolden Say," "Winin' Boy Blues," and "Don't You Leave Me Here," and some less effective band performances. Despite using some fine musicians, none of Morton's records sold that well, and he failed to create much of an impression during an era dominated by big bands.

Morton became frustrated when he was unsuccessful at making a major impact on the late 1930s music world. In 1940 he decided to try his luck in Los Angeles. By then his health was failing, and he died on July 10, 1941, at the age of fifty-five. Like Oliver, if he had lived a few more years, he would have been one of the main beneficiaries of the Dixieland revival movement. Despite his premature demise, Jelly Roll Morton is today thought of as one of the major greats of early jazz.

JAMES P. JOHNSON AND THE DEVELOPMENT OF STRIDE PIANO

At the same time as the traditions and the roles of the cornet/trumpet, trombone, and clarinet were formed in New Orleans prior to 1920, the stride piano was developing on the East Coast and flourished in New York. Pianists, who of course were not part of parade and marching bands, developed their technique independently of the other instruments. Since they often functioned as one-man bands at parties and dances, pianists had to be able to not only keep a steady beat going but play for many hours, often with few rests.

James P. Johnson was chiefly responsible for developing the definitive stride piano style. He kept time by "striding" with his left hand back and forth between bass notes and chords that were an octave or two higher on the keyboard, while his right hand created variations of the melody, turning his piano into a miniature orchestra. Because this style caught on and was utilized by most jazz pianists up until the bebop era of the mid-1940s, and because Johnson was the star of many late-night jam sessions and cutting contests in Harlem, he became known as the "king of stride pianists."

Johnson's solo playing was well documented on records and piano rolls. He was also a notable songwriter who, unknown to most of the white world, wrote "The Charleston," which by 1925 symbolized the Jazz Age. He wrote other standards, including "Old Fashioned Love" and "If I Could Be with You One Hour Tonight," composed piano features, including "Carolina Shout," "Jingles," and "Riffs" that would be test pieces for young pianists, proved to be a masterful accompanist on records with classic blues singers, especially Bessie Smith and Ethel Waters, led bands, and wrote for shows.

James P. Johnson, like Scott Joplin, had more ambitious dreams beyond being a pianist and jazz composer. In July 1928 his extended work *Yamekraw* with Fats Waller on piano debuted at Carnegie Hall. He spent most of the 1930s out of the limelight, working on composing large-scale orchestral works, including *Harlem Symphony, Jassamine, Symphony in Brown,* and a blues opera called *De Organizer*. Unfortunately much of that music was never performed and is lost. Beginning in 1938 Johnson returned to active playing, and until a stroke ended his career in 1951, four years before his death, he was back on the scene, playing his invigorating brand of stride piano with Dixieland and classic jazz groups.

The king of stride pianists, James P. Johnson defined jazz piano in the 1920s.
Photo courtesy of the Wayne Knight Collection, Star Line Productions.

When Johnson went to after-hours sessions, he rarely traveled alone, bringing with him some of the most talented stride pianists around. Willie "The Lion" Smith was his best pal. Born William Henry Joseph Bonaparte Bertholoff, Smith was playing piano in Atlantic City clubs as early as 1912. After serving with the army in France during World War I, where he earned the title "The Lion," he became a fixture in New York of the 1920s. Smith usually wore a derby, had a cigar in his mouth, and bragged a bit, although he came across as much more lovable than Jelly Roll Morton. His playing was often surprisingly sensitive and lyrical. Unlike Johnson, Smith barely recorded in the 1920s, but he received his chance in the late 1930s when he was documented playing such impressionistic and original compositions as "Echoes of Spring," "Morning Air," and "Passionette." He outlived most of the other stride pianists and was always a colorful figure, keeping stride piano alive in the 1950s and 1960s, and passed away in 1973.

By 1923 Johnson and Smith were often joined in their sessions by nineteen-year-old Thomas "Fats" Waller. Waller was Johnson's protégé, in time surpassing his teacher. Waller began on piano when he was five. His father was a church minister who disapproved of him playing anything other than religious music. When his mother died, he left home and befriended James P. Johnson who became his inspiration. In 1919 when he was just fifteen, Waller was working at the Lincoln Theatre, playing pipe organ as accompaniment for silent movies. He was already a talented composer, writing "Squeeze Me," which became a standard.

Waller's life was a whirlwind of activity with a constant excess of food, liquor, women, and music. In the 1920s he made twenty piano rolls, recorded as a solo pianist—including his dazzling "Handful of Keys"—and as a solo organist, backed classic blues singers, guested with a variety of combos and orchestras, led his own band dates, and wrote music. Often teaming with lyricist Andy Razaf, Waller composed the bulk of the music for the shows *Keep Shufflin'* (1928), *Hot Chocolates* (1929), and *Load of Coal*, including such songs as "Ain't Misbehavin'," "Honeysuckle Rose," and "Black and Blue." Other than one obscure vocal in 1927, "Red Hot Dan," Waller did not sing on records until 1931, and his comic personality would not become world famous until near the beginning of the swing era. He was already a very busy and productive musician, on his way to becoming one of the greats.

Other New York–based stride pianists of the 1920s included Cliff Jackson, Claude Hopkins, and the young Duke Ellington.

BIX BEIDERBECKE

Although Louis Armstrong's work during the classic jazz era made him immortal, it was only the start of a long career. Bix Beiderbecke did not survive past 1931. Beiderbecke, a cornetist with a beautiful tone and harmonically advanced style, was a quieter and cooler-toned player than Armstrong and is today thought of as his closest competitor among brassmen. Beiderbecke was also early proof that jazz, although founded by African Americans based in the South, could be played just as creatively by whites and other races or by anyone who had the musical ability and the chance-taking spirit.

Beiderbecke's life was the stuff of legend, as was his unusual name, even while he was alive. He rose to prominence in the 1920s, hit his peak in 1927, and then quickly declined from an overindulgence of bootleg liquor. Along the way he intuitively created great music while remaining largely unknown to the general public.

Born in Davenport, Iowa, in 1903 to a conservative middle-class family, Beiderbecke showed a natural ability for the piano early in life, playing songs by ear at four. Although he was given classical piano lessons, they did not last long because he preferred to "improve" the written music, which he memorized after hearing once rather than learning to read music. He discovered jazz in 1918 when his older brother brought home a record by the Original Dixieland Jazz Band, and he surprised his parents by buying a cornet and practicing it constantly.

Since his life seemed to be directionless to his parents, they enrolled Beiderbecke at Lake Forest Military Academy in 1921, not knowing that the school was located just thirty-five miles north of Chicago, the center of jazz. After violating curfew a few too many times to sit in with groups in Chicago, Beiderbecke was expelled. He became a fulltime musician, playing throughout the Midwest. In October 1923 he joined the Wolverines, a new group that was influenced by the New Orleans Rhythm Kings. The band caught on for a time, recording sixteen songs in 1924. Although their recordings are mostly concise jam sessions, Beiderbecke's cornet playing was already so lyrical and haunting that he gained a strong reputation among musicians. On "Big Boy," Beiderbecke even took a piano solo in addition to leading the ensemble on cornet.

The Wolverines visited New York in the fall of 1924 and fared quite well. When Beiderbecke was hired away by Jean Goldkette's orchestra, the Wolverines faded into history. He was soon fired for being unable to read music, although Goldkette promised him his job back after he mastered sight-reading.

Much of 1925 was spent in obscurity as Beiderbecke had a short stint with Charlie Straight's band but was again fired for his inability to read music. He spent two weeks at the University of Iowa but was expelled after a drunken brawl. While gigging in St. Louis with C-melody saxophonist Frankie Trumbauer's orchestra, Beiderbecke worked on his sight-reading with the bandleader, and in March 1926 returned to New York and was rehired by Goldkette; Trumbauer also joined the band.

One of jazz's great legends, cornetist Bix Beiderbecke's life rose and fell with the Roaring Twenties.
Photo courtesy of the Wayne Knight Collection, Star Line Productions.

The Jean Goldkette Orchestra of 1926 and 1927, potentially the leading big band in jazz, also featured clarinetist Don Murray, trombonist Bill Rank, the swinging bassist Steve Brown, and arrangements by Bill Challis. Unfortunately Goldkette had signed with the Victor label, and the record producer who worked with the band hated jazz and disliked Beiderbecke's ad-libbing. With a couple of exceptions, most notably "Clementine" and "My Pretty Girl," these Goldkette recordings are disappointing. The songs are inferior, the guest vocalists do not cut it, and the band is not allowed to cut loose except occasionally during the final chorus.

For Beiderbecke 1927 was the high point of his career. In addition to working with Goldkette during the first half of the year, he began recording as the star sideman with groups led by Frankie Trumbauer. Their classic recording of "Singin' the Blues," which has Beiderbecke's most famous solo and a memorable statement from Trumbauer, is one of the first recorded jazz ballads. Their other record gems included "I'm Comin' Virginia" and "Way Down Yonder in

New Orleans." Beiderbecke, under the title of Bix and His Gang, also led a series of freewheeling dates that are highlighted by "Royal Garden Blues," "At the Jazz Band Ball," and "Jazz Me Blues." In addition, Beiderbecke composed four impressionistic piano pieces that year, futuristic music that included "Candlelight," "Flashes," "In the Dark," and "In a Mist," recording the latter as a piano solo.

The Jean Goldkette Orchestra broke up in the summer, and after a brief time performing in New York with a jazz band led by bass-saxophonist Adrian Rollini, both Beiderbecke and Trumbauer joined the Paul Whiteman Orchestra. Although billed as "The King of Jazz," Whiteman was aware that his over-sized big band was more of a concert orchestra. Because he liked jazz, at least in small doses, he went out of his way to sign up some of the best talent. It was a prestigious association for Beiderbecke, playing with the most famous orchestra of the era.

At first the matchup worked well, but soon Beiderbecke became worn out by Whiteman's nonstop schedule of recording dates, radio shows, and live appearances. Many records featured his short solos, including "There Ain't No Sweet Man That's Worth the Salt of My Tears," "San," "Dardanella," "You Took Advantage of Me," and the original recording of George Gershwin's *Concerto in F*. His drinking, which was troublesome by 1925, became uncontrollable by 1928.

Near the end of that year, Beiderbecke was out of action altogether, and he suffered a nervous breakdown in January 1929. Andy Secrest, a younger cornetist with a similar sound, had been filling in for Beiderbecke. Throughout 1929 he continued to decline, and on September 13 he collapsed and was sent home to Davenport. He checked into a hospital for a time and gamely tried to kick his alcoholism. In 1930 he was well enough to return to New York and make three recording dates, but his tone had deteriorated, and he returned to excessive drinking.

All of his recordings are well worth hearing, even when he was slipping. On August 6, 1931, when he was just twenty-eight, Bix Beiderbecke died from pneumonia. If he had quit drinking, he would have become one of the swing era's stars. Instead, because of his tragic death, he is permanently associated with the 1920s.

PAUL WHITEMAN

Prior to 1920 jazz and big bands were separate, with the latter playing strictly melodic dance music. As jazz became popular, the orchestras began to open up their arrangements a bit to satisfy the dancing customers, adding short solos and more flexible rhythms.

One of the first commercial orchestras to incorporate jazz was led by Paul Whiteman. Whiteman started playing violin at seven, and he worked with the Denver Symphony Orchestra from 1907 to 1914. After a stint leading a

Paul Whiteman, an important bandleader who was billed inaccurately as "The King of Jazz," in the mid-1940s with the great European guitarist Django Reinhardt.
Photo courtesy of the Wayne Knight Collection, Star Line Productions.

forty-piece band during a brief period in the navy, in 1918 Whiteman founded his own dance band in San Francisco. Originally it was just seven pieces with cornetist-trumpeter Henry Busse, trombone, clarinet, piano, banjo, tuba, and drums, but by 1921 it was up to a dozen musicians with the addition of a second trumpet, trombone, two more reeds, and violin. Whiteman relocated his band to New York in 1920, and his hit recordings of "Whispering," "Three O'Clock in the Morning," "Japanese Sandman," "Wang Wang Blues," and "Hot Lips" made him the most famous bandleader in America.

Although he was billed as "The King of Jazz" by the mid-1920s, Whiteman never intended jazz to be more than a small part of his repertoire. He was wise enough to hire technically skilled musicians who could play anything, and he utilized the talents of Ferdie Grofe, who was among the first to incorporate a jazz feeling in his arrangements. Whiteman's goal was to "make a lady out of jazz" by taming and civilizing the wild music and performing it for a large audience. Much of the time prior to 1927, all he succeeded at was performing first-class dance music containing a bit of watered-down jazz. An early highpoint for Whiteman was a prestigious concert on February 24, 1924, at Aeolian Hall that featured the debut of George Gershwin's *Rhapsody in Blue*, with Gershwin on piano.

By the mid-1920s Whiteman began to realize that, although he might have been called "The King of Jazz," there were few actual jazz musicians in his over-sized orchestra. In 1926 cornetist Red Nichols, trombonist Tommy Dorsey, and clarinetist Jimmy Dorsey played in his band, and the following year he added the remnants of Jean Goldkette's big band, including Bix Beiderbecke and Frankie Trumbauer, plus the Rhythm Boys with Bing Crosby. By 1929 Whiteman had also hired violinist Joe Venuti and guitarist Eddie Lang, and his large orchestra consisted of four trumpeters, four trombonists, six reed players, a full string section, two pianos, banjo, guitar, bass sax, tuba, bass, drums, and up to six vocalists. Although some of Whiteman's music from 1927 to 1929 was semi-classical or just plain dance music, he recorded enough jazz arrangements to be considered one of the more significant big bands of the time. After the Depression hit, Whiteman cut back his giant orchestra and became less important, being more of a historic figure rather than a relevant force by the time the swing era was flourishing.

THE PACESETTERS IN NEW YORK JAZZ OF THE 1920s

During the 1920s many unique musicians appeared on the jazz scene in New York, lending their highly individual voices to the music. The role of the cornet, and its successor the trumpet, in the 1920s was still the lead voice in ensembles and the horn usually most responsible for stating the melody. Louis Armstrong widened its range and potential, while Bix Beiderbecke offered an alternative voice. Joe Smith with Fletcher Henderson's orchestra had a mellow tone, one that Bessie Smith enjoyed hearing behind her on her recordings. In 1929 Henry "Red" Allen, Jabbo Smith, and Reuben "River" Reeves were all recorded by labels hoping that their hot style of trumpet playing could compete with Louis Armstrong. Allen would have a long career, while the other two soon faded away, although Jabbo Smith's fiery and explosive playing with his Rhythm Aces had an influence on Roy Eldridge later in the 1930s. Cootie Williams succeeded Bubber Miley, a master at using mutes. The lyrical Arthur Whetsol and Freddie Jenkins added further color and variety to Duke Ellington's trumpet section.

As a cornetist, Ernest Loring "Red" Nichols was technically skilled if emotionally a bit bland. In great demand for record dates from 1925 to 1932, Nichols also led many sessions of his own under other names, with his best known being Red Nichols and his Five Pennies. Nichols and his trombonist through 1928, Miff Mole, often employed unusual interval jumps, radical-sounding whole-tone runs, and a mixture of arranged and jammed ensembles.

During the 1920s the trombone evolved from a novelty instrument used for its effects, primarily in New York before New Orleans and Chicago, to playing percussive harmony and emerging as a solo instrument. Kid Ory's rhythmic approach was influential in the early days, but as the decade progressed, other trombonists helped free the instrument from such a subsidiary role. Charlie

Green with Fletcher Henderson and Bessie Smith displayed a bluesy and swinging style. Tricky Sam Nanton with Duke Ellington became Bubber Miley's equivalent on trumpet as an innovator with mutes. Miff Mole, particularly with Red Nichols, had plenty of technique and adventurous ideas, even if his phrasing was rhythmically awkward. Jimmy Harrison, featured with Fletcher Henderson, displayed a smooth legato style, but his early death kept him from having a bigger influence.

Jack Teagarden created a sensation among musicians in 1928 and 1929 after he arrived in New York. He played the trombone with the authority of a trumpeter, certainly had no difficulty with either blues or complex pieces, and displayed outstanding musicianship; he was also a superior blues singer. Teagarden liberated the trombone from its earlier role, no longer restricted to being merely a supportive instrument.

The clarinet had already been "freed" during the New Orleans years. In fact, the big three 1920s clarinetists were all from New Orleans: Sidney Bechet, Johnny Dodds, and Jimmie Noone. Bechet was a child prodigy who played clarinet in public at age eight and as a teenager performed with all the top bands in New Orleans. By 1914 when he was seventeen, he was already traveling throughout the South with different shows, landing in Chicago by 1917. As a member of Will Marion Cook's Southern Syncopated Orchestra, Bechet traveled to Europe in 1918 where his virtuoso solos and wide vibrato made him very popular. While in London, he bought a soprano sax that eventually became his main horn. Bechet was a very passionate player, and he could be quite fiery as an individual, too, often getting in fights. Back in New York, in 1923 he made his first recordings and was showcased as jazz's first major non-piano soloist on "Wild Cat Blues" and "Kansas City Man Blues" with Clarence Williams' group. After two years of recordings, including matchups with Louis Armstrong, he spent most of the 1920s in Europe, limiting his influence on American players.

Jack Teagarden was both a masterful trombonist (who played his horn with the fluidity of a trumpet) and a fine jazz singer.
Photo courtesy of the Wayne Knight Collection, Star Line Productions.

Although it seems like the saxophone was always associated with the music, it was rarely ever used in jazz before the early 1920s and was quite insignificant before 1925. There were six types of saxes used in the 1920s: the soprano, alto, C-melody, tenor, baritone, and bass. Sidney Bechet started doubling on soprano in 1920 and carved out such a distinctive voice on the instrument that few others played it for decades. The C-melody sax, which is voiced between the tenor and the alto, was the vehicle for Frankie Trumbauer, best known for his association with Bix Beiderbecke and for his recordings with his own combos and with Paul Whiteman's orchestra. The bass sax, which was mastered by Adrian Rollini, was sometimes substituted for tuba or string bass in the rhythm section. Although Bechet, Trumbauer, and Rollini were three of the greatest saxophonists of the 1920s, the soprano would be a minor instrument until the 1960s, the C-melody never caught on beyond Trumbauer, and the bass sax became largely extinct by the 1930s except on rare occasions.

At first it looked like there was no role for the tenor sax in jazz either. Sometimes used as a poor substitute for a trombone, at other times utilized for comedy effects, the tenor did not appear in jazz until Coleman Hawkins joined Mamie Smith's Jazz Hounds in 1921. Hawkins joined Fletcher Henderson's orchestra in 1923, and although technically skilled, he employed slap-tonguing and odd tonal distortions in some of his early solos. After Louis Armstrong joined Henderson, Hawkins learned quickly, smoothed out his style, and became the first great tenor saxophonist. His 1926 recording with Henderson, "The Stampede," has what is considered the first important tenor sax solo on records. Hawkins' thick tone and mastery of chords made him the pacesetter in his field. Most other tenor saxophonists who arrived on the scene up to the mid-1930s sounded a great deal like Hawkins, including Chu Berry and Ben Webster. The only important exception was Bud Freeman whose tone was softer than Hawkins and choice of notes more angular. Otherwise Hawkins towered over the field on tenor.

The first great tenor saxophonist, Coleman Hawkins was a continually modern soloist for forty years.
Photo courtesy of the Wayne Knight Collection, Star Line Productions.

The alto sax was used as an extra instrument on jazz recordings in the early 1920s, giving a sweeter sound to the ensembles. Although it worked well as a lead horn with larger ensembles, it did not attract any major soloists until Jimmy Dorsey emerged in 1926. He was soon joined by Johnny Hodges with Duke Ellington's band and Benny Carter. The baritone sax was only used in the 1920s as a substitute for the bass sax, at least until Harry Carney became the first important jazz baritonist when he joined Duke Ellington in 1927.

Because the best stride pianists kept time with their powerful left hands, other rhythm instruments in the 1920s tended to be optional, particularly in small groups. The banjo was favored over the guitar during much of the era simply because it could be heard better. Most banjoists simply kept time, strumming their strings on every beat; the remarkable Harry Reser, who could play with the facility of a pianist, was one of the few exceptions.

After electrical recording developed, the more flexible guitar began to take over, and the banjo became a much rarer instrument in jazz. Eddie Lang was the leading guitarist from 1926 to 1933 because he could play both complex chords and single-note solos. He was in great demand for studio sessions with both jazz and commercial groups, often teamed with violinist Joe Venuti on some classic sessions. Only his premature death in 1933 stopped him from being a major force for many decades to come. A few other guitarists, most notably bluesman Lonnie Johnson, Carl Kress, Dick McDonough, and Teddy Bunn, also proved to be fine soloists. Usually the guitar assumed the same role formerly held by banjoists, keeping the rhythm steady and being felt more than heard.

Many of the earliest jazz dates did not use a bass instrument because, with piano and banjo being employed, the tuba could get in the way or overwhelm the other instruments on the recording. With larger groups, the tuba was used more often than a bass because it could be better heard. Since tuba players had to breathe, they usually only played on every other beat, one and three, while drummers emphasized two and four. Solos were very rare and brief.

Even before the switch over to electrical recording, there were some string bassists who were being used on records. The first major players were the New Orleans pioneer Bill Johnson and Steve Brown, who added a real lift to the final choruses of Jean Goldkette's records. The improvement in recording quality doomed the tuba because bassists could play four beats to a bar and really drive a band. During 1928 and 1929, Wellman Braud, with Duke Ellington, and Pops Foster became the leading bassists. All bassists during this period were restricted to providing accompaniment for bands, very rarely taking more than a two-bar break and never having a full-length solo.

Drummers faced a major dilemma between 1917 and 1927. They were forbidden to use their full drum set, especially the bass drum, on record dates because it was felt that they would destroy the recording balance and drown out the other instruments. Drummers had to become subtle percussionists, using woodblocks, cowbells, cymbals, and sometimes washboards. In 1927 recording techniques finally allowed full drum sets to be recorded, starting with a set by the McKenzie-Condon Chicagoans that featured Gene Krupa. By the end of the decade Krupa, Dave Tough, and Chick Webb were the leading drummers in New York. As with bassists and guitarists, their primary role was to accompany the soloists because the real stars were the horns, singers, and pianists.

There were three very impressive jazz violin soloists who first made an impression in the 1920s. Eddie South and Stuff Smith recorded a few obscure titles and would find greater recognition during the swing era. Joe Venuti was the leader in his field during the classic jazz era. Venuti was a major soloist by 1925 at twenty-two, often teaming up with Eddie Lang on studio dates, jazz sessions, and for heated violin-guitar duets. His small group recordings from the era are a real joy. After Lang's premature death, from a botched tonsillectomy in 1933, Venuti continued working, although his big band during the swing era was quite obscure and he maintained a low profile in the 1950s. Rediscovered in 1967, Venuti made a full comeback and played at his absolute prime during the decade before his death in 1978. Even if he had not been such an exciting jazz violinist, Joe Venuti might still be famous as a practical joker. In one of his many stunts he once called up a couple of dozen bassists, offering them a gig and telling them to meet him on a busy intersection; Venuti watched the ensuing chaos from a safe distance!

THE EARLY JAZZ SINGERS

Very few male singers who appeared on jazz records before 1928 are considered worth hearing. In the early days, vocalists were chosen to record because they could enunciate clearly so as to satisfy song promoters and publishers; the actual sound of their voice was secondary. Male studio singers who were not associated with the musicians were usually hired for the record dates, and most were interchangeable. Some were boy tenors, others were semi-operatic baritones, and they often took up a chorus on even the best jazz performances, particularly those of larger ensembles.

Among the very few early male jazz singers was Cliff Edwards, known as "Ukulele Ike," who also played ukulele and kazoo. He hit it big in 1924 when he introduced "Fascinatin' Rhythm" in the George Gershwin show *Lady Be Good*. Edwards was an early scat-singer, often sang in a falsetto voice, and held his own with the jazz musicians who accompanied him. He debuted "I'll See You in My Dreams" in the 1927 *Ziegfeld Follies* and introduced "Singing in the Rain" in the film *Hollywood Revue of 1929*. Unfortunately Edwards' addiction to alcoholism and gambling hurt his life, and few realized his importance to jazz history. He spent the 1930s playing comedy relief in mostly forgettable B movies. Although he became immortal as the voice of Jiminy Cricket in *Pinocchio*, including singing "When You Wish upon a Star," his excessive drinking eventually led to him becoming completely destitute.

Although Cliff Edwards was arguably the first recorded jazz singer, Louis Armstrong made a much bigger impact. Other than one brief spot with Fletcher Henderson, Armstrong first started singing on records in late 1925. His horn-like phrasing, choice of notes, brilliant scat-singing, and sense of swing became extremely influential, particularly after he moved back to New York in 1929 and started singing current pop songs. Jack Teagarden, who had a lazier style, was touched by Armstrong's singing, as was Bing Crosby.

Crosby, the most popular singer of the 1930s, was responsible for bringing jazz phrasing and swinging into pop music. Harry Lillis "Bing" Crosby sang with his high school band in Washington state, was self-taught on drums, and while studying law at Gonzaga University in Spokane, he met vocalist Al Rinker. After graduating in 1925, Crosby dropped any plans to be a lawyer and instead formed a duo with Rinker. They soon moved to Los Angeles and, through Rinker's sister Mildred Bailey, met and were hired by Paul Whiteman. He teamed them with singer-pianist-songwriter Harry Barris, billing them as the Rhythm Boys. They were a popular attraction with Whiteman's Orchestra from 1927 to 1930, sometimes recording as a separate unit. During this period, Crosby learned from the singing of Armstrong and Teagarden and was also very impressed by the playing of Bix Beiderbecke. Unfortunately, the Rhythm Boys' constant carousing were a problem for Whiteman, and when he had to cut his budget in 1930, they were among the first to go. The Rhythm Boys sang for a time with Gus Arnheim's orchestra in Los Angeles, but by then Crosby's ballad solos were receiving much more attention than the rest of the group. They broke up, and Bing Crosby became a solo singer.

The development of the microphone and electrical recording in the mid- to late 1920s facilitated Bing Crosby's rise. Rather than having to shout out lyrics to be heard, Crosby had a more intimate style and sounded much more natural, relaxed, and accessible. His series of fifteen-minute CBS radio programs were very successful, his records became major sellers and introduced scores of future standards, his club appearances were very well attended, and he began appearing regularly in movies. Although Bing Crosby moved away from jazz by 1935 and emphasized ballads and novelties, he always retained a love for the music of his youth and for Louis Armstrong, occasionally recording in Dixieland settings during the next few decades.

The first female singers to make an impact in jazz were the classic blues singers, most notably Bessie Smith. After the late 1920s, several vocalists faded from the scene, with the major exception of Ethel Waters. Born in 1896, Waters started her career as a teenager singing in Philadelphia and Baltimore. She moved to New York in 1917 and already at that point had both clear enunciation and a solid sense of swing. She was among the first of the classic blues singers to be recorded after Mamie Smith and was the main star of the Black Swan label, the first record company owned by African Americans. Waters was too versatile a singer to be confined solely to blues, and by the time she signed to the larger Columbia label in 1925, her repertoire was divided between blues and popular songs. She introduced the standard "Dinah," recorded a series of wonderful performances while accompanied by James P. Johnson, and in 1929 sang "Am I Blue" in the underrated movie *On with the Show*.

Like Louis Armstrong, by 1929 Waters stretched out toward popular music, still remaining a jazz singer at heart even in the most commercial settings. A strong influence on the singing of such vocalists as Mildred Bailey and Lee Wiley, Waters also developed into a fine actress, not only appearing in such major all-black musical films as the 1943 *Cabin in the Sky* but also getting non-musical parts in both dramas and comedies. She was the best-known black female singer during the first half of the 1930s, and even in the 1940s when much of her time was taken up by acting, she was one of jazz's top vocalists. In her later years before her death in 1977 Waters focused on religious singing.

Although most female singers, outside of the classic blues artists, on the late 1920s records were frivolous and lightweight, a few were on a much higher level. Ruth Etting could be thought of as the female Bing Crosby, a likable singer who brought jazz phrasing and swing into pop music. Etting had a colorful, if at times unfortunate, life story, working as a chorus girl, dancer, and singer in Chicago starting in 1915. She married the gangster "Moe the Gimp" in 1922, and he helped her push her way to the top in New York, although his tactics were really not necessary since she had the talent. In addition to recording steadily from 1926 to 1937, Etting appeared in such shows as the *Ziegfeld Follies of 1927*, *Whoopee*, and *Simple Simon*, was featured in thirty-five film shorts and three full-length movies, and helped make famous such songs as "Ten Cents a Dance," "Love Me or Leave Me," and "You're the Cream in My Coffee." Due to her husband's activities in the criminal world, there were scandals and heartbreak along the way, and she retired in 1937, only making brief comebacks in later years.

Annette Hanshaw retired at twenty-four, much earlier than Etting, due to her reluctance to sing in public. Hanshaw, who would be much better known today if she had not withdrawn from the jazz scene, was one of the first significant white female jazz singers. She debuted on records in 1926 when she was just fifteen, showed from the start that she could swing, sometimes wrote additional lyrics to songs, and was billed as "The Personality Girl." In one of Hanshaw's first records she concluded a song by saying "That's all," which became her trademark. From 1926 to 1934 she recorded in jazz-oriented settings including definitive versions of "I'm Gonna Meet My Sweetie Now," "It All Depends on You," "Get Out and Get under the Moon," "Daddy, Won't You Please Come Home," "Lovable and Sweet," and "My Future Just Passed." She was never hungry to perform, was nervous when she had to appear in public, and was relieved in 1934 when she decided to retire from music, get married, and work in office jobs. Though she lived until 1985, Annette Hanshaw never sang in public again.

Vocal groups in jazz are quite rare, but two of the very best made a strong impression in the early 1930s. The Boswell Sisters, Connie, Martha, and Helvetia, were raised in New Orleans, and each of the sisters learned instruments, although Martha, on piano, was the only one who pursued it. They recorded initially in 1925 as teenagers, gained experience working regularly on radio in Los Angeles, and began recording regularly after moving to New York in 1930. Their adventurous arrangements featured plenty of surprising tempo and key changes. The Boswells all had beautiful voices and could sing lyrics well in addition to scatting up a storm. Connie Boswell took occasional solos,

Bing Crosby, a hugely influential singer who brought jazz phrasing into pop music, and the Boswell Sisters, one of the major jazz vocal groups.
Photo courtesy of the Wayne Knight Collection, Star Line Productions.

but it was the advanced vocal harmonies and the arrangements that made the sisters a hit. They appeared in several movies in the 1930s, the best being the 1932 *Big Broadcast*, and often used all-star jazz greats on their records, although they were quite capable of singing just accompanied by Martha's piano. Despite the successes, in 1936 when Martha and Helvetia got married, they decided to retire from show business. Connie Boswell continued as a solo singer. Although her own career went fine, it lacked the uniqueness and endless potential of the Boswell Sisters.

Another unique group in the early 1930s was the Mills Brothers. Still famous today for their pop successes of the 1940s and 1950s, the Mills Brothers started out as an innovative jazz group. John, Herbert, Harry, and Donald Mills began singing in vaudeville shows in the late 1920s in their native Ohio. They developed the uncanny ability to imitate instruments, often sounding as if they were playing trumpet, trombone, tuba, and bass even though they only used an acoustic guitar. When they moved to New York and started appearing on records and national radio in 1931, they caused a sensation. Throughout the 1930s the "four boys and a guitar" were kept busy, appearing in several movies and touring Europe. John Mills' death in 1935 was a major loss, but with their father in his place, they continued performing top-notch jazz into the early

1940s. After having a pop hit with "Paper Doll" in 1942, they dropped their original approach and became more conventional and middle-of-the-road, using a full rhythm section and sometimes a full band while sticking to singing lyrics. The early Mills Brothers were so much more interesting, showing how quickly the art of jazz singing had moved from 1927 to 1932.

HARLEM

For many African Americans in the 1920s and early 1930s, Harlem was the promised land. The black district of New York City was one of the few places in the United States where African Americans could be themselves and have a certain amount of freedom and independence from the white establishment. The freedom was a bit of an illusion, but at least during what became known as the Harlem Renaissance, African Americans could express themselves artistically in poetry, prose, theater, dancing, and music. Although jazz was somewhat separate from the Renaissance movement, both predating and outliving it, it provided the soundtrack for some of the artistic innovations.

Having set the standards for big bands in the 1920s, Fletcher Henderson's orchestra at Roseland was a major influence on the many Harlem-based big bands by the early Depression years. The orchestras not only performed swinging jazz but also backed dance acts, variety shows, and singers, and provided dance music for customers. Among the many notable clubs that flourished in Harlem during this period were the Alhambra Ballroom, the Bamboo Inn, Barron's, the Capitol Palace, Connie's Inn, the Lafayette Theatre, the Lenox Club, the Nest Club, the Cotton Club, Small's Paradise, and the Savoy Ballroom, where Chick Webb and his band reigned supreme.

DUKE ELLINGTON

It is impossible to overstate Duke Ellington's vast accomplishments as a composer, arranger, bandleader, and pianist. He wrote thousands of pieces in his career, scores of which became standards. His arrangements, written specifically for his sidemen, were so inventive that he was able to blend together very different individualists into a unified group sound. Ellington led a band that for forty-nine years, from 1926 to 1974, always ranked near the top with no real down period artistically. As a pianist, he was initially a fine stride player, influenced by Willie "The Lion" Smith and James P. Johnson, who through the decades always remained modern.

Born April 29, 1899, in Washington, DC, Edward Kennedy Ellington began playing piano when he was seven and seemed to be destined to become an artist, even earning an art scholarship to Brooklyn's Pratt Institute. By then he had been hanging out nightly at local clubs and parties where he was impressed by the local ragtime and stride pianists. Already nicknamed "Duke" due to his suave, sophisticated nature, Ellington partly learned how to play jazz piano by slowing down James P. Johnson piano rolls to half-speed so he could copy the fingering. In 1917 he composed his first song, "Soda Fountain Rag," and although he only knew a few tunes at the time, he was soon supplying several groups a night for parties and dances, having taken out a very large Yellow Pages ad about his band before it even existed. Although he was making a good living in Washington, DC, in 1923 Ellington traveled to New York to join Wilbur Sweatman's band. Sweatman was well known at the time for his ability to play three clarinets at once, but he was not much of a jazz player. When the engagement ended, Ellington returned home. A few months later, banjoist Elmer Snowden formed the Washingtonians with Ellington and some of his friends, and they worked steadily in New York. A money dispute resulted in Snowden being ousted and Duke becoming the leader.

The Washingtonians worked at the Kentucky Club from 1924 to 1927, during which Ellington developed quickly as a pianist and a writer. Although the group sounded good on the two songs they recorded in December 1924, that was just a false start, and it was not until late 1926 before the Ellington sound started to emerge on records. By then the band featured trumpeter Bubber Miley and trombonist Tricky Sam Nanton, both of whom were masters at distorting their sounds with mutes to get otherworldly effects, which were nicknamed "the jungle sound." In 1927 Ellington retained Irving Mills as his manager, started recording frequently for many different labels under a variety of names, and introduced the eerie "Black and Tan Fantasy" and "Creole Love Call," the latter with a pioneering wordless vocal from Adelaide Hall. The most important event took place on December 4, 1927, when the Duke Ellington Orchestra became the house band at Harlem's Cotton Club. In addition to playing its own music, the Ellington big band was now performing for shows, and they gained a great deal of publicity broadcasting regularly from the establishment. Soon they were being billed accurately as Duke Ellington's Famous Orchestra.

With Ellington writing prolifically, the band introduced such originals from 1926 to 1931 as their theme song "East St. Louis Toodle-oo," "The Mooche," "Black Beauty," "Old Man Blues," "Mood Indigo," "Rockin' in Rhythm," and "Cotton Club Stomp." In 1929 he recorded his first extended piece, a rendition of *Tiger Rag* that took up two sides of a 78, totaling nearly six minutes. In 1931 Ellington wrote his initial extended work, the two-part *Creole Rhapsody*, but that was just the first step in his desire to write lengthy suites.

In Ellington's band, more than in most others, his sidemen were of major importance. Many of the pieces Duke wrote were collaborations with his players, and virtually all of his musicians were potentially significant soloists. Rather than hiring musicians because they played ensembles well or were good sight-readers, Ellington was most interested in gathering unique voices and writing for them.

Most important in his early band was trumpeter Bubber Miley, who greatly extended the expertise that King Oliver had shown with mutes. The tones that he achieved from his horn were eerie and quite unforgettable. Unfortunately Miley became an alcoholic, and in early 1929, Ellington reluctantly fired him after he had become quite unreliable. Cootie Williams took his place and proved in future years to be more of an all-round player, very capable of utilizing mutes but also able to play open solos influenced by Louis Armstrong. In the trumpet section next to Miley or Williams were the lyrical trumpeter Arthur Whetsol, whose tone was haunting in a different way, and the more conventional but hot soloist Freddy Jenkins. The trombonists were Joe "Tricky Sam" Nanton, Miley's equivalent with tone distortions but much more reliable, and the versatile valve trombonist Juan Tizol, who did not solo much but could fill in for any players including the saxophonists.

Altoist Johnny Hodges had a beautiful tone and the ability to sound very much at home on blues, stomps, and ballads. Barney Bigard was a New Orleans native who had played fine tenor sax with King Oliver's Dixie Syncopators from 1924 to 1927 but switched permanently back to clarinet to play with Ellington. His presence allowed Ellington to use the New Orleans sound in unexpected and sophisticated settings. Harry Carney, who joined Duke in 1927 and stayed forty-eight years even after Ellington's death, was the first important baritone saxophonist in jazz, and his huge sound is still definitive. The sax section also included Otto Hardwicke, an altoist with a sweet tone that contrasted well with Miley and Nanton, although he played elsewhere between 1929 and 1931. In addition to Ellington on piano, the rhythm section consisted of banjoist Fred Guy, who switched to the nearly inaudible guitar in the early 1930s, the excellent string bassist Wellman Braud, and the colorful drummer Sonny Greer.

Duke Ellington's orchestra was based at the Cotton Club from 1927 to 1931 and then hit the road, its real home for the next four decades. The band toured Europe for the first time in 1933 and crisscrossed the United States countless times.

There were several important new additions to the band's personnel in the 1930s. Cootie Williams was joined in the trumpet

A true genius, Duke Ellington was an innovative composer, arranger, pianist, and bandleader for a half century.
Photo courtesy of the Wayne Knight Collection, Star Line Productions.

section by cornetist Rex Stewart, who became a key soloist in 1934. Stewart's half-valve technique of bending notes, featured on numbers including

"Boy Meets Horn," gave Ellington a new voice to blend into the ensembles. Lawrence Brown played trombone, in addition to the tonal distortions of Tricky Sam Nanton and the fluent playing of valve trombonist Juan Tizol. Brown had strong technique, a swinging style, and a distinctive sound of his own. The saxophone section, including altoist Johnny Hodges, clarinetist Barney Bigard, and baritonist Harry Carney, was occasionally joined by Otto Hardwicke on second alto. With all of those distinctive players, the rhythm section was often overlooked. While guitarist Fred Guy was largely inaudible and drummer Sonny Greer primarily added colors, Ellington was a superior forward-looking stride pianist, and Wellman Braud was one of the top bassists of the early 1930s. When Braud departed later in the decade, he was replaced by Billy Taylor, no relation to the later pianist, with Hayes Alvis sometimes on second bass. In addition, in 1932 Ellington hired Ivie Anderson, his first fulltime singer, who had an immediate hit with "It Don't Mean a Thing If It Ain't Got That Swing," a tune written by Ellington three years before the swing era began.

The 1930s found Ellington writing many songs that became standards, including "Sophisticated Lady," "Drop Me off in Harlem," "Solitude," "In a Sentimental Mood," "I Let a Song Go out of My Heart," and "Prelude to a Kiss." In addition, his recordings included a remarkable musical recreation of a train trip called "Daybreak Express," the melancholy four-part "Reminiscing in Tempo," and many underrated gems. Ellington was the arranger and pianist for a series of small group dates headed by his sidemen including Cootie Williams, Rex Stewart, Johnny Hodges, and Barney Bigard.

The rise of the swing era did not cause Ellington any difficulty because he was well established before any of the potentially competitive big bands had been formed. During 1939 and 1940 his superb orchestra became even stronger with three new additions. Billy Strayhorn, a promising young pianist-composer-arranger from Pittsburgh, became an integral, if often invisible, part of the band, contributing songs, including the new Ellington theme song "Take the 'A' Train," collaborating with Duke on arrangements, and working behind the scenes. Ben Webster became Ellington's first major tenor sax soloist, and Jimmy Blanton, who was just twenty-one when he joined Ellington in 1939, revolutionized the string bass. In addition to playing inspiring accompaniment to soloists and in the ensembles, Blanton could solo on the bass with the fluency of a guitar. He had short solos with the full band and recorded six duets with Ellington in which the pianist mostly backed the bassist instead of the other way around. Tragically Blanton's life was very short; he was struck down by tuberculosis in late 1941 and passed away the following year. His legacy lived on through the playing of Oscar Pettiford, Ray Brown, and virtually every acoustic bassist in future years.

The period from 1939 to 1942 is considered to be the absolute peak for the Duke Ellington Orchestra, although the band never really had an off period. When Cootie Williams left in 1940 to join Benny Goodman this was not a fatal blow because he was immediately replaced by Ray Nance, who not only could play cornet solos in a style similar to Williams' but also was a fine singer and a violin soloist. Among the scores of classic Ellington recordings from this period are "Portrait of the Lion," a tribute to Willie "The Lion" Smith, "Ko-Ko," "Concerto for Cootie," a feature for Cootie Williams that with lyrics was renamed "Do Nothing till You Hear from Me," "Cotton Tail," featuring Ben Webster, "Harlem Air Shaft," "All Too Soon," the original recording of "Take the 'A' Train," "I Got It Bad (And That Ain't Good)," "Just A-Settin' and A-Rockin," "Jump for Joy," Strayhorn's "Chelsea Bridge," Juan Tizol's "Perdido," "The 'C' Jam Blues," Mercer Ellington's "Things Ain't What They Used to Be," and a non-Ellington song that became a big hit for his new vocalist Herb Jeffries, "Flamingo."

The Duke Ellington Orchestra was in the legendary, if short-lived, show *Jump for Joy* in 1940. It debuted at Carnegie Hall in 1943, introducing his fifty-minute suite *Black, Brown and Beige* that musically depicted the history of blacks in America. Although the piece only gained mixed reviews because it was too original to be accepted by the conservative critics of the time, one section became a definitive spiritual, "Come Sunday." Between 1943 and 1950 Ellington appeared annually at Carnegie Hall, and in addition to playing the usual repertoire, he normally debuted an extended work each year. Among those compositions were the *Perfume Suite*, *A Tonal Group*, *The Liberian Suite*, *The Tattooed Bride*, and *Harlem*. Ellington, who did not like the word "jazz" because he felt that it was a restriction on his music, considered his extended works to be among his most important accomplishments.

During the 1940s there was more turnover in Ellington's band than before. Among the new members were trumpeters Taft Jordan, Shorty Baker, and Cat Anderson, who became the greatest high-note trumpeter, trombonist-vibraphonist Tyree Glenn, who succeeded Nanton after Tricky Sam's death, tenor-saxophonist Al Sears, the cool-toned clarinetist Jimmy Hamilton, and singer Al Hibbler. Ellington had further hits in "I Ain't Got Nothing but the Blues," "I'm Beginning to See the Light," and "Don't Get Around Much Anymore."

Duke was able to keep his big band together after the end of the swing era in 1946, partly by financing the orchestra during lean times with his song royalties. In 1951 things looked bleak when Johnny Hodges, Sonny Greer, and Lawrence Brown all departed to join Hodges' new combo. Ellington retorted with what was called "the great James robbery" by adding drummer Louie Bellson, altoist Willie Smith, and Juan Tizol, who had departed earlier, from Harry James' band. Ellington recorded some fine records in the early 1950s and had his last pop hit with "Satin Doll," but the first half of the 1950s was a struggle, and it was not a foregone conclusion that he would be able to keep his big band together.

Things changed during 1955 and 1956. Hodges gave up on his group and rejoined Ellington. At the 1956 Newport Jazz Festival on a blues interlude between "Diminuendo in Blue" and "Crescendo in Blue," Ellington turned his tenor-saxophonist Paul Gonsalves loose. Gonsalves played twenty-seven choruses, practically causing a riot, and the performance gained worldwide headlines. Duke Ellington was back, and his band was never in danger of breaking up again.

Although always playing some of his older hits and never completely discarding the Harlem jungle sound of the 1920s, Ellington constantly looked ahead. His band was open to the influence of bebop in the 1950s, and new soloists kept Duke's music stimulating. Among his stars of the era were trumpeters Clark Terry, Ray Nance, Cat Anderson, and Willie Cook, trombonists Quentin Jackson, Buster Cooper, and Britt Woodman, and a saxophone section— Hodges, Hamilton, Carney, Gonsalves, and clarinetist-altoist Russell Procope— that was unchanged between 1955 and 1968. Counting Ellington on piano, his band had up to thirteen possible soloists in the late 1950s. Ellington kept his own piano style modern, influencing Thelonious Monk with his percussive approach. In the early 1960s he recorded collaborations with Louis Armstrong, John Coltrane, Coleman Hawkins, a trio with bassist Charles Mingus and drummer Max Roach, and a double big band set with the Count Basie Orchestra.

Ellington did not slow down in the 1960s, constantly circling the globe with his orchestra. He and Billy Strayhorn wrote such works as an adaptation of Tchaikovsky's *Nutcracker Suite*, the 1963 shows *My People*, *The Far East Suite*, and *Night Creature*. Cootie Williams returned to the band in 1961 after a twenty-one-year "vacation," and for a short time it appeared that Duke was ageless, but inevitably his key collaborators began to pass away. Strayhorn's passing in 1967 was a major blow, as was Johnny Hodges' death in 1970. Some replacements, such as tenor-saxophonist Harold Ashby, altoist Norris Turney, and trumpeter Barry Lee Hall, were major assets during the last years. Ellington's seventieth birthday was celebrated at the White House in 1969, and among the projects that meant the most to him during this last period was writing the music for his three sacred concerts. It all came to an end in 1974 when Duke Ellington died from cancer a few weeks after his seventy-fifth birthday. His accomplishments during his half century in the limelight are so enormous that no other jazz musician's work is comparable.

AN OVERVIEW OF THE SWING YEARS

Between 1935 and 1946, jazz was a major force in popular music. From its beginnings in New Orleans, jazz had usually been played for dancers. In 1935 when teenagers discovered the new swing music, its popularity skyrocketed due to its danceability. Although there were hundreds of big swing orchestras all over the United States, with just a few exceptions, such as Earl Hines' big band in Chicago, all major names were eventually based in New York.

The Wall Street crash of 1929 and the Depression between 1930 and 1934 pushed most jazz underground. Although the music was still alive and evolving, most of its former fans were more concerned with surviving economically. When they heard music on the radio or at nightclubs, it tended to be straight dance music and sentimental ballads. Much of the best jazz of this period was performed in Harlem by such black big bands as those led by Duke Ellington, Cab Calloway, Chick Webb, and Fletcher Henderson, but mainstream America rarely heard that music, and teenagers of the era must have been a bit bored with the pop music scene, such as it was.

That all changed during 1934 and 1935 as the Benny Goodman Orchestra on the *Let's Dance* radio series broadcast the new swing music nationwide. Even Goodman had no idea as to his music's potential popularity, and it was only when his legendary cross-country tour in 1935 ended that he knew he had made it big.

Swing became the pop music of its day. Teenagers and young people wanted more exciting music to dance to than the smooth ballads that had previously dominated. Although the Depression did not really end until World War II, the gradual improvement of economic conditions allowed Americans to pay a little more attention to the music scene. In a time when money was short, radio broadcasts of swing bands gave listeners free entertainment, and the hundreds of inexpensive dance halls permitted dancers and fans in smaller towns opportunities to see their heroes in person. Not all big bands were jazz oriented and not all swing bands were big orchestras, but it is the swinging large ensembles that are most remembered today.

Jazz musicians were more than ready for the swing era to begin. Some of the top white players of the 1920s, those with strong technical skills, survived the early Depression years by playing in the New York studios and commercial radio bands. Many dance records from the early 1930s have brief solos from the likes of clarinetist Benny Goodman, altoist-clarinetist Jimmy Dorsey, trombonist Tommy Dorsey, the new trumpeter Bunny Berigan, and other survivors from the earlier era. Although the pay was lucrative, these and other jazz musicians were bored by the music they had to play during their day jobs, and many searched for nighttime jam sessions where they could play the music they loved. The black musicians did not have the option of playing in studio and radio bands for the music scene. The more fortunate players caught on with the Harlem big bands or were able to play in local black dance orchestras. Many others dropped out of music altogether for long stretches, and some were never able to come back, for example King Oliver.

In 1935, however, the climate began to change. Benny Goodman's surprise success led to him being crowned "King of Swing" and becoming a household name. Musicians everywhere were inspired by both his music and his success at attracting a huge dancing audience. Scores of bands were formed within a year, and by 1937 there were hundreds all over the United States. Goodman would always be famous, but he soon had close competition. Tommy Dorsey caught on in 1937, the following year Artie Shaw surpassed Goodman in popularity, and in 1939 Glenn Miller topped everyone. Count Basie arrived out of Kansas

City in late 1936, Jimmy Lunceford had some hit records, and Goodman alumni Gene Krupa and Harry James had bands that became very successful. Charlie Barnet, Cab Calloway, Bunny Berigan, and Bob Crosby all made an impact. In addition, throughout this era, Duke Ellington wrote one memorable song after another while his orchestra remained in its own special category.

It was a magical time when new hit songs seemed to be written every week and bandleaders were celebrities. Even the outbreak of World War II did not slow swing's acceptance as a new and superior form of popular music. A combination of forces between 1943 and 1946 ended the swing era, and this golden age of popular music came to a conclusion.

BENNY GOODMAN: THE KING OF SWING

Unlike Paul Whiteman, whose title of "The King of Jazz" should have gone to either Louis Armstrong or Jelly Roll Morton, Benny Goodman did deserve to be known as "The King of Swing." Although the clarinetist did not invent swing music or have the first swing band, a distinction given to Fletcher Henderson's orchestra of 1924 and 1925, Goodman's orchestra was the one that caught on and launched the swing era. And besides that, BG was one of the greatest clarinetists of all time.

Born in 1909 Benny Goodman grew up in poverty in Chicago but early on found his direction in life. He began playing clarinet at eleven and within five years had impressed many in the local scene. At sixteen he became the top soloist in Ben Pollack's orchestra, making his recording debut with it a year later in 1926. After four years with Pollack, Goodman worked with Red Nichols' Five Pennies before becoming a very busy studio musician in New York. He appeared on a countless number of sessions during the first half of the 1930s, being a very good sight-reader and a technically skilled player. Goodman was bored with playing bland dance music, and he dreamed of leading his own band.

In 1934 he formed a big band, played regularly at Billy Rose's Music Hall, and made some records. More importantly, the band won an audition to become one of the three orchestras appearing on the new *Let's Dance* radio series, providing the jazz that contrasted with Xavier Cugat's Latin music and Del Murray's more commercial band. Goodman at first did not have enough material constantly to play new pieces on the radio programs, but producer John Hammond, a significant force in swing music, convinced him to hire Fletcher Henderson to contribute arrangements. Henderson's band was struggling, and the bandleader was happy to get the extra money. Goodman would always credit Henderson's writing with helping his band become successful.

The *Let's Dance* series ended in May 1935, leaving Goodman struggling for work. In July he recorded two songs for the Victor label, "King Porter Stomp" and "Sometimes I'm Happy," that became popular. With his regular drummer Gene Krupa and guest pianist Teddy Wilson, he made the first recordings of the

Benny Goodman Trio. It was not definite, however, that his orchestra would be able to stay together long without a regular engagement.

A top booking agent, Willard Alexander, convinced Goodman that a cross-country tour would be the best thing for his orchestra and would help determine if it had a future. Goodman and his musicians were booked in small towns all the way to the West Coast, and many of their appearances were failures. Some club owners insisted that the orchestra emphasize waltzes, tangos, and dance music, and there were many nights when there was hardly anyone in the audience. Few people had apparently heard of Goodman. As the band made its way to California, the future looked dismal. An engagement in Oakland was well received, but an August 21 concert at the Palomar Ballroom appeared to be the band's last chance. During the first few sets, Goodman played it safe, performing polite dance music before a large but mostly quiet audience. Finally, the clarinetist decided there was nothing left to lose, and he called a hot swing number. The audience exploded in happiness, and teenagers began to dance in the aisles. Goodman was quite surprised and called one jazz tune after another, to the crowd's delight. The performance made headlines and launched the swing era.

How was Benny Goodman's big band different than the ensembles in the 1920s, and what was the cause of its success as opposed to other orchestras that were struggling in 1935?

The Fletcher Henderson Orchestra in 1927 consisted of two trumpets, two trombones, three reeds, piano, banjo, tuba, and drums. The Goodman band in 1935 had three trumpets, two trombones, the leader's clarinet, two alto saxes, two tenor saxes, piano, guitar, bass, and drums, fourteen pieces in all, compared to Henderson's eleven in the earlier days. The piano-guitar-bass-drums rhythm section had become standard and kept a steady and uncluttered beat that was very easy to follow. Goodman was quite skilled at setting the perfect dance tempo for each song while alternating wild "killer dillers" with slower ballads. In addition to Henderson and his younger brother Horace, Goodman employed top arrangers such as Jimmy Mundy, Deane Kincaide, Edgar Sampson, and Spud Murphy who put the melody first but included rhythmic figures in their charts and wrote arrangements that built to a logical climax. In 1935 Goodman did not have many major soloists in his band. Unlike Duke Ellington who went out of his way to hire unique individualists, Goodman was most concerned that his musicians read music perfectly, blended together naturally, and did not mind being subservient to the leader. It was the sound of the ensembles, the swinging rhythm section, and the leader's fluent clarinet that proved to be irresistible to his young and eager listeners.

After Bunny Berigan was Goodman's trumpet soloist for a few months, including on the first hit records and during the legendary cross-country tour, he soon returned to the studios. Otherwise there were no real individual stars in Goodman's 1935 band except the appealing singer Helen Ward. Even drummer Gene Krupa was then primarily a supportive player. Things gradually changed during 1936 and 1937. Ziggy Elman joined and took heated trumpet solos. Krupa, increasingly assertive in his playing, became the most popular drummer in swing. The Benny Goodman Trio, a regular feature of the band's broadcasts and performances, broke down racial boundaries with the inclusion of Wilson. In 1936 after Goodman, Wilson, and Krupa jammed with vibraphonist Lionel Hampton, they formed the Benny Goodman Quartet. The Trio and Quartet helped start a trend of swing bands, adding variety by featuring a small jazz combo drawn from its personnel on occasional numbers.

Goodman's big band was a major sensation at New York's Paramount Ballroom. Although Helen Ward's decision to retire and get married was unfortunate for the band, she was replaced successfully by Martha Tilton. By 1937 Goodman's orchestra had become more exciting with the addition of Harry James who, with Elman and Chris Griffin, formed an unbeatable trumpet section. Krupa, showcased on the studio version of "Sing Sing Sing," was on his way to becoming a superstar, and the King of Swing's dominance of popular music continued to grow. Goodman's band was featured on the very popular *Camel Caravan* radio series, its records sold steadily, and every night his orchestra played before huge crowds. Among its more popular recordings were "Stompin' at the Savoy," "Goody Goody," "Don't Be That Way," and "Avalon" by the Quartet.

Benny Goodman was just twenty-eight when he reached the height of his career at the January 16, 1938, concert at Carnegie Hall. It was the first full-length jazz concert held at the temple of classical music, and the clarinetist and his musicians were initially nervous. The opening number, "Don't Be That Way," featured some Krupa drum breaks that woke up both the band and the audience. Throughout the night the many highlights included a brief "History of Jazz" medley reaching back to 1917, a jam session on "Honeysuckle Rose" that included some stars from the Duke Ellington and Count Basie bands, features for the Benny Goodman Trio and Quartet, and most notably, a lengthy version of "Sing, Sing, Sing" that alone would have made Gene Krupa into a superstar, although Jess Stacy's impressionistic piano solo almost stole the show. The concert was a huge success. And unknown to most, the concert was recorded, although it would have to wait until 1950 and the LP era before it was released to the public.

Benny Goodman would never quite reach that height again, but he continued leading one of the most popular of all swing bands. Gene Krupa, whose playing had become too flashy for Goodman, departed a month after the Carnegie Hall concert due to personality clashes to form his own band. Harry James left on more amicable terms in early 1939 because he had also become a big star. Ziggy Elman filled in for James and had a hit for Goodman with "And the Angels Sing." In mid-1939 Goodman had a very important new addition to his band, electric guitar pioneer Charlie Christian, an integral part of his sextet for the next two years. Christian played his guitar with the fluency of a tenor sax, revolutionizing the instrument and inspiring Goodman to create some of his finest solos in the small group.

Although Goodman had to break up his big band for two months in mid-1940 due to health problems, he was soon back with a similar band. Lionel Hampton left to form his own big band, and Ziggy Elman joined Tommy Dorsey in the interim. Goodman hired trumpeter Cootie Williams, who had just ended eleven years with Duke Ellington, and tenor-saxophonist Georgie Auld, formerly with Artie Shaw, for both his big band and septet. He also used Eddie Sauter's very advanced arrangements, along with some durable swingers by Fletcher Henderson and others, and Helen Forrest on vocals. By 1942 he was featuring singer Peggy Lee, who had a hit with "Why Don't You Do Right," and pianist Mel Powell. Goodman broke up his band twice during the war years but had another fine swing orchestra during 1945 and 1946. By then, however, the rapid evolution of jazz was starting to pass him by, and Goodman's swing clarinet sounded old-fashioned next to the boppish trumpet playing of Dizzy Gillespie.

The King of Swing Benny Goodman with the first great electric guitarist, Charlie Christian.
Photo courtesy of the Wayne Knight Collection, Star Line Productions.

Goodman persevered. He had a flirtation with bop during 1948 and 1949, placing his clarinet in more modern settings and utilizing a few adventurous arrangements for his big band. He did not sound all that comfortable and in 1950 returned permanently to swing. Other than an attempt to bring back the long-gone swing era in 1952 with what would be a short-lived orchestra, Benny Goodman spent the rest of his career alternating between playing with swinging small groups and putting together a big band for special occasions. Always retaining his enthusiasm for both swing music and the clarinet, he remained active up until his death in 1986, never relinquishing his title of "The King of Swing."

THE DORSEY BROTHERS

The story of Tommy and Jimmy Dorsey is particularly colorful because, although the two brothers loved and greatly respected each other, their fighting earned them the nickname "the battling Dorseys." Jimmy was born in 1904, and Tommy followed twenty-one months later. Their coal miner father also worked as a music teacher and a band director. He started Jimmy on the cornet, although he switched to alto sax and clarinet by the time he was eleven. Tommy was taught trombone and trumpet.

The Dorsey brothers began their careers as teenagers co-leading Dorsey's Novelty Six and Dorsey's Wild Canaries. After a stint with Billy Lustig's Scranton Sirens, they moved to New York in 1924. Jimmy emerged as one of the first significant jazz soloists on alto, and his clarinet playing also ranked near the top. He appeared on a countless number of records in the 1920s, including with the California Ramblers, Jean Goldkette, Paul Whiteman, and Red Nichols's Five Pennies. Tommy, who occasionally played some rough sounding trumpet, developed a very smooth tone on trombone and appeared in some of the same groups with his older brother.

Beginning in 1928 they co-led the Dorsey Brothers Orchestra that for the first five years was just a recording group. Both of the brothers were in great demand during the early Depression years for commercial and jazz sessions where their impeccable sight-reading abilities came in handy. In 1934 at about the time that Benny Goodman was thinking of starting a big band, the Dorsey brothers formed their own orchestra, having a bit of initial success. Glenn Miller provided some of the arrangements, Bob Crosby was one of their vocalists, and the band worked steadily and recorded prolifically for a year. Unfortunately, the fighting between the competitive brothers was constant, and in May 1935, while playing onstage at the Glen Island Casino, they had an argument over the tempo of "I'll Never Say 'Never Again' Again." Tommy Dorsey stormed off the bandstand and never returned. Jimmy Dorsey became the sole leader of the Dorsey Brothers band while his brother soon took over the struggling Joe Haymes Orchestra.

Tommy Dorsey's band caught on first. Although he enjoyed taking an occasional chorus on freewheeling jazz, Dorsey emphasized the pretty side of his tone and featured himself on ballads, being billed as "The Sentimental Gentleman of Swing." His theme song was "I'm Getting Sentimental over You." In 1937 when trumpeter Bunny Berigan was in his band for six weeks, Dorsey had two major hits in "Marie" and "Song of India." Tommy Dorsey featured a wide variety of music, ranging from up-tempo swing tunes and some Dixieland—particularly from the Clambake Seven, a combo taken out of his big band—to vocal ballads from Edythe Wright and Jack Leonard, and dance music. The Tommy Dorsey Orchestra hit its peak from 1939 to 1944, using Sy Oliver arrangements, heated solos from trumpeter Ziggy Elman and drummer Buddy Rich, a full string section by 1942, and such vocalists as Frank Sinatra, Jo Stafford, and the Modernaires. Among the hit records were "I'll Never Smile Again" and "Opus #1." While he had to cut back a bit after World War II, eliminating the string section, Dorsey was considered a legend and a world-famous celebrity so was able to keep his big band working.

The Jimmy Dorsey Orchestra took longer to hit it big. Other than Jimmy Dorsey and a few of his sidemen, including pianist Freddie Slack and drummer Ray McKinley, his band did not have its own musical personality during the second half of the 1930s, although it worked steadily. In 1941 when his singers Helen O'Connell and Bob Eberle began sharing records, it was the equivalent of hitting a jackpot. O'Connell sang a relatively hot chorus, Eberle sounded warm on a ballad chorus, and Dorsey provided an instrumental interlude. Hit records of "Amapola," "Green Eyes," "Tangerine," and "Brazil" followed, and the Jimmy Dorsey band was finally competitive with that of his brother.

The Dorsey brothers had long since made up, but since both of their orchestras were quite successful, their collaborations in the 1940s were very rare, other than co-starring in the semi-fictional and sometimes laughably bad movie *The Fabulous Dorseys*. The band business started to go bad after 1945, and by 1952 both orchestras, particularly Jimmy's, was in danger of collapsing financially. They decided to pool their resources, with Jimmy and a couple of his sidemen joining Tommy's big band that was renamed the Dorsey Brothers Orchestra. The new group emphasized nostalgia swing and dance music, although occasionally playing with some excitement. The brothers had mellowed to an extent with age while still being quite capable of arguing. Things were mostly peaceful during the last years, which included co-hosting a television series that introduced Elvis Presley to a wide public. Tommy's sudden death in November 1956 cut short their success. A heartbroken Jimmy Dorsey, who was already ill with cancer, ironically had his first pop hit in a decade, "So Rare," during a final record date before his own death in June 1957.

ARTIE SHAW

Artie Shaw was an odd person to become so famous during the swing era. As an intellectual, he wished his audience would sit quietly rather than dance wildly to his music, he hated hype, and he did not care about success except as a means for him to perform the music he enjoyed. It seemed as if the more he ran away from success, the easier it was for success to find him.

Born in 1910 Shaw started on clarinet and saxophone at the age of twelve. At fifteen he was touring with bands. After moving to New York in 1930, he settled into the life of being a studio musician, hating the music while saving his money. In 1934 Shaw quit music for the first time, moved to a farm, and worked on a novel until the money ran out and he was forced to return to the studios. For a major big band concert held on April 8, 1936, he was hired to lead a group for ten minutes between sets by more famous names. Instead of putting together an orchestra, he performed "Interlude in B Flat" on clarinet with a string quartet and a rhythm section, stealing the show and making headlines. Soon he took the radical step of putting together an ensemble consisting of four horns, a string quartet, and a four-piece rhythm section. The band lasted for a year but was too unusual to make it in the swing world.

Shaw then formed a more conventional big band, and after an initial struggle, in mid-1938 the Artie Shaw Orchestra became famous with its recording of "Begin the Beguine." Shaw's further successes included "Softly as in a Morning Sunrise," his theme song "Nightmare," "Carioca," and "Traffic Jam." Until late 1939 he led one of the major big bands, an orchestra that surpassed the popularity of Benny Goodman and Tommy Dorsey. When the pressure of leading the top swing band began to get to Shaw, he shocked the music world in November 1939 by spontaneously leaving his orchestra while they were still performing and fled to Mexico.

A few months later Shaw returned because he needed to make some money. He led a record date on March 3, 1940, that featured a thirty-two-piece orchestra including thirteen strings. One of the six songs they recorded was "Frenesi," which immediately became as big a hit as "Begin the Beguine." Shaw was reluctantly on top again. Since he always wanted to work with strings, the clarinetist put together a twenty-three-piece band, with nine strings, that included trumpeter Billy Butterfield, trombonist Jack Jenney, and pianist Johnny Guarnieri among the soloists. Their recordings included the definitive version of Hoagy Carmichael's "Star Dust," a perfect performance with brilliant solos from Butterfield, Shaw, and Jenney, and the extended *Concerto for Clarinet*. Also during this period, Shaw had fun playing with his small combo drawn from the big band, the Gramercy Five, that had Guarnieri switching to harpsichord; their recording of "Summit Ridge Drive" was another giant hit.

Roy Eldridge, one of the major trumpeters who emerged during the swing era, played with clarinetist Artie Shaw's big band in 1945.
Photo courtesy of the Wayne Knight Collection, Star Line Productions.

In the spring of 1941 Shaw broke up his third orchestra, but after a few months he was back with his fourth big band, a fun group featuring trumpeter-singer Hot Lips Page, trumpeter Max Kaminsky, a string section, and some alumni, including Jenney, Guarnieri, and tenorman Georgie Auld. It lasted until shortly after Pearl Harbor when Shaw broke up the band and enlisted in the navy. While in the military, Shaw led an undocumented navy band until he became seriously ill in late 1943. After his discharge he recovered and returned to the swing world. Shaw's orchestra in 1944 and 1945 featured trumpeter Roy Eldridge, pianist Dodo Marmarosa, and guitarist Barney Kessel. On a few numbers, Shaw showed that he was not only aware of the bebop movement but could play credible bop solos himself.

The clarinetist, however, was tired of the music world, and by 1946 he recorded with a studio orchestra rather than a regular touring band. He was semi-active for a few years, led a short-lived bebop big band in 1949 that soon flopped despite playing exciting music, and emerged for the last time during

1954, heading a new version of the Gramercy Five that featured guitarist Tal Farlow and pianist Hank Jones. During this last period, Shaw showed that he was a very talented modern jazz player even if the clarinet was forever associated with the swing era.

Frustrated by the public indifference toward the Gramercy Five and the constant requests to play "Begin the Beguine," Artie Shaw retired before the end of 1954, even though he was still only forty-four. Although he remained active as an author and a public speaker, Shaw never played in public again. He died on December 30, 2004, at age ninety-four.

CAB CALLOWAY

A famous name by 1932 and a celebrity throughout his life, Cab Calloway was the "Hi-De-Ho Man." He grew up in Baltimore and Chicago, gaining some experience appearing in revues, including one in which he was the relief drummer, though he was never really a musician. Calloway found his niche as an exciting vocalist and showman, influenced to various degrees by Louis Armstrong, Al Jolson, and opera singers. For a few months in 1929 he led and sang with the Alabamians at New York's Savoy, but the band was not strong enough to survive. Calloway gained some recognition when he appeared in the *Hot Chocolates* show, a revue that had both Fats Waller's music and Louis Armstrong. In 1930 Calloway took over the Missourians, a superior jazz band that had recorded fourteen numbers during the past year but was on the verge of breaking up due to the Depression and the lack of work. The ensemble was renamed the Cab Calloway Orchestra, Calloway made his recording debut with the band in July 1930, and in February 1931 the group became the house band at the Cotton Club, succeeding Duke Ellington who had gone on the road. As they had with Ellington, the regular radio broadcasts soon made Calloway famous, and after he recorded "Minnie the Moocher" on March 3, 1931, he was destined for stardom.

Calloway not only had a strong voice, but he was an inventive scat-singer whose dancing,

"Mr. Hi-De-Ho," Cab Calloway was a spectacular showman who was also a colorful singer.
Photo courtesy of the Wayne Knight Collection, Star Line Productions.

exaggerated conducting, and gyrations on stage defined showmanship. Sometimes it seemed almost beside the point that his orchestra was full of talented musicians because Calloway usually dominated every live performance. Some of their recordings were instrumentals, and many top players passed through the band in the 1930s and 1940s, including tenors Chu Berry and Ike Quebec, trumpeter Jonah Jones, bassist Milt Hinton, drummer Cozy Cole, and the young Dizzy Gillespie from 1939 to 1941, whose adventurous playing Calloway called "Chinese music."

Although Calloway made many popular recordings including "St. James Infirmary," "Blues in My Heart," "Bugle Call Rag," "Trickeration," "Corinne Corinna," "The Old Man of the Mountain," "F. D. R. Jones," and a variety of sing-alongs à la "Minnie the Moocher," it was his series of tunes that featured the adventures of Minnie and Smoky Joe that were particularly famous. Their tales often referred to drugs, but these were largely overlooked or not understood by the general public in the 1930s. In addition to "Minnie the Moocher," their exploits are covered in such songs as "Kickin' the Gong Around," "Minnie the Moocher's Wedding Day," "Reefer Man," "Mister Paganini," "Swing for Minnie," and "The Ghost of Smoky Joe."

Cab Calloway was at the height of his fame in 1943 when he appeared in the film *Stormy Weather*. After the big band era ended, he was forced to cut back to a sextet, then a quartet. In the 1950s he found additional fame playing "Sportin' Life" in a successful revival of *Porgy and Bess*, which seemed only right since George Gershwin had originally based the character on Calloway. After that show ran its course, Calloway was mostly semi-retired, performing now and then up until his death in 1994, always happy to sing "Minnie the Moocher" for new generations of fans.

CHICK WEBB

Chick Webb, stricken in childhood with tuberculosis of the spine, grew up as a dwarf with a hunched back. Despite this major handicap, he found success in a very unlikely profession as a drummer. He was born in Baltimore, moved to New York in 1925, and was generally a leader from that point on. Webb first recorded in 1929, and in 1931 his orchestra became the house band at the Savoy Ballroom. The orchestra resided there for the rest of the decade, with Webb and his big band playing for some of the most talented, and demanding, dancers in the country on a nightly basis. Fortunately Webb and his musicians always swung hard at danceable tempos, and they became a major attraction. They also engaged in legendary "battle of the band" contests, usually winning, including against Benny Goodman and Count Basie, thanks to a home court advantage, apparently only losing once to Duke Ellington.

Among the main talents in the group was altoist Edgar Sampson, a skilled songwriter who in 1934 wrote "If Dreams Come True," "Don't Be That Way," and "Stompin' at the Savoy." Although Benny Goodman had bigger hits with the latter two, Webb's band recorded them first and had the initial success. Another early star of the band was saxophonist Wayman Carver who occasionally took flute solos. Only Alberto Socarras in the late 1920s preceded Carver on an instrument that would not catch on in jazz until the 1950s.

In 1935 eighteen-year-old Ella Fitzgerald joined Webb's orchestra. She had struggled through a rough childhood, including being homeless, and eventually found her way out of poverty through music. She won an important amateur contest at the Apollo Theatre the previous year, but due to her appearance and shoddy clothes, she was turned down for a job with Fletcher Henderson. Benny Carter talked Webb into giving her a chance, and when the drummer saw the audience's enthusiastic response to her singing, Ella was hired. She quickly grew to be Webb's biggest attraction, and although many of the songs given her to sing and record between 1935 and 1939 were juvenile novelties, she was particularly skilled on ballads. In 1938 she had a huge hit with the nursery rhyme "A-Tisket, A-Tasket" and became a famous name.

Unfortunately, by then Chick Webb's health was beginning to fail. He had heart troubles and pleurisy and on June 16, 1939, passed away at the age of thirty-seven. His final words were "I'm sorry, but I gotta go."

Because the band was successful and had a steady engagement at the Savoy, Ella Fitzgerald was picked to lead the orchestra although she actually had nothing to do with its musical direction. After two years, by the summer of 1941, she was so popular that she went out on her own, and the vestiges of the Chick Webb orchestra broke up.

JIMMIE LUNCEFORD

Jimmie Lunceford's orchestra was famous for its musicianship, the tightness of the ensembles, and its showmanship. Considered to be one of the finest orchestras of the late 1930s, part of its appeal was visual, and therefore its recordings are not always up to that level, rarely approaching the heights of Duke Ellington, Benny Goodman, Count Basie, or Artie Shaw. Lunceford grew up in Denver, took music lessons from Paul Whiteman's father, and had extensive training on many instruments. He earned a music degree from Fisk University in 1926, taught music at Manassas High School in Memphis, and gradually formed a band, the Chickasaw Syncopators, comprising his students. They recorded two numbers in both 1927 and 1930, and then Lunceford decided the band should become professional and move up North. After time in Cleveland and Buffalo, they moved to New York in 1933, and the following year they caught on.

The inventive arrangements of Sy Oliver and Ed Wilcox were a major asset as were several musicians' ability to sing in a sort of glee club, the high note trumpet work of Tommy Stevenson, and the fine solos of altoist Willie Smith, tenor-saxophonist Joe Thomas, trumpeter Oliver, and by 1937 trombonist Trummy Young. There was also less-inspiring ballad singing from Dan Grissom. Since none of the soloists were all that major, with the possible exception of Willie Smith, the emphasis was on the ensemble sound and the arrangements rather than free-flowing blowing.

The formula worked for quite a few years. Among the band's best-loved recordings were "Rhythm Is Our Business," "Swanee River," "Organ Grinder's Swing," "For Dancers Only," "Tain't What You Do," "Margie," "Uptown Blues," and "Lunceford Special." When Sy Oliver was lured away by Tommy Dorsey in 1939, it was a major blow, although the young Gerald Wilson proved to be a very able replacement. Because Lunceford paid his sidemen very little, Willie Smith left in 1942. Although the band was struggling after World War II, it was still touring regularly in 1947 when Lunceford died suddenly, probably poisoned by a racist restaurant owner who had been forced to serve the black orchestra. Ed Wilcox and Joe Thomas kept the band together as best they could, but it permanently broke up in 1949.

BUNNY BERIGAN

One of the giants of the trumpet, Bunny Berigan could always be relied upon to take an exciting solo that would uplift any performance. He never should have been a bandleader because his alcoholism and general attitude made him unfit to discipline others, but he was always a star.

One of the most exciting trumpeters, Bunny Berigan took plenty of chances in both his solos and in his life.
Photo courtesy of the Wayne Knight Collection, Star Line Productions.

Berigan gained early experience playing in local bands and college groups in the Midwest. By 1930 he was strong enough to be a soloist with Hal Kemp's orchestra. An excellent sight-reader, Berigan had a beautiful sound, a range that included deep low notes and upper register shouts, and the right spirit to play jazz, always taking chances in his solos. He was a member of Fred Rich's CBS studio band between 1931 and 1935, other than a few uneventful months with Paul Whiteman, and appeared on numerous records, often contributing brief solos. He was at his best during this era when featured with the Dorsey Brothers Orchestra.

In 1935 Benny Goodman talked him into joining his orchestra. Berigan's solos on "King Porter Stomp" and "Sometimes I'm Happy" made those recordings Goodman's first hits, and he was part of the big band as it toured west, climaxing in the Palomar Ballroom engagement. Soon afterwards, Berigan went back to New York and the studios that paid much more. In 1937 he emerged again, spending six weeks with Tommy Dorsey's band and recording famous choruses on the hits "Marie" and "Song of India." By now Berigan was seriously considering starting his own orchestra.

At first the Bunny Berigan Orchestra was off to a good start, recording regularly for Bluebird and having a major hit with his theme song, the dramatic "I Can't Get Started." Berigan never built on that success, and by 1938 the big band was struggling despite the leader's fine playing. The trumpeter's constant drinking led to lost opportunities, and he tried to let the band run itself, a fatal mistake. By the end of 1939 he was forced to declare bankruptcy and break up his orchestra. Berigan rejoined Tommy Dorsey's big band for a few months, but this time the association did not work out, with his excessive drinking making him very erratic. In 1941 Berigan formed another orchestra, and it struggled along for a year until his health declined, and he died on June 2, 1942, when he was only thirty-three. His best recordings show just how powerful and colorful a trumpeter Berigan could be, but it is a tragedy that this great talent did not take care of himself.

BOB CROSBY

It is difficult to listen to Bob Crosby sing and not feel a little sorry for him. The younger brother of the most popular vocalist of the 1930s, Bob Crosby could never hope to be on Bing's level. He did find a niche for himself as a bandleader, but ironically his biggest hits were recordings on which he did not sing!

Crosby had gained experience singing with the Dorsey Brothers Orchestra in 1934. At year-end Ben Pollack's musicians became disillusioned with their leader spending all his time promoting his girlfriend Doris Robbins' singing career. When that band broke up they needed an ideal frontman. Jack Teagarden was their first choice, but he was unavailable, tied up in a five-year contract with Paul Whiteman. Crosby, who certainly had name recognition, accepted the offer, and at first the Bob Crosby Orchestra was a typical run-of-the-mill, second-level swing band. By 1936 the band began to form its own identity as a New Orleans–style big band, one that mixed together Dixieland and swing. By November 1937 its small group, the Bob Crosby's Bobcats, became a major attraction. With such fine musicians as trumpeters Yank Lawson and Billy Butterfield, trombonist Warren Smith, clarinetists Irving Fazola and Matty Matlock, tenor-saxophonist Eddie Miller, pianists Bob Zurke or Joe Sullivan, guitarist-singer Nappy Lamare, bassist-arranger Bob Haggart, and drummer Ray Bauduc, both the Bobcats and the full orchestra were quite strong and exciting. Such hits emerged as "Gin Mill Blues," "Little Rock Getaway," "South Rampart Street Parade," Bob Haggart's "What's New," and a famous bass-drum duet on "Big Noise from Winnetka."

After several years of success, in 1940 Crosby and his musical director Gil Rodin messed with the orchestra's formula, moving towards commercial swing, hoping to expand their audience. When the band's music became more routine, its audience shrunk. Coupled with the attack on Pearl Harbor, this resulted in Crosby breaking up his orchestra at the end of 1942. After spending time in the marines in 1944 and 1945, Bob Crosby starred in some B movies, hosted a television show, worked as a personality and an occasional singer in the 1950s, and hosted several reunions of the Bobcats during the fifty years between his big band breaking up and his death in 1993. He never did emerge from Bing Crosby's shadow.

GENE KRUPA

Gene Krupa was the first superstar drummer. Before Krupa made it big with Benny Goodman, drummers were almost completely restricted to the background, with the occasional exception of Chick Webb, and solos were very rare. Krupa was part of the Chicago jazz scene of the 1920s and worked in the New York studios in the early 1930s before joining the new Goodman big band in December 1934. Gradually during the next three years, he became more assertive in his playing, not just as a member of the Benny Goodman Trio and Quartet but also with the orchestra. Krupa had the ability to make everything look colorful and a bit more difficult than it really was, adding a flourish to simple breaks while chewing gum and looking slightly possessed. By 1937 he was a major name, and his showcase on "Sing, Sing, Sing" drove young audiences wild.

After the success at Goodman's Carnegie Hall concert on January 12, 1938, Krupa and Goodman had an argument that resulted in the drummer leaving to form his own big band. Although his fame allowed him to work regularly, the orchestra did not develop its own personality beyond the leader until 1941. At that time, with trumpeter Roy Eldridge and singer Anita O'Day becoming major stars, the Krupa band had hits in "Let Me Off Uptown" and "Thanks for the Boogie Ride" even if Eldridge and O'Day, who shared some hip conversation on these two recordings, actually did not care for each other. O'Day was a major new voice, while Eldridge was taking his place as one of the great trumpeters, as he showed on Krupa's recordings of "After You've Gone" and "Rockin' Chair."

The Gene Krupa big band was forced to break up in May 1943 when Krupa was framed on a marijuana rap by narcotics agents who wanted to generate headlines by arresting a celebrity. The drummer was in jail for a short time before being cleared of all charges. Benny Goodman symbolically welcomed him back to jazz, having him rejoin his orchestra for a few months. After spending half of 1944 playing with Tommy Dorsey, in August 1944 Krupa formed a new big band, one that was called "the band with strings that swings." Although the string section was dropped in early 1945, Krupa kept this big band together through 1951.

Although very much a swing drummer who emphasized the bass drum, Krupa kept his big band open to the innovations of bebop, for a time featuring trumpeter Red Rodney and the Charlie Parker–influenced altoist Charlie Kennedy.

Gene Krupa was the first drummer to become a matinee idol.
Photo courtesy of the Wayne Knight Collection, Star Line Productions.

His most popular features after 1945 tended to be with a trio that highlighted the rambunctious tenor playing of Charlie Ventura; their version of "Dark Eyes" was often requested. After Krupa broke up his big band in 1951, he led a small group, went on some tours with Jazz at the Philharmonic, ran a drummer school with Cozy Cole, and had occasional reunions with Benny Goodman. Although easily surpassed by more modern drummers, he remained a very popular figure up until his death in 1973.

GLENN MILLER

Ultimately the most popular big band of the swing era was Glenn Miller's, although it did not catch on until four years after Benny Goodman's initial successes. Miller had played trombone and arranged for Ben Pollack from 1926 to 1928. When Jack Teagarden joined Pollack, Miller immediately realized that his future was more in writing than in performing music, though he continued playing trombone, mostly in sections, throughout his life. He worked in the studios and was with the Dorsey Brothers Orchestra in 1934 and 1935 and with Ray Noble's American band. In 1937 Miller put together his first orchestra, but it only lasted a year. The problem was that few had ever heard of Glenn Miller, and his ensemble had not developed its own sound.

In the spring of 1938 Miller tried again. By then he had adopted a signature ensemble sound, having the clarinet double the melody an octave above the sax section. This first came about years earlier when he had written some arrangements, and trumpeter Pee Wee Erwin insisted that his part be written high. When Erwin left the band, few other trumpeters could play his part so a clarinet was substituted. Miller's second orchestra mostly struggled through 1938, and 1939 looked like its final year. Then the magic started to come together. On April 4 Miller's band recorded its romantic theme song "Moonlight Serenade." On April 10 its record date generated two hits in "Little Brown Jug" and "Sunrise Serenade." The band's fourteen-week period at the Glen Island Casino, from mid-May to the end of August, for the first time beamed Glenn Miller's music out to the masses, and it soon became obvious that his band was the hit of the year. Its fate was sealed after recording "In the Mood" on August 1.

Why did Glenn Miller's orchestra ultimately catch on so big? As with Paul Whiteman's in the 1920s, Miller expertly used jazz as an important, but not dominant, ingredient in what was really a musical variety show. He alternated ballad vocals by Ray Eberle with novelty numbers featuring singer Marian Hutton, likable jazzy romps with Tex Beneke on vocals and tenor, some swinging and usually repetitive instrumentals, and set-ending "killer dillers," up-tempo pieces often involving a drum solo. The formula worked remarkably well, and Miller had other big hits with "Pennsylvania 6-5000," "Anvil Chorus," "Song of the Volga Boatmen," "Perfidia," "Chattanooga Choo Choo," "I Know Why," "Elmer's Tune," "A String of Pearls," "Moonlight Cocktail," "Don't Sit under the Apple Tree," "American Patrol," "I've Got a Gal in Kalamazoo," "Serenade in Blue," "At Last," "Juke Box Saturday Night," and "Tuxedo Junction," easily outselling Erskine Hawkins' earlier recording.

The only thing that stopped Glenn Miller's success was the advent of World War II and his desire to serve his country. In mid-1942 after he was accepted as a captain in the Army Air Force, he broke up his band, easily the most popular in the world, on September 27. It was Miller's dream to form a giant military orchestra and play for the troops. He had an uphill battle against red tape and conservatives who felt that military bands should stick to Sousa tunes, but he succeeded and by mid-1943 was leading the Army Air Force Band. This orchestra had a full string section, several very talented jazz musicians—pianist Mel Powell, clarinetist Peanuts Hucko, trumpeter Bobby Nichols, and drummer Ray McKinley among them—and the versatility to play anything from mood music and sentimental ballads to heated versions of the latest jazz standards. Although none of its recordings were released to the general public, the Glenn Miller Army Air Force Band popularized "St. Louis Blues March."

Glenn Miller looked forward to having his orchestra, which was based in England by 1944, performing on the European continent. The band ultimately did just that, but Miller was not there to see it. His plane to France on December 15, 1944, was shot down over the English Channel, and his body was never found. The Army Air Force Band, led by Ray McKinley, continued for one more year. Since the end of World War II, a posthumous Glenn Miller Orchestra has always been popular, playing Miller's hits from 1939 through 1942 for newer generations.

HARRY JAMES

One of the top young trumpeters of the second half of the 1930s, Harry James became a famous star with Benny Goodman's orchestra. A natural player, he learned trumpet from his father and at twelve was leading his own band for the Christy Brothers Circus. After working in territory bands and with Ben Pollack from 1935 to 1936, he joined Goodman when he was still just twenty-one. James' technique was always very impressive, and he had the ability to uplift the Goodman band with his spirited and exciting solos.

In early 1939 James formed his own big band. As with Gene Krupa, it took some time for him to become successful despite his name recognition. James alternated swinging instrumentals with vocal ballads, which for a few months featured Frank Sinatra, but was unable to connect with the public. Then in 1941 after adding a small string section, he recorded an instrumental recording of an Al Jolson hit that Judy Garland had recently revived, "You Made Me Love You." That song was such a success that James was finally in the big leagues. Other hits followed, including "The Mole," "Strictly Instrumental," "Sleepy Lagoon," "Cherry," "I'm Beginning to See the Light," "It's Been a Long, Long Time" in 1945, and three that featured singer Helen Forrest: "I Don't Want to Walk without You," "I Had the Craziest Dream," and "I've Heard That Song Before." James' ability to play heated jazz, sentimental ballads, and schmaltz made him top the polls, and when Glenn Miller went into the Army Air Force in mid-1942, James had the most popular big band in the country. His popularity grew even more when he married movie star Betty Grable. At its peak, his orchestra consisted of thirty-two pieces, including fourteen strings.

Plenty of fireworks occurred anytime that trumpeter Harry James and drummer Buddy Rich performed together. *Photo courtesy of the Wayne Knight Collection, Star Line Productions.*

When the big band industry collapsed in 1946, James dropped the string section. Near the end of the year, he broke up his orchestra but was soon back on the road with a similar big band. James experimented with bebop a bit in 1948 and 1949 but the next year had reverted to swing and nightly nostalgic remakes of his hits. By then James was patterning his band after Count Basie's, which seemed logical since his "Two O'Clock Jump" was just a copy of Basie's "One O'Clock Jump." Although he had fine soloists in altoist Willie Smith and tenor-saxophonist Corky Corcoran and he personally enjoyed the music of such trumpeters as Dizzy Gillespie, Miles Davis, and Chet Baker, James stopped evolving. Due to his fame, he was able to keep his big band going most of the time between 1950 and his death in 1983, but there were few surprises along the way, and he was content to play his trumpet on the same basic tunes as he had performed in the 1940s.

LIONEL HAMPTON

Because of the shows he put on, which inevitably climaxed with "Flying Home," no band wanted to follow that of vibraphonist Lionel Hampton.
Photo courtesy of the Wayne Knight Collection, Star Line Productions.

Lionel Hampton was one of the most loyal of Benny Goodman's sidemen, staying with the clarinetist until mid-1940 even though he had already been famous for over three years. Hampton was originally a drummer with Paul Howard's Quality Serenaders in Los Angeles in 1929 and 1930. He had lessons on the xylophone and practiced vibes, so when Louis Armstrong on a record date in 1930 asked Hampton if he could play a bit of vibes behind his vocals, Hamp was ready. His spots on "Memories of You" and "Shine" were the first appearances of the vibes on jazz records. Based in Los Angeles, Hampton continued playing in obscurity for a few more years, working with Les Hite between 1932 and 1934 and leading his own local orchestra. In the summer of 1936 Benny Goodman was alerted about Hampton's musical abilities so one night Goodman, Gene Krupa, and Teddy Wilson sat in with the vibraphonist, and the results were magical. Soon Hampton joined the Benny Goodman Quartet.

In addition to playing vibes, Hampton could also fill in on drums, sing, play speedy two-finger runs on the piano, dance, and excite musicians, fans, and Goodman with his enthusiasm and brilliance. From 1937 to 1940 he led a series of all-star record dates for the Victor label, using major sidemen drawn from the top swing big bands. In mid-1940 when Goodman temporarily broke up his big band to take care of health problems, Hampton decided to form his own orchestra. Since he was a household name and a crowd pleaser, it was not long before the Lionel Hampton Big Band was quite popular. The leader was never shy about going out of his way to get applause, whether it involved literally jumping on his drum set, having his brass section screaming out high notes, or inspiring his reeds to honk away. His 1942 recording of "Flying Home," featuring a classic tenor solo by Illinois Jacquet, became so famous that it virtually launched r&b, inspiring other saxophonists who wished to become popular to use repetition, honking, and screaming sounds.

With their exciting shows, the Lionel Hampton Big Band survived after the collapse of the swing era, mixing together swing, r&b, and bebop. Hampton led big bands on and off for the next five decades, helping to introduce such notables as singer Dinah Washington, bassist Charles Mingus, singer Betty Carter, and guitarist Wes Montgomery, a decade before he became well known. The great trumpeter Clifford Brown played on the 1953 European tour. Hampton also appeared with small groups during special concerts, had many reunions with Benny Goodman, and remained a major attraction until his death in 2002 at the age of ninety-three.

OTHER BIG BANDS

The other most obvious jazz orchestras of the swing era are those of Count Basie, Andy Kirk, and Jay McShann. Although each made it big nationally after moving to New York, they formed their sounds in Kansas City and will be discussed in chapter five.

In 1927 Don Redman left the Fletcher Henderson band for the opportunity to lead McKinney's Cotton Pickers. A decent clarinetist and alto-saxophonist, Redman also had strong writing abilities. He was one of the very first arrangers, with Ferdie Grofe, to divide a big band into brass and reed sections. Redman developed the ability to write ensembles that sounded like harmonized solos, heard early on in his arrangements for Henderson of "Sugar Foot Stomp," which was really King Oliver's "Dippermouth Blues," and "The Stampede." Between 1928 and 1931 McKinney's Cotton Pickers competed favorably with Henderson's big band, introducing such songs as "Baby Won't You Please Come Home," "I Want a Little Girl" and "Gee Baby, Ain't I Good to You." When Redman left the Cotton Pickers in the summer of 1931 to form his own big band, the orchestra's days were numbered; its creative vision was gone. The Don Redman Orchestra worked regularly from 1931 to 1940 but surprisingly never really caught on.

Benny Carter, who briefly led McKinney's Cotton Pickers in 1931 and 1932, on a few occasions made attempts to lead big bands of his own in 1932, 1933, and on and off between 1939 and 1946. Despite his musicianship and resulting high-quality music, his band failed to have any hits or establish a strong identity with the public. Coleman Hawkins in 1940 and Teddy Wilson in 1939 and 1940 had the same difficulty, as did Jack Teagarden, whose big band managed to last from 1939 to 1946, eventually bankrupting him.

The Casa Loma Orchestra was arguably the first white swing band, preceding Benny Goodman by six years. Originally known as the Orange Blossom Band and based in Detroit, it was scheduled to play at the Casa Loma Hotel in Toronto, Canada. When that hotel never opened, the band was reformed as a co-op and took the Casa Loma. Saxophonist Glen Gray was elected the band's president, and eventually he would take over the orchestra. In the early days, guitarist Gene Gifford was the Casa Loma's most important member contributing most arrangements, using heated riffs in many of the charts. Among the early tunes that showed the potential of swing, even if the band sometimes sounded a bit mechanical, were "Black Jazz," "White Jazz," "Casa Loma Stomp," and the haunting "Smoke Rings," the band's theme song. When the swing era began, the Casa Loma Orchestra was soon overshadowed by Goodman and the other new bandleaders, although it had hits with the two-part remake of "Casa Loma Stomp," the two-sided "No Name Jive," and "Memories of You," a high-note feature for trumpeter Sonny Dunham. The Casa Loma Orchestra survived until 1950, although Glen Gray kept the name alive later in the decade with a series of swing era recreations that covered many orchestras and featured sympathetic studio musicians.

Charlie Barnet was an unusual swing-era big bandleader in that he came from a very rich family. Although his parents wanted him to become a lawyer, in time Barnet prospered more than if he had pursued law. It took the tenor saxophonist six years, until 1939, before his band caught on, but that year's recording of "Cherokee," his theme song arranged by Billy May, became his first hit. Others included "Redskin Rhumba," "Pompton Turnpike," "Southern Fried," "Charleston Alley," and 1944's "Skyliner." Barnet, one of the first white bandleaders to have an integrated orchestra, also played alto and soprano, often paying tribute to Duke Ellington and Count Basie. He featured important contributors such as Lena Horne, singer Kay Starr, trumpeter-singer Peanuts Holland, pianist Dodo Marmarosa, guitarist Barney Kessel, and trumpeter Roy Eldridge. Barnet's group remained popular during the 1940s, and he even led a bebop orchestra in 1949, with trumpeters Maynard Ferguson and Doc Severinsen, before he broke up his band, choosing to lead part-time swing groups until his retirement in the mid-1960s.

Red Norvo had an unusual big band since he played xylophone, not switching to vibes until 1943. Norvo was married to singer Mildred Bailey, the star on many of his orchestra's records. Eddie Sauter's arrangements for the group between 1936 and 1938 made it possible for Norvo's quiet instrument to be heard over the horns, and Norvo was able to keep the band together into the early 1940s. In later years Norvo worked with the Benny Goodman Sextet and Woody Herman's First Herd, led a cool jazz trio in the early 1950s with guitarist Tal Farlow and bassist Charles Mingus, and stayed active until the mid-1980s.

Erskine Hawkins, who was billed as "The 20th-century Gabriel," could hit high notes on the trumpet yet never dominated his own band's music. His orchestra was originally known as the 'Bama Street Collegians and was attached to the State Teachers College in Montgomery, Alabama. By 1934 it had become independent, moved to New York, and was on its way. Hawkins was particularly adept at picking out swinging tempos that excited dancers. Based at the Savoy Ballroom for a long time, the Hawkins big band also featured trumpeter Dud Bascomb, tenors Paul Bascomb and Julian Dash, and pianist Avery Parrish. Their main hits were "Tuxedo Junction," the 1945 "Tippin In," and "After Hours," which featured Parrish's blues piano.

Trombonist Will Bradley most enjoyed playing ballads, but despite his wishes, he is best remembered for his big band's exuberant boogie-woogie records. Born Wilbur Schwichtenberg, Bradley was happy as a studio musician in the 1930s but was convinced by promoter Willard Alexander to lead a big band with drummer-singer Ray McKinley as his unofficial co-leader. With pianist Freddy Slack as a major soloist, the Will Bradley Orchestra had their first hit, the eccentric "Celery Stalks at Midnight," and another in 1940, the two-sided "Beat Me Daddy, Eight to the Bar." The boogie-woogie craze was at its peak during this period so Bradley reluctantly recorded such numbers as "Rock-A-Bye the Boogie," "Scrub Me Mama with a Boogie Beat," "I Boogied When I Should Have Woogied," "Chicken Gumboogie," "Boogie Woogie Conga," "Bounce Me Brother with a Solid Four," "Booglie Wooglie Piggy," and "Fry Me Cookie with a Can of Lard." Bradley soon became bored with much of the music, and in February 1942 he broke up the band, permanently returning to the studios.

Of all the swing-era big bands, the one that lasted the longest under the same leader was Les Brown's Band of Renown that survived for sixty-two years. Brown, who played clarinet and saxophones, was a reliable musician although never overly exciting, and the same can be said for his orchestra. He led a big band in 1935 while attending Duke University, the Duke Blue Devils. After a period freelancing, in 1938 he formed the Les Brown Orchestra. His first major hit was the 1944 "Sentimental Journey" featuring the young singer Doris Day. Other popular Brown recordings included his theme song "Leap Frog," "Bizet Has His Day" and "I've Got My Love to Keep Me Warm." Brown's orchestra was able to survive for decades after the end of the swing era because they worked steadily as the backup band for Bob Hope's many shows and tours. The big band was at its best for a period in the 1950s when it featured tenor-saxophonist Dave Pell, trumpeter Don Fagerquist, and singer Lucy Ann Polk, but it remained pretty consistent for decades, lasting until Les Brown's death in early 2001.

SMALL GROUPS DURING THE SWING ERA

While big bands dominated jazz from 1935 to 1946, providing employment for most musicians, the top jazz soloists often preferred to play at late-night jam sessions where they could stretch out beyond their brief solos with even the most jazz-oriented orchestras. Small group jazz never completely disappeared, and its main center became New York's legendary Fifty-second Street, which was nicknamed Swing Street. Within two blocks, on a typical night clubs like the Famous Door, Jimmy Ryan's, the Onyx Club, and Kelly's Stables were featuring Art Tatum, Coleman Hawkins, Billie Holiday, Eddie Condon's Dixieland band, Stuff Smith's Onyx Club Boys, and Louis Prima plus other up-and-coming bands. During its prime decade, Fifty-second Street was jazz heaven.

Although most jazz combos of the swing era were short-term affairs, gatherings of all-stars put together for a week or two, some had independent lives and made a strong impact through their recordings and live appearances. It is remarkable how many were based in New York during this era.

FATS WALLER AND HIS RHYTHM

One of the great stride pianists of the 1920s, Fats Waller developed into a comic personality in the 1930s. He did not neglect his piano, songwriting, or his occasional organ playing but began to sing frequently on records and show off his highly appealing sense of humor. Between 1934 and 1942, Waller recorded an extensive series of performances with his Rhythm, a sextet that usually included trumpeter Herman Autrey, Gene Sedric on tenor and clarinet, guitarist Al Casey, and drummer Slick Jones with various bassists. Throughout these dates, except when playing his own tunes and superior standards, Waller displayed his ability to turn trash into treasures. When faced with an inferior song pushed by his label, Fats often satirized the lyrics mercilessly, often to hilarious effect. Since the tunes often had no potential at all, the label was happy, as was the public who found Waller's brand of hilarity quite refreshing.

Waller became quite famous during the second half of the 1930s, appearing regularly on the radio, recording constantly, and appearing briefly in two movies. Among his best recordings are "A Porter's Love Song to a Chambermaid," "I'm Gonna Sit Right Down and Write Myself a Letter," "Floatin' Down to Cotton Town," "Swingin' Them Jingle Bells," "The Joint Is Jumpin'," "Hold Tight," "Your Feet's Too Big," and one of the first jazz waltzes, "The Jitterbug Waltz." Waller was also able to make such odd numbers as "Fat and Greasy," "Little Curly Hair in a High Chair," "You're a Square from Delaware," "My Mommie Sent Me to the Store," "Abercrombie Had a Zombie," and "Come Down to Earth, My Angel" sound worthwhile through his satire and humor.

Fats Waller would have been a natural to appear on television in the 1950s, but he was long gone by then. The partying, excessive liquor, and overeating took its toll, and on December 14, 1943, he passed away from pneumonia at the age of thirty-nine.

As a stride pianist, pioneering jazz organist, songwriter, comic vocalist, and personality, very few were ever on the level of Fats Waller.
Photo courtesy of the Wayne Knight Collection, Star Line Productions.

STUFF SMITH'S ONYX CLUB BOYS

Stuff Smith, possibly the hardest swinging jazz violinist ever, had great success for a few years playing with his band at the Onyx Club on Fifty-second Street. Hezekiah "Stuff" Smith started working professionally in 1924 when he was fifteen. He was one of the key soloists with Alphonso Trent's territory band from 1926 to 1930 and led groups in Buffalo for a few years. In 1936 his Onyx Club Boys were one of the biggest attractions on Fifty-second Street. The sextet matched his violin with the heated trumpet solos of Jonah Jones, with Cozy Cole driving the band on drums. The band had a hit with the novelty "I'se a Muggin'" and recorded such exciting jams as "I Hope Gabriel Likes My Music," "You'se a Viper," "Old Joe's Hittin' the Jug," and the classic "Here Comes the Man with the Jive." The band lasted until 1940 when Jones and Cole departed to join Cab Calloway.

Smith led trios in the 1940s with one of his best-known tunes of the era, the atmospheric "Desert Sands." He was somewhat neglected in the 1950s until producer Norman Granz recorded him on several albums for the Verve label during which he demonstrated that he could keep up with Dizzy Gillespie. Smith moved to Copenhagen in 1965 and showed during the two years before his death in 1967 that he could still play with plenty of spirit and fire.

THE JOHN KIRBY SEXTET

John Kirby was the only bassist to be a successful bandleader during the swing era, and he did it not by being a virtuoso soloist but by having a vision. He originally played tuba in the late 1920s before switching to bass and working with Bill Brown's Brownies from 1928 to 1930, the Fletcher Henderson Orchestra from 1930 to 1933 and in 1936, Chick Webb from 1933 to 1935, and the Mills Blue Rhythm Band in 1936 and 1937. Kirby developed his sextet during the eleven months that he led a group at Fifty-second Street's Onyx Club.

By mid-1938 Kirby had settled on the brilliant twenty-one-year-old trumpeter Charlie Shavers, clarinetist Buster Bailey, altoist Russell Procope, pianist Billy Kyle, and drummer O'Neill Spencer for his sextet. These technically superior musicians fit together very well, were able to play explosive but concise solos, and had cool soft tones, particularly when Shavers played muted. Their light and mellow sounds looked towards cool jazz of the 1950s, yet their repertoire included swinging versions of classical pieces, atmospheric works such as "Dawn on the Desert" and "Nocturne," and transformations of such standards as "Rose Room" and "Royal Garden Blues." During their prime from 1938 to 1941, the John Kirby Sextet had their own unique place in music, being a major contrast to the much louder and less subtle swing orchestras.

Unfortunately, the glory did not last long. In mid-1941 Spencer was forced to leave the band after contracting tuberculosis, which killed him three years later, and Procope and Kyle were drafted a year later. All three were replaced by musicians who sounded similar, but in 1943 Shavers departed to work as a freelancer, and he was irreplaceable. Kirby struggled on, sticking to the same sound. By 1946 the band was considered old hat, and Kirby reluctantly broke up the sextet. He never gave up his dream and even had a reunion for a 1950 Carnegie Hall concert, but that event was poorly attended and both Shavers, who was with Tommy Dorsey, and Procope, who worked with Duke Ellington, had permanent jobs waiting for them elsewhere. Some say that John Kirby died of a broken heart in 1952 when he was just forty-three.

THE RAYMOND SCOTT QUINTETTE

Pianist-arranger Raymond Scott, who was born Harold Warnow, led one of the great novelty groups of all time. A studio musician who worked for CBS, Scott organized his Quintette in 1937. During its two years, it certainly made an impact. Its episodic music had no improvising, with every note including the solos being worked out beforehand, and quite remarkably, the very complicated parts were memorized rather than written down. The Raymond Scott Quintette had hits with "Powerhouse," "Twilight in Turkey" and "The Toy Trumpet" and recorded such picturesque numbers as "New Year's Eve in a Haunted House," "Dinner Music for a Pack of Hungry Cannibals," "Reckless Night on Board an Ocean Liner," "Bumpy Weather over Newark," and "War Dance for Wooden

Indians." Many of the songs became a staple of Warner Bros. Cartoons. Raymond Scott, having made his point, returned to the studios where he conducted much more conventional music during the rest of his career.

TWO GREAT TENOR SAXOPHONISTS: COLEMAN HAWKINS AND LESTER YOUNG

By the end of the swing era, Coleman Hawkins and Lester Young exemplified the two main approaches to playing tenor sax. Throughout his career, the soft-spoken and distinguished Coleman Hawkins always took pride in his ability to be modern and open to newer ideas. He had emerged in 1921 with Mamie Smith's Jazz Hounds and joined Fletcher Henderson's orchestra in 1923 as the first tenor saxophone jazz soloist, but although technically skilled, his style was rhythmically awkward. After playing next to Louis Armstrong on a nightly basis, he smoothed out his style, discarded his reliance on effects, and learned to create meaningful improvisations. A master at chordal improvising, Hawkins was never bothered by later developments; he was usually ahead of the game. While with Henderson from 1923 to 1934, he easily dominated other tenor players with his large, thick tone. Frustrated by the Henderson band's lack of progress compared to that of Duke Ellington, he left the orchestra after eleven years to spend five years in Europe, playing with local orchestras on the Continent and in England.

With Hawkins gone, other tenor players, most notably Lester Young, Ben Webster, and Chu Berry, emerged as rivals. When he returned in 1939 and played in jam sessions, Hawkins showed that he was still the king of tenors, and that he had not stood still while overseas. That year, apparently as a last minute throwaway at a record date, he recorded a famous version of "Body and Soul" that has two choruses in which he barely hints at the melody, creating new ideas of his own.

In 1940 Hawkins led a big band, but it never caught on and soon broke up. Instead, he led a series of combos that often performed at Fifty-second Street. Between 1943 and 1946 he recorded one gem after another, including a classic version of "The Man I Love" and sets in which he welcomed such younger bebop musicians as drummer Max Roach, trombonist J. J. Johnson, trumpeters Dizzy Gillespie, Fats Navarro, and Miles Davis, and pianist Thelonious Monk, who made his recording debut with Hawkins. Although most tenors now had a lighter sound than Hawkins, harmonically he was keeping up with the next generation. With his rhythms considered old-fashioned, he was a bit overlooked during the first half of the 1950s but was an early influence on the young tenor Sonny Rollins. By 1957 his longevity and consistent greatness was being recognized, and Hawkins recorded everything from Dixieland and swing to bop, and a date led by his former pianist Monk that found him holding his own alongside John Coltrane. Hawkins continued to be a major force until 1966 when bad health caused his rapid decline and death three years later.

Lester Young was always an individualist, a quiet revolutionary who blazed his own musical path. As a child he played trumpet, violin, drums, and alto with his father in the Young Family Band. Lester settled on alto but switched to tenor when he worked with Art Bronson's Bostonians in 1928 and 1929. After playing with the Original Blue Devils in 1932and 1933, Count Basie in 1934, Bennie Moten, and King Oliver, he got his big break as Coleman Hawkins' replacement with Fletcher Henderson's orchestra. His radical style was too different to suit the Henderson sidemen, and he was reluctantly let go after three months. Young sounded like he was playing a new instrument altogether. His tone was very light, he floated over bar lines, and he always sounded relaxed, even when the tempos were fast. He was the epitome of "cool."

After Young rejoined the Count Basie band in 1936, he was a major part of their success during the next four years, traveling to New York and being its top soloist. On the very first record date in late 1936, Young emerged fully formed, taking a perfect solo on "Lady Be Good." He recorded frequently with Basie, and starting in 1937 often with Billie Holiday, a close friend. He named her "Lady Day" and she called him "Pres."

For some reason, maybe because he did not want to record on Friday the thirteenth, Lester Young left the Basie band in December 1940. The next two years were largely uneventful; he made relatively few recordings, and his own band did not catch on. In October 1943 he rejoined Basie, and although the recording strike kept the full orchestra off records, Young made some classic small-group records and appeared in the Academy Award–winning short film *Jammin' the Blues*.

In the summer of 1944, Young was drafted. The military was the wrong place for the introverted and sensitive saxophonist, and he experienced a horrible year, including time in a military prison. Young was unsuited for military life and the institutional racism of the period. The experience left him emotionally scarred and depressed. After his discharge, Young at first played at his peak. He led combos during the next decade, toured with Jazz at the Philharmonic, and was well paid. He was greatly respected by the younger musicians; many copied his sound and approach. But his drinking increased and his state of mind gradually deteriorated during the 1950s. By then he had invented a language of his own, full of eccentric slang that was only understood by his closest friends, shielding himself as best he could from the world. Although he rallied on several occasions and often played quite well, Lester Young eventually drank himself to death, passing away in 1959 at the age of forty-nine.

ART TATUM

Art Tatum was arguably the most remarkable musician ever to play jazz. His blinding speed on the piano was without precedent outside of classical music, the way that he voiced chords and his unusual harmonies were at least thirty years ahead of their time, and his imagination was always very fertile. There have been several cases through the years of young pianists hearing an Art Tatum record and being convinced that at least two if not three pianists were playing.

Tatum was born with cataracts causing total blindness in one eye and partial vision in the other. There is no explanation for where his musical genius came from. Having started on piano as a child, he was working regularly at sixteen in his hometown of Toledo, Ohio, in 1926. Tatum appeared often on the radio and in 1932 was moved to New York as one of two pianists to accompany Adelaide Hall's singing. After his recording debut backing Hall, he recorded several solos, most notably an incredible version of "Tiger Rag" in 1933. From then on, he was primarily heard as a solo pianist. Some criticized him for not being able to play with other musicians, but as it turned out the opposite was true. Most other musicians were simply afraid to get on the bandstand with Tatum for he could make anyone sound old-fashioned in comparison.

Because he was black, nearly completely blind, and beyond any simple musical category, Tatum spent much of his life playing solo piano in bars and at parties. He loved to perform at late-night jam sessions, and once when he dropped in on a Fats Waller performance, Waller announced to the audience, "God is in the house."

After years of mostly playing solo, from 1943 to 1945 Tatum led a trio on Fifty-second Street that also included guitarist Tiny Grimes and bassist Slam Stewart. The trio gave Tatum a rare opportunity to play off other musicians, and even if he could not change keys and tempos at will in this format, he enjoyed exchanging witty ideas with the other musicians.

Tatum was occasionally presented at concerts and appeared on television in the 1950s but was always largely unknown to the general public. Producer Norman Granz recorded Tatum extensively in the 1950s, both as a soloist and in all-star groups with the likes of Lionel Hampton, Buddy Rich, clarinetist Buddy DeFranco, Ben Webster, Benny Carter, and Roy Eldridge. Art Tatum died from a blood disease, uremia, in 1956 at the age of forty-seven. His playing has still never been equaled.

BOOGIE-WOOGIE

Boogie-woogie, when a pianist's left hand plays a double-time repetitive eight-note pattern on blues, was very popular in the late 1930s and early 1940s. In the late 1920s it was a great favorite at parties and jam sessions, especially with Meade Lux Lewis' famous "Honky Tonk Train Blues." With the rise of the Depression, boogie-woogie largely disappeared except as an influence. Later in the decade, however, the Tommy Dorsey Orchestra's recording of "Boogie Woogie," based on Pinetop Smith's 1920 recording, became a hit, soon followed by Will Bradley's "Beat Me Daddy, Eight to the Bar," and other big band boogie-woogie records. At the height of the boogie-woogie fad, the Andrews Sisters had their big seller in "Boogie-Woogie Bugle Boy."

At John Hammond's Spirituals to Swing concert in December 1938, boogie-woogie was presented at Carnegie Hall featuring three pianists playing as a remarkable trio. Albert Ammons, who performed in Chicago clubs in the late 1920s, had started recording in 1936 with his Rhythm Kings. Meade Lux Lewis worked during the Depression at manual labor shovel gang and driving a taxi. He had been rediscovered by producer Hammond, who got him to record a newer version of "Honky Tonk Train Blues" and revived his career. Pete Johnson had started out as a drummer in Kansas City, not switching to piano until 1926 at age twenty-two. He was part of the city's legendary late-night jam sessions, often teaming up with Big Joe Turner, who worked as a singing bartender. Although Johnson and Turner were featured at the Spirituals to Swing Concert, including on "Roll 'Em Pete," they had not yet recorded.

The successful concert resulted in Ammons, Johnson, and Lewis all having productive careers, recording as a trio, in various duets, and as soloists. Big Joe Turner went on to fame as an unchanging but always spirited blues singer, performing swing, r&b, rock and roll, including a major hit in "Shake, Rattle and Roll," and jazz until his death in 1985.

There were other fine boogie-woogie pianists during the swing era. Most notable was Jimmy Yancey, who was the movement's father figure. Yancey, a groundskeeper at Comiskey Park for the Chicago White Sox, had a gentle and subtle style which was perhaps most notable for his funny habit of ending every song in E-flat, no matter what the tune's key.

Boogie-woogie's popularity peaked between 1938 and 1942 but has survived through the years. Its influence can be heard at least indirectly in the playing of many modern jazz and rock and roll pianists.

OTHER TOP NEW YORK–BASED MUSICIANS OF THE SWING ERA

Roy "Little Jazz" Eldridge was one of the most competitive of all jazz musicians. Always challenging himself, he loved to top rivals at trumpet battles and often ended solos on a difficult-to-reach high note. Often described as a link between Louis Armstrong and Dizzy Gillespie in the trumpet's evolution, Eldridge in reality he had his own crackling sound, chance-taking style, and legacy.

Eldridge began playing with groups in 1927 and gained some early attention for playing Coleman Hawkins' tenor solo from "The Stampede" on trumpet. He freelanced with many different orchestras before finally recording in 1935. Eldridge recorded with Billie Holiday, helped make Fletcher Henderson's version of "Christopher Columbus" a hit in 1936, and the next year led a Chicago octet. His recordings as a leader from 1937 to 1939 are outstanding, full of exciting trumpet solos that seem to be bursting at their seams. His harmonically advanced ideas were a major influence on the young Dizzy Gillespie. Eldridge was one of the stars of Gene Krupa's orchestra in 1941 and 1942 despite having difficulties being a black trumpeter touring with a white orchestra. He had similar problems with Artie Shaw's band in 1944 and 1945 but played brilliantly despite it all. Eldridge toured with Jazz at the Philharmonic and had his own short-lived big band but by 1950 was having self-doubts. Formerly among the most modern players in jazz, he felt a bit lost during the bebop revolution, wondering if he should modernize his style to keep up with Gillespie and the younger beboppers.

In 1950 Eldridge visited Europe with Benny Goodman and stayed an extra year. During this period his confidence was restored, and he realized that it was much more important to be himself than to worry about always being the most modern trumpeter. In the decade after returning to the United States, he made many recordings, often teamed up with Coleman Hawkins in a quintet and remained as competitive as ever. Although his range gradually decreased during the 1960s and 1970s, Roy Eldridge never lost his fire and spirit until a serious stroke in 1980 forced him to stop playing, nine years before his death.

Among the other impressive trumpeters of the swing era, Louis Armstrong, Bunny Berigan, and Harry James were the pacesetters. Ziggy Elman starred with Benny Goodman from 1936 to 1940 where he had a hit with "And the Angels Sing." He was featured with Tommy Dorsey between 1940 and 1947 but waited too long to form his own orchestra, spending his last active years as a studio musician. Charlie Shavers, who came to fame with the John Kirby Sextet, also had a long association with Tommy Dorsey after succeeding Elman and was a spectacular player who successfully battled Roy Eldridge at Jazz at the Philharmonic. Orin "Hot Lips" Page had been a star in Kansas City in the late 1920s with Walter Page's Blue Devils and in the early 1930s with Bennie Moten. He was briefly Count Basie's main trumpet soloist but left in Kansas City to precede him to New York. Although his own big band in 1937and 1938 did not catch on, Page was a fixture on Fifty-second Street and at late-night jam sessions where his colorful trumpet solos and exuberant blues vocals were greatly in demand. Buck Clayton and Harry "Sweets" Edison came to fame with the Count Basie Orchestra, as did Cootie Williams, Rex Stewart, and Ray Nance with Duke Ellington.

Jack Teagarden and Tommy Dorsey were the swing era's main trombonists. Dorsey's beautiful tone and popular band made him famous, but he always felt a bit shy about playing jazz, knowing that Teagarden was around. Teagarden sounded at his best with small groups, so he was overshadowed during these years, first buried in Paul Whiteman's Orchestra and then leading an unsuccessful big band of his own. Other key trombonists included Dickie Wells with Count Basie, Tricky Sam Nanton, Lawrence Brown and Juan Tizol with Duke Ellington, and Trummy Young with Jimmie Lunceford's orchestra.

One of Coleman Hawkins' closest competitors during the 1930s, Leon "Chu" Berry, had a sound and style that were very influenced by Hawkins, whose shadow he never completed escaped. He made an impression playing with the big bands of Teddy Hill from 1933 to 1935, Fletcher Henderson in 1936, and finally Cab Calloway from 1937 to 1941. He wrote the catchy instrumental "Christopher Columbus" and had a notable ballad showcase with Calloway on "Ghost of a Chance" but was at his best on up-tempo material. Tragically, Chu Berry's life was cut short in a car accident in 1941 when he was just thirty-three. With the premature death of Chu Berry, Ben Webster became Coleman Hawkins' top rival among tough-toned tenors. Webster had a raspy tone that in his early days was similar to Hawkins' tone although not as harmonically sophisticated. In time Webster developed two very different musical personalities, being brutish and roaring on up-tempo tunes while purring sensuously during ballads. Part of the early 1930s Kansas City scene, Webster worked with Bennie Moten in 1932 and passed through many big bands including those of Andy Kirk, Benny Carter, Cab Calloway, Teddy Wilson, and Fletcher Henderson, where he replaced Lester Young. He came to fame with Duke Ellington between 1940 and 1943 with classic solos on "Cottontail" and "All Too Soon." After leaving Ellington, Webster mostly led small groups, other than a second stint with him in 1948 and 1949, toured with Jazz at the Philharmonic, and made recordings including jam sessions and dates with string sections. Overshadowed by newer tenor players and weary of the U.S. racial problems, in 1964 Ben Webster moved permanently to Europe where he spent his last nine years playing in his unchanged but still viable style.

Whereas Chu Berry's chances at fame were cut short by his early death, Don Byas' were hurt by geography. Originally an altoist, Byas started playing professionally in 1927 and was part of the Kansas City scene with Bennie Moten and Walter Page's Blue Devils. In the 1930s he had many short-term associations with Lionel Hampton, Buck Clayton, Ethel Waters, and Andy Kirk but gained much more recognition as Lester Young's replacement with the Count Basie band from 1941 to 1943. Although his tone was very similar to Coleman Hawkins, he proved to be even more advanced harmonically and able to play fast runs full of exciting ideas.

Byas fit into early bebop groups without any difficulty, appearing on Fifty-second Street with Dizzy Gillespie and recording prolifically in a variety of settings between 1944 and 1946. After touring Europe with Don Redman's big band in 1946, he decided to settle overseas where work was plentiful and racism was minor in comparison to the United States, returning only once briefly in 1970. Although he played and recorded fairly frequently in Europe, Don Byas was largely forgotten stateside. The world was a much larger place in the 1950s then it is now, his recordings were rarely available in the United States, and Byas was unknown to most contemporary American jazz listeners, except as a historic figure, by the time he passed away in 1972. In addition to Lester Young, top tenors of the era included Buddy Tate and Herschel Evans with Count Basie, Georgie Auld with Benny Goodman, Eddie Miller who starred with Bob Crosby, Bud Freeman, and Illinois Jacquet.

The three top altoists were Johnny Hodges with Duke Ellington's Orchestra, Willie Smith with Jimmie Lunceford and later Harry James, and Benny Carter.

Also well worth mentioning are Tab Smith with Count Basie, Jimmy Dorsey, and Woody Herman.

Benny Carter had a long career that was filled with consistency, professionalism, and a flexible but largely unchanging alto style. In the 1920s he was already a significant player and arranger for Charlie Johnson's Paradise Ten, Fletcher Henderson's orchestra, and McKinney's Cotton Pickers, where he briefly succeeded Don Redman as leader. Carter, who also played trumpet, clarinet, tenor and piano, led his own big band from 1932 to 1935. He following Coleman Hawkins to Europe in 1935, spending three productive years playing and writing, including "When Day Is Done" and "Waltzing the Blues," with European orchestras. He returned to the United States in 1938, led a big band from 1939 to 1941, and two years later relocated to Los Angeles. Carter wrote for the studios, led occasional orchestras, and in the 1950s recorded some of his finest small group work. After being too busy writing to play his alto much between 1967 and 1975, Carter then made a full comeback and was active as a player, arranger, and composer until he retired in 1997 at the age of ninety. He passed away five years later. Throughout his career, Carter's solos were thoughtful, logical, and distinctive, as was his writing.

Teddy Wilson was the definitive pianist of the swing era, a very tasteful player with a light touch who could swing hard without looking as if he were sweating. Wilson began gigging in 1929 when he was sixteen, played with Speed Webb's unrecorded territory band from 1929 to 1931, and worked with several Chicago groups, including Louis Armstrong's big band. A favorite of producer John Hammond, he was recorded as the leader of all-star swing combos between 1935 and 1942, often featuring Billie Holiday. Wilson gained fame as a member of the Benny Goodman Trio and Quartet from 1935 to 1939, breaking down many racial boundaries with one of the first interracial groups to perform regularly in public. When Wilson left Goodman, he formed a big band, but it only lasted a year. He had a successful sextet between 1940 and 1944 and played in reunions with Benny Goodman and occasional all-star sessions in later years. Wilson was content to perform the same swing era standards with trios in the 1935 style until his death in 1986.

Until the guitar was electrified in 1938, acoustic guitarists were always hard to hear. The guitar was mostly utilized to state the rhythm, hitting a chord on each beat, with only very infrequent solos Freddie Green with Count Basie's orchestra was a prime example of how the guitar was used during the swing era.

By 1938 some players were starting to experiment with the new electric guitar. Les Paul had experimented with electronics earlier, and George Barnes began playing electric guitar on blues records, beginning a long career as a studio musician and a swing soloist. Eddie Durham, a trombonist and arranger for Count Basie, doubled on guitar and can be heard playing electric guitar in 1938 with the Kansas City Five and Six, small groups drawn from Basie's band. It would be up to Charlie Christian, however, to revolutionize the instrument.

Charlie Christian, an innovator on the electric guitar, first liberated his instrument from its quiet part in the rhythm section. Christian grew up in Oklahoma City, started on the acoustic guitar when he was twelve, and played locally. In 1937 he switched to the new electric guitar. Christian quickly realized the instrument's potential, soloing like a saxophonist while not worrying about being heard over horns. He was a master at coming up with riff-filled ideas that included new melodies and infectious swinging rhythms. Several top musicians, including Teddy Wilson and Mary Lou Williams, heard Christian playing in Oklahoma City, and word got back to producer John Hammond. Hammond flew to Oklahoma and was also amazed by Christian's playing, so he flew the guitarist to Los Angeles where Benny Goodman was playing. The clarinetist was not impressed by Christian's flashy clothes, but after much persuasion, he was persuaded to audition the guitarist. He called out the song "Rose Room," and forty-five minutes later Goodman and Christian were still playing the tune. Christian immediately became a key member of the Benny Goodman Sextet.

During the next two years, Christian starred with Goodman's combo, playing next to Lionel Hampton and trumpeter Cootie Williams, inspiring the other musicians. He was also featured on a rare occasion with the Goodman big band, including his showcase "Solo Flight." Other guitarists listened closely and were greatly influenced by Christian, including Tiny Grimes, Slim Gaillard, and Oscar Moore, with the King Cole Trio. Tragically in June 1941, Charlie Christian was stricken with tuberculosis, confined to a sanitarium, and never recovered, dying on March 2, 1942, at the age of twenty-five. It was the late 1960s before other jazz guitarists began to surpass Christian, a major influence on Barney Kessel, Herb Ellis, Tal Farlow, Wes Montgomery, George Benson, and countless other players.

Even after the bass assumed the former role of the tuba, the role of string bassists was very set until 1939. They accompanied soloists and ensembles by playing one note on each beat, four-to-the-bar except in rare cases when they played two-to-the-bar. Bass solos were extremely rare, usually when other musicians dropped out leaving the bassist playing four-to-the-bar. The top bassists of this period included Milt Hinton with Cab Calloway and Slam Stewart, whose bowed solos with Slim Gaillard were both impressive and witty.

The bass was liberated when twenty-one-year-old Jimmy Blanton joined Duke Ellington in the fall of 1939. Blanton had started out as a violinist, switching to bass in 1936. He gained experience working with territory bands, and by the time he joined Ellington, he was a top-notch accompanist, playing advanced ideas behind soloists. He was much more than a mere timekeeper, soloing with the fluidity of a guitarist or saxophonist, often playing unprecedented double-time runs. While with Ellington, Blanton often had short solos, recording six duets accompanied by him. He was also a fine bower. In general Blanton sounded twenty years ahead of his contemporaries, and it was the late 1950s before other bassists caught up and surpassed him. Unfortunately Blanton was long gone by then, having contracted tuberculosis, dying in 1942 at the age of twenty-three.

The drums first really gained recognition when Gene Krupa became a star with Benny Goodman from 1935 to 1938. Later drummers who had lighter touches and were more musical included Big Sid Catlett, Cozy Cole, Dave Tough, Ray McKinley, Ray Bauduc, O'Neill Spencer, and Jo Jones, who shifted the timekeeping function from the bass to the hi-hat. The most spectacular soloist, then and now, was Buddy Rich who, with Artie Shaw and Tommy Dorsey, began to set a standard that no one else could reach.

THREE MAJOR SWING SINGERS: BILLIE HOLIDAY, ELLA FITZGERALD, AND DINAH WASHINGTON

Billie Holiday's life would make a classic Hollywood movie, but unfortunately the fictional and mundane *Lady Sings the Blues* is not it; the truth behind this great legend of jazz is much more interesting. Born April 7, 1915, Eleanora Harris Holiday was the daughter of Fletcher Henderson's guitarist Clarence Holiday, but he never did marry her mother. Holiday had a very difficult childhood, growing up feeling alone and unloved, acquiring a life-long inferiority complex.

Things began to improve in 1933. Holiday, who was struggling in poverty, was discovered singing in a Harlem club by John Hammond, who became a major booster. He arranged for Holiday to record two songs with a Benny Goodman small group, and although those performances were not memorable, it was a start. Holiday free-lanced in 1934, appeared in a short film with Duke Ellington, and thanks to Hammond began recording with all-star combos led by Teddy Wilson in 1935. The series, which continued until 1942, were quite jazz oriented with Holiday sharing the spotlight with top soloists.

Lady Day, a nickname given to her by her good friend Lester Young, had a small voice and her improvising was basic, but her behind-the-beat phrasing and emo-

One of the great legends, Billie Holiday (Lady Day) was in her own special category.
Photo courtesy of the Wayne Knight Collection, Star Line Productions.

tional intensity were eerie and haunting. Holiday had stints with the big bands of Count Basie in 1937 and Artie Shaw in 1938, but those associations went almost completely undocumented. Much more significant were her small group sessions, with and without Teddy Wilson, that resulted in such classic recordings as "What a Little Moonlight Can Do," "I Cried for You," "Billie's Blues," "I Can't Give You Anything but Love," "Sugar," "Some Other Spring," "Falling in Love Again," "Them There Eyes," "Gloomy Sunday," and her famous "God Bless the Child." Also in 1937 Holiday recorded for the first time with tenor-saxophonist Lester Young and trumpeter Buck Clayton, two soloists who fit her singing perfectly. Young's very light tone and lyrical style echoed Lady Day's phrasing, and they often sounded as if they were making love through music. Among their many special collaborations are "This Year's Kisses," "Mean to Me," "Foolin' Myself," "Easy Living," "Without Your Love," "When You're Smiling," "I Can't Believe That You're in Love with Me," and "All of Me."

In 1939 Holiday began working regularly at New York's interracial Café Society club. At this time she added "Strange Fruit" to her repertoire, a somewhat scary and picturesque anti-lynching poem/art song. Her fame continued to grow, and in 1944 she signed with the Decca label, having her biggest selling record, "Lover Man," backed by a string section. But all was not well.

Lady Day's insecurities led her to constantly picking the wrong boyfriends and husbands. She preferred tough men who could protect her, but quite often they turned on her. Worse yet, her early reliance on alcohol evolved into a heroin habit by the mid-1940s that made her life very difficult. Ironically, Holiday's voice was at its prime then, and her popular recordings included "Good Morning Heartache," "Don't Explain," "Fine and Mellow," and "Ain't Nobody's Business if I Do." In 1946 she appeared in her only motion picture, *New Orleans*, opposite her hero Louis Armstrong, who she considered her main influence along with Bessie Smith. Shortly afterwards she was arrested for possession of heroin and jailed for a year. The notoriety followed her throughout the rest of her career.

In the 1950s Holiday's voice gradually declined, although she mostly recorded in very favorable jazz-oriented settings. For a time her emotional intensity and her desire only to sing lyrics that she had lived made up for her weakening voice. Her unhappy relationships and reliance on liquor and heroin continued, however, and although she occasionally rallied, by 1958 she sounded like she was seventy-three rather than forty-three. On July 17, 1959, Billie Holiday passed away, after being arrested for heroin possession on her deathbed. She left behind scores of classic recordings but proved to be her own worst enemy.

Ella Fitzgerald began her solo career in the fall of 1941 when her orchestra, the Chick Webb ghost band, broke up. At twenty-four she was already a mature ballad singer, finally free of juvenile novelties. During the next few years her fame and power grew, and in the mid-1940s she learned how to scat-sing so well that she became the leader in that field. Fitzgerald by then had the ability to outswing any other singer: her voice was perfectly in tune, and her interpretations were generally full of the joy of singing. Although some criticized her for always sounding so happy, perhaps it was simply her way of showing relief at escaping her early poverty, and for the joy she felt at being paid well for something she loved.

In 1946 Fitzgerald began working regularly for Norman Granz's Jazz at the Philharmonic, and Granz became her manager. Her scat-filled recordings of "Lady Be Good," "How High the Moon," and "Flying Home" forever gave her stature as one of the premiere jazz singers, yet her straightforward versions of George Gershwin songs in 1950, while backed by pianist Ellis Larkins, reminded listeners that she was also a superb interpreter of lyrics.

In 1956 Granz started the Verve label, initially to feature Fitzgerald. During the next few years she recorded extensive songbooks of the music of Cole Porter, George and Ira Gershwin, Rodgers and Hart, Duke Ellington, Harold Arlen, Jerome Kern, and Johnny Mercer. She mostly stuck to the melody, except during the Ellington project, showing other singers how the songs should sound.

Throughout the 1950s, 1960s, and 1970s, Fitzgerald constantly toured the world, performing and recording frequently and earning her title of "The First Lady of Song." By the late 1970s Ella's voice was declining, and erratic health plagued her during the next decade. Even in her last performances before retiring in the early 1990s, Ella Fitzgerald retained her joyful swinging style until her death in 1996. She was one of the most beloved of all performers in the jazz world.

One of the most versatile and accessible singers of the 1940s through early 1960s, Dinah Washington was able to sing anything. Born Ruth Jones, she sang with a church choir before performing in night-clubs at age fifteen in 1940. Renamed Dinah Washington, she worked with Lionel Hampton's big band between 1943 and 1946. Although she recorded very little with Hampton, her own initial record date as a leader created the hit "Evil Gal Blues." After leaving Hampton, Washington became a popular attraction, singing jazz, blues, r&b, and pop music with equal enthusiasm and skill. Among her hits were "I Wanna Be Loved," "New Blowtop Blues," "T.V. Is the Thing This Year," and "Teach Me Tonight." Whether it was performing with a big band, a studio orchestra, an all-star combo, or a classic set with trumpeters Clifford Brown, Maynard Ferguson, and Clark Terry, she sounded quite at home, uplifting every set with her voice.

The First Lady of Song, Ella Fitzgerald out sung all other singers for over forty years.
Photo courtesy of the Wayne Knight Collection, Star Line Productions.

In 1959 Washington's career changed permanently with her giant pop hit "What a Difference a Day Makes." During the next three years her recordings were backed by orchestras that often played country-oriented arrangements in hopes of duplicating the hit. She recorded some popular duets with Brook Benton and in clubs showed that she could sing any style, including swinging jazz. On December 14, 1963, Dinah Washington died from an accidental overdose of liquor and diet pills when she was just thirty-nine.

OTHER VOCALISTS

Vocalists were in great demand during the swing era, with virtually every jazz big band featuring a female singer and often a male vocalist too. Those who could swing the words were always able to find work singing the many high-quality songs by George Gershwin, Cole Porter, Harold Arlen, Hoagy Carmichael, Jerome Kern, Richard Rodgers, Harry Warren, Irving Berlin, Duke Ellington, and others, with words by Porter, Berlin, Al Dubin, Ira Gershwin, Larry Hart, Johnny Mercer, Yip Harburg, Andy Razaf, and other major lyricists.

The swing era's top male jazz vocalists in addition to Bing Crosby, who had moved largely to pop music, were Louis Armstrong, Jack Teagarden, Big Joe Turner, Billy Eckstine with Earl Hines, and the best of the male band singers, Jimmy Rushing. Like Frank Sinatra with Tommy Dorsey, most other male vocalists with big bands, unless they were musicians, focused on ballads.

Nearly every big band had a female vocalist. Among the best were Ella Fitzgerald with Chick Webb, Helen Ward with Benny Goodman, Helen Humes with Count Basie, Ivie Anderson with Duke Ellington, Anita O'Day with Gene Krupa, Peggy Lee with Benny Goodman, Dinah Washington with Lionel Hampton, Billie Holiday with Count Basie and Artie Shaw, and Helen Forrest with Artie Shaw, Benny Goodman, and Harry James. Four other singers had important careers that went beyond singing with a particular orchestra: Mildred Bailey, Lena Horne, Maxine Sullivan, and Lee Wiley.

Although always suffering from an inferiority complex due to her weight, Mildred Bailey was one of the finest jazz singers of the 1930s and 1940s. After going to school in Spokane, Washington, she moved to Los Angeles in 1926 where she sang on the radio. After Paul Whiteman heard her sing at a party in 1929, she joined his orchestra, becoming the first fulltime female singer. Bailey was inspired by Ethel Waters and Bessie Smith but had a very distinctive little girl-like voice that contrasted with her appearance. A fine blues singer, she helped to popularize "Georgia on My Mind," which she recorded in 1931, and "Rockin' Chair." After marrying xylophonist Red Norvo in 1933, she co-led a big band with her husband during the first half of the swing era. They were dubbed "Mr. and Mrs. Swing," but neither the band nor the marriage lasted, and they were divorced in 1943. At the height of her career in 1944 and 1945, Bailey hosted a regular radio series, but her health soon faded, and she died in 1951 when she was just forty-four.

Early in her career, Lena Horne was part of the jazz world. Famous for being a beauty, she started singing and dancing at the Cotton Club in 1934, worked with Noble Sissle's Orchestra in 1935 and 1936 and Charlie Barnet in 1940 and 1941, and recorded with Artie Shaw. With her looks she was naturally picked to appear in movies, but being black during an era when black actors and actresses usually had terrible stereotyped roles was difficult. Because Horne would not accept undignified parts during her years at MGM, other than the major black films *Cabin in the Sky* and *Stormy Weather*, she was confined to cameo appearances in a variety of white films, usually just performing a song that could easily be cut from versions shown to the South's segregated audiences. There was no room for glamorous black movie stars in the 1940s. So instead, Lena Horne continued singing, drifting away from jazz toward cabaret and middle-of-the-road pop music by the 1950s.

Throughout her career, Maxine Sullivan uplifted tunes by singing them fairly straight, swinging lightly and changing notes here and there. A very subtle singer, she had a pleasing voice that was influential. At sixteen she was discovered while singing on the radio in Pittsburgh and was soon making records with pianist Claude Thornhill as her musical director. Her second record date in 1937 produced a huge hit with a lightly swinging version of the Scottish folk song "Loch Lomond." Soon Sullivan was recording other folk songs, including "If I Had a Ribbon Bow," "Annie Laurie," and "Down the Old Ox Road," and adding her warm voice to such ballads as "The Folks Who Live on the Hill" and to light swing tunes. After marrying John Kirby in 1938, she recorded often with that cool jazz band, which perfectly framed her voice. Sullivan had a radio show for two years, *Flow Gently Sweet Rhythm*, spent a dozen years outside of music after retiring in the mid-1950s, later in life married stride pianist Cliff Jackson, and made a full comeback starting in 1966. Maxine Sullivan's final twenty years before her 1987 death were busy, and she never seemed to get tired of singing "Loch Lomond" for her fans.

Lee Wiley, a smoky cabaret singer with indescribable charisma, was a favorite of Eddie Condon and some of the traditional jazz musicians. She started out singing commercial music with Leo Reisman in the late 1920s and for a few years was closely tied with composer Victor Young, performing with radio orchestras. She was the first singer to record complete songbooks dedicated to the work of one composer. Between 1939 and 1943 she recorded songs by the Gershwins, Cole Porter, Rodgers and Hart, and Harold Arlen in sets of eight songs, including definitive versions of "I've Got a Crush on You," "Glad to Be Unhappy," "Down with Love," and "Let's Fall in Love." Wiley was married to pianist Jess Stacy for a time in the mid-1940s and sang with his short-lived big band. Often backed by Eddie Condon's Dixieland musicians, her ballads provided a break from the more freewheeling performances. Although she recorded some excellent albums in the 1950s, including *Night in Manhattan*, most did not sell well, and she recorded only once after 1957.

JOHN HAMMOND: A TALENT SCOUT AND PROMOTER FOR SWING

One of the most important non-musicians in jazz history, John Hammond made a major impact on jazz, particularly in the swing era. Born in late 1910, Hammond was part of a wealthy family and was educated at Yale. From the beginning, he had a great love for black music and was an early fighter against racism. By 1932 when he was twenty-one, he was already working hard in the music business, setting up a record date for the Fletcher Henderson orchestra. He discovered Billie Holiday in 1933 and arranged for her first record dates, produced Bessie Smith's final record session, and produced American jazz sessions for the European market when there seemed to be no market for free-wheeling jazz in the United States. He was a friend of Benny Goodman, later his brother-in-law, encouraged him to form his first big band, and persuaded him to fill his library with Fletcher Henderson arrangements. In 1935 Hammond teamed Billie Holiday with Teddy Wilson for a series of classic recordings, and he was a behind-the-scenes force in forming Benny Goodman's trio with Wilson and Gene Krupa. Late that year in Chicago, he was scanning the radio dial and discovered Count Basie's orchestra broadcasting from Kansas City. After writing about Basie in some publications, he persuaded Basie to come East in 1936.

It is difficult to imagine the swing era without John Hammond. In 1938 and 1939 he organized two famous Spirituals to Swing concerts at Carnegie Hall. Among those featured at the 1938 concert were Big Joe Turner, the Count Basie Orchestra, the New Orleans Feetwarmers with Sidney Bechet, several major blues artists, and the Boogie Woogie Trio of Albert Ammons, Meade Lux Lewis, and Pete Johnson. If they had survived, Bessie Smith and Robert Johnson would have certainly been at the concert. The 1939 Spirituals to Swing concert featured James P. Johnson, Ida Cox, Basie's band, the Kansas City Six, and the Benny Goodman Sextet. One of the stars was guitarist Charlie Christian, who Hammond had discovered a few months earlier and had flown from Oklahoma City to Los Angeles to meet Benny Goodman. Hammond also produced many records for Columbia between 1937 and 1943.

After serving in the military, Hammond felt out of touch with the jazz world and never developed a taste for the new bebop music. In the 1950s he produced a series of superior mainstream swing dates for the Vanguard label that featured top swing era veterans, and from 1959 to 1975 he was an important force at Columbia Records. During that era he helped discover guitarist George Benson, Aretha Franklin, Bob Dylan, and Bruce Springsteen. In 1967 Hammond organized a third Spirituals to Swing concert, and he produced sessions as late as the 1980s, passing away in 1987. Although his dominant personality and self-righteous views could rub some people the wrong way, Hammond deserves to be saluted for his fights against racism and his skills as a talent scout.

THE END OF THE SWING ERA

Swing was king from 1935 to 1942, but the deepening of U.S. involvement in World War II and a variety of other factors killed the big band era by 1946. With wartime gasoline rationing, it became much more difficult for big bands to travel. The draft claimed some key players who were often replaced with teenagers, and some bandleaders enlisted, including Glenn Miller, Bob Crosby, and Artie Shaw.

The Musicians Union called a recording strike for August 1, 1942, to protest against radio stations broadcasting records for free. No commercial records were made until the Decca label settled in September 1943, with some of the larger companies, Columbia and Victor, not recording until November 1944. Non-union singers were free to record, and this twenty-seven-month gap allowed them to take over popular music. There were still broadcasts, radio transcriptions—recordings made specifically to be played on the radio—and "V Discs," records that were made for servicemen overseas, but the ban made it very difficult for new orchestras to catch on. The broadcasts, radio transcriptions, and V Discs add a great deal to the legacy of big bands from the first half of the 1940s, but they were not for sale to the general public then.

In addition to the lack of opportunities for new big bands during 1942 to 1944, many of the established orchestras, other than Duke Ellington's, were simply running out of ideas and becoming predictable if not stale. The younger creative musicians were starting to look elsewhere, participating in late-night jam sessions that resulted in bebop, getting more lucrative work in smaller r&b groups, or finding joy in reviving Dixieland. This drain of creativity hurt swing.

Particularly ruinous was the cabaret tax enacted in 1941, forcing clubs and dance halls to pay 30 percent of their ticket sales if they permitted dancing. Big swing bands became too expensive, and smaller nightclubs with combos made more money than large dance halls. Dancing was separated from jazz, and jazz's audience shrunk dramatically.

After World War II ended in 1945, musicians who had worked for next to nothing during the Depression wanted livable salaries, which were mostly impossible due to the smaller audience. Big bands also had the difficulty now of being associated with the World War II years, and they were thought of as old-fashioned. Even if the swinging orchestras had somehow survived these difficulties, they would have been killed by the rise of television, which encouraged people to get free entertainment at home rather than go out dancing.

Many big bands broke up in 1946, the survivors, in 1949 and 1950. Since then many have asked, When are the big bands coming back? Until thousands of fans rediscover the joy of dancing to swing orchestras, the answer is, never, at least not on the level of the swing era. Fortunately, records do survive.

RECOMMENDED RECORDINGS

Art Tatum. *Classic Early Solos*. GRP/Decca, 607.

Art Tatum. *The Complete Pablo Group Masterpieces*. Pablo, 4401, 6 CDs.

Artie Shaw. *Self-Portrait*. Bluebird, 09026-63808, 5 CDs.

Ben Webster. *See You at the Fair*. GRP/Impulse, 2126.

Benny Carter. *Further Definitions*. GRP/Impulse, 229.

Benny Goodman. *The Birth of Swing*. Bluebird, 61038, 3 CDs.

Benny Goodman. *Carnegie Hall Jazz Concert*. Columbia, 65167, 2 CDs.

Benny Goodman. *The Complete Small Group Recordings*. RCA, 68764.

Bessie Smith. *The Collection*. Columbia/Legacy, 44441.

Billie Holiday. *The Complete Decca Recordings*. GRP/Decca, 2-601, 2 CDs.

Billie Holiday. *The Quintessential, Volume 4*. Columbia, 44252.

Billie Holiday. *The Quintessential, Volume 5*. Columbia, 44423.

Bing Crosby. *1926–1932*. Timeless, 1-004.

Bix Beiderbecke. *Singin' the Blues*. Columbia, 45450.

Bob Crosby. *South Rampart Street Parade*. GRP/Decca, 615.

Boswell Sisters Collection. Vol. 1. Nostalgia Arts, 3007.

Bunny Berigan. *The Pied Piper 1934–40*. Bluebird, 66615.

Cab Calloway. *1931–1932*. Classics, 526.

Charlie Barnet. *Clap Hands Here Comes Charlie*. Bluebird, 6273.

Charlie Christian. *The Genius of the Electric Guitar*. Columbia, 40846.

Chick Webb. *1929–1934*. Classics, 502.

Coleman Hawkins. *A Retrospective*. Bluebird, 66617, 2 CDs.

Dinah Washington. *Dinah Jams*. Emarcy, 814 639.

Duke Ellington. *The Blanton-Webster Band*. Bluebird, 5659, 3 CDs.

Duke Ellington. *The Carnegie Hall Concerts—January 1943*. Prestige, 34004, 2 CDs.

Duke Ellington. *Early Ellington*. Bluebird, 6852.

Duke Ellington. *Okeh Ellington*. Columbia, 46177, 2 CDs.

Duke Ellington. *70th Birthday Concert*. Blue Note, 32746, 2 CDs.

Ella Fitzgerald. *The Complete Ella in Berlin*. Verve, 314 519 584.

Ella Fitzgerald. *75th Birthday Celebration*. GRP/Decca, 2-619, 2 CDs.

Erskine Hawkins. *The Original Tuxedo Junction*. Bluebird, 9682.

Ethel Waters. *1925–1926*. Classics, 672.

Fats Waller. *The Early Years, Part 1*. Bluebird, 66618, 2 CDs.

Fats Waller. *The Last Years*. Bluebird, 9883, 3 CDs.

Fats Waller. *Turn on the Heat*. Bluebird, 2482.

Fletcher Henderson. *A Study in Frustration*. Columbia/Legacy, 57596, 3 CDs.

Gene Krupa. *Uptown*. Columbia, 65448.

Glenn Miller. *The Popular Recordings*. Bluebird, 9785, 3 CDs.

Glenn Miller Army Air Force Band. Bluebird, 63852, 4 CDs.

Harry James. *Snooty Fruity*. Columbia, 45447.

Jabbo Smith. *1929–1938*. Retrieval, 79013.

Jack Teagarden. *The Indispensable Jack Teagarden*. RCA, 961 327, 2 CDs.

James P. Johnson. *Harlem Stride Piano*. Hot 'N' Sweet, 151032.

Jimmie Lunceford. *For Dancers Only*. GRP/Decca, 645.

Jimmy Dorsey. *Contrasts*. GRP/Decca, 626.

Joe Venuti and Eddie Lang. *The 1920s and 1930s Sides*. JSP, 3402, 4 CDs.

John Kirby Sextet. *1938–1939*. Classics, 750.
Lester Young. *The Complete Aladdin Sessions*. Blue Note, 32787, 2 CDs.
Lester Young. *The Complete Lester Young on Keynote*. Mercury, 830920.
Lionel Hampton. *Hamp!* GRP/Decca, 652, 2 CDs.
Louis Armstrong. *1934–1936*. Classics, 509.
Louis Armstrong. *Plays W.C. Handy*. Columbia / Legacy, 64925.
Louis Armstrong. *Pops: 1940s Small Band Sides*. RCA / Bluebird, 6378.
Louis Armstrong. *St. Louis Blues, Vol. 6*. Columbia / Legacy, 46996.
McKinney's Cotton Pickers. *Put It There, Vol. 1*. Frog, 25.
Mills Brothers. *Chronological, Vol. 1*. JSP, 301.
Original Dixieland Jazz Band. *75th Anniversary*. Bluebird, 61098.
Pete Johnson. *1938–1939*. Classics, 656.
Raymond Scott. *Reckless Nights and Turkish Twilights*. Columbia, 53028.
Red Nichols and Miff Mole. Retrieval, 79010.
Roy Eldridge. *Little Jazz*. Columbia, 45275.
Stuff Smith. *1936–1939*. Classics, 706.
Tommy Dorsey. *Yes, Indeed*. Bluebird, 9987.
Various Artists. *Jazz in the Thirties*. DRG/Swing, 8457/8458, 2 CDs.
Various Artists. *From Spirituals to Swing*. Vanguard, 169/71, 3 CDs.

5

Kansas City Swing, the Territory Bands, and the San Francisco Revival

BEYOND CHICAGO AND NEW YORK

Although the early history of jazz is often depicted as a move from New Orleans to Chicago and New York, other significant cities were involved in its evolution, most notably Kansas City. Many jazz groups in the 1920s, 1930s, and into the 1940s were based in smaller cities, spending time on the road, usually in the Midwest and the Southwest. These territory bands, as they were called, had strong reputations and followings in certain parts of the country, but because they did not record extensively, most were unknown outside their territories.

Both the territory bands and the Kansas City jazz scene were at their peak during the classic jazz and swing eras.

KANSAS CITY

By 1929 of all the cities outside of New York, Kansas City had the strongest and most intriguing jazz scene. Although Prohibition was in force during the 1920s, Kansas City was a wide-open city run by a corrupt government that encouraged, and profited from, bootleg liquor, gambling joints, and around-the-clock nightclubs. There was always a great need for black musicians to play at these clubs. Although the hours were long and the pay was low, the musicians appreciated the work and experience, particularly during the early

Depression years. The late-night jam sessions often went past dawn, with the top players in town battling the nationally famous greats who were passing through Kansas City.

While jazz, particularly in New York, became more sophisticated during the 1920s and 1930s, developing more complex chords, adventurous solos, and trickier arrangements, the musicians in Kansas City never lost sight of the basics, specifically the blues. A vocalist who could not sing the blues stood little chance of getting much work there. The same was true for a pianist or horn soloist. Even while creating new ideas and trying to top each other in jam sessions, a performer was doomed to failure if he lost sight of the blues.

Best known among the regular Midwestern bands of the 1920s and early 1930s was Bennie Moten's Kansas City Orchestra. Moten was a decent ragtime-based pianist whose sextet expanded to becoming a big band in 1922 and 1923. He hired the best musicians in the city, becoming so dominant that some bands had to break up when they lost their key sidemen. Moten recorded frequently between 1923 and 1931, having a hit record with "South." Along with playing standards and spirited originals, his band performed a fair number of blues.

For a period Moten's main competitor was the Blue Devils, a small combo led by bassist Walter Page that included pianist Bill "Count" Basie, singer Jimmy Rushing, and trumpeter Hot Lips Page. In time, however, Moten hired all of Page's top players, including the bassist leader. Although Moten played piano, he hired Basie because he enjoyed the younger pianist's playing and used him on all of his recordings after October 1929.

On December 13, 1932, the Bennie Moten band made its final record, and it was quite significant. With Hot Lips Page, tenor-saxophonist Ben Webster, and Basie as key soloists, the orchestra sounded similar to Count Basie's big band five years in the future. The clean riff-filled ensembles, the purposeful and hard swinging solos, and the use of space would become Basie trademarks. On such numbers as "Blue Room," "Lafayette," and "Moten Swing," the music pointed directly towards swing, serving as a symbolic close to the classic jazz era.

Count Basie

Count Basie had originally been a stride pianist influenced by his friend Fats Waller. After a traveling show left him stranded in Kansas City in 1927, Basie decided to stay because of the very active local music scene. He joined Walter Page's Blue Devils in 1928 and starred with Bennie Moten's Orchestra between 1929 and 1935. After Moten died due to complications from a tonsillectomy in 1935, Basie went out on his own and soon was leading one of the top local groups.

Basie's band had a different sound, mainly due to the rhythm section. He left a lot of space in his piano playing, having pared down the stride style to the essentials to make every note count. The timekeeping role was assumed by the 4/4 playing of bassist Walter Page, while drummer Jo Jones shifted the emphasis from the bass drum to the cymbals, giving the rhythm section a much lighter sound. After the band settled in New York in 1937, Freddie Green became the rhythm guitarist, playing quiet chords right on the beat which made the band swing even more. Even after decades away from Kansas City, Basie's band continued to define the Kansas City sound, never losing sight of its roots.

The use of space and lighter tone was a major part of the Kansas City heritage, which had developed during the legendary late-night jam sessions. Basie's main soloist, Lester Young, developed a floating tone on tenor that sounded as if he were playing a different instrument altogether than Coleman Hawkins, who up until the early 1940s was the dominant force on tenor saxophonists.

After producer John Hammond heard the Basie band in a 1936 broadcast from Kansas City, he persuaded Basie to take the band east. Despite growing pains from quickly expanding to thirteen pieces from nine, the Count Basie Orchestra was one of the hottest big bands of 1937 and, even with personnel changes along the way, ranked near the top for the next dozen years. Basie's theme song, "One O'Clock Jump," and "Jumpin' at the Woodside" became standards, Billie Holiday sang with the orchestra in 1937, and other important sidemen included trumpeters Buck Clayton and Harry "Sweets" Edison, trombonist Dickie Wells, singers Jimmy Rushing and Helen Humes, and tenor-saxophonist Herschel Evans, whose hard tone contrasted with that of Young. The Basie band's reliance on blues and riffing originals became the epitome of swing. When Evans' death in 1939 left a void, tenor-saxophonist Buddy Tate filled in for ten years, and Young's departure in 1940 opening up a position filled at times by tenors Don Byas, Illinois Jacquet, Lucky Thompson, and Paul Gonsalves. Other later soloists included altoist Tab Smith, trombonist Vic Dickenson, and trumpeter Clark Terry.

Count Basie, the leader of the most famous Kansas City swing orchestra, shares the piano with the incredible Art Tatum.
Photo courtesy of the Wayne Knight Collection, Star Line Productions.

The Basie orchestra, which was nationally famous by 1938, remained popular, but money problems resulted in the orchestra reluctantly breaking up in 1949. Basie led a septet for two years, featuring Terry, clarinetist Buddy DeFranco, and tenor-saxophonist Wardell Gray, before re-entering the big band world with a new orchestra in 1952. Although including few alumni from the 1940s, other than

Freddie Green and trumpeter Joe Newman, the band retained the Basie Kansas City sound even with more tightly arranged ensembles and more modern soloists than before. With its 1954 recording of "April in Paris," the band had a new hit. The following year's addition of singer Joe Williams was a major coup. His version of "Everyday I Have the Blues" was quite popular, proving him to be a superb blues singer even though he preferred ballads. The new Basie orchestra caught on so well that it is still active today.

In the 1950s its main soloists were trumpeters Joe Newman and Thad Jones and tenors Frank Foster and Frank Wess, but the ensemble sound and the arrangements were more significant than any individual stars. That has been an important factor in the band's longevity; as major soloists gradually left the band, the Basie Kansas City sound still remained the same. There have been features along the way for the passionate tenor of Eddie "Lockjaw" Davis, trombonist Al Grey, drummer Butch Miles, and tenor-saxophonist Jimmy Forrest among others, but even when these were absent, the Basie orchestra never stopped swinging. In fact Count Basie's death in 1984 did not stop the band either, and it has continued touring the world ever since as jazz's number one swinging institution.

Other Kansas City Bands

Although Bennie Moten and later Count Basie were the most famous regular bands in Kansas City, they had their competitors. George E. Lee's Singing Orchestra was popular in the 1920s, most notable for featuring pianist-singer Julia Lee, George's sister. By 1929 Andy Kirk's Twelve Clouds of Joy was a major band, particularly due to the piano solos and arrangements of Mary Lou Williams. Kirk's band made its debut recordings in 1929 and 1930. Although not documented at all from 1932 to 1935, the orchestra continued to evolve and worked steadily in Kansas City. In 1936 they were signed to the Decca label, traveled east to New York, and had its biggest hit, a vocal ballad "Until the Real Thing Comes Along" that featured Pha Terrell's high-note vocal. The band's best performances were the instrumental arrangements by their pianist Mary Lou Williams, a brilliant and always modern player. Also quite impressive was tenor-saxophonist Dick Wilson. After Wilson died from tuberculosis in 1941 and Williams left the band, it quickly declined. The 1944 edition featured Howard McGhee and Fats Navarro on trumpets playing early bebop, but that band barely recorded, and a few years later the Kirk Orchestra faded into history.

Following Count Basie and Andy Kirk, pianist Jay McShann had the last important Kansas City big band. McShann was part of the Kansas City jazz scene by the mid-1930s and formed his big band in 1937. Although his orchestra was excellent, it will always be best remembered as an important musical home for the young altoist Charlie Parker. In 1940 McShann brought the orchestra to New York, and in 1941 and 1942 they recorded for Decca. The label typecast McShann's orchestra as a blues band, especially after "Confessin' the Blues," which featured Walter Brown's vocal, became a hit. Unfortunately many of the band's more swing-oriented arrangements were not recorded. The McShann Orchestra lasted until 1944 when the leader was drafted. Since then Jay McShann has led combos and been featured as a pianist and singer who loves the blues but can also play hard-driving swing too.

The arrival of Count Basie's orchestra in New York had revitalized the swing era by infusing the mainstream of jazz with two specific aspects of Kansas City jazz, a much lighter rhythm section and more of an emphasis on the blues. Charlie Parker's period with Jay McShann and training in Kansas City prior to being the leader of bebop resulted in the blues becoming a significant part of even the most complex bop tunes in the late 1940s.

Even though the Kansas City jazz scene declined with the discovery and relocation of most of its top players, it has continued to have an influence on jazz to the present day.

TERRITORY BANDS

Although most of the main jazz innovators gravitated to large cities to gain the most exposure, have opportunities to play with their peers, and hopefully make a decent living, the smaller cities and rural areas also had a demand for danceable jazz music from 1920 to 1945. This was the prime era of the territory bands.

The surviving recordings of the territory bands that were fortunate enough to be documented demonstrate some regional differences in the 1920s and 1930s and a wide range of quality. Typically the territory bands comprised up-and-coming talents who usually left the ensemble after a short time to venture to one of the big cities, veterans from earlier eras, local legends who had no desire to live in New York or Chicago, and lesser players who probably would not have made it in one of the famous bands. In general the territory bands were between two and five years behind the pacesetting bands of New York and Chicago, the musicianship and quality of the instruments was rougher with shakier intonation, and soloists ranged from inspired to weak. Still, the best territory bands had their own charm and special personality.

Most of the key American cities in the Midwest, South, and West had one or two top territory bands by the late 1920s. Texas was home for the Don Albert band, the highly rated Alphonse Trent Orchestra from Dallas, Boots and His Buddies, and the Troy Floyd Orchestra. Omaha, Nebraska, featured frequent appearances from Red Perkins' Dixie Ramblers, Hunter's Serenaders, and the sadly unrecorded Nat Towles Orchestra. Other notable ensembles were Miami's Ross De Luxe Syncopators, Milwaukee's Grant Moore, Kansas' Art Bronson's Bostonians, Denver's George Morrison, Memphis' Snooks and His Memphis Stompers, Ohio's Chubb-Steinberg Orchestra, Birmingham, Alabama's Carolina Cotton Pickers, St. Louis' Original St. Louis Crackerjacks, Hot Springs, Arkansas' Original Yellowjackets, and the Midwest's Zach Whyte's Chocolate Beau Brummels and Jeter-Pillars Club Plantation Orchestra. Of the many undocumented bands from this era, drummer Speed Webb's orchestra is the major omission. Texas pianist Peck Kelly, leader of Peck's Bad Boys, was famous for his refusal to make records, though he was later captured on some private sessions cut in the 1950s.

By the mid-1940s, territory bands were on their way out, mainly due to the rise of radio, the increase in record sales, and the growth in mass communication. Those factors helped to erase most, but not all, regional differences in jazz music. Radio offered free entertainment and gave listeners and local musicians continuous opportunities to hear the major bands. Shortly after Benny Goodman caught on, there were scores of new orchestras formed that played in a similar style; the same thing happened when Count Basie hit it big and when Glenn Miller became a national sensation. As time went on, the territory bands declined in importance due to the sheer quantity of major swing bands and the general urbanization of the United States. It was no longer considered acceptable for territory bands to lag behind the major jazz groups, not when radio brought the most modern swing bands into the home on a regular basis.

During their peak years, however, the territory bands brought exciting entertainment to rural and isolated areas, serving an important purpose.

WESTERN SWING

Swing was so big by the mid-1930s that it was played everywhere, not just in the major metropolitan areas. Often overlooked in jazz history books, the variation of swing called Western Swing was performed in the Southwest, primarily Texas and Oklahoma. A fusion between early country music and jazz of the 1920s and 1930s, Western Swing featured country musicians playing jazz on fiddle, guitar, mandolin, banjo bass, and other string instruments, often adding piano and a few horns. Their repertoire was jazz standards that often sounded quite different in this context, Western ballads, and unusual material.

In 1932 singer Milton Brown and fiddle player Bob Wills were part of the Fort Worth Doughboys quartet that recorded two numbers at the first Western Swing recording session. Brown went out on his own later that year, forming Milton Brown and His Musical Brownies, the first fulltime Western Swing band. They were quite popular and recorded prolifically from 1934 to 1936. A very promising career ended when Brown died after falling asleep while driving.

With Brown's passing, Bob Wills became the undisputed leader of Western Swing. After leaving the Light Crust Doughboys in 1933, he formed his Texas Playboys, a band comprising a piano, guitar, banjo, steel guitar, bass, drums, and a horn section plus two fiddles including Wills. After the band caught on in Oklahoma and Texas, its fame became nationwide. Wills expanded the group to become an eighteen-piece big band by 1940, performing a mixture of pure country music, ballads, and swinging jazz. By 1940 there were dozens of other top-notch Western Swing bands in the Southwest, including Bill Boyd's Cowboy Ramblers, the Tune Wranglers, Jimmie Revard's Oklahoma Playboys,

Cliff Bruner's Wanderers, the Modern Mountaineers, Adolph Hofner's Texans, and Hank Penny's Radio Cowboys. Although the style dropped in popularity by the 1950s, Spade Cooley and Bob Wills kept the idiom alive for many years, and it has been occasionally revived, most notably by Asleep at the Wheel in the 1970s.

Western Swing was a rare instance where swing music was played with a southern accent.

SAN FRANCISCO JAZZ

At the same as the territory bands were bridging the gap between classic jazz and swing, in San Francisco a revival movement brought back the freewheeling jazz of the 1920s two decades later. Swing-oriented big bands completely dominated the musical landscape by the late 1930s, but not all young musicians wanted to be part of orchestras, playing arrangements and waiting for their brief solos. In San Francisco, trumpeter Lu Watters led an important movement that looked backwards rather than ahead.

After a period playing with swing orchestras in San Francisco, Lu Watters desired to play more spontaneous music that was based in the past, so in 1939 he founded the Yerba Buena Jazz Band. It was one of the very first revival bands, as opposed to groups featuring veterans playing in the style that they had helped originate years earlier. With Bob Scobey on second trumpet, trombonist Turk Murphy, and clarinetist Bob Helm, Watters had a solid front line to his octet. Although King Oliver's 1923 Creole Jazz Band was the original role model, the Yerba Buena Jazz Band also performed vintage songs by Jelly Roll Morton and Louis Armstrong plus their own originals. Watters and his musicians were based at the Dawn Club in San Francisco from 1939 to 1942, took a hiatus during World War II, and were at their best after regrouping in 1946. The Yerba Buena Jazz Band was based at Hambone Kelly's in El Cerrito from 1947 until Watters broke up the group in 1950. He retired shortly afterwards, other than a brief comeback in 1963, feeling that he had made his contribution to jazz history, to pursue other interests.

The music of Watters' sidemen who went out on their own, trombonist Turk Murphy and trumpeter Bob Scobey, is considered part of the San Francisco jazz tradition although it differed, with both of their units only having one trumpet and Scobey's rhythm section actually playing in four beats rather than the two-beat music of Yerba Buena band. Bob Scobey was with Watters from 1940 to 1942 and 1946 to 1949 before forming his own Frisco Jazz Band. During the 1950s Scobey worked regularly, often using banjoist Clancy Hayes, another alumnus of the Yerba Buena Jazz Band, on vocals. While many Dixieland musicians take occasional vocals without impressing anyone, with his strong voice Hayes was one of the best singers of the Dixieland movement. Scobey's career was cut short when he died of cancer in 1963 at the age of forty-six.

Trombonist Turk Murphy had a much longer career. He left Watters' band in 1947, forming his own group that often did not utilize drums and had a lighter feel than the Yerba Buena Jazz Band. Always based in San Francisco and with a home base at Earthquake McGoon's starting in 1960, Murphy's group featured many obscure gems in its repertoire, clean ensembles, and some excellent trumpeters in Don Kinch, Bob Short, and Leon Oakley. Until Turk Murphy's death in 1987, his band was considered an institution on the Dixieland circuit.

Other San Francisco–style groups have appeared on the scene since the passing of Watters, Scobey, and Murphy, keeping the vintage style fresh and exciting.

RECOMMENDED RECORDINGS

Andy Kirk. *Mary's Idea*. GRP/Decca, 622.
Bob Scobey. *Scobey and Clancy*. Good Time Jazz, 12009.
Bob Wills. *Take Me Back to Tulsa*. Proper Box, 1032, 4 CDs.
Count Basie. *April in Paris*. Verve, 314 521 407.
Count Basie. *The Complete Decca Recordings*. GRP/Decca, 611, 3 CDs.
Count Basie. *Count Basie Swings, Joe Williams Sings*. Verve, 314 519 832.
Lu Watters. *The Complete Good Time Jazz Recordings*. Good Time Jazz, 4409, 4 CDs.
Turk Murphy. *Jazz Band Favorites*. Good Time Jazz, 60-011.

6

New York Bebop, Latin, and Cool Jazz

BOP TAKES OVER

Because many of the top jazz musicians moved to New York during the second half of the 1920s, the Big Apple became the center of classic jazz. It was also the main home for the top swing bands with many major black orchestras based in Harlem during the Depression years, and the studios employing such future bandleaders as Benny Goodman, the Dorsey brothers, and Artie Shaw.

Although swing was accepted nationwide as soon as it was exposed on the radio and records by Benny Goodman, bebop was a different matter. The first joint recordings of altoist Charlie Parker and trumpeter Dizzy Gillespie in 1945 were considered so radical that many swing fans were confused and doubted that it was jazz or even music at all. With all of its early innovators based in New York in the mid-1940s, it would take five years before bebop had caught on elsewhere to the point where it was mainstream jazz. Its basic approach, however, has dominated jazz ever since.

WHAT IS BEBOP?

Although the melody can usually be heard in the solos of even the most advanced swing players—Art Tatum, Lester Young, and Roy Eldridge among them—in bebop the theme is usually discarded after the first chorus, and the improvising is based much more on the chord structure. Because the chords are often much more complex than those used in swing, there were many cries of, Where's the melody? from conservative listeners and record executives who found it difficult to recognize the tune during the solos.

Musically, bebop is a logical evolutionary step ahead of swing. In a classic bebop performance, the melody is stated for a chorus or two. While in older styles, a second or third horn plays harmonies, the theme in bop is played in unison because the melody is often jagged and filled with fast runs. Many swing melodies are instantly singable, but it often takes repeated listenings to comprehend bop themes. After the theme, individual soloists play their variations over the chord changes, creating new melodies and ideas that often are only abstractly connected to the first chorus. Generally at the end of the song, the opening melody is repeated. In some cases familiar chord changes were used, but a new melody was written, with Paul Whiteman's 1920 hit "Whispering" being transformed into "Groovin' High," "How High the Moon" becoming "Ornithology," and many songs using either the blues chord changes or that of "I Got Rhythm" or "Lady Be Good."

In addition to the melodies and the chords becoming more complex, the rhythm section's function changed. Although Count Basie's piano style in the late 1930s had moved the piano away from being a timekeeper, Bud Powell took it much further. While his right hand played rapid single-note lines like a horn, his left hand played chords on an irregular basis, accompanying like a drummer without keeping time, acting more as a guidepost. Although Jimmy Blanton had liberated the bass, most musicians still played strict 4/4 time and were valued for their endurance, particularly if they could play up-tempo tunes for a half-hour straight, then for their ability to solo. Because bassists were primarily responsible for keeping the music moving at a steady pace, rhythm guitars became much less common. On drums, Jo Jones with Count Basie's band had kept time on the hi-hat cymbal rather than the bass drum, giving the music a lighter feel. Kenny Clarke switched that function to the ride cymbal and used the bass and snare drums to comment on what was going on in what was called "dropping bombs." Although the music was still danceable, the rhythms were not as smooth as in swing due to these explosions.

Bebop did not become popular with a mass audience like swing for a variety of reasons. While the music of bebop was an evolutionary step, the attitude of bop musicians to the public was more revolutionary. Many bop players felt that their music was an art form and that it should not be thought of as part of the entertainment world. Although the swing big bands made certain compromises, including playing at danceable tempos, emphasizing ensembles over individual solos, utilizing glamorous female vocalists, and covering some commercial material, beboppers felt that the music should be allowed to speak for itself. Many of the musicians largely ignored the audience in favor of just playing music. They discouraged and sneered at dancers, so the dancing audience went elsewhere, to the ballad vocalists and r&b. It did not take long for jazz to lose two-thirds of its audience, and it separated permanently from the pop music world.

The recording strike from 1942 to 1944 made it look like bebop emerged fully formed as a type of alien art form from nowhere. Because it did not have time to evolve gradually on records, the public was not ready for it; servicemen returning from World War II were not ready for Dizzy Gillespie when they were expecting Harry James. Because heroin had become a plague in the jazz world, it was easy to portray beboppers as unreliable nuts who spoke and played music that was incoherent. Swing had had both white and black heroes, but because most of bop's early exponents were black, racism played a part in keeping it from catching on with the general public.

To a large extent, bebop was the invention of its two main innovators, Charlie Parker and Dizzy Gillespie, although jazz was heading in this direction anyway. By the early 1940s, many swing bands had simply run out of fresh ideas, leading to the popularity of Dixieland and r&b. The more creative young jazz musicians wanted opportunities to stretch beyond the brief spots given them in the big band arrangements, so they tried out new ideas at late-night jam sessions. Two New York clubs, Minton's Playhouse and Monroe's Uptown House, were very much open to these jams, with Minton's using as a house band pianist Thelonious Monk, drummer Kenny Clarke, bassist Nick Fenton, and trumpeter Joe Guy. The new music's beginnings are evident in the solos of Gillespie with Cab Calloway's band from 1939 to 1941 and Charlie Parker with Jay McShann in the same period, but they are only hints. In 1944 Coleman Hawkins led a bebop session that featured Gillespie, and he used Monk on a quartet date. It was in 1945, however, when bebop seemed to explode in the jazz world.

Bebop was the last form of jazz to rise to prominence during the 78s era when most studio recordings were limited to three minutes. Live performances from swing bands of the 1930s did not differ much from their studio work, other than occasionally having an extra chorus or two for solos; the arrangements kept the renditions concise. Bebop numbers, however, were much longer in their live versions than on record, often five to ten minutes long. Live recordings from the era are particularly valuable in showing how inventive the best bop players could be when they were not restricted to short improvisations.

Although criticized by conservative critics and fans, by 1947 bebop was making strong inroads. So strong in fact that the record labels jumped on the bandwagon briefly. A second Musicians Union recording strike kept most music off records during 1948, but the next year some of the major labels persuaded their artists to record bebop. Such swing bands as those of Benny Goodman, Charlie Barnet, Lionel Hampton, Gene Krupa, Artie Shaw, Harry James, and Les Brown were somewhat bop-oriented. By 1950 the labels realized that bop was not going to catch on commercially like swing had fifteen years ago, and most of the remaining big bands switched back to swing.

However bebop did not die in 1950. The veterans of the era who survived were still important forces in the 1950s, 1960s, and 1970s. Despite all of its problems, bebop did catch on in jazz. Bebop, one of the most exciting styles of music ever created, became the foundation for all of the styles that followed, particularly cool jazz and hard bop.

CHARLIE PARKER

Charlie "Bird" Parker was one of the most brilliant musicians to ever play jazz and arguably its finest saxophonist. Parker's ideas became a major part of the jazz vocabulary, and he had the ability to play perfectly coherent solos at ridiculously fast tempos. He was born in 1920 in Kansas City, Kansas, growing up across the state line in Kansas City, Missouri. Parker's first instrument was the baritone horn, but he switched to alto sax when he was ten. Because he loved the Kansas City jazz scene of the era, he dropped out of school at fourteen to become a professional musician. At first it seemed like a foolhardy move because his ability was not up to the level of the musicians he met in jam sessions and he was humiliated a few times. Parker was determined, however, and he spent a summer practicing to Lester Young records. When he emerged in the fall, he was strong enough for the local players to accept him.

Parker worked with several orchestras in Kansas City including Jay McShann's band from 1937 to 1941. In 1940 the orchestra traveled to New York where Parker made his recording debut. He already sounded original in his few short solos, although they only hint at what he was to become.

Parker met Dizzy Gillespie in the early 1940s, played at jam sessions, and in 1943 became a member of the Earl Hines Orchestra on tenor. The performances by the first bebop orchestra, which had Gillespie on trumpet along with a few other modernists, are lost to history, because no recordings were made, and not even a radio broadcast survives. Hines' singer Billy Eckstine started his own bop big band in 1944, and Parker and Gillespie joined with Parker back on alto, but Bird departed before that orchestra ever recorded. Parker did make a small

Charlie Parker permanently changed jazz with his spontaneous ideas, which immediately became an important part of the jazz vocabulary.
Photo courtesy of the Wayne Knight Collection, Star Line Productions.

group record date led by guitarist Tiny Grimes, and he appeared on Fifty-second Street (an area of New York that was filled with jazz clubs and nicknamed "Swing Street"), co-leading a group with Gillespie.

In 1945 Parker and Gillespie were finally fully documented, and their music, issued under the latter's name, shocked many contemporary listeners. Their performances of such songs as "Groovin' High," "Dizzy Atmosphere," "Shaw 'Nuff," "Salt Peanuts," and "Hot House" were unprecedented for the period, displaying a radically different musical language than did contemporary swing records. Parker and Gillespie's solos seemed to have little relation to the melody, but they were connected. It was a giant step forward for jazz. Later in the year, Parker had his first record date as a leader, using nineteen-year-old trumpeter Miles Davis and performing such pieces as "Now's the Time," "Billie's Bounce," and a classic solo on "Ko Ko," an original based on the chord changes of "Cherokee." Parker's distinctive sound, complete control of his horn, and endless flow of original ideas resulted in his records being memorized worldwide by other musicians.

In the fall of 1945, Gillespie and Parker traveled to Hollywood. Parker had been a heroin addict since he was a teenager, unlike the clean Gillespie, and heroin supplies were difficult to get during that period in Los Angeles. After a few months, in the spring of 1946, Gillespie and his sidemen flew back to New York. Parker instead cashed in his plane ticket to buy drugs and decided to remain on the West Coast. He had a productive recording date with such songs as "Moose the Mooche," "Yardbird Suite," and "Ornithology," each of which became bop standards. Parker was soon struggling, however, trying to substitute an excessive amount of alcohol for the heroin he craved but couldn't obtain. His next recording, in which he was barely able to play, should never have been released. After a chaotic scene at his hotel that resulted in his mental breakdown, he was arrested and committed to Camarillo State Hospital for six months.

When Parker was released from Camarillo in early 1947, he was completely recovered and in top health. Back in New York, he led a classic quintet that included trumpeter Miles Davis, pianist Duke Jordan, bassist Tommy Potter, and drummer Max Roach. Until December 1948 this was his regular group, and for two years after that he continued leading quintets, with Kenny Dorham or Red Rodney on trumpet. In 1949 Parker was at his peak, visiting Europe, signing with Norman Granz's Clef label, touring with Jazz at the Philharmonic, playing brilliantly at an all-star bebop Carnegie Hall concert on Christmas Eve and recording "Bird with Strings." He seemed to really be making it and was still just twenty-nine.

Unfortunately the next five years were a gradual decline for Parker, not in his playing, but in the effects of heroin and alcohol abuse on his personal life and his state of mind. Some highpoints along the way included a concert at Canada's Massey Hall in 1953 with Gillespie, Bud Powell, Charles Mingus, and Max Roach, but Parker worked only infrequently in 1954. On March 12,

1955, while watching the Dorsey brothers' television show, Charlie Parker died suddenly. The doctor who was called to the scene guessed Parker's age at sixty. He was thirty-four.

DIZZY GILLESPIE

The Dizzy Gillespie story is happier than that of Charlie Parker. Gillespie, a different type of performer than Bird, was an extroverted musician influenced by Louis Armstrong and Fats Waller in his showmanship and use of humor, although like Satchmo and Fats, he was serious about his music. He was a mentor who taught younger musicians how to play bop, helping to make it the mainstream music of jazz. And, unlike too many of the bop musicians, Gillespie stayed away from hard drugs completely and lived a long life.

Even more than Parker, Dizzy Gillespie took very complex solos, having the ability to play the oddest note in the most unlikely spot and somehow make it fit. Parker's playing was based more on the blues, Lester Young, and the Kansas City players, and Gillespie took Roy Eldridge's most adventurous ideas and greatly extended them. It made him a bit of an outcast during the swing era, but a leader when bebop took over.

Dizzy Gillespie was born in 1917 to a poor family in South Carolina. After winning a scholarship to an agriculture school where he studied music, Gillespie dropped out in 1935 to work as a musician. In 1937 he worked and recorded in New York with Teddy Hill's orchestra, and from 1939 to 1941 he was a member of Cab Calloway's orchestra. With the latter Gillespie took many chances in his solos, often improvising over more complex chords than the rhythm section was playing. Calloway was dismayed by some of Gillespie's odder solos, calling his playing "Chinese music." Some spitballs were thrown at Calloway on stage once, and since Gillespie was infamous for fooling around, he was blamed. A fight took place backstage, and Dizzy was fired. Years later it was revealed that trumpeter Jonah Jones had actually been the culprit.

Dizzy Gillespie with Charlie Parker founded bebop, was one of the leaders in Latin jazz, and was quite significant as both a bandleader and a teacher of bop to younger generations. *Photo courtesy of the Wayne Knight Collection, Star Line Productions.*

Gillespie had short-term associations with many big bands during the next few years, met Charlie Parker, and was a member of Earl Hines' unrecorded band in 1943, contributing some advanced arrangements including one of what would become his most famous composition, *A Night in Tunisia*. After leaving Hines, Gillespie led a group on Fifty-second Street with bassist Oscar Pettiford and spent part of 1944 with Billy Eckstine's orchestra. He was with Eckstine long enough to record a few solos and also appeared on Coleman Hawkins' pioneering bop dates.

In 1945 Gillespie made his famous records with Charlie Parker, led a short-lived and unsuccessful bop big band, and started to create a major stir. When his band toured the South, the audiences complained that they could not dance to the music. The trip with Parker to Los Angeles in late 1945 was unsuccessful for the group, but the following year Gillespie formed a second big band, one that lasted over three years and is now considered a classic. Such top players as trombonist J. J. Johnson, pianist John Lewis, vibraphonist Milt Jackson, bassist Ray Brown, drummer Kenny Clarke, and saxophonists James Moody, Jimmy Heath, Cecil Payne, Yusef Lateef, and John Coltrane were among the sidemen. The ensemble showed that bebop could be orchestrated and performed by a big band. Its version of "Things to Come" still sounds advanced, and the band swung hard on "Our Delight," "One Bass Hit," and "Ray's Idea." In addition Gillespie was a major force in forming Afro-Cuban or Latin jazz that can be heard on "Manteca."

Against all odds the Dizzy Gillespie big band lasted into 1950 before breaking up. Gillespie was at the peak of his playing powers throughout the 1950s, keeping bebop alive and viable even after the death of Charlie Parker. Dizzy led small groups, toured with Jazz at the Philharmonic, teamed up on records with his old idol Roy Eldridge, Sonny Rollins, Sonny Stitt, and Stan Getz, and in 1956 and 1957 headed a big band that in some ways topped the power of his 1946 to 1949 group. This orchestra, which at times included trumpeters Lee Morgan and Joe Gordon, trombonist Al Grey, altoist Phil Woods, tenors Billy Mitchell and Benny Golson, and arranger Quincy Jones, toured the world for the State Department. Bebop, or at least the colorful Dizzy Gillespie, had become acceptable enough to represent the United States overseas.

Except for special big band projects, Gillespie led small groups during the 1960s and 1970s, and his popularity in the jazz world never faded, even as his trumpet playing started to slip after the mid-1970s. He made the transition from young radical to a universally loved veteran. Dizzy Gillespie led a final big band, the United Nation Orchestra, during 1988 to 1991, passing away at the age of seventy-five in early 1993.

BUD POWELL

Other than James P. Johnson and Bill Evans, Bud Powell was one of the few musicians who changed the way that the piano is played in jazz. A major innovator who defined bebop piano, Powell had a tragic life. Born in 1924, he left school at the age of fifteen to work as a fulltime musician. He sat in at Minton's Playhouse and was a member of the Cootie Williams Orchestra during 1943 and 1944. Near the end of his period with Williams, Powell was beaten on the head during a fight with racist police, although he had been an innocent bystander, and he suffered from mental illness from then on. Powell alternated productive periods with stays in institutions that always returned him to the jazz world in a little worse shape than he had been before.

From 1945 to 1951, Powell was at his prime, performing with the top musicians of the bop era and with his own trio. He recorded memorable sessions for the Roost, Verve, and Blue Note labels, and his compositions included "Bouncing with Bud," "Parisian Thoroughfare," "Celia," "Budo," "Un Poco Loco," and "Tempus Fugit." After being in an institution during parts of 1951 through 1953, he was released in time to appear at the famous Massey Hall Concert with Charlie Parker and Dizzy Gillespie. Powell's playing was erratic in the late 1950s, ranging from stunning to indifferent depending on his mood. After moving to Paris in 1959, he was treated well and made a short comeback, assisted by a fan, Francois Paudras, who helped extend his life. Powell often led The Three Bosses, a group including bassist Pierre Michelot and drummer Kenny Clarke.

In 1964 Powell decided to return to the United States and that proved to be a bad move. After performing at Birdland and recording two albums, he disappeared for long periods of time and declined quickly. The troubled Bud Powell died in 1966 at the age of forty-one, having changed the world of music while being unable to save himself from his inner turmoil.

THELONIOUS MONK

Although jazz is a music that prizes individuality, sometimes a performer appears on the scene whose uniqueness is not appreciated at the time. Bebop was thought of as a rather radical music from 1945 to 1949, but Thelonious Monk, as a pianist and composer, was considered even too advanced and oddball for the boppers. He had to wait through years of neglect for the world to catch up to him before he received the acclaim that he deserved.

The ironic part is that aspects of Monk's style were actually old-fashioned, but in an abstract and unusual way. His solos kept the melodies in mind, he sometimes played a light stride piano when unaccompanied, and one of his early musical heroes was James P. Johnson. Not a virtuoso like his good friend Bud Powell, Monk had a unique touch on the piano, making every chord sound different than expected. Some of his runs with his right hand were like Art Tatum's with two-thirds of the notes purposely missing, playing only the essential ones, and he used space and dynamics dramatically. His compositions had their own logic, but took some time to master, and many of the players of the 1940s considered his songs to be too difficult to play; he was simply ahead of his time. It did not help that he was an introvert who did not care that much about communicating verbally with people, so it was easy to stereotype him as some sort of intuitive nut.

Thelonious Sphere Monk was born in North Carolina, moving to New York as a child. He started on piano at six, had his first job accompanying an evangelist, and was a member of the house band at Minton's Playhouse from 1940 to 1943. In those early jam sessions, Monk sounded a bit like Teddy Wilson, playing stride and swing piano, but he gradually developed his unusual style. Monk worked for a few months with Lucky Millinder's big band in 1942 and with Coleman Hawkins in 1944. The Cootie Williams Orchestra was the first to record his compositions: "Epistrophy" in 1942 and "'Round Midnight" two years later. During 1947 and 1948 Monk made his earliest recordings as a leader, introducing such songs as "Ruby My Dear," "Well You Needn't," "Off Minor," "In Walked Bud," and "Evidence" plus recording his most famous song, "'Round Midnight," for the first time. These Blue Note records did not sell well, but producer Alfred Lion believed in the music and recorded Monk again during 1951 and 1952, including such complex pieces as "Four in One" and "Criss Cross."

While Monk worked a bit during the bebop era, he rarely performed from 1951 to 1954, mostly staying at home practicing and writing songs. He did introduce such songs on his Prestige records as "Little Rootie Tootie," "Monk's Dream," "Bye-Ya," "Twinkle Tinkle," "Bemsha Swing," "Nutty," and "Friday the 13th." Two of his untitled tunes ended up being called "Let's Call This" and "Think of One."

In 1955 Monk's life began to change. Orrin Keepnews of the Riverside label devised a strategy to help him. To show that the pianist was not all that forbidding, his first project for Riverside was a set of Duke Ellington songs played in a trio. Next Monk recorded a set of standards. Then since the jazz public had become a little more accustomed to Monk, Keepnews had the pianist make an album of his own music, *Brilliant Corners*, with tenor-saxophonist Sonny Rollins and trumpeter Clark Terry among his sidemen. It received good reviews. In 1957 the jazz world finally fully discovered Monk when he played much of the summer at New York's Half Note, leading a quartet that included tenor-saxophonist John Coltrane. The combination of Monk and Coltrane was magical, and finally the pianist-composer was being thought of as a genius rather than an eccentric nut.

From then on, Monk's life was different. He worked regularly, crowds were large, and his recordings sold well, even though his music was similar to his 1947 sound. His 1958 quartet with tenor-saxophonist Johnny Griffin was rewarding, and in 1959 Charlie Rouse became his tenor player, staying for a decade. During this time Monk's fame continued to grow, he signed with the Columbia label, and in 1964 he was even on the cover of *Time* magazine. Two notable band concerts were recorded in 1959 and 1963, featuring some transcriptions of Monk's piano solos played by the ensemble.

During 1971 and 1972, Monk toured with The Giants of Jazz, an all-star sextet including Dizzy Gillespie, altoist Sonny Stitt, trombonist Kai Winding, bassist Al McKibbon, and drummer Art Blakey, and recorded an extensive set of solo and trio performances. This stopped, however, when Thelonious Monk succumbed to mental illness and lost all interest in playing, feeling that he could no longer perform at his best. He spent his last years in isolation before his death in 1982. Monk's music was later rediscovered; "'Round Midnight" was recorded so much that it almost was a pop hit, and he was fully recognized as a unique genius, one of jazz's finest composers, and most individual pianists.

THE PACESETTERS OF THE NEW YORK BOP SCENE

Trumpeters

While Dizzy Gillespie was the leading bop trumpeter, there were several close competitors during the 1945 to 1950 period, most notably Howard McGhee and Fats Navarro. McGhee started his career playing in low-level bands before spending part of 1941 with Lionel Hampton. He made an impression while with Andy Kirk's orchestra during 1941 and 1942, being featured on Kirk's recording of "McGhee Special." From the start he had a crisp sound influenced by Roy Eldridge while displaying his own musical personality. After working with Charlie Barnet, McGhee was with Kirk for a second time during 1943 and 1944 where he influenced another player in the trumpet section, Fats Navarro. As a member of the Coleman Hawkins Quintet in 1945, McGhee made some major recordings, matched wits with the great tenor, and played in a boppish style that was tied to the swing era yet increasingly influenced by Gillespie. When Hawkins took the group to the West Coast, McGhee decided to stay in Los Angeles for two years, though he returned to New York by the late 1940s. McGhee was just thirty-two in 1950, but his most significant years were over. He was a heroin addict, and other than a USO tour during the Korean War and some records during 1955 and 1956, the decade was largely a waste for him. He emerged from 1960 to 1962, making some excellent recordings, but then was largely off record again until 1976. In the next four years, he made his final comeback when he still had strong ideas, even if his tone was fading, but it was too late. Howard McGhee died in 1987, having largely wasted his potential.

Theodore "Fats" Navarro had even more problems than McGhee with heroin, and as an indirect result, his life was significantly shortened. Once Navarro had fully emerged, he became one of the most important influences on other trumpeters, even more than Gillespie whose playing was too complex for most trumpet players to emulate. Navarro worked with the big bands of Snookum Russell in 1941 and 1942 and Andy Kirk in the following two years before succeeding Dizzy with the Billy Eckstine bebop big band of 1945 and 1946. Navarro also worked with Tadd Dameron, Illinois Jacquet, Lionel Hampton, and briefly with the Benny Goodman Orchestra. Otherwise he led groups around the New York area and played with fellow bebop all-stars. Along the way he headed a few record dates and recorded with Eckstine, the Bebop Boys, tenor-saxophonist Eddie "Lockjaw" Davis, Coleman Hawkins, Dameron, Jacquet, Goodman, and

Bud Powell. In a live set with Charlie Parker from 1950, the trumpeter was in excellent form, but the date is probably inaccurate, for by then Fats Navarro was very ill with tuberculosis which, coupled with his heroin addiction, caused him to waste away. He died on July 7 when he was just twenty-six. Navarro's sound and style lived on in the playing of Clifford Brown in the mid-1950s, and through Brownie his sound can be heard in the recordings of Lee Morgan, Freddie Hubbard, and Woody Shaw from later decades.

Miles Davis made his debut during the bebop era, although it was only the first step in a remarkably productive career. Born May 25, 1926, Davis grew up in a middle-class family in East St. Louis, Illinois. He started on trumpet when he was thirteen, playing with Eddie Randall's Blue Devils during 1941 to 1943. Davis met Charlie Parker and Dizzy Gillespie when the Billy Eckstine Orchestra passed through town in 1944, having an opportunity to sit in with the innovative band. When he went to New York in September 1944 to study at the Julliard School of Music, he first wanted to find Charlie Parker, whose music he greatly admired. Soon he had dropped out of school and was working on Fifty-second Street with Coleman Hawkins. Then he had a tiny range, a soft sound, and just so-so technique, but Hawkins and others saw the potential in Davis' ideas and determination. He made his recording debut in April 1945 with singer-dancer Rubberlegs Williams but sounded better later in the year when he recorded "Now's the Time" and "Billie's Bounce" with Charlie Parker. When Parker went to Los Angeles in the fall, Davis joined Benny Carter's orchestra specifically because the big band was also relocating to Los Angeles. During his few months on the West Coast, Davis recorded with Parker, including "Yardbird Suite" and "Ornithology," showing that he was growing as a trumpeter. When Parker's mishaps in Los Angeles were finished, he formed a quintet in New York that included Miles Davis. He picked the twenty-year-old because Davis' relaxed solos were a contrast to Parker's heated improvisations, and the young trumpeter had a complementary (rather than competitive) style.

Because Miles Davis had a much simpler style than Dizzy Gillespie and less technique than Fats Navarro, but fit well into bebop, he became a key influence on trumpeters who wished to play in a more relaxed and calm fashion, including the ones who were prominent during the cool jazz era of the 1950s. Miles Davis would help pioneer cool jazz with his "Birth of the Cool" recordings of 1948 through 1950.

When Davis left the Charlie Parker Quintet in December 1948, his replacement was Kenny Dorham. Dorham spent his life being overshadowed by other trumpeters, but he made a strong contribution both to the bebop era and to the later hard bop movement. A solid improviser with a distinctive tone that was touched by Fats Navarro, Dorham worked with the first unrecorded Dizzy Gillespie big band, Billy Eckstine's orchestra, and Lionel Hampton before he spent a year with Parker's group. In later years he worked with the initial edition of Art Blakey's Jazz Messengers, led the Jazz Prophets, gigged with Max Roach from 1956 to 1958, and headed his own groups including a 1960s quintet with tenor-saxophonist Joe Henderson. His health faded after the mid-1960s, and Dorham died in 1972 at forty-eight. Despite his talents, he was never able to escape from the shadow of such trumpeters as Gillespie, Davis, Clifford Brown, and Lee Morgan.

When Dorham departed from Parker's quintet, Red Rodney took his place. Rodney, who was born Robert Chudnick, one of the first important white trumpeters to fully comprehend bebop, was only fifteen during 1942 and 1943 when he played with Jerry Wald's orchestra. He played with many big bands for a short period of time, originally idolizing Harry James until he discovered Dizzy Gillespie's playing in 1945. Rodney helped give the Gene Krupa Orchestra an infusion of bebop in 1946, and he also worked with Buddy Rich, Claude Thornhill, and Woody Herman's Second Herd before joining Parker. When Parker toured the South, he got away with using a mixed group by having Rodney billed as blues singer "Albino Red." Unfortunately Rodney emulated Parker's heroin habit, and he was busted in 1951. He spent much of the 1950s going in and out of prison. Unlike Navarro, Rodney did eventually kick the habit. After a long period playing in Las Vegas in the 1960s, his jazz chops were rusty, but he made a gradual comeback in the 1970s and by the latter part of the decade was playing at his very best. By 1980 he was co-leading a modern jazz group with trumpeter-saxophonist Ira Sullivan, being constantly challenged by the new compositions of pianist Garry Dial. He lived long enough to see himself portrayed favorably in the movie *Bird*, playing the trumpet parts for his character, and to be recognized as a living legend. Red Rodney died in 1994 at the age of sixty-six.

Two other short-lived trumpeters from the bebop era are worth mentioning, although both died from overdoses of drugs. Freddie Webster, a player with a haunting tone who was cited by Miles Davis as an important early inspiration, only lived to 1947, while Sonny Berman, a star with Woody Herman's First Herd, just made it to the age of twenty-one.

Trombonists

When bebop emerged, it caused a major dilemma for trombonists. How could they keep up on the rapid lines with trumpeters and saxophonists?

J. J. Johnson could, and he became the dominant force on trombone. With complete mastery of his horn, he knew all the short cuts and relied more on hitting notes like a trumpet rather than using the slide excessively. Born James Louis Johnson he was always nicknamed J. J. Johnson emerged from Indianapolis to play with territory bands before gaining recognition while with Benny Carter's orchestra from 1942 to 1945 and Count Basie from 1945 to 1946. Johnson was considered the Charlie Parker of the trombone, and he showed that he could keep up with him on one record date where he was added to the Parker Quintet. He also fared well during stints with Illinois Jacquet's jump band from 1947 to 1949 and the Dizzy Gillespie big band. Although J. J. Johnson saved the trombone from suffering the fate of the clarinet during the bebop era, he still had difficulty finding work in the early 1950s, mostly dropping out of music for two years to work as a blueprint inspector. In August 1954, however, he teamed up with fellow trombonist Kai Winding in a quintet. Their catchy arrangements and the interplay of the two trombones made the group popular during its two years. In addition to being the top jazz trombonist, Johnson was an adventurous composer who in the 1950s wrote classical-oriented works and more conventional songs including his most famous, "Lament." He was quite active during the hard bop era as both a trombonist and writer, but eventually became very busy writing for the studios and barely played at all during 1970 to 1976. He made a full comeback as a trombonist during his final twenty years and showed that he still had no peers. J. J. Johnson died in 2001.

Other important trombonists of the bebop era included Kai Winding, who came to prominence with Stan Kenton, Woody Herman's Bill Harris, and Bennie Green who worked with Earl Hines. The latter two were swing players who adjusted their style to fit in more boppish situations. Otherwise most modern trombonists by 1950 sounded very much like J. J. Johnson.

Clarinetists

Although the trombone was saved to a certain extent by J. J. Johnson and it would have continued being an important part of big bands, the clarinet became practically extinct in jazz styles more modern than swing. It was so closely associated with the swing era and Benny Goodman that it was considered old-fashioned by modernists, some of whom probably also realized that it is more difficult to play than a saxophone. Buddy DeFranco did his best to keep the clarinet alive in bebop but with much less of an impact than Johnson had with the trombone.

Because Benny Goodman and Artie Shaw became world-famous celebrities and Buddy DeFranco was on their level in technique and creativity, he can be forgiven if he thought his career would be similar. Born Boniface Ferdinand Leonard DeFranco, he developed quickly as a clarinetist after starting at the age of nine and at eighteen was a member of Gene Krupa's band in 1941. He also worked with the orchestras of Charlie Barnet in 1943 and 1944 and Boyd Raeburn in 1946, and most importantly starred with Tommy Dorsey off and on during 1944 through 1948. DeFranco's style, originally based in swing, became more bop-oriented as the 1940s progressed, and he had no close competitors in that area. After working with the Count Basie Septet during 1950 and 1951, DeFranco mostly led his own groups, emphasizing up-tempo renditions of standards. Although he recorded regularly, holding his own with Art Tatum on one album, and won jazz polls, DeFranco struggled to find work at times because there was not much demand for a clarinetist who did not play nostalgic swing or Dixieland. From 1966 to 1974 he gave up to an extent, leading the Glenn Miller ghost band even though he was really not a swing player. After eight years of playing the same old Miller hits every night, DeFranco resumed his solo career, and since then he has been in greater demand, particularly when playing with vibraphonist Terry Gibbs.

Only a few other clarinetists attempted to forge a career in bebop. Stan Hasselgard, who was born in Sweden, had great potential. After being influenced by Benny Goodman and working during the second part of the swing era, he moved to the United States in 1947 and immersed himself in bop, playing with tenor saxophonist Wardell Gray and pianist Dodo Marmarosa. Hasselgard was such an impressive player that he was the only clarinetist Benny Goodman ever added to his own small groups, being part of a two-clarinet septet for a few months in 1948. After the combo broke up, Hasselgard freelanced and then was tragically killed in a car crash in November at the age of twenty-six.

Tony Scott, one of the best clarinetists of the 1950s, had a much cooler tone than DeFranco. Born Anthony Sciacca, he freelanced during the bebop era with Buddy Rich, Ben Webster, the Claude Thornhill Orchestra, and others. Scott mostly led his own combos in the 1950s and during part of 1959 had pianist Bill Evans in his quartet. After becoming frustrated with the American jazz scene and the lack of demand for clarinetists, Tony Scott became a world traveler, spending most of the past four decades overseas and exploring folk music from other countries.

Although the clarinet has had a few modern jazz practitioners since 1960, most notably Eddie Daniels and Don Byron, it is still rare to hear it featured in any style more recent than swing.

Saxophonists

Alto saxophonists had a different dilemma than that of trombonists and clarinetists during the bebop era. The problem was to master bebop and yet not sound like a mere copy of Charlie Parker. Since it took time for his music to be learned and assimilated, some altoists responded by switching to tenor, including Jimmy Heath, who had been called "Little Bird," and James Moody. Sonny Stitt, who also began doubling on tenor by 1949, kept the alto as his main ax and mastered Parker's music so well that he sometimes seemed like his duplicate.

Stitt always claimed that his style developed before hearing Parker, although that seems rather doubtful considering how similar they sounded. Stitt, who was four years younger than Bird, played with the Billy Eckstine Orchestra in 1945, worked with Dizzy Gillespie in 1946, and recorded a classic session with Bud Powell in 1949. During 1950 to 1952 Stitt co-led a quintet with Gene Ammons, having a minor hit in "Blues Up and Down." After the group ran its course, Stitt mostly freelanced the rest of his life, having occasional reunions with Ammons. Like Roy Eldridge, he had a gladiator's spirit, arriving in a town, picking up a rhythm section, and then successfully battling all of the local musicians. Stitt knew bebop backwards and forwards and could play the standards in any key and tempo. No matter what the setting, he stuck to bop, and he never declined on alto or tenor, where he sounded a little like Lester Young, being bebop's top combatant until his death in 1982.

Harry Carney was the only significant baritone saxophonist of the swing era. As the baritone became essential in all big bands, a few new soloists emerged during the bebop era. Serge Chaloff was one of the "Four Brothers" with Woody Herman's Second Herd and a major soloist, while Cecil Payne was the anchor with the Dizzy Gillespie orchestra during 1946 to 1949. Leo Parker's deep guttural tone was featured with Billy Eckstine in 1944 and 1945, Dizzy Gillespie's big band, and Illinois Jacquet in 1947 and 1948. He would have been a natural to star in r&b during the early 1950s, but drug abuse knocked him out of action. Parker's 1961 comeback did not last long; he died of a heart attack the following year when he was thirty-six.

Although the dominant influence of Charlie Parker was very difficult to escape on alto, tenor players had several major giants to draw from. Illinois Jacquet had been one of the first to combine aspects of Coleman and Lester Young's styles, and the tenors of the bebop generation followed his example, also using some of Parker's ideas in their playing.

Dexter Gordon was one of the first tenor saxophonists to play bop. Nicknamed "Long Tall Dexter" for his height and mellow personality, Gordon had a colorful career that included three separate comebacks. He originally played clarinet and alto, switching to tenor when he was seventeen in 1940. Gordon was with Lionel Hampton's orchestra from 1940 to 1943 but had little solo space. After stints with the big bands of Fletcher Henderson and Louis Armstrong, he was an important member of the Billy Eckstine Orchestra in 1944, trading off with Gene Ammons on the band's hit recording of "Blowin' the Blues Away." Gordon started leading record dates of his own in 1945. He spent a few years in his native Los Angeles, and then as with too many others, drugs fouled up the 1950s for Gordon, who only played occasionally. By 1960 he was

Dexter Gordon had a colorful career with three separate comebacks and scores of rewarding recordings.
Photo courtesy of the Wayne Knight Collection, Star Line Productions.

ready for his first comeback, and he made some outstanding recordings, helping to define bebop/hard bop tenor. Gordon moved to Europe in 1962 where he stayed for fourteen years, playing at his best but being somewhat forgotten in his native land. When Dexter returned to the United States in 1976 when fusion was dominating jazz, his brilliant playing in his acoustic quartet/quintet made him a major celebrity frequently attracting long lines at clubs where he performed. His health began to fade in the early 1980s before he received his final big break, starring in the 1985 film *Round Midnight* for which he received an Academy Award nomination. That third comeback was his last, and Dexter Gordon passed away in 1990 at the age of sixty-seven.

Wardell Gray had a softer tone than Gordon and was more influenced by Lester Young. He was featured with the Earl Hines big band from 1943 to 1945, settled in Los Angeles for a few years, and played with the groups of Benny Carter, Billy Eckstine, and Tadd Dameron. Gray's playing was admired by swing and bop musicians alike, and he was flexible enough to fit in both Charlie Parker's group and Benny Goodman's bands of 1948 and 1949. Gray was with the Count Basie Septet in 1950 and 1951 and had a classic solo on a Basie big band date, "Little Pony." His solo on "Twisted" became the basis for Annie Ross's famed vocalese. Unfortunately Wardell Gray got involved in drugs, and he died in 1955 under mysterious circumstances when he was just thirty-four.

Drugs also played a major part in Gene Ammons' life, splitting his career into two. The son of boogie-woogie pianist Albert Ammons, he gained recognition for his work with Billy Eckstine's orchestra from 1944 to 1947. He was a soloist with Woody Herman's Second Herd in 1949 and co-led a group with Sonny Stitt from 1950 to 1952. His 1950s series of jam session recordings for the Prestige label included much of his best playing, teaming him with some of the top Young Lions of the era. Unlike his good friend, Sonny Stitt, Ammons was very flexible. He had a huge sound that was recognizable in two notes, and in addition to bebop, he sounded quite comfortable caressing ballads or in a soul/r&b setting. He was jailed on two occasions for possession of drugs from 1958 to 1960, and when he was arrested in 1962, it was decided to make an example of him. He languished in jail for seven years before finally being released. Ammons made a comeback, sometimes playing bop and at other times exploring music that was more influenced by either the avant-garde or the pop music of the era. He had nearly regained his former stature when he died from cancer in 1974 at the age of forty-nine.

James Moody has had a much more consistent life. After serving in the air force during World War II, Moody became a member of the Dizzy Gillespie big band from 1946 to 1948, mostly featured on tenor but also doubling on alto. From 1948 to 1951 he was in Europe, and while there, he recorded a version of "I'm in the Mood for Love" that was a minor hit. A few years later Eddie Jefferson wrote vocalese for it, and as "Moody's Mood for Love," it became a trademark song for both Jefferson and Moody. In the 1950s Moody, who took up the flute and later the soprano sax, led a septet that often featured Jefferson's singing. He had a joyful and rewarding experience as a key member of the Dizzy Gillespie Quintet from 1963 to 1968, and other than playing in Las Vegas from

1975 to 1979, he continues to be an important leader in the jazz scene. Moody, like Gillespie, sees nothing wrong with including humor and showmanship in his performances, and he remains a modern bop-oriented soloist more than fifty-five years after first entering the jazz major leagues.

The Rhythm Section

Nearly all of the pianists to emerge during the bebop era sounded very influenced by Bud Powell, struggling to find their own voice within his conception. Al Haig was one of the best of the Powell followers. He worked with Ben Webster, Fats Navarro, Coleman Hawkins, and Gillespie during 1945 and 1946—including traveling to Los Angeles with Gillespie and Bird—in addition to being in the Charlie Parker Quintet from 1948 to 1950 and with Stan Getz. Haig faded out of the major league jazz scene after that, playing at obscure clubs on the East Coast for twenty years before having a higher profile during the decade before his death in 1982.

Dodo Marmarosa had a short-lived but brilliant career. He started off working in his native Pittsburgh and had stints with the big bands of Gene Krupa in 1942 and 1943, Tommy Dorsey, Charlie Barnet, and Artie Shaw. As early as 1944, Marmarosa had evolved into a top bop pianist. He made many recording appearances from 1946 to 1949 with Lester Young, Lucky Thompson, Howard McGhee, Stan Hasselgard, and Charlie Parker. Unfortunately mental and personal problems plagued Marmarosa, and after 1950 he disappeared for a decade. He emerged briefly in Chicago during 1961 and 1962, appearing on a few final records before retiring permanently to his native Pittsburgh, a lost talent.

George Wallington, another early bop pianist, also retired early but for different reasons. Wallington was on the level of Al Haig and played with Dizzy Gillespie's early combo in 1943 and 1944. He worked with the who's who of bop including Charlie Parker, Kai Winding, Terry Gibbs, Gerry Mulligan, and Red Rodney. A member of the Lionel Hampton big band in 1953, Wallington led groups of his own from 1954 to 1960, featuring such top young players as trumpeter Donald Byrd and Jackie McLean or Phil Woods on alto. Frustrated by the lack of work, in 1960 Wallington dropped out of music altogether to work in his family's air conditioning company when he was thirty-six. He returned in 1984 to record three albums of originals, showing that his boppish style was still very much intact, passing away in 1993.

Duke Jordan gained his greatest fame for being the pianist with the Charlie Parker Quintet of 1947 and 1948. Jordan's single-note lines and thoughtful but swinging style was particularly effective. He worked early on with Coleman Hawkins, the Savoy Sultans, and the 1946 Roy Eldridge big band. After being part of Parker's classic group, Jordan played with Stan Getz and led his own trios. He has lived in Denmark since 1978. Other significant bop era pianists include Hank Jones, Claude Williamson, and John Lewis. Barry Harris has been a major force since then in keeping bebop piano alive.

Three major pianists became prominent during the bop era but have always stretched far beyond bop. Actually George Shearing was a star in England by 1940. Born blind in 1919, he started on piano when he was three, and his original influences were Teddy Wilson and Fats Waller. He first appeared on records in 1937 and in the early 1940s worked with Stephane Grappelli. In 1947 Shearing visited the United States and began to become interested in bop. He moved permanently to New York in 1949, putting together a quintet that matched his piano with vibraphonist Marjorie Hyams, guitarist Chuck Wayne, bassist John Levy, and drummer Denzil Best. With its tight harmony between piano, vibes, and guitar, the George Shearing Quintet had its own sound and became very popular, making bop accessible to a mass audience. Shearing, whose "Lullaby of Birdland" became a standard, kept the quintet together through many personnel changes for nearly thirty years. A masterful accompanist, Shearing also recorded notable albums backing Nat King Cole, Nancy Wilson, and Peggy Lee. Since breaking up the quintet, Shearing has mostly played in duets and trios, recording frequently, including a series of gems with Mel Torme. A senior statesman in jazz, Shearing in his mid-eighties still plays at his best and with enthusiasm.

Erroll Garner was a pianist who did not fit into any style but his own. His playing was so infectious that it was immediately popular, and he never had to alter it to remain both modern and accessible. On medium-tempo numbers he emulated a swinging big band by stating the beat with his left hand like a rhythm guitar while his right hand played chords slightly behind the beat, creating an echo effect. Garner's ballads were full of feeling, he enjoyed playing free-form introductions to songs so as to confuse his sidemen, and his technique was particularly impressive considering he never learned to read music. Born in Pittsburgh, Garner moved to New York in 1944 when he was twenty-three, worked with Slam Stewart's trio for a year, and then led his own successful trios starting in 1946. He grew in popularity during the 1950s, wrote a standard in "Misty," and had the ability to go into a recording studio and make three albums in a day, all first takes. Until ill health forced his retirement in 1975 two years before his death, Erroll Garner was a constant on the jazz scene, a regular guest on television variety shows, and always a joy to hear.

Also emerging during the second half of the 1940s was Oscar Peterson, one of the most remarkable jazz pianists of all time, and one of the few who can be mentioned in the same breath with Art Tatum. Peterson's style was most influenced by Nat King Cole although his technique is comparable with Tatum, and he has always fit into both swing and bop settings while sounding like himself. Born in Montreal, Canada, in 1925, Peterson developed very quickly after starting classical piano lessons when he was six. He was featured on a weekly radio show in Montreal at the age of fourteen and in the mid-1940s worked with Johnny Holmes' orchestra. He began recording in Montreal in 1945 and in his early days was a swing player who could also play rapid renditions of boogie-woogie. In 1949 producer Norman Granz discovered him playing live on the radio and presented him as a surprise guest at a Jazz at the Philharmonic concert. Granz began recording him prolifically, Peterson had a hit with his version of "Tenderly," and he often was heard in a duo with bassist Ray Brown. In 1952 he formed a trio with Brown and guitarist Barney Kessel. After Kessel tired of the road, Herb Ellis took his place. The Peterson-Ellis-Brown Trio of 1953 to 1958 was the pianist's greatest group, one in which the musicians constantly challenged each other. Peterson, with his speed and ability to outswing anyone, enjoyed the complex arrangements devised by Ellis and Brown. When Ellis left the band in 1958 was replaced by drummer Ed Thigpen, the sound of the group changed.

The Peterson-Brown-Thigpen Trio, which had the pianist as the dominant voice, lasted until 1965. In 1968 Peterson made his first set of unaccompanied solos, sounding quite brilliant. In the 1970s he recorded constantly for Granz's Pablo label, often teamed up with guitarist Joe Pass and bassist Niels Pederson. As in the 1950s, Peterson also appeared on many records with bop and swing all-stars. Occasionally he also recorded on electric piano and featured his own compositions; best known is his *Canadiana Suite* from 1964. A serious stroke in 1993 knocked Peterson out of action for two years. Since then he has resumed touring the world although his left hand is barely used at all. However even as a one-handed pianist, Oscar Peterson still plays more notes than most musicians, and he is impossible to beat in a cutting contest.

Charlie Christian's death in 1942 left a giant hole among his many contemporary jazz guitarists who were very influenced by him. These include Tiny Grimes who was with the Art Tatum Trio in 1945 before shifting towards r&b, Billy Bauer with Woody Herman and Lennie Tristano, the adventurous Bill DeArango who after making some impressive records moved permanently home to Cleveland in 1948, Mary Osborne, Remo Palmieri who worked mostly in the studios after 1946, and Chuck Wayne, a member of the George Shearing Quintet from 1949 to 1952 who also only played jazz part-time after becoming a studio musician in the 1950s. Barney Kessel had a bigger impact on later years, particularly in his string of recordings for the Contemporary label in the 1950s. There was, however, no jazz guitarist, other than Django, of Christian's stature during this period, and the guitar was not yet fully accepted as a major solo instrument in jazz.

Lionel Hampton and Red Norvo, who switched from xylophone in 1943, were the two leading vibraphonists as the bebop era began. They were soon joined by two other very impressive players. Milt Jackson was greatly in demand by 1946. He had played guitar, piano, violin, and drums in addition to singing gospel music before he switched to the vibes as a teenager. By slowing down the speed of the vibraphone's oscillator, Jackson achieved a different sound than Hampton. Soon after Dizzy Gillespie heard him in Detroit, he was in New York playing with Gillespie and Parker. Jackson joined the Dizzy Gillespie big band, recorded with Thelonious Monk, and played with Woody Herman's Second Herd. He would make a major impact in the 1950s playing cool jazz with the Modern Jazz Quartet and hard bop on his own soulful and swinging sessions.

Terry Gibbs, a fast talker, plays runs on his vibes faster than he speaks and always conveys plenty of excitement. Born Julius Gubenko, he started on xylophone, drums, and tympani. After serving in the military, he switched to vibes and played on Fifty-second Street. Gibbs worked with Tommy Dorsey, Buddy Rich, Woody Herman's Second Herd, Benny Goodman, and Chubby Jackson, as one of the first bop groups to tour Scandinavia. Gibbs freelanced, moved to Los Angeles in 1957, worked in the studios and led a swinging orchestra called the Terry Gibbs Dream Band from 1959 to 1961. He was the musical director of the *Steve Allen Show* in the 1960s, sometimes jammed in combos with Buddy Rich, often teamed up with clarinetist Buddy DeFranco in the 1980s and 1990s, and today still has as much energy and enthusiasm as ever.

Jimmy Blanton may have liberated the bass in the early 1940s, but few other bassists during the bebop era took the plunge and were featured as soloists. The bass had become more significant due releasing the pianist's left hand from keeping time, so bassists were valued for their endurance at rapid tempos; solos were much less important. Tommy Potter, a member of the Charlie Parker Quintet from 1947 to 1949, and Curly Russell, who also worked with Parker in addition to Gillespie, Dexter Gordon, Sarah Vaughan, Bud Powell, and Fats Navarro, were kept quite busy. Al McKibbon was important not just as a swinging accompanist with Coleman Hawkins, Bud Powell, and Thelonious Monk but for his ability to play Latin rhythms with the Dizzy Gillespie big band and the George Shearing Quintet.

Ray Brown, after playing locally in Pittsburgh, arrived in New York in 1945 just in time to play a large part in the bebop era. In fact his first day in town he jammed with a group consisting of Dizzy Gillespie, Charlie Parker, Bud Powell, and Max Roach! Brown worked with Gillespie in both his big band, where he was featured on "One Bass Hit" and "Two Bass Hit," and combos. He played with Jazz at the Philharmonic in 1947 and was married to Ella Fitzgerald from 1948 to 1952. In 1949 he met Oscar Peterson, and after they worked as a duo, he played in the Oscar Peterson Trio from 1952 to 1966. Brown, who always had a huge tone and could swing at any tempo, was greatly in demand for sessions from the 1950s on. After his long period with Peterson ended, he settled in Los Angeles, played with altoist Bud Shank in the L. A. Four, and led his own trios that along the way featured pianists Gene Harris, Benny Green, and Geoff Keezer. Ray Brown had many reunions with Peterson and was very active up until the day of his death in 2002.

Of the bassists who came up after Jimmy Blanton's death, Oscar Pettiford was the heir apparent and the top bass soloist of the bop era and the 1950s. One of eleven children, he played in a family band led by his father. Pettiford worked with Charlie Barnet in 1942 and started making records the following year, including sets with Coleman Hawkins, Ben Webster, and Earl Hines. After stints with Roy Eldridge, Dizzy Gillespie, and Hawkins, he played in Duke

Ellington's orchestra from 1945 to 1948, filling in for Blanton who had died three years earlier. In 1949 Pettiford worked with Woody Herman's Second Herd but was sidelined after breaking his arm playing baseball. Pettiford spent the time learning to play solos on the cello; only Harry Babasin preceded him as a jazz cellist.

In the 1950s Pettiford was one of the few bassists to work regularly as a leader, doubling on cello. He also recorded with Miles Davis and Thelonious Monk. Pettiford moved to Copenhagen in 1958, playing with touring Americans and top European jazzmen. He worked steadily until a bicycle accident caused his death in 1960 when he was not quite thirty-eight. By then the bass was going through a new round of liberation, but Oscar Pettiford is still considered one of the finest bass soloists of all time.

Although the guitar and bass did not evolve that much during the bop era, drumming did change. No longer restricted to playing quiet rhythms, drummers interacted much more with the lead voices, took more frequent solos and "dropped bombs" during their accompaniment, pushing the ensembles and soloists.

Kenny Clarke originally defined bebop drumming by shifting the time-keeping role from Gene Krupa's bass drum or Jo Jones's hi-hat cymbal to the ride cymbal. Born in 1915, he had already enjoyed a substantial career during the swing era, playing with Roy Eldridge, the Jeter-Pillars band, Claude Hopkins, Teddy Hill, and the Edgar Hayes Orchestra in1937 and 1938. Clarke was a member of the house band at Minton's Playhouse in the early 1940s, and at those jam sessions he developed his style. The irregular bombs, or unexpected accents, that he played behind the other musicians earned him the nickname "Klook-Mop." Clarke would have become more of a force during the bebop era, but he had to serve in the military from 1943 to 1946. When he was discharged, the bebop era was already very much under way, and Max Roach was considered its leading drummer. Clarke, however, worked with most of the top bop players including Fats Navarro, Kenny Dorham, Sonny Stitt, Bud Powell, Tadd Dameron, and the Dizzy Gillespie big band, and led a few record sessions of his own. He was an original member of the Modern Jazz Quartet from 1951 to 1955 but felt restricted by its highly arranged music and low volume. After a bit of freelancing, Clarke permanently moved to France in 1956 where he worked with Bud Powell and top French musicians and co-led a major big band from 1961 to 1972 with pianist Francy Boland. Although Kenny Clarke, who was active up until his 1985 death, was not as famous as some contemporaries due to missing the initial bebop sessions and spending his last twenty-nine years in Europe, he ranks as one of the most important players of the bop era.

Max Roach, like Coleman Hawkins, was always a modern player open to later styles and ideas. He started on drums when he was ten, was well trained at the Manhattan School of Music, played with the house band at Monroe's Uptown House in 1942, and was soon working with Coleman Hawkins and Benny Carter's big band. Roach was at the forefront of the bebop movement, working with Dizzy Gillespie on Fifty-second Street and Charlie Parker on his famous "Ko Ko Session," gigging with Stan Getz and becoming an important member of Parker's 1947 to 1949 quintet. A potentially explosive player, Roach was a rarity among drummers in that he emphasized the value of space, constructing his solos like an architect. His improvisations told a story.

Max Roach was a major force for many decades after the bebop era ended. He played on some of the recordings by Miles Davis' *Birth of the Cool* nonet, played everything from r&b and cool jazz to Dixieland during the early 1950s, and in 1954 formed a classic hard bop quintet with trumpeter Clifford Brown. Among the sidemen in his later groups were tenor saxophonist Sonny Rollins, the modern tuba of Ray Draper, and trumpeters Kenny Dorham, Booker Little, and Freddie Hubbard. Roach's music evolved from bop to hard bop and post-bop with some of his recordings being closer to free jazz and the avant-garde. He was married to singer Abbey Lincoln from 1962 to 1970. They worked on some adventurous and political music projects including *We Insist! Freedom Now Suite*, a classic civil rights set. As jazz moved forward, so did Roach. Among his most interesting ventures of the past thirty years have been the ten-piece all-percussion ensemble M'Boom, his longtime pianoless quartet, and a set of duet recordings with the likes of saxophonists Anthony Braxton and Archie Shepp and pianists Cecil Taylor and Abdullah Ibrahim. Through it all Max Roach never turned his back on bebop and is quick to praise Charlie Parker, Dizzy Gillespie, and Coleman Hawkins as continual inspirations.

Other top drummers of the bebop era include Denzil Best, Roy Haynes, J. C. Heard, Tiny Kahn, Stan Levey, Roy Porter, and Art Blakey, who made a much bigger impact in the 1950s. After these and other fine players arrived on the scene, drummers would no longer be restricted merely to background timekeeping.

Sarah Vaughan had a wondrous voice and was one of the first singers to understand how to use bop in her style.
Photo courtesy of the Wayne Knight Collection, Star Line Productions.

SARAH VAUGHAN

The most significant singer to fully emerge during the bebop era, Sarah Vaughan always had a wondrous voice with a very wide range. She often gave the impression that she could do anything with her voice, and her training in bebop really opened up her singing possibilities even when performing pop music. Born in 1924 Vaughan started off singing in church as a child, and she had extensive piano lessons throughout the 1930s. After winning an amateur contest at the Apollo Theatre in 1943, she was hired by Earl Hines for his orchestra as a singer and second pianist. Although that band unfortunately never recorded, Sassy, her lifelong nickname, picked up invaluable experience singing with a big band that included Dizzy Gillespie, Charlie Parker, and Billy Eckstine. The following year Eckstine formed his own orchestra, and Vaughan joined him, along with Gillespie and Parker. She only recorded one number with the Eckstine band, "I'll Wait and Pray," but at year-end was featured on her own recording that introduced her voice to a larger audience. Her singing was quite bop-oriented, and she was one of the very first singers to fully grasp the potential of bebop.

Other than singing with the John Kirby Sextet in1945 and 1946, Sarah Vaughan was a solo artist from then on. She recorded many gems for the Musicraft label from 1946 to 1948 including "If You Could See Me Now," "Everything I Have Is Yours," "Tenderly," and "It's Magic." After being signed to Columbia in 1949, some of her recordings were more commercial, with backing by orchestras and strings, but Vaughan always had occasional jazz dates, including a notable set in 1950 with Miles Davis. As with Ella Fitzgerald, Vaughan's fame grew during the 1950s. She recorded frequently for the Mercury label and its jazz subsidiary Emarcy, Roulette, Mainstream, and during her final period from1977 to 1982 with Pablo. Whether it was a classic album with Clifford Brown, her making the wide interval jumps of "Misty" sound effortless, or an odd project in which she sang the poems of Pope John Paul II, Vaughan always sounded strong. She retired before she ever declined, passing away in 1990 when she was sixty-six. Sarah Vaughan still ranks at the very top of female jazz singers along with Ella Fitzgerald and Billie Holiday.

THE BEBOP AND VOCALESE SINGERS

With the collapse of the big band era, the singers who were formerly employed by orchestras either drifted toward pop music, like Frank Sinatra and Doris Day, found a medium between jazz and pop like Ella Fitzgerald, Peggy Lee, and Anita O'Day, or gradually went into obscurity. The most promising new voices were Sarah Vaughan and Billy Eckstine, but there was also a new category of singers who were more closely associated with bebop.

To an extent, the bop singers were an extension of such jive singers as Slim Gaillard, Leo Watson, and Fats Waller, all of them influenced initially by Louis Armstrong. They scatted wildly, and the better ones performed adventurous solos although none were on the level of an Fitzgerald or Vaughan. Dave Lambert and Buddy Stewart's 1945 recording of "What's This" with Gene Krupa's orchestra is considered the first bop vocal. Stewart, also a fine ballad singer, would most likely have had a significant career had he not died in a 1950 car crash.

Joe "Bebop" Carroll was a limited singer but never lacked enthusiasm. He is best known for singing with Dizzy Gillespie's big band in 1949 and with some of his small groups in the 1950s. Kenny "Pancho" Hagood had a heavier voice than is usually heard in this music but could also sing effective bebop, as he showed with the Gillespie orchestra from 1946 to 1948 on "Oop-Pop-A-Da" and "Ool-Ya Koo." Dizzy, who dueted with Hagood on those two songs, developed into a phenomenal scat-singer over time, using his vocalizing for variety and his harmonic knowledge and daring to create some miraculous scatting. Babs Gonzales always knew how to promote himself, and although he was not a great singer, he became well known. In 1946 he put together the Three Bips and a Bop and during the next few years had such notable sidemen as Tadd Dameron, tenorman Sonny Rollins, trombonists Bennie Green and J. J. Johnson, Julius Watkins on French horn, violinist Ray Nance, altoist Art Pepper, Don Redman on soprano, and flutist Alberto Socarras, a veteran of the 1920s. Among Gonzalez's better recordings were "Oop-Pop-A-Da," "Weird Lullaby," "Professor Bop," "Prelude to a Nightmare," and "Real Crazy." Gonzales, whose emphasis on vowels in his scatting could often sound weird, faded from the scene long before his 1980 death. Also well worth mentioning is Jackie and Roy, singer Jackie Cain and singer-pianist Roy Kral, who sang some colorful and crazy bop with Charlie Ventura in the late 1940s, later going on their own where their singing remained colorful if becoming more conventional.

While bebop singing was considered a novelty and became less common after 1950, vocalese, a new concept altogether, did not develop until after the bop era. Vocalese is writing lyrics to a recorded solo and using that solo as the basis for the song. When the solo is complex, the singer has to be quite adept at spitting out the words and hitting the same notes as the original soloist. The first example of vocalese is very obscure, Bee Palmer singing part of the Bix Beiderbecke and Frankie Trumbauer's solos to "Singin' the Blues" on her 1929 recording. However that performance went unreleased for over a half century—Palmer was not a very good singer—and had no influence at all. More importantly, in the late 1940s Eddie Jefferson began writing lyrics to some of his favorite bop and swing solos. Already in his thirties, Jefferson had been singing and dancing for a decade and never did have that strong a voice, but he could swing hard and was quite skilled as a lyricist. When James Moody recorded a catchy alto solo on "I'm in the Mood for Love," Jefferson wrote vocalese for the solo, and it became "Moody's Mood for Love" which King Pleasure turned into a hit. Jefferson, who worked with James Moody from 1953 to 1957 and 1968 to 1973 and often performed with altoist Richie Cole during his later years, also wrote the vocalese for such performances as Coleman Hawkins' "Body and Soul," Miles Davis' "So What," Cannonball Adderley's "Jeannine," Charlie Parker's "Now's the Time," and even such impossible to sing pieces as "Freedom Jazz Dance" and "Bitches Brew."

King Pleasure had the strongest voice of the vocalese vocalists and could have made it as a regular singer if he had had the interest. Born Clarence Beeks, he had a mysterious life. In 1951 he won an amateur contest singing Eddie Jefferson's lyrics for "Moody's Mood for Love," and the following year he recorded it before Jefferson, having the hit record. In 1953 Pleasure recorded his own words for Bird's "Parker's Mood," which predicted Charlie Parker's

DAVE LAMBERT
ANNIE ROSS & JON HENDRICKS
of
LAMBERT, HENDRICKS & ROSS

Dave Lambert, Jon Hendricks, and Annie Ross formed a remarkable vocal group featuring three masters of vocalese.
Photo courtesy of the Wayne Knight Collection, Star Line Productions.

death, a second hit. King Pleasure also recorded memorable versions of "Red Top," "D. B. Blues," and "Jumpin' with Symphony Sid," the latter two based on Lester Young solos, but after 1962 he disappeared for unknown reasons, passing away in 1981.

Three of the most skilled vocalese lyricists and singers came together to form what was arguably the top jazz vocal group ever, Lambert, Hendricks, and Ross. Dave Lambert started his career first, working as a drummer in 1937. He gained some recognition for recording "What's This" with Buddy Stewart when they were with the Gene Krupa orchestra in 1945. Lambert struggled for the next decade, occasionally leading a vocal ensemble and first collaborating with Jon Hendricks in 1955. Hendricks, who was one of seventeen children, sang with Art Tatum when he was a youth in Ohio and played drums for two years in the 1940s without much success. In 1952 he arrived in New York and had one of his songs, "I Want You to Be My Baby," recorded by Louis Jordan but only worked in music on a part-time basis until 1957.

In 1957 Lambert and Hendricks planned to use a vocal ensemble to record vocalese versions of a set of Count Basie big band recordings. As it turned out, none of the singers that auditioned could swing very well except for one, Annie Ross. Ross had been a child actor, a nightclub singer in England, and had already recorded three vocalese classics on her own in "Farmer's Market," "Jackie," and "Twisted," based on a Wardell Gray tenor solo. After much thought, Lambert and Hendricks decided to form a vocal trio with Ross and overdub their voices so as to simulate the Basie orchestra. Their 1957 album, *Sing a Song of Basie*, is a classic, and it launched Lambert, Hendricks, and Ross.

During the next five years, the group recorded five additional albums with such vocalese songs as "Cloudburst," "Come on Home," "Cookin' at the Continental," Hendricks' humorous "Gimme That Wine," and "Going to Chicago," which had Joe Williams singing while the other three vocalists weave lines around him. In 1962 Ross quit the group, citing bad health. Yolande Bavan replaced her, and the reorganized group became Lambert, Hendricks, and Bavan. In 1964 the vocal trio broke up altogether. In future years both Ross and Bavan worked primarily as actresses although Ross occasionally came back to the jazz scene. Lambert died in a car accident in 1966. Jon Hendricks, the genius of vocalese, has continued singing and writing up to the present time, having a very successful solo career and sometimes singing with his wife Judith, daughter Michelle, and a fourth vocalist as The Hendricks Family.

Anita O'Day, who came to fame with Gene Krupa's orchestra during 1941 and 1942 and sang with Stan Kenton in 1944, was one of the main swing era singers to embrace bebop. She recorded her finest work during the 1950s and hit the peak of her career at the 1958 Newport Jazz Festival, which was filmed as part of the documentary *Jazz on a Summer's Day*. A drug addict by then, she almost died in the 1960s but made a full comeback in the 1970s.

O'Day's style of singing and phrasing were early influences and inspirations for June Christy, who succeeded her with Stan Kenton's orchestra. After Christy left Stan Kenton in 1951, she had a very successful solo career, recording steadily for Capitol and making the haunting "Something Cool" famous. Until she lost interest in singing and retired in 1965 when she was thirty-nine, Christy was a major influence on a generation of cool-toned singers that included Chris Connor, Helen Merrill, and Julie London. Christy's successor with Stan Kenton, Chris Connor, had a trademark song with "All About Ronnie" and recorded prolifically for Atlantic during the second half of the 1950s. Her deep, low voice was distinctive and fit the era well. Although Helen Merrill did not sing with Kenton, she also fit into the cool style. Merrill has recorded infrequently in her career, but nearly every one of her recordings has been a major event, particularly her session with trumpeter Clifford Brown, one with arranger Gil Evans, and some later albums with pianist Dick Katz's inventive arrangements. Actress Julie London, who had a hit with "Cry Me a River," was at her best in intimate small-group settings, as well known for her sensuous album covers as for her singing.

TADD DAMERON

Although classic bebop is primarily thought of as combo music with only the theme written, that is not always true. Some small groups utilized arranged ensembles, and not all of the big bands were gone by 1946. Some of the more important arrangers of the era included Gil Evans with Claude Thornhill and the Miles Davis Nonet, Gil Fuller with the Dizzy Gillespie big band, Boyd Raeburn's George Handy, Ralph Burns, Pete Rugolo, and Neal Hefti. While most of these concentrated on big bands, Tadd Dameron emerged as one of the definitive arranger-composers for smaller bop groups.

During the swing era Dameron picked up experience freelancing with several groups as a pianist-arranger. He wrote for Harlan Leonard's Kansas City Orchestra in 1940, which recorded some of his work, and contributed charts to the big bands of Jimmie Lunceford, Count Basie, Billy Eckstine, and Dizzy Gillespie, plus recordings by Sarah Vaughan. During 1948 and 1949 Dameron led a sextet that featured Fats Navarro and his successor Miles Davis. Among the standards that he wrote during this era were "Hot House," "Good Bait," "Our Delight," "Lady Bird," and "If You Could See Me Now."

Dameron should have had a prosperous life, but some bad business deals and drug problems made that impossible. He led a group that included trumpeter Clifford Brown in 1953 and recorded "Mating Call" with John Coltrane in 1958 but was in jail much of 1959 to 1961. After his release he resumed writing including for Sonny Stitt, Milt Jackson, and Benny Goodman, recording a final album in 1962. Tadd Dameron died of cancer in 1965 at the age of forty-eight.

BIG BANDS

After 1946 there was only a fraction of the many large jazz orchestras that had been active in 1942. Dancers were more attracted to small r&b combos, and the modern jazz big bands made the mistake of discouraging dancing. As a result audiences became a lot smaller than they had been for the swing orchestras. Still it was prestigious to lead an orchestra, and a few bandleaders had brief success with boppish bands.

Billy Eckstine

The first bebop big band, Earl Hines Orchestra in 1943, never recorded due to the Musicians Union strike, and not even a radio broadcast has survived. The second bop orchestra was headed by Hines' former singer, Billy Eckstine, an unlikely but influential bandleader, who had a warm and deep baritone voice and was particularly skilled on romantic ballads. While with Hines from 1939 to 1943, he displayed his versatility by having a minor hit on the blues "Jelly, Jelly" and showed that he could sing jazz too. In 1943 he persuaded Hines to hire Charlie Parker, Dizzy Gillespie, and Sarah Vaughan, and the following year he took them as the nucleus of his newly formed band. His key soloists included tenors Dexter Gordon and Gene Ammons, baritonist Leo Parker, drummer Art Blakey, and himself on valve trombone. The band alternated bop tunes and catchy numbers with smooth ballads. "Blowing the Blues Away" was a minor hit and has a heated trade-off of heated phrases by Gordon and Ammons. Sonny Stitt and Fats Navarro ably replaced Parker and Gillespie, and later on the trumpet section also included Miles Davis and Kenny Dorham.

Eckstine kept the band together as long as possible, into 1947, but it was a losing battle since swing audiences and dancers were not interested. After he reluctantly broke up the orchestra, Billy Eckstine had a very successful career in middle-of-the-road pop music, occasionally singing a bit of jazz and reminiscing about the bebop days.

Boyd Raeburn

Boyd Raeburn, like Eckstine, was also an unlikely choice to lead a big band. Raeburn started on tenor, switched to bass sax and baritone sax, and never really soloed. He was more of a figurehead, leading commercial orchestras starting in the late 1930s. His big band became more swing-oriented in 1944, sounding a bit like Count Basie's and sometimes featuring the Johnny Hodges–influenced altoist Johnny Bothwell with such guests as Roy Eldridge, Oscar Pettiford, trombonist Trummy Young, and Dizzy Gillespie. Raeburn's band was one of the first to feature Dizzy's *A Night in Tunisia* with such numbers as "Hep Boyd," "March of the Boyds," "Early Boyd," "Boyd Meets the Duke," "Boyd Meets Girl," and "Little Boyd Blue." In 1945 the orchestra changed considerably when

George Handy became its main arranger, contributing radical charts that were quite dissonant and eccentric. Although the singers Ginnie Powell and David Allyn were potentially commercial, the ensembles behind them constantly exploded and were quite dissonant, hinting at modern classical music. Despite the fact that the band did not stand a chance of succeeding commercially, it soon expanded to twenty pieces with the addition of French horns and a harp. Its personnel included Lucky Thompson, Dodo Marmarosa, and Buddy DeFranco. Among the band's more outlandish recordings are "Tonsillectomy," "Dalvatore Sally," "Rip Van Winkle," and "Boyd Meets Stravinsky," plus radical remakes of "Over the Rainbow," "Body and Soul," and "Temptation."

The Boyd Raeburn Orchestra, which never caught on but did record a great deal of intriguing music, broke up at the end of 1947.

Woody Herman

While the Billy Eckstine and Boyd Raeburn big bands did not continue past 1947, the orchestras of Woody Herman and Stan Kenton survived the end of both the swing and bop eras, joining Duke Ellington and Count Basie as the main big bands of the 1950s, 1960s, and 1970s.

Herman, who was born in 1913, sang as a child in vaudeville and grew up around show business. He started on saxophone at eleven, clarinet at fourteen, and became a professional musician by the time he was fifteen. After playing with some obscure bands, he was well featured on clarinet, alto, and vocals with Isham Jones Orchestra from 1934 to 1936. When Jones broke up the band, the twenty-three-year-old Herman took the remnants and formed his own orchestra. The band never quite caught on big during the swing era but worked steadily, mostly featuring the leader's ballad vocals during the first few years along with some instrumentals. In 1939 its theme "At the Woodchopper's Ball" became a hit, and Herman's orchestra was billed as "The Band That Plays the Blues." Still the band did not break out from the second level of swing orchestras during this period.

Many changes began in 1943 when the draft from World War II forced a large turnover in Herman's band. At first, their music was influenced by Duke Ellington, but by the end of 1944 Herman's band finally had its own sound. It was an advanced swing band that was not unaware of bebop, featuring very spirited ensembles, colorful soloists, some up-tempo romps, and lots of humor. Trombonist Bill Harris and tenor saxophonist Flip Phillips were major soloists with other important voices including trumpeters Sonny Berman and Pete Candoli, drummers Dave Tough and Don Lamond, arrangers Ralph Burns and Neal Hefti, and bassist Chubby Jackson, the band's cheerleader who often yelled out encouragement during performances. With Herman contributing clarinet and alto, the band, first known as Herman's Herd and later renamed The First Herd, was the most exciting new big band of 1944. Its versions of "Apple Honey," "Caldonia," and "Bijou" were memorable. Igor

Stravinsky was so impressed with the band in general that he wrote *Ebony Concerto* for it.

At the end of 1946, family problems led to Woody Herman breaking up The First Herd, his only financially successful orchestra, at the peak of its fame. After a few months off the scene, Herman formed the Second Herd. It was unusual in that the saxophone section, in addition to Herman and lead altoist Sam Marowitz, consisted of baritonist Serge Chaloff and three cool-toned tenors influenced by Lester Young, Stan Getz, Zoot Sims, and Herbie Steward. When the tenors and Chaloff were featured on the hit recording of "Four Brothers," the orchestra became unofficially known as The Four Brothers Band. It was more bop-oriented and at first seemed a bit too serious, but over time Bill Harris and Chubby Jackson joined, and some of the old spirit returned. Among the band's recordings were "Early Autumn," a Ralph Burns ballad that made Stan Getz into a star, "The Goof and I," and "Keen and Peachy," based on the chord changes of "Fine and Dandy." Al Cohn eventually replaced Steward, and some of Herman's musicians from 1949 included Gene Ammons, Oscar Pettiford, Terry Gibbs, and drummer Shelly Manne. Despite the great music that it produced, the Second Herd lost money, and Herman broke up the band at the end of 1949.

After playing briefly with a small group, Herman formed The Third Herd to fulfill some obligations. This orchestra performed the hits of the first two Herds but also played at more danceable tempos, sounding conservative when it was necessary. Many fine musicians passed through the band before it broke up in 1956. Herman kept on playing, leading various small groups. After a specially assembled orchestra was a hit at the 1959 Monterey Jazz Festival, Herman formed The Young Thundering Herd, an exciting big band that has lasted up to the present time. The early 1960s version featured exciting playing from the powerful tenor Sal Nistico, trombonist Phil Wilson, pianist-arranger Nat Pierce, and high-note trumpeter Bill Chase. Herman, an underrated altoist, clarinetist, and soprano sax, proved to be most important as an inspiration to his younger players, urging them to contribute new music to his book. This included playing cover versions of some rock tunes during 1968 to 1975 and sometimes veering close to commercialism and irrelevancy. However Herman's band was always full of up-and-coming talent, and when he celebrated his fortieth anniversary as a bandleader with a Carnegie Hall concert in 1976, his orchestra was back to playing mostly straight-ahead jazz.

The Woody Herman Orchestra made it to its fiftieth anniversary in 1986, and with Frank Tiberi assuming some of the leadership, it was a tight, if somewhat predictable, band. Unfortunately Herman was not able to enjoy his last years because the Internal Revenue Service constantly hounded him for thousands of dollars of taxes that a crooked manager had not withheld from his sidemen's salaries in the 1960s. In order to make payments, Woody Herman had to be on the road constantly, which helped contribute to his failing health. He passed away in 1987 at the age of seventy-four. Frank Tiberi still leads the Herman

Orchestra on a part-time basis, but without its leader, the Herman Big Band has stopped evolving.

AFRO-CUBAN (OR LATIN) JAZZ

The term "Latin jazz" has often been applied to the very different styles associated with Cuba and Brazil. While the latter, founded by composer Antonio Carlos Jobim and guitarist Joao Gilberto, was based in Brazil even although bossa novas became a part of many jazz musicians' repertoires, Afro-Cuban jazz was born in New York City.

Afro-Cuban jazz is a mixture of Cuban and African polyrhythms with jazz improvising. Although it includes many complex rhythms, all Cuban music is based on an offbeat rhythmic pattern called the clave. The clave, also the name for two wooden sticks that originally made the rhythm, is stated or at least implied over every two bars. The infectious clave rhythm is achieved by clapping on beats 1, 2½, and 4 in the first bar and on beats 2 and 3 in the second. Sometimes during solos the pattern is reversed, with beats 2 and 3 accented in the first bar, and 1, 2½, and 4 emphasized in the second.

Prior to the 1940s Cuban music and jazz were separate. American musicians of the swing era did not have much interest in playing Latin rhythms—no swing band used a percussionist—and Cuban groups emphasized ensembles, singing, and rhythms without much soloing. The first band to combine Cuban rhythms with American jazz was Machito's Afro-Cubans. Formed in 1940 the New York–based orchestra was originally a Cuban dance band. The next year Mario Bauza, Machito's brother-in-law who had previously played trumpet with Chick Webb and Cab Calloway's bands, became Machito's musical director and key arranger. He encouraged Machito to hire jazz musicians for the horn sections and in 1943 wrote "Tanga," the first Afro-Cuban jazz song. The rise of bebop in 1945 was a giant step forward for Afro-Cuban jazz because bop's rhythms were much more flexible than the strictly 4/4 swing of the big bands. All that the formative music needed was a catalyst, and that soon came in the short-lived but potent musical partnership of an American trumpeter and a Cuban conga player.

DIZZY GILLESPIE AND CHANO POZO

Dizzy Gillespie, who with Charlie Parker led bebop, was always interested in his African heritage and in complex rhythms. He had written *A Night in Tunisia* in 1943 when he was still with Earl Hines' big band, a song that became a classic of both bop and African Cuban jazz. In 1947 Gillespie casually asked Mario Bauza, his fellow trumpeter in Cab Calloway's band, whether he knew of a good percussionist who he could add to his big band. Bauza suggested Chano Pozo.

Pozo had a colorful past as a street fighter, a reform school attendee, and a dancer in Cuba. He was also a skilled choreographer and a popular songwriter whose tunes were in the repertoire of Machito, Xavier Cugat, and other New York Cuban bands, even though he did not know how to read or write music. Most significantly, Pozo was a charismatic conga player and singer who, before being introduced to Gillespie, had struggled since arriving in New York in May 1946.

Although Dizzy knew no Spanish and Pozo spoke no English, musically they communicated immediately. At first Pozo's rhythms clashed with Gillespie's American rhythm section, but bassist Al McKibbon joined the band in August and bridged that gap. A Carnegie Hall concert on September 29, 1947, introduced Pozo as Gillespie's percussionist, symbolically launching African Cuban jazz. Later in the year Pozo recorded eight selections with the big band including features on "Cubana Be," "Cubana Bop," and the original version of "Manteca," a song he co-wrote with Gillespie. They would also co-compose "Tin Tin Deo."

The 1948 recording strike kept Pozo off records during that period although broadcasts exist of him inspiring the Gillespie orchestra. Tragically it all ended on December 2, 1948, when Chano Pozo was fatally shot in a bar brawl; he was just thirty-three.

Through the years, Gillespie occasionally used percussionists, particularly for special projects, playing both bebop and African Cuban jazz and frequently performing *A Night in Tunisia* and "Manteca." Late in life, Dizzy encouraged quite a few Latin American musicians, especially after he visited Cuba in 1977. When altoist Paquito D'Rivera and trumpeter Arturo Sandoval defected from Cuba, Gillespie helped sponsor and employ them, including in his last major project, the United Nation Orchestra from 1988 to 1991.

CUBOP

The mixture of bebop and Afro-Cuban rhythms was soon dubbed "Cubop." Stan Kenton in 1947 revived "The Peanut Vendor" quite memorably, and Jack Costanzo played bongos in his orchestra for a time. Other big bands of the late 1940s added percussionists, briefly including Benny Goodman, who had a bebop orchestra in 1949.

In the 1950s the top three Latin big bands—those led by Tito Rodriguez, Machito, and Tito Puente, who unlike the other bandleaders was born in New York—all included jazz soloists, showing that the two types of music could mix quite well. Generally these orchestras consisted of trumpet, trombone, and saxophone sections plus piano, bass, congas, bongos, and timbales. The Palladium in New York was one of the major centers of African Cuban jazz, with the two Titos often competing to gain top billing and to win acclaim from the enthusiastic dancing audiences. Machito's band in particular went out of its way to feature guest jazz players in the late 1940s and 1950s, including projects with Charlie Parker, Buddy Rich, tenors Flip Phillips and Brew Moore, trumpeters

Howard McGhee and Harry "Sweets" Edison, flutist Herbie Mann, trombonist Curtis Fuller, and altoist Cannonball Adderley. Arranger Chico O'Farrill, who moved to the United States from Cuba in 1948, wrote the *Afro-Cuban Jazz Suite* for Machito, the four-part *Manteca Suite* for Gillespie, and recorded a series of exciting Afro-Cuban jazz sets of his own during the first half of the 1950s. Tito Rodriguez, a singer whose music was usually further removed from jazz than the other big bands, had such greats as pianist Eddie Palmieri, tenor saxophonist Mario Rivera, and lead trumpeter Victor Paz in his band for a time.

Tito Puente, who outlasted all of his competitors, was billed as "El Rey" and "King of the Mambo." A colorful and exciting performer, he played timbales and vibes and wrote and arranged music. Puente picked up experience with Machito in 1942 and Pupi Campo's orchestra during 1947 and 1948 before beginning his fifty-one-year career as a bandleader in 1949. In the mid-1950s when he had Mongo Santamaria on congas and Willie Bobo on bongos, Puente's rhythm section was nicknamed "Ti-Mon-Bo." Through all of the changes in Latin music, Puente kept his sound flexible without losing his musical identity and never lost his popularity.

By the early 1950s, it was not unusual for a conventional bop combo to play an occasional Latin-oriented piece even without adding a percussionist. Important African Cuban musicians of that era included percussionists Ray Barretto, Candido, Patato Valdes, Sabu Martinez, Armando Peraza who guested regularly with George Shearing, and Jack Costanzo who was a member of the Nat King Cole Trio during 1949 to 1951. In 1960 when the United States froze relations with Fidel Castro, the steady influx of Cuban musicians stopped altogether, and the Cubop era began to come to a close.

AFRO-CUBAN JAZZ TODAY

As jazz evolved, so did Afro-Cuban jazz, with bands experimenting on instrumentation. Herbie Mann's Latin jazz band of 1959 through 1967 used the leader's flute, John Rae on vibes and timbales, a bassist, drummer, two percussionists, and trumpeter Doc Cheatham. Eddie Palmieri had a frontline consisting of a flute and two trombones that his older brother pianist Charlie Palmieri called a "trombanga." Eddie Palmieri in time brought the influences of McCoy Tyner and Chick Corea into his piano playing, sounding much more modern than the usual Latin jazz pianist of the 1950s. Soul jazz and r&b were often mixed into Afro-Cuban jazz in the 1960s, resulting in music called "bugalu." Some of the records were big sellers, including Ray Barretto's "El Watusi," Joe Cuba's "Bang Bang," and several recordings by Mongo Santamaria, who wrote "Afro Blue" and popularized Herbie Hancock's "Watermelon Man."

In the 1970s salsa caught on big. It is basically Latin dance music that is dominated by vocals in Spanish, tight structures, and a pop sensibility. Although in existence since the 1940s, the word became so popular in the 1970s that it sometimes was applied to all types of Latin music rather than the non-jazz style that it really represents. Salsa can be thought of as the pop equivalent of Afro-Cuban jazz, with vocals in place of the solos.

In 1977 when relations between the United States and Cuba had temporarily thawed, Dizzy Gillespie, Stan Getz, and a few other top American jazz musicians made a rare visit to Cuba. This was the symbolic beginning of the modern era of Afro-Cuban jazz. Gillespie was amazed to discover the high level of musicianship that was prevalent on the island, including the group Irakere. When Castro began to crack down on Cuban musicians, several key players defected, including altoist Paquito D'Rivera in 1980 and trumpeter Arturo Sandoval in 1990; both became major jazz artists in the United States. Some other top Cuban musicians worked out agreements with Castro and became important forces on the U.S. scene, including pianists Gonzalo Rubalcaba and Chucho Valdes, whose remarkable technique and creativity makes him the Art Tatum of Cuba.

While New York has many of the top Afro-Cuban jazz performers, Los Angeles is the second main center of Afro-Cuban jazz in the United States. Los Angeles is the home for such performers as conguero Poncho Sanchez and his spirited band, saxophonist Justo Almario, violinist Susie Hansen, the Estrada Brothers, and percussionists Alex Acuna, Francisco Aguabella, and Pete Escovedo. Other major forces in today's African Cuban jazz scene, most of whom play regularly in New York, include the avant-Latin tenor-saxophonist David Sanchez; pianists Danilo Perez, Hilton Ruiz, Michel Camilo, and Hilario Duran; percussionists Giovanni Hidalgo and Bobby Sanabria; drummers Steve Berrios and Ignacio Berroa; trumpeters Claudio Roditi, Charlie Sepulveda, and Ray Vega; flutist Dave Valentin; Ray Barretto's band, and the groups Cubanismo and Los Hombres Calientes.

While some other styles of jazz have struggled commercially during the past two decades, Afro-Cuban jazz remains one of the most popular styles due to the danceable rhythms and the infectious grooves.

NEW YORK COOL JAZZ

Although early cool jazz was centered and popularized in Los Angeles and elsewhere on the West Coast, it was influenced by bands from other areas. In addition to the quiet tone of Lester Young, the use of space and swing by Count Basie's orchestra, and the sound of the John Kirby Sextet, three groups based in New York affected the early development of cool jazz. This will be discussed at much greater length in chapter seven.

The Claude Thornhill Orchestra

Claude Thornhill always had an unusual band. Its repertoire emphasized ballads, particularly in its early days, and the instrumentalists utilized very little vibrato. The ensemble's long floating tones and unique tone colors were quite individual, and sometimes as many as six clarinets playing in unison. The orchestra's music fell between sweet and swing. Thornhill, who was a studio musician in the 1930s and had worked with singer Maxine Sullivan, formed his first orchestra in 1940. Until Gil Evans joined in 1942, he and Bill Borden wrote most of the arrangements. The Thornhill Orchestra was best known for its haunting theme song "Snowfall," adapting some classical themes to its dance band style, having a hit in "Where or When," and introducing "Autumn Nocturne." In 1942 the band widened its sound by adding two French horns, but when Thornhill enlisted in the navy, the orchestra broke up.

In 1946 Claude Thornhill formed a new big band, initially similar to the first one. With two French horns and, in 1947, a tuba joining all the clarinets, the orchestra was unlike any other at the time. In 1947 it featured trumpeter Red Rodney and altoist Lee Konitz among the soloists. Gil Evans arranged memorable versions of some bebop standards for Thornhill, including "Anthropology," "Robbins' Nest," and "Yardbird Suite," and he met Miles Davis when the trumpeter asked Evans for his arrangement of "Donna Lee." To a large extent, Miles Davis's *Birth of the Cool Nonet* was based on the Thornhill sound.

Although they had a hit with Fran Warren's vocal on "A Sunday Kind of Love," the Claude Thornhill Orchestra broke up in 1950, but the genesis of cool jazz can still be heard in Thornhill's music.

The Miles Davis Nonet

Miles Davis was a member of the Charlie Parker Quintet until December 1948, but two months before he left, he had already formed a nonet that was the next step beyond bebop. Davis was very impressed by the sound of the Claude Thornhill Orchestra, particularly when they played Gil Evans charts, and he wanted to form a smaller group based on their sounds and tone colors. With Evans, altoist Lee Konitz, and baritonist Gerry Mulligan being key members, Davis put together a nonet that from September 4 to 18 performed as the intermission band for Count Basie at the Royal Roost. The band was unusual in that it prominently featured a French horn and a tuba in the ensembles, in addition to trumpet, trombone, alto, baritone, piano, bass, and drums. Despite the band's distinctive sound and music, the Royal Roost engagement was its only gig. Thirteen songs were recorded during three record dates for Capitol in 1949 and 1950, with the arrangements provided by Mulligan, Lewis, Evans, Davis, and Johnny Carisi. Among the most memorable performances are "Move," "Boplicity," "Israel," the haunting "Moon Dreams," and "Godchild." When the studio recordings were released two years later on an album, they were billed as "Birth of the Cool," and they became highly influential on the West Coast jazz movement.

Miles Davis' quiet trumpet sound became a key voice in cool jazz, influencing Shorty Rogers and Chet Baker, even though by 1953 he had moved on and was playing early hard bop.

Lennie Tristano

Lennie Tristano was both an innovator in the cool jazz movement and a founder of his own style of music. Blind from childhood, Tristano connected to the piano from an early age and gained a degree from the American Conservatory of Music in 1943. After teaching music in Chicago, he moved to New York in 1946. Soon he was at the center of a jazz cult, surrounded by eager and talented students. Among his key "pupils" were guitarist Billy Bauer, altoist Lee Konitz, and tenor-saxophonist Warne Marsh, although many musicians and singers studied with him, including veteran tenor Bud Freeman.

Tristano enjoyed playing long melodic lines with unusual accents; he was also a master at reharmonizing songs. While he was very advanced melodically and harmonically, rhythmically Tristano preferred that his bassists and drummers simply keep time, staying almost static, while he and the horn players improvised endlessly, usually over common chord changes that were slightly disguised. Variations of tone and rhythmic excitement were sacrificed in the name of melodic development. Sometimes Tristano featured two or three soloists at once or had his group play free improvisations, a very radical step for the late 1940s. Because Tristano was a virtuoso and quite original in his ideas, he was greatly respected by bop musicians, even performing on a few occasions with Charlie Parker and Dizzy Gillespie. In 1949 he recorded his most important works in a sextet with Konitz. His songs from that year featured some stunning unisons from Konitz and Marsh, particularly on "Wow," colorful interplay on "Sax of a Kind," and the very first recorded free improvisations in "Intuition" and "Digression," a decade before avant-garde jazz began to have an impact.

In 1951 Tristano founded a school of jazz that lasted for five years. His live performances became much less frequent, and even after the school ended, he spent most of his time teaching privately. Tristano continued making occasional recordings including an intense and atonal "Descent into the Maelstrom" in 1953 and an album in 1955. *The Lennie Tristano Quartet*, which includes some overdubbing of extra pianos and a few numbers with the piano purposely speeded up. Being unable to bend notes on the piano, Tristano was experimenting with new sounds; that particular album was considered quite controversial.

Tristano's later recordings are more conventional but no less original, performed with as much fire and focus as ever. After his last recordings in 1965, he was a bit of a recluse until his death in 1978, although he never stopped teaching, influencing a later generation of jazz musicians including pianists Connie Crothers and Liz Gorrill.

The Modern Jazz Quartet

One of the top cool jazz bands to debut in the 1950s, the Modern Jazz Quartet (MJQ), was a rarity in that it was based in New York rather than on the West

Coast. Pianist John Lewis, vibraphonist Milt Jackson, bassist Ray Brown, and drummer Kenny Clarke first came together as the rhythm section of the 1946 Dizzy Gillespie Orchestra. They were occasionally given features at the time, and their paths crossed occasionally during the next five years. In 1951 the same musicians recorded as the Milt Jackson Quartet. Brown could not commit himself to the group because he was busy playing with Oscar Peterson, so when the MJQ was formed in 1952, Percy Heath was on bass. Other than Connie Kay replacing Clarke when he chose to leave in 1955, there were no personnel changes for forty years.

Gradually John Lewis became the band's musical director, with Milt Jackson functioning as the key soloist. The MJQ's music included some classical-oriented pieces and originals but also featured their versions of bop standards and blues. During an era when jazz musicians were often stereotyped as unreliable and sloppily dressed, the members of the Modern Jazz Quartet were impeccably attired, never showed up late, and were quite distinguished. They often performed at prestigious venues, interacted with classical ensembles, and were considered pure class, while never forgetting how to play the blues. Among their most famous songs were Lewis' "Django" and Jackson's "Bags' Groove." They also performed on a few soundtracks and participated in some third stream concerts.

Stan Getz had such a beautiful tone on tenor that he became known simply as "The Sound."
Photo courtesy of the Wayne Knight Collection, Star Line Productions.

The MJQ worked steadily until 1974 when Milt Jackson, who was tired of the format and the musical restrictions, quit the group. The members scattered for seven years until a reunion in 1981 found them rekindling their musical magic. They resumed touring and recording, staying busy until Kay's death in 1995. Mickey Roker and Albert "Tootie" Heath were temporary replacements before the MJQ stopped performing two years later.

Stan Getz and the Cool-Toned Tenors

By 1950 Lester Young was the main influence on most young tenor saxophonists. In fact, on a record date from that period, Stan Getz, Zoot Sims, Al Cohn, Brew Moore, and Allan Eager all have solo space on tenor, and it is impossible to tell them apart. The Young style, first heard on records in 1936, featured a light tone and a relaxed approach even at faster tempos. The younger generation of cool tenors was also touched by the ideas of Charlie Parker, and the best players eventually developed their own voices within the style.

Stan Getz had such a beautiful tone, comparable to Johnny Hodges on alto, that he was nicknamed "The Sound." During World War II the draft depleted many swing bands of some of their musicians, so Getz worked regularly as a teenager, playing with Jack Teagarden in 1943 when he was sixteen and gaining important experience with the big bands of Stan Kenton, Jimmy Dorsey, and Benny Goodman. He became famous while playing with Woody Herman's Second Herd from 1947 to 1949, as one of the soloists on "Four Brothers," and taking a renowned ballad solo on "Early Autumn." When he left Herman, Getz became a leader of a series of small groups in the 1950s, including a quartet with the then-unknown pianist Horace Silver, a quintet that teamed him in exciting fashion with guitarist Jimmy Raney, and a group with valve trombonist Bob Brookmeyer. Although Getz became the symbol of the "cool school," he could also swing very hard, holding his own on records with Dizzy Gillespie, Lionel Hampton, and J. J. Johnson. After spending 1958 to 1960 in Europe, Getz recorded a classic album with Eddie Sauter's orchestra Focus and in 1962 became a major force in launching the bossa-nova movement. Getz's cool tone perfectly fit bossa nova, and he made hit records with guitarist Charlie Byrd, Antonio Carlos Jobim, Astrud Gilberto, and Joao Gilberto.

Rather than stick to bossa nova the rest of his career, Getz continued to evolve and search for stimulating settings. He had a pianoless quartet with vibraphonist Gary Burton, used Chick Corea as his pianist for a time, and in the late 1970s even utilized an Echoplex on his tenor to create distorted electronic effects, although the novelty quickly wore off. During the final decade before his death in 1991, Stan Getz was mostly heard leading an acoustic quartet, showing that his brand of cool-toned swinging was quite timeless.

While Getz evolved and was heard in many different situations in his career, most of the other Lester Young–influenced tenors found their sound early and were content to grow from within. Zoot Sims, who also was a member of Woody Herman's Second Herd, was famous for his ability to swing no matter what the setting; he never played an uninspired solo. Sims worked with Benny Goodman, Stan Kenton, Gerry Mulligan, and his good friend Al Cohn, but was mostly heard with quartets, always sounding consistent. The same can be said for Al Cohn, whose tone during much of his career was nearly identical to Sims', except that Cohn was also skilled as an arranger-composer. Cohn played next to Getz and Sims in Herman's Second Herd, and after a stint with Artie Shaw's bebop orchestra in 1949, he worked as a single, freelanced as a writer, and co-led a two-tenor quintet with Sims. Cohn's tone deepened in his later years, but his cool jazz/swing style remained the same, and he could always be relied upon to produce high-quality music. He passed away in 1988.

Allen Eager was one of the first of the Lester Young–inspired tenors, emerging in 1946. After less than a decade of playing, however, he lost interest in music and faded out of the scene by 1956. Brew Moore was more active, but he never achieved any real fame. From 1948 to 1953 he played with Claude Thornhill's orchestra, Machito, Kai Winding, and Gerry Mulligan. Moore spent seven years living in San Francisco, sometimes playing with vibraphonist Cal Tjader, and ended his career and life in Europe where he always did his best to sound like Lester Young. No one, however, came closer to sounding like Young than Paul Quinichette. He stood out on a few levels. Quinichette was black while all of the other Four Brothers–type tenors were white, and he emulated Lester Young from the 1950s rather than Young's sound in the 1930s. Quinichette was so close to sounding like Young, who was nicknamed Pres, that he became known as "the Vice Pres." Quinichette worked with a variety of big bands including Jay McShann and Count Basie in 1952 and 1953 but was at his best when playing with combos where he sounded like an exact duplicate of his musical idol.

Other tenors playing in a modernized Lester Young style in the 1950s included Bill Perkins, whose tone is remarkably cool on John Lewis' Grand Encounter album, Bob Cooper, Richie Kamuca, and Jack Montrose, who was also a skilled arranger, each of whom made many worthy recordings in their careers.

The Third Stream Movement

Some of the New York–based cool jazz musicians became involved with third stream music in the mid-1950s. Composer-educator Gunther Schuller coined the "third stream" title to describe a blending of jazz and classical music. During the second half of the 1950s, special recordings and concerts were held, but third stream music never really caught on except as an ideal.

The problem with combining jazz and classical music is that in most cases classical musicians are not able to improvise and swing, so their presence on jazz recordings tends to weigh down the music. As early as Igor Stravinsky's 1918 "Ragtime," which despite its name captures very little of the joyful syncopations of ragtime, Paul Whiteman's recording of George Gershwin's Rhapsody in Blue in 1924, and Bix Beiderbecke's "In a Mist," third stream was a concept that interested some composers. During the swing era, several big bands, most successfully Artie Shaw, added string sections that occasionally hinted at classical music, while classical themes were sometimes jazzed up and swung in arrangements by other groups, including the John Kirby Sextet. The best jazz musicians were always aware of classical music, and to an extent by the late 1940s the opposite was also true, with Stravinsky writing Ebony Concerto for Woody Herman's Herd. Stan Kenton's Innovations Orchestra of 1950 and 1951 was an ambitious attempt to have a classical jazz orchestra.

In 1955 Gunther Schuller formed the Jazz and Classical Music Society, two years before he came up with the third stream name. Among the jazz writers who composed third stream works during the second half of the 1950s were J. J. Johnson, Jimmy Giuffre, William Russo, and John Lewis. During that era when musicians were asked where the future of jazz was going, many speculated that jazz and classical music would eventually combine as one idiom.

Despite some successful works in the 1950s and in later decades, that particular fusion never really happened. Clarinetist Eddie Daniels' "Breakthrough" from 1986 is a rare classic in this idiom. Many of the third stream works were simply too dry and difficult to catch on with jazz audiences, and most classical composers preferred to stay in their own musical world without having to deal with improvisation. The rise of free jazz and the avant-garde in the 1960s ended whatever hopes third stream advocates had of being dominant in jazz. There are still new third stream works being written, however, often featuring virtuoso jazz soloists in a classical setting. It continues on as a minor movement and a possibility for future jazz musicians to explore.

RECOMMENDED RECORDINGS

Anita O'Day. *Anita Sings the Most*. Verve, 829 577.
Arturo Sandoval. *The Latin Train*. GRP, 9818.
Babs Gonzales. *Weird Lullaby*. Blue Note, 84464.
Billy Eckstine. *The Legendary Big Band*. Savoy, 17125, 2 CDs.
Boyd Raeburn. *Jubilee Broadcasts 1946*. Hep, 1.
Bud Powell. *The Complete Blue Note and Roost Recordings*. Blue Note, 30083, 4 CDs.
Chano Pozo. *El Tambor de Cuba*. Tumbao, 308, 3 CDs.
Charlie Parker. *The Complete Live Performances on Savoy*. Savoy, 17021, 4 CDs.
Charlie Parker. *Jazz at Massey Hall*. Original Jazz Classics, 044.
Charlie Parker. *Yardbird Suite: The Ultimate Charlie Parker Collection*. Rhino, 72260, 2 CDs.
Chico O'Farrill. *Cuban Blues*. Verve, 314 533 256, 2 CDs.
Chucho Valdes. *Solo Piano*. Blue Note, 80597.
Claude Thornhill. *Best of the Big Bands*. Columbia, 46152.
Coleman Hawkins. *Hollywood Stampede*. Capitol, 92596.
Coleman Hawkins. *Rainbow Mist*. Delmark, 459.
Cubanismo. *Jesus Alemany's Cubanismo*. Hannibal, 1390.
Danilo Perez. *The Journey*. Novus, 63166.
David Sanchez. *Street Scenes*. Columbia, 67627.
Dexter Gordon. *Doin' Alright*. Blue Note, 84077.
Dexter Gordon. *Settin' the Pace*. Savoy, 17027.
Dizzy Gillespie. *The Complete RCA Victor Recordings*. Bluebird, 66528, 2 CDs.
Dizzy Gillespie. *At Newport*. Verve, 314 513 754.
Dizzy Gillespie. *With Roy Eldridge*. Verve, 314 521 647.
Dizzy Gillespie. *Sonny Side Up*. Verve, 825 674.
Eddie Daniels. *Breakthrough*. GRP, 9533.
Eddie Jefferson. *Letter from Home*. Original Jazz Classics, 307.

Eddie Palmieri. *Arete*. RMM, 81657.

Erroll Garner. *The Complete Savoy Master Takes*. Savoy, 17025-26, 2 CDs.

Erroll Garner. *Concert by the Sea*. Columbia, 40859.

Fats Navarro. *Fats Navarro and Tadd Dameron*. Blue Note, 33373, 2 CDs.

Fats Navarro. *Goin' to Minton's*. Savoy, 92861.

Gene Ammons. *The Happy Blues*. Original Jazz Classics, 013.

George Shearing. *Jazz Masters 57*. Verve, 314 529 900.

Gonzalo Rubalcaba. *The Blessing*. Blue Note, 97197.

Gunther Schuller. *The Birth of the Third Stream*. Sony, 64929.

Helen Merrill. *With Clifford Brown*. Emarcy, 534 435.

Howard McGhee. *1948*. Classics, 1058.

June Christy. *Something Cool*. Capitol, 96329.

King Pleasure Sings/Annie Ross Sings. Original Jazz Classics, 217.

Lambert, Hendricks, and Ross. *The Hottest New Group in Jazz*. Columbia/Legacy, 64933, 2 CDs.

Lennie Tristano/Warne Marsh. *Intuition*. Blue Note, 52771.

Machito. *Mucho Mucho*. Pablo, 2625-712.

Miles Davis. *The Complete Birth of the Cool*. Capitol, 94550.

Modern Jazz Quartet. *The Last Concert*. Atlantic, 72189, 2 CDs.

Mongo Santamaria. *Watermelon Man*. Milestone, 47075.

Oscar Peterson. *Stratford Shakespearean Festival*. Verve, 314 513 752.

Oscar Peterson. *Trio Plus One*. Verve, 818 840.

Paquito D'Rivera. *40 Years of Cuban Jam Sessions*. Messidor, 15826.

Paul Quinichette. *For Basie*. Original Jazz Classics, 978.

Sarah Vaughan. *With Clifford Brown*. Emarcy, 814 641.

Sarah Vaughan. *No Count Sarah*. Emarcy, 824 057.

Sarah Vaughan. *Young Sassy*. Proper Box, 1027, 4 CDs.

Serge Chaloff. *The Fable of Mable*. Black Lion, 60923.

Sonny Stitt. *Endgame Brilliance*. 32 Jazz, 32009, 2 CDs.

Sonny Stitt/Bud Powell/J. J. Johnson. Original Jazz Classics, 009.

Stan Getz. *The Complete Roost Recordings*. Roulette, 59622, 3 CDs.

Thelonious Monk. *Big Band and Quartet in Concert*. Columbia/Legacy, 57636, 2 CDs.

Thelonious Monk. *Brilliant Corners*. Original Jazz Classics, 026.

Thelonious Monk. *The Complete Blue Note Recordings*. Blue Note, 30363, 4 CDs.

Tito Puente. *On Broadway*. Concord Picante, 4207.

Tito Rodriguez. *Tito Tito Tito*. Palladium, 139.

Woody Herman. *Keeper of the Flame*. Capitol, 98453.

Woody Herman. *The Thundering Herds 1945–1947*. Columbia, 44108.

Zoot Sims. *Zoot Sims and the Gershwin Brothers*. Original Jazz Classics, 444.

7

Los Angeles: West Coast Cool Jazz

JAZZ ON THE LEFT COAST

Cool jazz was one of the most popular jazz styles of the 1950s. Not all of the cool jazz leaders were based in California, and not all of the jazz there during the era was cool jazz; but the music made its greatest impact and reached the height of its popularity in Los Angeles.

Throughout jazz history, an extroverted musician's innovations have often been followed by those of a quieter, "cooler" stylist. Some examples are Louis Armstrong whose flamboyant personality and innovations were followed by the more subdued Bix Beiderbecke, Art Tatum and Teddy Wilson, Coleman Hawkins and Lester Young, and Dizzy Gillespie and Miles Davis. Cool jazz of the 1950s was in some ways a reaction to bebop, utilizing bop's harmonic complexity, but bringing back a few as pects from swing. The tones of the horns became softer, the volume quieter, the tempos usually slower, and the rhythms lighter and less jarring. Arrangements became important again, even in small groups, and the music was more accessible in general than bop.

Cool jazz began with the music of the John Kirby Sextet during the swing era, the Claude Thornhill Orchestra, and Lester Young's mellow-toned tenor, which became very influential by the late 1940s. As mentioned in chapter six, just three years after bebop made a big impact on jazz, Miles Davis formed his famous nonet, later billed "The Birth of the Cool." Pianist Lennie Tristano and his sidemen, including altoist Lee Konitz and tenor-saxophonist Warne Marsh, performed a variation on cool jazz, emphasizing melodic and harmonic sophistication while keeping the rhythm section in a quiet timekeeping role. It set the stage for what was to happen in Los Angeles.

AN UNDERRATED STYLE

The founder of "cool jazz," Lester Young was always the epitome of restrained hipness, both musically and in his personality.
Photo courtesy of the Wayne Knight Collection, Star Line Productions.

Although the recordings of the Miles Davis Nonet and Lennie Tristano were made in New York, cool jazz really caught fire on the West Coast, particularly Los Angeles during 1952 and 1953, with the success of Gerry Mulligan's pianoless quartet with Chet Baker, Howard Rumsey's Lighthouse All-Stars, and the recording bands headed by Shorty Rogers. At this time jazz started appearing much more regularly in Hollywood motion picture soundtracks where the cool jazz style fit in quite well with its subtlety, tight arrangements, and dramatic solos. Such groups as Shorty Rogers' Giants, the Jimmy Giuffre 3, Shelly Manne and His Men, and the Dave Pell Octet all worked regularly on the West Coast and contributed to the legacy of cool. In addition other cool jazz groups not based in Los Angeles, such as the Modern Jazz Quartet, Stan Getz's combos, and the Dave Brubeck Quartet that started in northern California, helped make the idiom into a viable style. The rise of the LP, which became common in 1949 and completely took over from 78s by 1953, led to a booming record industry, and new labels such as Contemporary, Pacific Jazz, and Nocturne documented scores of significant West Coast jazz sessions.

Despite all of the fine music, cool jazz has been underrated and sometimes dismissed outright in jazz history books. There are three main reasons for its critical neglect. First, the music was not centered in New York, so critics and jazz journalists who feel that all significant post-1930 jazz has to be based there to be taken seriously either overly criticized the music or ignored it.

Second, many of the cool jazz leaders, unlike those in most other styles of jazz, were white. This was not due to segregation in the jazz world; in fact mixed groups became more common in the 1950s and predated the civil rights movement. It was due to the segregation in the movie and television studios. Many big band veterans, particularly former members of the Stan Kenton and Woody

Herman orchestras, settled in Los Angeles to work at lucrative day jobs in the studios, playing jazz at night. Because arrangers and expert sight-readers were in great demand, and the studios with a few exceptions were closed to black musicians, there was a concentration of white jazz musicians and writers in Los Angeles during the era, many involved in cool jazz.

The third reason for cool jazz being underrated is that some cool jazz performances were overarranged and as close to background music as to jazz, deserving to be criticized as bland and unadventurous. The best cool jazz, however, perfectly balanced concise solos with colorful arrangements and lively harmonies.

JAZZ IN LOS ANGELES BEFORE COOL JAZZ

Los Angeles had its own viable jazz scene from 1920 to 1950, even if no major new style was born in that region. As early as 1909, New Orleans bassist Bill Johnson was playing and leading a band in the Los Angeles area. Five years later he sent for cornetist Freddie Keppard and other top New Orleans players, forming the Original Creole Orchestra, which played the vaudeville circuit in Los Angeles before moving elsewhere. Pianist-composer Jelly Roll Morton was based mostly in Los Angeles from 1917 to 1922, and King Oliver took a successful West Coast tour with his Creole Jazz Band in 1921. The first jazz instrumental recordings by a black New Orleans band took place in Los Angeles by 1922 as trombonist Kid Ory, leading a group named Spike's Seven Pods of Pepper Orchestra, recorded "Ory's Creole Trombone" and "Society Blues."

During the 1920s a strong local jazz scene formed on Central Avenue, which at its prime was Los Angeles' equivalent to New York's Fifty-second Street, with quite a few major clubs lining both sides of the street. The difference was that Fifty-second Street was generally more integrated, but Central Avenue was dominated by black performers. Central Avenue actually outlasted Fifty-second Street, remaining a significant center for jazz into the early 1950s.

Los Angeles in the late 1920s had such major groups as Paul Howard's Quality Serenaders with drummer Lionel Hampton, Curtis Mosby's Blue Blowers, and Sonny Clay's Plantation Orchestra, but during the swing era its local big bands paled next to the major orchestras from New York. Still Los Angeles has the distinction of having officially launched the swing era when Benny Goodman was given a sensation reception at the Palomar Ballroom.

One of the most important groups to be born in Los Angeles during the swing years was the King Cole Trio. Nat King Cole, who was born in Montgomery, Alabama, grew up in Chicago where he enjoyed hearing radio broadcasts by his main influence, pianist Earl Hines. Cole first recorded with his brother bassist Eddie Cole's Solid Swingers in 1936. Two of his other brothers, pianist Ike and pianist-singer Freddie Cole, also became musicians. After touring with a revue that broke up in Los Angeles in 1937, Cole settled in the city. He formed the King Cole Trio with guitarist Oscar Moore and bassist Wesley

Nat King Cole first came to fame in Los Angeles as the pianist and occasional singer of the King Cole Trio.
Photo courtesy of the Wayne Knight Collection, Star Line Productions.

Prince. They recorded an extensive series of radio transcriptions from 1938 to 1941 and made their first official studio recordings in the latter two years, including "This Will Make You Laugh," "Hit That Jive Jack," and "Sweet Lorraine," Nat King Cole's first solo vocal. These and many other records showed him to be one of the best jazz pianists of the later swing era.

The King Cole Trio grew in popularity throughout the 1940s and eventually inspired other drumless piano-guitar-bass trios, including groups led by Art Tatum, Oscar Peterson, and Ahmad Jamal. While in its early period, the trio often featured group vocals, but it was becoming obvious by 1946 that Cole's singing was a major factor in the group becoming nationally famous. Among the many hits were "Straighten Up and Fly Right," "It's Only a Paper Moon," "The Frim Fram Sauce," "For Sentimental Reasons," "Come to Baby, Do," the original version of Bobby Troup's "Route 66," "The Christmas Song," and "Nature Boy." The trio's personnel changed with Irving Ashby taking over on guitar in 1947, then expanded to a quartet when Jack Costanzo was added on bongos.

A much bigger change took place when Nat Cole recorded "Mona Lisa" in 1950 with a large orchestra. The song, which contained no piano playing by Cole, became a number one hit, speeding up his evolution from a jazz pianist to a pop crooner. His trio merely became his rhythm section, often buried in a much larger orchestra. Cole only played piano as a novelty and for special projects, shifting the focus entirely to his soothing and likable vocals. By 1955 most of Nat King Cole's fans did not even know that he had once been a major pianist. He enjoyed great commercial success until his death from lung cancer in 1965.

Although swing groups did well in Los Angeles and on Central Avenue, it took longer for bebop to catch on. In the fall of 1945, Gillespie and Parker traveled to Hollywood, but their music had never been heard before on the West Coast, and their audiences were small and indifferent. For some of the young local musicians, however, the visit of Parker and Gillespie was an important and inspiring event. Also significant was an earlier visit by the Coleman Hawkins Sextet, because Hawk's trumpeter Howard McGhee decided to stay in Los Angeles, where he led boppish combos that demonstrated the style to local players.

By 1947 the Central Avenue club scene featured many bop groups, and Los Angeles was nearly on par with New York. During this period Los Angeles was particularly strong in tenor saxophonists. Dexter Gordon spent 1946 to 1949 based in his native Los Angeles, often engaging in saxophone battles on Central Avenue with Wardell Gray and Teddy Edwards. Gray's recording of "The Chase" is a good example of how the tenor battles sounded.

Teddy Edwards should have been as famous as Gordon, but he chose to spend most of his life in Los Angeles and never garnered many headlines. Born in Jackson, Mississippi, Edwards started playing professionally in 1936 when he was just twelve. After freelancing on clarinet and alto, he switched to tenor and moved to Los Angles in 1945. Edwards worked with Howard McGhee and was part of the jam sessions on Central Avenue. A natural-born leader, Edwards mostly led his own combos throughout his career, providing not just the tenor solos but arrangements and compositions. His best-known song was "Sunset Eyes." Teddy Edwards was a major force on the West Coast jazz until his death in 2003.

STAN KENTON

Stan Kenton had an unusual career. He had little interest in leading a swinging big band for dancers because his goal was to have a concert orchestra.

Despite his noncommercial goals and the complex music that he often performed, Kenton kept his big band together whenever he wanted throughout his career, when not on a voluntary sabbatical, becoming both a household name and a cult figure.

Born in Wichita, Kansas, Kenton grew up in California and played piano; Earl Hines was his main influence. Never a virtuoso or a major soloist, Kenton nevertheless had little difficulty finding work in the Los Angeles area, and during the 1930s he also developed into a skilled arranger. In 1940 when he was twenty-eight, he organized his first rehearsal band. The next summer the Stan Kenton Orchestra made a strong impression playing regularly at the Rendezvous Ballroom in Balboa Beach near Los Angeles.

Even at that early stage, the Kenton band had its own sound with a screaming brass section, thick-toned tenors, and ambitious arrangements. The orchestra recorded nine selections during 1941 and 1942, but none sold that well. A gig as the house band on the Bob Hope radio show was unsatisfying. Kenton wanted his band to be featured much more rather than backing someone else, but Les Brown would eventually get the job.

Much more important was landing a contract with the Capitol label in late 1943. Kenton's recording of "Eager Beaver" sold well, as did his waxing of his theme song "Artistry in Rhythm" and the vocals of Anita O'Day. By 1945 Kenton had a major band. Pete Rugolo was Kenton's main arranger, extending the leader's ideas and creating a series of ambitious works. Vido Musso and the softer-toned Bob Cooper gave Kenton two major tenor sax soloists, while June Christy's popular vocals, including "Tampico" and "Across the Alley from the Alamo," helped keep the band solvent. Kenton called this period of his band's music "progressive jazz."

In 1947 Kai Winding, who made the trombone a major instrument in Kenton's ensembles, joined the band's key players, including altoist Art Pepper, bassist Ed Safranski, drummer Shelly Manne, and high-note trumpeters Ray Wetzel and Al Porcino. Certainly the arrangements, which could be bombastic, of such tunes as "Southern Scandal," "Opus in Pastels," the catchy "Intermission Riff," "Artistry in Percussion," "Concerto to End All Concertos," "Monotony," "Elegy for Alto,"

Stan Kenton's "progressive jazz" was either loved or despised but never ignored.
Photo courtesy of the Wayne Knight Collection, Star Line Productions.

"Thermopylae," and the riotous "The Peanut Vendor" gave the versatile Kenton band its own unique sound and musical personality. Although influenced by bebop, it was not really bop or swing but a new kind of "progressive jazz," one that did not mind sacrificing swinging for dense ensembles and unusual sounds.

By the end of 1948, Kenton was exhausted, so he broke up his big band and took a year off. In 1950 he came back with his most radical band, the thirty-nine-piece Innovations in Modern Music. The huge ensemble, which had sixteen strings, two French horns, and a woodwind section, performed modern classical charts leavened by an occasional swinger. Although it included the high-note trumpeter Maynard Ferguson, altoists Art Pepper and Bud Shank, Bob Cooper, guitarist Laurindo Almeida, Shelly Manne, and June Christy in its personnel, it did not survive. Two tours and some remarkable recordings resulted before Kenton cut back to back to a more conventional nineteen-piece big band.

Considering the extroverted, occasionally bombastic, and intense music that Stan Kenton's orchestra created, it is ironic that many of its players, when they settled in Los Angeles after touring, became prime exponents of cool jazz.

For the remainder of the 1950s Kenton once again confounded expectations and led his most swinging bands. Although some of the arrangements were very complex as usual, others let the musicians stretch out. Many all-stars passed through the orchestra, including trumpeters Conte Candoli, Sam Noto, and Jack Sheldon; trombonists Frank Rosolino and Carl Fontana; altoists Lee Konitz and Charlie Mariano; tenors Richie Kamuca, Zoot Sims, Bill Perkins, Arno Marsh, and Lucky Thompson; and baritonist Pepper Adams. Kenton always encouraged arrangers to contribute to his library, and among the better writers were Shorty Rogers, Gerry Mulligan, Lennie Niehaus, Marty Paich, Johnny Richards, the radical Bob Graettinger, and especially Bill Holman and Bill Russo.

From 1960 to 1963 Kenton had his last major band, a unit that featured four mellophoniums, which sounded a bit like French horns. After 1963 Stan Kenton's orchestra declined in originality, while he became quite significant as an educator. Because his big band worked closely with college and high school musicians in band camps and fought to get jazz taught in school, many of the resulting college bands sounded a lot like the Kenton Orchestra. At the same time, Kenton's own orchestra became filled with recent college graduates who were eager to learn and were relatively inexpensive, so his outfit sounded like a professional stage band rather than an innovative orchestra. Instead of his sidemen considering their period with Kenton to be an early step in an important jazz career, many of them it was the highpoint of their playing days before they became college educators.

Stan Kenton continued touring with his big band until shortly before his death in 1979, having made a major contribution to jazz during the preceding forty years.

GERRY MULLIGAN AND CHET BAKER

Although the Claude Thornhill Orchestra, the Miles Davis Nonet, and Lennie Tristano all developed their music on the East Coast, the first superstars of West Coast jazz were Gerry Mulligan and Chet Baker. Mulligan was actually born in New York and spent relatively little time on the West Coast. He started on piano and clarinet before switching to saxophones, not settling permanently on baritone until he was twenty-one in 1948. In his early days, Mulligan was better known as an arranger than as a soloist, contributing music to a variety of big bands, most notably those of Claude Thornhill and Gene Krupa, starting in 1946. In 1948 he became part of the Miles Davis Nonet, providing some of the charts and playing baritone with the group.

Mulligan was still relatively unknown when he hitchhiked his way to Los Angeles in the fall of 1951. At first he wrote some arrangements for Stan Kenton and worked at the Lighthouse. He began a more important regular Monday night engagement at the Haig. Because his group was playing opposite that of Red Norvo whose vibes took up a large part of the stage, Mulligan decided to experiment by leading a group without a piano. The baritonist enjoyed the

Baritonist Gerry Mulligan played his horn with the lightness of an alto.
Photo courtesy of the Wayne Knight Collection, Star Line Productions.

freedom from the piano's constant chord statements, and he soon realized that, musically at least, he and trumpeter Chet Baker often thought alike.

Chet Baker, who was from Oklahoma, moved to California by 1940. In 1952 he started his career at the top by impressing Charlie Parker at an audition and working with him in Los Angeles. Baker emphasized his middle register and had a thoughtful and relaxed style that Mulligan discovered meshed perfectly with his approach.

To everyone's surprise, the Gerry Mulligan Quartet, with Bob Whitlock or Carson Smith on bass and Chico Hamilton or Larry Bunker on drums, became a national sensation. Dick Bock started the Pacific Jazz label originally to record Mulligan's group. Among the classic recordings by the group were "Bernie's Tune," "Nights at the Turntable," "Walkin' Shoes," "Line for Lyons," "Bark for Barksdale," and "My Funny Valentine," a song that would always be associated with Baker.

The band lasted until the summer of 1953 when Mulligan was arrested for possession of heroin. By the time the baritonist was released in the spring of 1954, Baker had built upon his success with his own quartet and the Mulligan-Baker collaboration was in the past. They only had two brief reunions in future years.

Gerry Mulligan continued as a major name and an influential force throughout his long career. His sound on baritone was much lighter than that of Harry Carney, almost sounding like a tenor at times, and his solos were full of his sly humor. Mulligan led one impressive group after another, including a pianoless quartet with valve trombonist Bob Brookmeyer, a 1959 quartet with trumpeter Art Farmer, his Concert Jazz Band from 1960 to 1964, and a pianoless sextet with Brookmeyer, trumpeter Jon Eardley, and tenor-saxophonist Zoot Sims. The latter was a big band featuring arrangements by Mulligan and Brookmeyer. He also shared albums with some of his favorite players including altoists Paul Desmond and Johnny Hodges, pianist Thelonious Monk, and tenors Stan Getz and Ben Webster. Mulligan toured with the Dave Brubeck Quartet from 1968 to 1972, led a new big band called The Age of Steam, toured with a quartet that did include piano, and led a Rebirth of the Cool band that revived the music of the Miles Davis Nonet. Gerry Mulligan stayed quite active until his death at age sixty-eight in 1996.

Chet Baker had a roller-coaster life and career. After Mulligan was jailed, Baker formed a quartet that featured pianist Russ Freeman. His popularity really rose in 1955 when he started singing in a limited and vulnerable high-pitched voice that appealed to a large female audience. Soon he was winning popularity polls, even though his trumpet playing could not compare to that of Dizzy Gillespie and Clifford Brown. With his good looks, Baker could have become a movie star, and Hollywood was showing some interest. But after a European tour in late 1955 and early 1956, Baker became a heroin addict, having not learned from the examples of Mulligan and the recently deceased Charlie Parker.

Baker played well during the mid- to late 1950s, but his lifestyle as an unapologetic drug addict began to seriously affect his career, with occasional busts damaging his reputation. In 1959 he moved to Europe where he worked steadily for a few months before getting arrested for drugs and spent time in an Italian jail. After his release, he was temporarily clean and played quite well, but was soon on heroin again. He returned to the United States, made a few fine records in the mid-1960s, scuffled a bit, and then hit a low point in 1968 when his teeth were knocked out during a botched drug deal. Miraculously, particularly for a trumpeter, Baker made a gradual comeback and by 1974 was recording and gigging again, soon moving permanently to Europe. By 1976 Baker's vocalizing and general appearance had seriously declined, but amazingly his trumpet playing was often quite strong during this final period. Chet Baker lived as a nomad, without a home or even a checking account during his last decade, never trying to kick drugs or organize his chaotic life. He died in 1988 at the age of fifty-eight, after either falling or pushed out of a window in Amsterdam.

HOWARD RUMSEY'S LIGHTHOUSE ALL-STARS

While Gerry Mulligan and Chet Baker were the first cool jazz celebrities, West Coast jazz had been played in Los Angeles for a few years before they made it big in 1952. Howard Rumsey, the original bassist with the Stan Kenton Orchestra, moved to Los Angeles after leaving Kenton in the mid-1940s. In 1949 he convinced the owner of the Lighthouse, an establishment in Hermosa Beach near Los Angeles, to feature jazz by his pickup group on Sundays. Within two years Rumsey's band, renamed the Lighthouse All-Stars, was playing nightly at the club, with its marathon Sunday sessions from 2:00 p.m. to 2:00 a.m. becoming particularly legendary, or from the musicians' standpoint, infamous.

The Lighthouse All-Stars first recorded in 1952 when it comprised trumpeter Shorty Rogers, trombonist Milt Bernhart, Bob Cooper and Jimmy Giuffre on tenors, pianist Frank Patchen, drummer Shelly Manne, and Rumsey. The band's string of recordings for the new Contemporary label made it famous, and it worked steadily throughout the 1950s. Among its many key players at this time were trumpeters Rolf Ericson and Conte Candoli, Stu Williamson on trumpet and valve trombone, trombonist Frank Rosolino, Bob Enevoldsen on tenor and valve trombonist, Bud Shank on alto and flute, altoist Herb Geller, Bob Cooper on tenor, oboe, and English horn, pianists Marty Paich, Claude Williamson, and Dick Shreve, and drummers Max Roach and Stan Levey. The band, with its "coolest" music during the Rogers-Giuffre period and when Cooper and Shank played oboe and flute together, gradually became a hard bop band when the cool jazz era ended.

By the early 1960s, all of the group's main sidemen had their own solo careers, and the Lighthouse All-Stars was no more. Rumsey retired from playing bass, booked other major groups at the Lighthouse, and switched to managing a nearby club, Concerts by the Sea. The Lighthouse All-Stars was revived in the 1980s as an all-star band that included Rogers, Candoli, Cooper, Shank, pianist Pete Jolly, bassist Monty Budwig, and drummer Larance Marable, but that was only a short-term project that hinted at the band's past glories.

SHORTY ROGERS AND HIS GIANTS

Shorty Rogers was a major force in the West Coast jazz scene as a trumpeter, arranger, composer, bandleader, and as an organizer and catalyst of sessions and events. His middle-register trumpet solos were definitive of the idiom, and he led bands for his own records and in the studios. Born Milton Rajonsky, he gained some early recognition as a trumpeter and arranger with Woody Herman's First Herd and Second Herd and with Stan Kenton's Innovations Orchestra in 1950 and 1951. Rogers settled in Los Angeles in 1952 where he was a member of the Lighthouse All-Stars before leading his own band, Shorty Rogers and His Giants, starting in 1953. He was significant in getting jazz music onto soundtracks, starting with Marlon Brando's *The Wild One*, and jazz musicians into the commercial studios.

Rogers' first recording as a leader in 1951 is closely based on the style and instrumentation of the Miles Davis Nonet, but his later record dates range from big bands to a notable mid-1950s quintet, also featuring Pete Jolly, bassists Curtis Counce and Shelly Manne, and Jimmy Giuffre on tenor, clarinet, and baritone. Each of those performers in time became bandleaders. Most of the West Coast jazz all-stars of the 1950s worked for Rogers at one time or another, as he kept the local musicians very busy. After 1962 Rogers stopped playing for twenty years because he was in such demand as a writer in the studios, working on television and films. In 1982 he became active as a player again, reorganizing the Lighthouse All-Stars and mostly playing flugelhorn during his last decade before passing away in 1994.

SHELLY MANNE AND HIS MEN

Shelly Manne, a very versatile drummer, was underrated except by other musicians. Although he started as a saxophonist, Manne switched to drums when he was eighteen in 1938. He played with several swing groups and big bands before making his mark with two of Stan Kenton's top orchestras from 1946 to 1948 and in 1950 and 1951.

Manne settled in Los Angeles in December 1951, worked with the Lighthouse All-Stars and played with Shorty Rogers' Giants during 1953 to 1955. During this period he became one of the busiest of all studio drummers, participating in countless record dates. Two of the most interesting are from 1954 and hint at the avant-garde of the future. One session has Manne in a trio with Rogers and Jimmy Giuffre with no piano or bass, some of the six numbers being freely improvised. The other is a set of duets with pianist Russ Freeman that is also quite advanced and unpredictable.

In 1955 he formed the quintet Shelly Manne and His Men to play in public, and in 1960 he opened up his own club in Hollywood, Shelly's Manne-Hole. His bands through the years featured such top players as trumpeters Stu Williamson, Conte Candoli, and Joe Gordon, valve trombonist Bob Enevoldsen, altoists Joe Maini, Charlie Mariano, Herb Geller, and Frank Strozier, tenors Bill Holman and Richie Kamuca, pianists Russ Freeman and Mike Wofford, and bassists Ralph Pena, Leroy Vinnegar, Chuck Berghofer, and Monty Budwig. Manne also had the good fortune of being the leader of a trio with pianist Andre Previn and bassist Vinnegar that recorded songs from the play *My Fair Lady*. That album was such a big seller in the late 1950s that it launched a series of jazz albums of scores taken from various musicals, films, and television shows.

While Shelly Manne's groups were associated with the West Coast jazz movement during the 1950s, by the end of the decade his bands had a harder sound that fit much more into hard bop than cool jazz. Manne remained a very popular and busy drummer until his death in 1984.

THE JIMMY GIUFFRE 3

While many of the leaders of cool jazz, particularly those based on the West Coast, shifted to hard bop by the end of the 1950s, Jimmy Giuffre went in another direction altogether. Giuffre, who had soft, cool tones on clarinet, tenor, and baritone, played with the big bands of Boyd Raeburn, Jimmy Dorsey, and Buddy Rich. His composition "Four Brothers" became a hit for Woody Herman, and two years later he spent a few months as a member of Herman's Second Herd in 1949. After moving to Los Angeles, Giuffre worked with Howard Rumsey's Lighthouse All-Stars in 1951 and 1952 and Shorty Rogers' Giants from 1952 to 1956, leading his own record dates starting in 1954.

Giuffre was a quiet improviser who made every note count and was not shy to take chances. He often stuck to the lower register of his clarinet, and on some of his early records as a leader, the music is atonal in spots. After leaving Rogers, he formed the Jimmy Giuffre 3, which originally included guitarist Jim Hall and bassist Ralph Pena. Giuffre had a minor hit with "The Train and the River," a folk song that emphasized the picturesque melody and featured the leader switching between his three horns. In 1958 he led a particularly unusual trio with Hall and valve trombonist Bob Brookmeyer, one that did not use piano, bass, or drums. The group sometimes played free improvisations in concert although its recordings stuck to tunes. Brookmeyer did not stay too long, and Giuffre went back to leading reeds-guitar-bass trios for a time, cool jazz that looked towards the future. From 1961 to 1963, the Jimmy Giuffre 3 included pianist Paul Bley and bassist Steve Swallow. Their music was still quiet and mostly gentle with an emphasis on space, but the avant-garde explorations mystified audiences who expected to hear Giuffre embracing melodies rather than playing free jazz.

After 1963 Jimmy Giuffre primarily worked as an educator, occasionally reappearing on the scene during the next thirty-five years, including reunion tours and further recordings with Bley and Swallow, always going his own way musically.

THE CHICO HAMILTON QUINTET

Drummer Chico Hamilton had extensive experience before the cool jazz era began. He recorded with Slim Gaillard, toured with Lionel Hampton, and worked with Lester Young and Lena Horne. Hamilton was an original member of the Gerry Mulligan quartet during 1952 and 1953 where his flawless time and subtlety were greatly appreciated.

In 1955 Hamilton formed a chamber jazz group with Buddy Collette on reeds—flute, alto, tenor, and clarinet—guitarist Jim Hall, bassist Carson Smith and, most importantly, cellist Fred Katz. The latter's ability to improvise gave the group its own sound, as did Collette's versatility. The band's debut recording, which includes "A Nice Day," "Blue Sands," and "My Funny Valentine," is considered a classic. Initially based in Los Angeles, the Chico Hamilton Quintet became very popular, and there was strong interest in the group traveling east. Because Collette was helping to integrate the studios in Los Angeles, he dropped out of the group, being succeeded by Paul Horn, with John Pisano soon taking Jim Hall's place. There was no real change in the group's sound until the spring of 1958 when Eric Dolphy on flute, alto, and bass clarinet took over Horn's spot, and the new cellist was Nate Gershman, a classical player who did not improvise.

In late 1959 Dolphy departed, replaced by Charles Lloyd. By then the concept of the band was getting a bit old, and in the early 1960s Lloyd talked Hamilton into dropping the cello to add trombonist Garnett Brown. With Hungarian guitarist Gabor Szabo also in the band, the quintet was now radically different from the 1955 group, leaning more toward post-bop and being influenced by John Coltrane. The Chico Hamilton Quintet broke up in 1966. Hamilton, now in his early eighties, has stayed active, freelancing and leading adventurous combos.

THE DAVE PELL OCTET

Unlike the Jimmy Giuffre 3 and the Chico Hamilton Quintet, the Dave Pell Octet never attempted to move beyond West Coast jazz. In fact Pell's group defined the style with its modern harmonies, restrained ensembles, soft tones, and swing repertoire. Pell played with several big bands before becoming the tenor soloist with the Les Brown Orchestra from 1947 to 1955. He formed his own octet in 1953 from Brown's big band, and the combo was often featured during Les Brown concerts before it broke away in 1955. The octet in its prime also included trumpeter Don Fagerquist, trombonist Ray Sims, guitarist Tony Rizzi, bassist Rolly Bundock, drummer Jack Sperling, singer Lucy Ann Polk, several pianists, and Ronny Lang on baritone, alto, and flute. With arrangements by Shorty Rogers, Wes Hensel, Bill Holman, Jack Montrose, and Med Flory among others, the Dave Pell Octet sounded beautiful on such numbers as "Mountain Greenery," "Aren't You Glad You're You," "Imagination," and "The Blue Room." After the era ended, Pell broke up the octet and primarily worked as a record producer, including pop and rock music. He never lost his love for jazz, however, had a group in the 1970s called Prez Conference that played Lester Young solos, and in the 1980s revived the Dave Pell Octet. Usually featuring trumpeter Carl Saunders, the octet still performs on a regular basis in the Los Angeles area, keeping the legacy of cool jazz alive.

THE DAVE BRUBECK QUARTET

Dave Brubeck is one of those fortunate individuals who has been able to become prosperous and famous while playing the music he loves throughout his career without any compromise. From northern California, he was never based in Los Angeles, but his music fit very easily into West Coast jazz. Born in 1920 in Concord, California, Brubeck received classical piano training from his mother but had such a good ear that he merely duplicated what she played. He studied music at the College of the Pacific from 1938 to 1942 and had nearly received a music degree before it was discovered that he still did not know how to read music! Brubeck soon reluctantly learned. After serving in the army, in 1946 he started studying at Mills College with classical composer Darius Milhaud, who encouraged his students to use their classical training in playing jazz.

Brubeck was always interested in polyrhythms—playing two or three rhythms at once—and polytonality—performing in two keys at once—having a strikingly original style from an early age. He led the Dave Brubeck Octet from 1946 to 1949, a group mostly comprising fellow classmates, including altoist Paul Desmond and drummer Cal Tjader. The band's music was very radical, still sounding advanced today, often employing unusual time signatures and polytonality. Although the octet recorded one album, it rarely ever worked in public, so in 1949 Brubeck formed a trio with Tjader, doubling on vibes, and bassist Ron Crotty. That group was popular and on the brink of great success when Brubeck hurt his back during a serious swimming accident that put him out of action for several months in 1951.

When Brubeck returned, Paul Desmond talked him into forming a quartet. Desmond, with a very light tone on the alto, was a witty and melodic improviser whose sound was a major contrast to the much heavier chord-based playing of Brubeck. Desmond once explained that he wanted to sound like a dry martini. At first critics hailed the group as a fresh new voice, but as the quartet became very popular, they criticized Brubeck for his heavy approach and for not

The classic Dave Brubeck Quartet with Paul Desmond, Joe Morello, and Eugene Wright.
Photo courtesy of the Wayne Knight Collection, Star Line Productions.

sounding like Bud Powell. The pianist nevertheless went his own way and out-lasted his critics. Among the first jazz groups to be booked regularly on college campuses, the Dave Brubeck Quartet built up a large and enthusiastic audience, and by 1954 they were signed to Columbia, one of the era's most prestigious record labels. That year Brubeck appeared on the cover of *Time* magazine.

The Brubeck Quartet mixed together leader's originals, including "In Your Own Sweet Way" and "The Duke," with their own swinging versions of standards. Brubeck and Desmond brought out the best in each other. Originally the group featured quiet rhythm sections that for a period included drummer Joe Dodge. In 1956 the virtuosic drummer Joe Morello succeeded Dodge, and in 1958 Eugene Wright became the band's bassist.

Since Morello was adept at playing in different time signatures, he had no difficulty on Desmond's new tune in 1959, "Take Five," that became a million seller. For a few albums, the Dave Brubeck Quartet featured unusual time signatures, including the 5/4 "Take Five" and "Blue Rondo à la Turk," which starts in 9/4 time before becoming a 4/4 blues. The band's popularity continued growing in the 1960s, and they were a fixture at jazz festivals and major clubs. By 1967 Brubeck had tired of the constant traveling, and he broke up the quartet, partly to find time to write some classical-oriented religious works.

Brubeck was not off the jazz scene for long. Within a year he had a new quartet featuring Gerry Mulligan. He had several reunions with Desmond before the latter's death in 1977. Four of Brubeck's sons became musicians, and three were involved in his group Two Generations of Brubeck in the 1970s: keyboardist Darius Brubeck, Chris Brubeck on electric bass and bass trombone, and drummer Danny Brubeck. The youngest son, Matthew Brubeck, later became a cellist.

The Dave Brubeck Quartet featured tenor-saxophonist Jerry Bergonzi in the early 1980s, for many years had clarinetist Bill Smith as its horn, and during the past decade has usually featured altoist-flutist Bobby Militello. Brubeck has continued circling the globe, constantly performing and writing new compositions, up to the present time. Now in his eighties, Dave Brubeck is still enthusiastic about music and refuses to play it safe.

THE COOL JAZZ ALTOISTS

Art Pepper had a turbulent career similar to that of Chet Baker, except that no matter how bad his personal life was, his recordings were consistently brilliant. Pepper, although white, gained important experience playing with black groups on Los Angeles' Central Avenue in the 1940s and with Stan Kenton's orchestra at times during 1943 and 1947 to 1952. A heroin addict from an early age, Pepper had an erratic lifestyle, and he was in jail during two periods during 1953 to 1956. He recorded a series of classic albums for the Contemporary label in the 1950s including *Art Pepper + Eleven Plays Modern Jazz Classics*, which featured Marty Paich arrangements, and an encounter with Miles Davis' sidemen on *Meets the Rhythm Section*.

Pepper's career was interrupted with several long prison sentences in the 1960s. He had opportunities to play music while in prison, and during some of his brief releases, he showed that he was influenced by John Coltrane, adopting a harder tone and a much freer style. Pepper worked with Buddy Rich's big band in 1968 but then spent a few years trying to kick drugs and going through rehabilitation at Synanon. Due to the inspiration of his wife Laurie and very strong will power, Pepper had a major comeback starting in 1975. His solos during his final seven years were full of intensity and expression, ranking with some of the finest work, never coasting or sounding overly comfortable. Pepper played each solo as if it might be his last.

Another altoist, Herb Geller, combines Benny Carter and Charlie Parker in his solos. An important force in the Los Angeles area in the 1950s, he has lived in Europe, mostly Berlin, since 1962, growing as a boppish soloist and still playing at his prime today. Bud Shank was initially overshadowed by Pepper, working with Stan Kenton during 1950 and 1951 and with the Lighthouse All-Stars before heading his own groups. In the 1950s Shank had a very cool tone on alto and was skilled on flute too. He primarily played in the studios in the 1960s, then with guitarist Laurindo Almeida in the Los Angeles Four in the 1970s, and since giving up the flute in the mid-1980s, Shank has continued evolving as a major altoist, developing a much harder tone than in his early days.

Lennie Niehaus, although more important as an arranger, is also a top-notch West Coast–based alto saxophonist. He worked with Stan Kenton's band during two periods, led a series of excellent albums for the Contemporary label in the 1950s, then put his horn away for decades as he wrote for Hollywood movies, including quite a few Clint Eastwood films. In recent times he has resumed playing alto in his same timeless style of decades ago.

A FEW OTHER IMPORTANT WEST COAST JAZZ MUSICIANS

Many other musicians were involved in the prime years of cool jazz. Trumpeters looked towards the harmonically sophisticated Dizzy Gillespie and the mellow sounds of Miles Davis and Chet Baker for inspiration. Conte Candoli, who had played with the big bands of Woody Herman in 1944, 1945, and 1950 and Stan Kenton in 1948 and from 1952 to 1954, became one of the most popular Los Angeles–based trumpeters, playing with the Lighthouse All-Stars, the Terry Gibbs big band, the studios, and in a countless number of bop-oriented situations. Don Fagerquist had a soft tone but an underrated technique, being one of the stars of Dave Pell's octet during 1953 to 1959. Jack Sheldon, a boyhood friend of Chet Baker, could play anything from bop to Dixieland. His playing matured in the 1950s, and he has been very active ever since as a trumpeter with his own sound, a vocalist, a bandleader, and a hilarious, if generally off-color, comedian. He is still a great entertainer today.

Frank Rosolino was a very popular trombonist in the 1950s, always in demand for West Coast jazz dates. After playing with the big bands of Gene Krupa in 1948 and 1949, Stan Kenton from 1952 to 1954, and others, he worked with the Lighthouse All-Stars, in the studios, and wherever an extroverted and witty modern jazz trombonist was needed.

The top West Coast pianists managed to carve out their own voices from the Bud Powell style, including Hampton Hawes, Lou Levy, Pete Jolly, Claude Williamson, Carl Perkins, and Russ Freeman, who played with Chet Baker and Shelly Manne. Another was Vince Guaraldi who became famous in the 1960s for his jazz scores of the *Peanuts* cartoon series. Even Andre Previn, a precocious sixteen year old who wrote film scores in 1945, played a bit like Bud Powell during the era. Previn recorded a series of jazz dates, including Shelly Manne's hit record of *My Fair Lady*, before becoming more closely involved with the classical music world.

In the post–Jimmy Blanton era, bassists were still primarily responsible for keeping the rhythm steady, with their solo abilities being secondary. The bassists who were particularly active in the West Coast jazz scene never lacked for work: Red Callender, Monty Budwig, Leroy Vinnegar, Curtis Counce, and Red Mitchell, who was also a superior soloist, and others. They remained underrated parts of many ensembles. The role of the drummer in cool jazz was the same as in bop, except that the West Coast drummers tended to be quieter and smoother. Shelly Manne was the most famous Los Angeles–based drummer; the other key players included Stan Levey, Frank Butler, and Larance Marable.

The most famous singer to emerge during the cool jazz era was Mel Torme, one of the all-time great jazz vocalists. Torme first performed in public with the Coon-Sanders Orchestra in 1929 at the age of four. By the early 1940s he was working as a drummer in addition to singing and writing songs. When he was nineteen in 1945, he wrote "The Christmas Song," his most famous original. By then Torme was leading a vocal group, the Mel-Tones, and performing with Artie Shaw. He soon became a solo singer, performing both pop music and swing. One of his prime periods from the jazz standpoint was during 1956 to 1960 when he recorded regularly with a West Coast, cool jazz–style group, Marty Paich's Dek-tette. Torme survived a period of neglect to record a brilliant series of albums for the Concord label during 1983 to 1996 that found him excelling in jazz settings, including several albums with George Shearing. He was the only singer actually to improve while in his sixties. Only a stroke in 1996, which preceded his death by three years, stopped Torme. Whether scatting like Ella Fitzgerald or holding an endless long note on a ballad, Mel Torme, who was also a skilled arranger, composer, drummer and even pianist, ranked at the top of his field.

THE END OF COOL JAZZ

By the late 1950s cool jazz was rapidly running out of gas. Hard bop was taking over as the mainstream of jazz, avant-garde jazz was starting to make inroads, and the public's interest in West Coast jazz had dropped, although Dave Brubeck, Gerry Mulligan, and Chet Baker continued to be popular. Unlike most other jazz styles, West Coast jazz has largely ceased to exist as a separate style since 1960. It is occasionally revived at historic recreation concerts, often in the Los Angeles area, and its approach of tight arrangements, restrained sounds, and thoughtful solos have influenced later styles, including some avant-garde music, but the glory years of cool jazz, 1948 to 1960, are long gone.

LATER STYLES IN LOS ANGELES

While Los Angeles' role in jazz history was most significant during the 1950s cool jazz movement, other styles were affected by events in this area of the country. Free jazz is generally thought of as originating in New York, yet bassist Charles Mingus, multi-reedist Eric Dolphy, and altoist Ornette Coleman spent part of their formative years in Los Angeles, with Coleman recording his first two records for Contemporary before moving to New York. Los Angeles has had an underpublicized, but important avant-garde movement ever since with clarinetist John Carter, cornetist Bobby Bradford, pianist Horace Tapscott, bassist Roberto Miranda, and saxophonist Vinny Golia being among Los Angeles' unsung giants.

In the early 1970s pop/jazz, which later became known as smooth jazz, had some of its genesis in Los Angeles, particularly with the formation of saxophonist Tom Scott's L.A. Express. With the city's many studio top arrangers leading big bands part-time, some of the major jazz orchestras are based there, including those led by Gerald Wilson, Bill Holman, Bob Florence, Jack Sheldon, Tom Kubis, and Tom Talbert, plus the Clayton/Hamilton Jazz Orchestra.

Significant small group jazz also continues to invigorate the Los Angeles jazz scene, including interpretations of the great American songbook by the fine swing singer Judy Chamberlain, the inventive piano playing and arrangements of Bill Cunliffe, trios led by veteran pianists Page Cavanaugh and Pete Jolly, and such local heroes as trumpeter Carl Saunders, trombonist Andy Martin, tenor-saxophonist Pete Christlieb, and altoist Lanny Morgan.

Although New Yorkers often act as if the entire jazz world is confined to city limits, Los Angeles continues to have a viable and creative jazz scene in the twenty-first century, though it will probably always be best known for the cool jazz years.

RECOMMENDED RECORDINGS

Art Pepper. *Art Pepper + Eleven Plays Modern Jazz Classics*. Original Jazz Classics, 341.
Art Pepper. *Meets the Rhythm Section*. Original Jazz Classics, 338.
Chet Baker. *Chet Baker & Crew*. Pacific Jazz, 8267.
Chet Baker. *The Italian Sessions*. RCA/Bluebird, 68590.
Dave Brubeck. *At Carnegie Hall*. Sony, 61455, 2 CDs.
Dave Brubeck. *Jazz Goes to College*. Columbia/Legacy, 45149.
Dave Brubeck. *Time Out*. Columbia/Legacy, 65122.
Dave Pell. *Plays Rodgers and Hart*. Fresh Sound, 505.
Gerry Mulligan. *The Complete Pacific Jazz Recordings of the Gerry Mulligan Quartet with Chet Baker*. Pacific Jazz, 38263, 4 CDs.
Gerry Mulligan. *Concert Jazz Band at the Village Vanguard*. Verve, 589 488.
Herb Geller. *Herb Geller Quartet*. V.S.O.P., 89.
Horace Tapscott. *The Dark Tree Vol. 1*. Hat Art, 6053.
Howard Rumsey's Lighthouse All-Stars. *Music for Lighthousekeeping*. Original Jazz Classics, 636.
Jimmy Giuffre. *The Jimmy Giuffre 3/Music Man*. Collectables, 6248.
Mel Torme. *Lulu's Back in Town*. Bethlehem, 75732.
Mel Torme. *Night at the Concord Pavilion*. Concord Jazz, 4433.
Nat King Cole Trio. *Jumpin' at Capitol*. Rhino, 71009.
Shelly Manne. *My Fair Lady*. Original Jazz Classics, 336.
Shelly Manne. *Vol. 1: The West Coast Sound*. Original Jazz Classics, 152.
Shorty Rogers. *Martians Come Back/Way Up There*. Collectables, 6268.
Stan Kenton. *Retrospective*. Capitol, 97350, 4 CDs.
Vinny Golia. *Out for Blood*. Nine Winds, 0127.

8

New York: Hard Bop and Soul Jazz

WHAT IS HARD BOP?

Hard bop is sometimes referred to as a reaction to cool jazz, since white musicians dominated cool in Los Angeles, while primarily black musicians initially performed hard bop in New York. The hard bop supporters felt that cool had de-emphasized the blues too much, and they wanted to put more overt feeling and spontaneity back into the music. Hard bop was also a way for New York to again reign as the center of jazz, wresting control away from Los Angeles.

Hard bop, like cool jazz, was a natural outgrowth of bebop, rather than a radical new approach to playing music. Because it was the first style of jazz to fully take advantage of the LP, hard bop musicians were not restricted to the three minutes of a 78. LPs, which began replacing 78s in 1949 and completely took over the recording industry by the mid-1950s, frequently contained forty minutes of music, twenty minutes to a side. Soloists were therefore able to stretch out and build their improvisations slowly, rather than being forced to express all of their ideas in two choruses. Hard bop featured longer and simpler melody statements, much more freedom for string bassists who sometimes played catchy lines rather than being restricted to four-to-the-bar timekeeping, stronger interaction from the drummers, and generally a bluesier and more soulful approach than classic bebop. Particular emphasis was placed on developing a powerful tone, bending notes, infusing the performance with a blues feeling, and being open to the influence of church music while still swinging.

There is not one specific record session that stands out as the beginning of hard bop, although the 1952 and 1953 recordings of Miles Davis, an innovator in so many different styles, exhibit some early examples of the music and included two future hard bop leaders, pianist Horace Silver and drummer Art Blakey.

Classic bebop was largely frozen in time, the second half of the 1940s, but hard bop evolved during the 1950s and 1960s, in time utilizing modal improvising, playing off scales and staying longer on one chord, and more adventurous soloing influenced by the avant-garde. By 1960 hard bop was the modern mainstream of jazz and was even adopted by most of the West Coast jazz players.

CLIFFORD BROWN

A major transitional force between bebop and hard bop was trumpeter Clifford Brown, who fit easily into both styles with his very warm tone. Brown had complete control of his trumpet and could make the most difficult bop lines sound simple. He started playing trumpet in 1945 when he was fifteen and within three years was a professional musician with enormous potential, strongly influenced by Fats Navarro. Brown attended Maryland State University but was knocked out of action for most of a year after being seriously hurt in a car accident in June 1950. After he recovered he worked with Chris Powell's r&b band, the Blue Flames, in 1952 and then was ready to burst upon the jazz scene. In 1953 Brown worked and recorded with Tadd Dameron, made his first recordings as a leader, starred on sessions with altoist Lou Donaldson and trombonist J. J. Johnson, and played with Lionel Hampton's big band during the second half of the year. During a European tour, Hampton for unknown reasons forbade his sidemen to record, but most did anyway, resulting in the breakup of the band. Brown led dates with a quartet, sextet, and a big band while overseas, displaying his warmth on ballads and his creative imagination on up-tempo pieces.

Clifford Brown lived just long enough to be considered one of the greatest jazz trumpeters of all time.
Photo courtesy of the Wayne Knight Collection, Star Line Productions.

Back in the United States, Brown appeared at New York's Birdland as part of a quintet headed by Art Blakey and featuring

Donaldson, Horace Silver, and bassist Curly Russell. This engagement was extensively recorded and features Brownie in superb form. It also sounds as if Blakey were preparing to form his Jazz Messengers, though the trumpeter was never actually part of that group. In Los Angeles that summer, Brown did some local work and then formed a quintet that was co-led by drummer Max Roach. The band, whose personnel soon solidified around tenor-saxophonist Harold Land, bassist George Morrow, and pianist Richie Powell (Bud Powell's younger brother), became Brown's main association during what would be his final two years. The group, which recorded regularly for Emarcy, helped define the era, featuring originals including Brown's "Joy Spring" and "Daahoud" and spirited versions of bop standards. Brown also recorded a well-received album with strings.

When Land had to drop out of the group due to family problems in late 1955, he was replaced by Sonny Rollins, whose presence made the Clifford Brown/Max Roach Quintet into a true super group. Brown, who lived cleanly, was an inspiration to Rollins, who successfully kicked drugs, as was his musical consistency and brilliant playing. It all came to an end during the early morning hours of June 26, 1956. After playing at a recorded jam session in Philadelphia, Brown was riding in a car driven by the near-sighted wife of Richie Powell during a rainstorm when he was killed in a crash. In addition to pianist Powell and his wife, Clifford Brown, who was just twenty-five, died instantly.

After his death, Brown became the main influence on several generations of younger trumpeters including Lee Morgan, Freddie Hubbard, and Woody Shaw. Despite the passing of nearly a half century, Clifford Brown's playing has yet to be improved upon.

ART BLAKEY'S JAZZ MESSENGERS

When drummer Art Blakey and pianist Horace Silver formed the Jazz Messengers in 1954, hard bop had its leading group. Blakey, a top bebop musician whose explosive playing propelled the Billy Eckstine Big Band, had worked during 1951 to 1953 with clarinetist Buddy DeFranco and led a quintet at Birdland that featured Clifford Brown and Horace Silver. Tired of performing with pickup groups that merely jammed standards, Blakey wanted to form a band that emphasized new music and enthusiastic playing from young up-and-coming musicians. Silver, who was discovered by Stan Getz in 1951, had developed his own style inspired by Bud Powell, filling his solos with bluish phrases and witty references to other songs. A talented songwriter, he was the perfect musical partner for Blakey in founding the Jazz Messengers.

The original Jazz Messengers included trumpeter Kenny Dorham, tenor-saxophonist Hank Mobley, and bassist Doug Watkins. They performed Silver originals, including "The Preacher" and "Doodlin'," other songs from band members, and occasional standards. In 1956 Donald Byrd succeeded Dorham, and then the Jazz Messengers had a crisis. Silver had developed into too big a name to be just a co-leader, so he departed to form his own quintet, taking along Byrd, Mobley, and Watkins. Blakey had to start from scratch, but soon had formed the second version of the Jazz Messengers with trumpeter Bill Hardman, Johnny Griffin on tenor, pianist Sam Dockery, and bassist Spanky DeBrest. For the next thirty-four years, Art Blakey's Jazz Messengers was a type of jazz school where promising young musicians learned to swing hard and were encouraged to write new music. When Blakey felt that his sidemen were strong enough to become leaders themselves, he persuaded them to leave the group so he could informally tutor other young potential greats.

Drummer Art Blakey's Jazz Messengers served as a finishing school for young hard boppers for thirty-five years.
Photo courtesy of the Wayne Knight Collection, Star Line Productions.

After some struggling during its first couple years, Art Blakey's Jazz Messengers really caught on in 1958 with its Blue Note album *Moanin'*. By then its lineup consisted of trumpeter Lee Morgan, tenor Benny Golson, pianist Bobby Timmons, and bassist Jymie Merritt. Morgan, Timmons, whose "Moanin'" became a jazz hit, and Golson, who contributed "Blues March," "Along Came Betty," and "Are You Real," were all skilled composers as well as distinctive instrumentalists. During the next few years, first Hank Mobley and then Wayne Shorter took Golson's place on tenor. The Morgan-Shorter frontline resulted in many classic recordings, and such songs as Timmons' "Dat Dere" and Shorter's "Lester Left Town," a tribute to the recently deceased Lester Young, entered the band's repertoire. In 1961 Freddie Hubbard proved to be the perfect replacement for Morgan, and the addition of trombonist Curtis Fuller made the band a sextet. With pianist Cedar Walton and either Jymie Merritt or Reggie Workman on bass, the Messengers personnel was stable during 1961 to 1964, one of its great periods.

The sound of the Jazz Messengers was pretty well set by the early 1960s, although it continued evolving with the use of new players and their original compositions. In the 1960s, 1970s, and 1980s, many major young musicians benefited from playing with Art Blakey, who pushed them to constantly grow and stretch themselves: trumpeters Chuck Mangione, Woody Shaw, Wynton Marsalis, Terence Blanchard, Wallace Roney, Phillip Harper, Brian Lynch, and Valeri Ponomarev, a top soloist from the Soviet Union; trombonists Julian Priester, Steve Turre, and Robin Eubanks; tenors John Gilmore, Billy Harper, Carlos Garnett, Carter Jefferson, David Schnitter, Bill Pierce, Jean Toussaint, and Javon Jackson; altoists Gary Bartz, Bobby Watson, Branford Marsalis, Donald Harrison, and Kenny Garrett; pianists John Hicks, Joanne Brackeen, George Cables, Albert Dailey, James Williams, Donald Brown, Johnny O'Neal, Mulgrew Miller, Benny Green, and Geoffrey Keezer; and bassists Victor Sproles, Dennis Irwin, Charles Fambrough, Lonnie Plaxico, Peter Washington, and Essiet Essiet. Only Blakey's death in 1990 ended the pre-eminent hard bop institution.

HORACE SILVER

Horace Silver has been very important as a bandleader, songwriter, and the first soul jazz pianist. In 1951 he was part of a rhythm section that backed Stan Getz at a concert in Hartford, Connecticut. Getz was so impressed that he used the rhythm section for a year. After that, Silver worked in New York with Coleman Hawkins, Lester Young, and Oscar Pettiford, recording with Lou Donaldson and Miles Davis. Evolving from a bop-oriented pianist, Silver developed his own bluesy approach, often sounding as if he were bending notes, which is impossible on the piano. As early as 1952, he was writing such catchy originals as "Opus de Funk," and "Ecaroh," his name backwards. After co-leading the Jazz Messengers during 1954 to 1956, he took the group, except Blakey, and formed the Horace Silver Quintet. For the first few years, the personnel changed but the Silver quintet sound was emerging. He debuted "Home Cookin'" and had a hit with "Senor Blues." From 1959 to 1964 Silver led the most famous version of his quintet, featuring trumpeter Blue Mitchell, tenor Junior Cook, bassist Gene Taylor, and either Louis Hayes or Roy Brooks on drums. Among the songs he introduced during this period were "Come on Home," "Cookin' at the Continental," "Sister Sadie," "Filthy McNasty," and "Tokyo Blues."

In 1964 Blue Mitchell did the same thing to Silver that the pianist had done to Art Blakey eight years earlier, forming his own band from the group but excluding the leader. Silver quickly formed a new quintet that included trumpeter Carmell Jones, tenor-saxophonist Joe Henderson, bassist Teddy Smith, and drummer Roger Humphries, recording his biggest hit, "Song for My Father." Silver continued leading similar groups through the 1970s with such sidemen as trumpeters Woody Shaw, Charles Tolliver, Randy Brecker, and Tom Harrell; altoist-flutist James Spaulding; and tenors Stanley Turrentine, Bennie Maupin, Michael Brecker, and Bob Berg. Since that time he has generally had a lower profile, occasionally leading groups on tours, writing lyrics, running his own record label, and being involved in self-help projects.

JIMMY SMITH, JAZZ ORGANISTS, SOUL JAZZ, AND A PHILADELPHIA CONNECTION

Soul jazz began with the funky piano style of Horace Silver, who was soon joined by Bobby Timmons, Junior Mance, Les McCann, Ramsey Lewis, and Gene Harris, who led the Three Sounds. When organists began to play groove music as opposed to bebop, soul jazz really took off, becoming popular in small black clubs and bars. Soul jazz often emphasizes the catchy bass lines, with the bluesy solos being influenced even more by gospel music and r&b than hard bop.

Although the organ had rarely been used in jazz before the mid-1950s, most notably Fats Waller's pipe organ solos in the 1920s and the 1950s' jazz-oriented r&b by Wild Bill Davis and Bill Doggett, it caught on when Jimmy Smith exploded on the scene in 1955. Smith had actually been working on developing his technique for four years in Philadelphia before he was discovered, transferring the ideas of Charlie Parker and Bud Powell to the bulky instrument while infusing it with his own brand of soul.

Jimmy Smith recorded twenty-five albums for the Blue Note label during 1956 to 1960, establishing his reputation as the first significant player on the Hammond B-3 organ and becoming a force that still dominates today. Smith could swing as hard on his instrument as Oscar Peterson did on piano and could hold his own with the best young soloists, including trumpeter Lee Morgan, altoist Lou Donaldson, and tenor-saxophonist Stanley Turrentine. His work on foot pedals made the inclusion of a string bass unnecessary. Because of his success, many groups comprising organ, guitar, drums, and sometimes tenor sax formed in the late 1950s.

Jimmy Smith was just one of many organists who spent their formative years in Philadelphia. Others included Jimmy McGriff, Richard "Groove" Holmes, Charles Earland, Joey DeFrancesco in recent times, and Shirley Scott, who was married to Stanley Turrentine. The organ was very popular in that city during the 1950s and 1960s, and even those organists who did not spend extensive time in Philadelphia had opportunities to play occasional engagements there, including Brother Jack McDuff from Chicago, Don Patterson from Columbus, Ohio, Big John Patton from Kansas City, Johnny "Hammond" Smith from Cleveland, and Dr. Lonnie Smith from Richmond, Virginia.

Jimmy Smith, whose jam session albums and dates with his trio were succeeded in the mid-1960s by his encounters with big bands, mostly stuck to hard bop in his career. The organists who followed him generally played blues, ballads, swinging pieces, and groove music, with the latter often being lengthy one-chord jams. There were dozens of organ records released by the mid-1960s. In general the organists' careers followed similar paths: they gained prominence in the early to mid-1960s and started out playing straight-ahead material. As the 1960s progressed, their music became simpler and more commercial. After most of these organists experimented with electric keyboards in the 1970s as the organ became less popular, they fell into obscurity. Those that survived made a comeback by the mid-1980s, returning to their original brand of soul jazz/hard bop.

One organist, Larry Young, grew away from the Jimmy Smith influence and developed his own independent voice, playing post-bop, avant-garde jazz, and fusion. In the early 1960s he sounded a bit like Smith, but by the time he recorded *Unity*, a quartet album with trumpeter Woody Shaw, tenor-saxophonist

Joe Henderson, and drummer Elvin Jones, Young had an original style. He became an important force in early fusion music, playing with Tony Williams' Lifetime in the early 1970s, before passing away prematurely in 1978 when he was thirty-seven.

THE BLUE NOTE LABEL

Of the labels that documented hard bop and soul jazz, none were as significant or as consistent as Blue Note. Swing had been recorded by Columbia, Decca, and Victor (major record companies), whereas bebop had initially been documented by Guild, National, Dial, the relatively larger Savoy, and other tiny labels before the bigger companies caught on. Hard bop's main champions were Blue Note's Alfred Lion and Francis Wolff.

Childhood friends in Germany, they fled the Nazi regime with Lion arriving in the United States in 1938, Wolff following about a year later. Alfred Lion founded Blue Note at the beginning of 1939, recording boogie-woogie pianists Albert Ammons and Meade Lux Lewis on the first session. During 1939 to 1941, Blue Note mostly released records by swing and New Orleans players, including Earl Hines, clarinetist Edmond Hall, and Sidney Bechet, who had a hit with his version of "Summertime." After Lion served in the military, Blue Note was reactivated in late 1943. With the rise of bebop, Lion and Wolff took a year off to investigate the music, and in 1947 Blue Note recorded important sessions by Thelonious Monk, Bud Powell, and Fats Navarro.

By 1955 Blue Note was very much involved in hard bop, and through the years recorded the most important albums of Art Blakey's Jazz Messengers, Horace Silver, and Jimmy Smith. Unlike most other record companies, Blue Note paid musicians to rehearse, and they encouraged the recording of new original music. Musicians were urged to be themselves and sound original rather than merely copying the current trends. During 1955 to 1966, Blue Note documented one classic set after another by such additional artists as trumpeters Kenny Dorham, Lee Morgan, Donald Byrd, Freddie Hubbard, and Blue Mitchell; trombonist Curtis Fuller; altoist Jackie McLean; tenors Dexter Gordon, Hank Mobley, Joe Henderson, Stanley Turrentine, and Wayne Shorter; pianists Herbie Hancock, Gene Harris, Duke Pearson, and Herbie Nichols; and guitarists Grant Green and Kenny Burrell; plus avant-gardists Cecil Taylor, Ornette Coleman, Eric Dolphy, Andrew Hill, and Sam Rivers.

When Alfred Lion sold Blue Note to Liberty in 1966, it was the beginning of the end for the classic label. By then Blue Note was doing well with danceable boogaloo sessions such as Lee Morgan's *The Sidewinder* and soul jazz dates, but the new owners were less interested in the more creative projects. During 1967 to 1969 the label's output gradually declined, and by the early 1970s, Blue Note was concentrating mostly on commercial funk sessions. By the time Horace Silver, the last of the original artists, departed in 1980, Blue Note, which had just been purchased by EMI, was dead. Surprisingly five years later it was revived by its new president, Bruce Lundvall, reissuing older classics and recording newer artists. Although it is not as consistent as Alfred Lion's original company, Blue Note has once again become a significant jazz label that also records other music.

Miles Davis was an innovator in bebop, cool jazz, hard bop, post-bop, and fusion, always going his own way and looking ahead.
Photo courtesy of the Wayne Knight Collection, Star Line Productions.

MILES DAVIS, 1950 TO 1964

Throughout his career, Miles Davis was continually at the forefront of new musical movements. Unlike most musicians who develop their style early and do not evolve much, Davis was always looking ahead and not afraid of alienating his older audience in favor of playing new music with younger musicians.

After being an important force in forming cool jazz, Davis had an off period during 1950 to 1954 due to his heroin addiction. He struggled during those years, but quite typically, even during this time, he was at the forefront of a new style: hard bop. Davis used such sidemen as tenor-saxophonist Sonny Rollins, altoist Jackie McLean, Horace Silver, and Art Blakey on some of his projects. An October 5, 1951, record date with Rollins and McLean ranks as one of the first hard bop sessions.

In 1954 Davis quit heroin cold turkey and began his comeback, recording jam session versions of "Walkin" and "Blue 'n' Boogie" with an all-star group including trombonist J. J. Johnson and Lucky Thompson on tenor. Later dates included one with Sonny Rollins that debuted three of the tenor's most popular originals, "Airegin," "Oleo," and "Doxy," and a collaboration with Thelonious Monk and Milt Jackson.

At the second annual Newport Jazz Festival in 1955, Davis played "Hackensack" and "Now's the Time" with a sextet also including tenorman Zoot Sims, baritonist Gerry Mulligan, and Thelonious Monk. His version of "'Round Midnight" with Monk in a quartet so impressed the critics in the audience that it made headlines and led to many realizing that Miles Davis was back.

That year, Davis formed a classic quintet comprising pianist Red Garland, bassist Paul Chambers, drummer Philly Joe Jones, and tenor-saxophonist John Coltrane, a relatively unknown but promising player. They made one album for

Prestige in 1955, but it was the four that they cut for the label the following year that cemented the group's reputation. Davis' introverted trumpet contrasted well with Coltrane's explorative tenor, and the rhythm section was tight enough to stand by itself. Their music could be considered hard bop, although it had a special flavor of its own, especially after Davis signed with the Columbia label and the quintet recorded a classic album titled 'Round about Midnight.

Miles Davis became a celebrity during this period due to his anti-hero status—he rarely acknowledged his audience—his stylish taste in clothes, and his frequently romantic music. He often used a Harmon mute on his horn as he played softly, close to a microphone. In reality Davis was not a very friendly or pleasant person, often displaying a bad temper and treating women poorly. In spite of that, he became a role model of sorts, a fiercely independent black musician during a still segregated era, a distinctive, if never virtuosic, trumpeter, and a brilliant talent scout, seeing qualities in younger players that went unnoticed by other musicians. John Coltrane was his greatest discovery, though he fired 'Trane in early 1957 due to the saxophonist's drug use; he rehired him a year later when he was permanently clean.

In 1957 Davis recorded the first of his three full-length albums, Miles Ahead, with Gil Evans' orchestra and toured Europe. By the following year, he had organized a remarkable sextet, which at first was his 1956 quintet with Coltrane, Garland, Chambers, and Jones plus altoist Cannonball Adderley. On their album Milestones, the brilliance of this group is in full flight, with Adderley's jubilant playing contrasting with the much more serious sounding Coltrane and the melancholy Davis. During the year Bill Evans and Jimmy Cobb succeeded Garland and Jones, and the sextet's set at that year's Newport Jazz Festival is quite outstanding. Evans departed before year-end, being replaced by Wynton Kelly, but was used by Davis on four of the five selections recorded in 1959 for the monumental Kind of Blue. This subtle and impressionistic set became hugely influential due to the musicians' improvising off scales rather than chord structures. It introduced the blues "Freddie Freeloader," "All Blues," and "So What," a song with only two chords.

The sextet was full of too many stars for it to stay together long. Adderley left before the end of 1959 to form his own successful quintet, followed by Coltrane in mid-1960. Davis continued with the Kelly-Chambers-Cobb rhythm section for two years, with the tenor spot being filled by players including Hank Mobley. Davis' playing in 1961 was essentially bebop, and his technical skills were in prime form, but he was increasingly impatient to move ahead. Two years later, after Mobley had departed and the Wynton Kelly Trio had become an independent unit, Davis found himself without a band. After trying out various players, he settled on pianist Herbie Hancock, bassist Ron Carter, and seventeen-year-old drummer Tony Williams. These musicians had their own individual voices, they were much younger than Davis, and they were confident in their playing while being eager to inspire the trumpeter. George Coleman was the group's tenor saxophonist during 1963 and 1964, playing brilliantly on a series of live sessions. As the rhythm section's sound grew more abstract, however, they began to feel that Coleman's hard bop playing was old-fashioned, and by mid-1964 they had persuaded him to depart. For a short time Davis utilized the adventurous tenor-saxophonist Sam Rivers, but he did not work out, and Miles already had another saxophonist in mind for his new classic quintet: Wayne Shorter. The work of that important group is covered in chapter eight.

GIL EVANS

Like that of Miles Davis, arranger Gil Evans' music was very much beyond any specific category. He led his own band in California in the 1930s and gained recognition for his arrangements for Claude Thornhill's orchestra during 1942 and 1946 to 1948. Evans enjoyed utilizing French horns and a tuba as frontline instruments in the ensembles, and he was open to bebop. After meeting Miles Davis, he did some writing for the trumpeter's "Birth of the Cool" nonet during 1948, including "Moon Dreams" and "Boplicity." Evans was a bit of a recluse during the first half of the 1950s, but after writing inventive charts for a session by singer Helen Merrill, he had a reunion with Miles Davis. They collaborated on three major album-length projects: *Miles Ahead* in 1957, *Porgy and Bess* in 1958, and *Sketches of Spain* in 1960. Evans' big band inspired Davis to play some of his warmest solos throughout these classic sets. Evans, who was the trumpeter's best friend, would also be an influential force behind the scenes in some of Davis' musical developments into the 1970s.

While his projects with Miles Davis put the focus completely on Davis, Evans also led some colorful albums of his own during the second half of the 1950s, utilizing unusual blends of reeds and brass that sometimes added a bassoon to a French horn and tuba and featured such soloists as soprano-saxophonist Steve Lacy, Cannonball Adderley, and trumpeter Johnny Coles. In the 1960s Evans was less active but wrote for sessions featuring guitarist Kenny Burrell and singer Astrud Gilberto. Starting in 1969, he returned to the scene fulltime, blending electronic and acoustic instruments quite expertly on a few studio sets and leading his big band once a week in New York clubs. His personnel included top players from post-bop, the avant-garde, and r&b-oriented jazz, which he featured in an electrified setting that the musicians found quite stimulating. Gil Evans was one of the most respected arrangers on the scene until his death in 1988.

JOHN COLTRANE: THE SIDEMAN YEARS

Born in 1926 John Coltrane originally played alto sax. His earliest recordings are some private sides made while he was in the navy in 1946. After his discharge, he picked up experience playing with King Kolax, the Dizzy Gillespie Big Band in 1948 and 1949, Gillespie's sextet, Earl Bostic, Johnny Hodges, and Eddie "Cleanhead" Vinson, during which time he switched to the tenor. In 1955 Coltrane was still virtually unknown when Miles Davis recognized the potential in the tenor's sound and searching style and hired him for his new quintet. Although he did not sound quite ready for the big time at first, Coltrane developed quickly, and by 1956 he was becoming a major voice on his instrument.

Influenced in tone in the early days by Dexter Gordon, but sounding original by the time he joined Davis, Coltrane became a master at dissecting chord changes. Rather than concentrating on individual notes, his solos were waves of passion that writer Ira Gitler termed "sheets of sound." Coltrane's drug use prompted Miles Davis to fire him early in 1957, but within a few months he quit all of his bad habits, a move that accelerated his musical evolution. He spent the summer as a member of the Thelonious Monk Quartet, playing nightly at the Five Spot in New York and learning a great deal from the unique pianist-composer. In 1958 'Trane rejoined Davis and was part of the trumpeter's classic sextet that recorded *Kind of Blue* the following year.

From 1956 to 1959, Coltrane appeared on many hard bop jam session–style record dates, teaming up with many of the top young players of the era. His increasingly lengthy solos were original and way ahead of his time. Coltrane's lone album for Blue Note, the 1957 *Blue Train*, is a classic with Lee Morgan and Curtis Fuller, while his 1959 album *Giant Steps* was quite innovative. The title cut from *Giant Steps* finds Coltrane bringing bebop and chordal improvisation to its logical extreme, with the chords usually changing every two beats, requiring the listener to really study the song before attempting to come up with an original statement.

In the summer of 1960, John Coltrane left Davis to form his own group. He would make history during the next seven years.

CANNONBALL AND NAT ADDERLEY

Altoist Julian "Cannonball" Adderley was originally uncertain about making a career as a fulltime musician. He was working as a school band director in Florida in 1955 when he and his younger brother, cornetist Nat Adderley, visited New York during his summer vacation. They were in the audience at the Café Bohemia watching Oscar Pettiford's group play when they were asked to sit in. Cannonball's exuberant playing on "I Remember April" made the audience, which happened to include altoists Jackie McLean and Phil Woods, immediately realize that a new giant was on the scene. Within a few days the Adderleys were recording for Savoy and working towards forming their first quintet.

Although the first Cannonball Adderley Quintet never caught on and broke up after two years, it created some strong bop-oriented music. The problem was that Adderley's name was not known beyond New York, and their group had nothing that original to say, yet. Cannonball joined Miles Davis while Nat Adderley played with J. J. Johnson and Woody Herman. Cannonball recorded several notable albums as a leader for the Riverside label, and his association with Davis gave him some fame.

In October 1959 Cannonball Adderley tried again, this time with his brother, pianist Bobby Timmons, bassist Sam Jones, and drummer Louis Hayes in his new quintet. The key element in the early group was Timmons, a talented song-writer whose "This Here" became a funky soul jazz hit and launched the band. Cannonball, whose style was exuberant, as opposed to the more serious sound-ing modern players of the era, was also quite articulate, enjoying talking to the audience and explaining the music his band played. Mixing together aspects of the styles of Charlie Parker and Benny Carter while Nat hinted at Miles Davis, Cannonball recorded a series of exciting hard bop sets for Riverside during the early 1960s. Among the songs that his band made famous were Nat's "Work Song" and "Jive Samba," Duke Pearson's "Jeannine," Sam Jones' "Del Sasser," and Timmons' follow-up to "This Here" that he called "Dat Dere."

The finest Adderley band was the 1962 and 1963 sextet with Nat Adderley, Jones, Hayes, pianist Joe Zawinul, and the versatile Yusef Lateef on tenor, flute, and oboe. After Charles Lloyd took Lateef's place on tenor and flute during 1964, the group reverted to being a quintet. By then the Riverside label had gone bankrupt, and Adderley signed with Capitol. His recordings became more commercial after his hit with Zawinul's "Mercy, Mercy, Mercy," veering towards funk by the late 1960s. In the early 1970s, Adderley was utilizing George Duke on electric keyboards and playing relatively little himself. Things looked up after he switched to the Fantasy label in 1973, getting an opportunity to revisit the repertoire of his earlier days and showing that he could still play quite well. Unfortunately Cannonball Adderley died of a heart attack in 1975 when he was just forty-six. A heartbroken Nat Adderley continued, leading similar soulful hard bop groups until his own death twenty-five years later. Cannonball Adderley's joyful sound and rambunctious style remain strong influences on many of the altoists of today.

SONNY ROLLINS

In the 1950s Sonny Rollins emerged, with John Coltrane, as the top young tenor saxophonist. Unlike the cool school players who looked towards Lester Young, Rollins was originally influenced by Coleman Hawkins. Rollins devel-oped a discrete tone, adventurous style, and wit to form an influential approach of his own. As did Thelonious Monk, he often built his ideas off of the melody rather than just the chord structure.

Having made his recording debut in 1948 when he was eighteen, the next year he held his own on a record date with Fats Navarro and Bud Powell. Miles Davis was a champion of his, using him on records in 1951 and originally hoping that Rollins would be a member of his 1955 quintet. By then the young tenor had worked with Thelonious Monk, introduced such originals, and later jazz stan-dards, as "Airegin," "Oleo," and "Doxy," led several of his own record dates, and retired for the first time, to quit drugs and get his health together. When he returned in late 1955, he became a member of the Clifford Brown/Max Roach

Quintet, staying with the group for a year after Brownie's tragic death. As a leader, Rollins recorded one memorable set after another from 1956 to 1959 for the Prestige, Blue Note, Contemporary, and Riverside labels, making the calypso "St. Thomas" famous and having a famous engagement at the Village Vanguard, accompanied only by bass and drums. Rollins had the ability to take marathon solos without ever losing the interest of listeners. He also enjoyed exploring unlikely material including "I'm an Old Cowhand," "Toot, Toot Tootsie," and "Rock-A-Bye Your Baby with a Dixie Melody," showing that virtually any song could be turned into creative jazz.

It was a major surprise to the jazz world in 1959 when Rollins decided to retire from playing; he was still only twenty-eight. This caused much speculation, but he simply wanted time off to practice, relax, and recharge his batteries. He was spotted on a few occasions playing late at night on New York's Williamsburg Bridge, but otherwise not much was heard from Rollins until he returned to jazz in early 1962. At first his playing, in a pianoless quartet with guitarist Jim Hall, was largely unchanged from 1959, but soon he was exploring freer improvising, being intrigued by Ornette Coleman's music and using Coleman's sidemen, cornetist Don Cherry and drummer Billy Higgins, in his band during part of 1962 and 1963. Rollins' solos became increasingly eccentric during this era, as can be heard on his RCA recordings, which probably surprised his veteran fans. His Impulse albums of 1965 and 1966, while still being adven-

One of the major tenor saxophonists, Sonny Rollins' constant creativity and wit enlivened many marathon solos. *Photo courtesy of the Wayne Knight Collection, Star Line Productions.*

turous, were more tightly focused as Rollins more smoothly incorporated elements of the avant-garde into his style. In 1966 the thirty-six-year-old tenor decided to retire for the third time. This time he was off the scene for six years. When he returned in 1972, Rollins signed with the Milestone label that he still continues with and opened his music to the influences of rock and r&b. His tone became grittier, and sometimes his repertoire and his sidemen were not quite worthy of him, but Rollins has never stopped being an exciting performer, one whose go-for-broke improvising onstage, particularly when he explores standards and calypsos, continues to justify his reputation as one of jazz's true giants.

THE BILL EVANS TRIO

The piano playing of Bill Evans is difficult to classify: it could be considered anything from cool jazz to post-bop. Since he had a major impact in the 1950s and 1960s, and is still considered the prime influence on quite a few acoustic pianists, he fits well into this section.

With his advanced chords and close interplay with bassists and drummers, Bill Evans changed the way that the piano is played in jazz.
Photo courtesy of the Wayne Knight Collection, Star Line Productions.

Evans moved the jazz piano beyond Bud Powell. His complex yet subtle chord voicings were quickly emulated, as was his close interplay with his bassist and drummer. Evans always utilized bassists who were free to comment musically on what he was playing, as were his drummers. Unlike most piano trios where the pianist was dominant, Evans' groups matched him with near equals. After gaining experience with a variety of groups and serving in the army, in 1956 Evans moved to New York. He began leading record dates for Riverside and developing his approach to trios. Having impressed Miles Davis, Evans became a part of his sextet for much of 1958, returning to record most of the *Kind of Blue* album the following year. His impressionistic approach greatly appealed to Davis, who was reluctant to see him go out on his own.

From 1959 to 1961, Evans had a classic trio with bassist Scott LaFaro and Paul Motian. LaFaro was developing into a major soloist, but his life was tragically cut short by a car accident. After a period off the scene, Evans returned to leading trios, featuring Eddie Gomez as his bassist from 1966 to 1977 and becoming one of the more popular jazz artists of the 1960s. He became famous for his interpretations of ballads, although Evans could play quite heatedly when inspired. His final group, a trio with bassist Marc Johnson and drummer Joe LaBarbera, was one of his finest. If anything, the influence of Bill Evans, who passed away in 1980, has grown since his death.

DETROIT'S CONTRIBUTIONS TO HARD BOP

Because very little of its music was recorded locally during 1945 to 1960 and its top musicians all eventually moved to New York, Detroit can be thought of as a farm team for New York during the hard bop years. Many great young players spent important time in Detroit in the period after World War II, working on their skills and getting ready to eventually enter the big leagues. Among the performers who kept the scene quite lively during this era were pianist Hank Jones, who actually left town in 1944, his younger brothers, cornetist-arranger Thad Jones and drummer Elvin Jones, pianists Tommy Flanagan, Barry Harris, and Roland Hanna, tenor-saxophonist Billy Mitchell, Yusef Lateef on tenor, oboe, and flute, baritonist Pepper Adams, trumpeter Donald Byrd, trombonist Curtis Fuller, guitarist Kenny Burrell, bassist Paul Chambers, and drummer Louis Hayes.

All of these musicians had important and productive careers, but due to the dominance of New York by the mid-1950s, the chances are good that none of them would have become famous if they had not moved east.

Lee Morgan and the Trumpeters

The trumpeters of the hard bop/soul jazz era looked to Dizzy Gillespie, Miles Davis, and especially Clifford Brown for inspiration. Lee Morgan emerged shortly after Brownie's death, playing with Dizzy Gillespie's big band in 1956 when he was just eighteen. Morgan was heavily influenced by Brown at first but had his own brash style, maturing at a very young age. He began recording as a leader in 1956 for Blue Note, leading twenty-five albums, and in 1958 became an important member of Art Blakey's Jazz Messengers. During his three years with Blakey, Morgan played alongside Benny Golson, Hank Mobley, and Wayne Shorter, setting a high standard for other trumpeters to follow. After two years off the scene, he returned in late 1963 with his hit recording of "The Sidewinder." Morgan was back with Blakey during 1964 and 1965 before freelancing as both a leader in clubs and often a sideman on records, playing everything from hard bop and soul jazz to adventurous dates that were nearly avant-garde. His music became funkier in the late 1960s but was always of strong value, and Lee Morgan should have certainly had a long career. After jilting an older girlfriend for a younger woman, he was shot to death in 1972 when he was just thirty-three.

A brash, soulful, and versatile soloist, Lee Morgan was one of the major trumpeters of the 1960s.
Photo courtesy of the Wayne Knight Collection, Star Line Productions.

Freddie Hubbard, who was born three months before Morgan, was originally in his shadow, emerging two years later, though in time he surpassed him. Hubbard, whose style was touched by Clifford Brown and Morgan, developed his own powerful voice on the trumpet. He succeeded Morgan with the Jazz Messengers from 1961 to 1964 yet was flexible enough to appear on such important records as Ornette Coleman's *Free Jazz*, John Coltrane's *Ascension*, and Oliver Nelson's *Blues and the Abstract Truth*. He led sessions of his own in the 1960s for Blue Note and Atlantic. From 1970 to 1974 Hubbard was a big star, recording gems for the CTI label and impressing listeners with both his technique and his warm sounds on trumpet and flugelhorn. After leaving CTI and signing with Columbia, Hubbard's recording career became aimless and often very commercial, although he continued playing quite well in clubs. At his most creative, Hubbard was the top trumpeter in jazz during the 1980s, even if his evolution had stalled. Unfortunately physical problems in the early 1990s caused a rapid decline in his playing, and he has rarely performed since 1993, but his best early records rank with the finest in his field.

Freddie Hubbard followed in Lee Morgan's footsteps and eventually surpassed him as a fiery and explosive trumpeter. *Photo courtesy of the Wayne Knight Collection, Star Line Productions.*

Donald Byrd, a young hard bop trumpeter in the 1950s, recorded a series of superior Blue Note albums in the 1960s, effectively utilizing a gospel choir on *A New Perspective*, resulting in the minor hit "Cristo Redentor." He also co-led a combo with baritonist Pepper Adams and became an important jazz educator. Byrd made a big name for himself while ruining his reputation in jazz in the early 1970s after he recorded commercial funk, having a hit with his album *Black Byrd*, with his trumpet in a minor role compared to the popish rhythms and vocals. Byrd played less and less on his own strong-selling records until becoming only semi-active by the late 1970s. His later comeback records from 1987 to 1991 find him gamely struggling to regain his chops, but the trumpet is not an instrument that can be neglected!

Of the other top hard bop trumpeters, the veteran Kenny Dorham, who was with Charlie Parker's quintet in 1948, led a series of strong sets for Blue Note. The mellow-toned Art Farmer, who switched to the softer flugelhorn in the early 1960s, co-led the Jazztet with tenor-saxophonist Benny Golson from 1959 to 1962. Thad Jones came to fame as a trumpet soloist and arranger with Count Basie before co-leading the Thad Jones/Mel Lewis Orchestra. Blue Mitchell, who had an original cry in his trumpet sound, was part of Horace Silver's best-known quintet before leading his own combos.

Woody Shaw and Charles Tolliver were among the last major trumpeters to emerge from the hard bop movement. Shaw, who worked with Max Roach, Art Blakey in 1973, and Dexter Gordon in addition to heading his own groups, sounded a lot like Hubbard in tone, although his ideas were generally more advanced; his prime years were from 1970 to 1987. Charles Tolliver had a briefer prime, 1968 to 1976, but was brilliant during that period in hard bop, free, and post-bop settings before maintaining a lower profile; he is still active today although greatly underrated.

JACKIE MCLEAN, LOU DONALDSON, AND THE ALTOISTS

Charlie Parker's dominant influence was felt in the playing of all the hard bop and soul jazz altoists to various degrees, but the best altoists of the era were able to develop their own individual voices, such as Cannonball Adderley. Jackie McLean and Lou Donaldson were both strongly touched by Bird but then evolved into different directions.

Jackie McLean always plays with great intensity, using a slightly sharp tone. At nineteen he made his recording debut in 1951 with Miles Davis. He appeared on many jam session–style records in the 1950s, as a leader and as a sideman for the Prestige label. After being a member of the Jazz Messengers during 1956 to 1958, he signed with the Blue Note label, recording twenty-one albums as a leader in the next nine years. Although initially a hard bop player, McLean was open to the newer innovations of the 1960s, and on some of his albums, including *One Step Beyond* and *Destination Out*, he's playing quite freely in a manner not that far from the free jazz of Ornette Coleman. McLean's sound became much more expressive and explosive, with honks, screams, and squeals as part of his musical vocabulary, but he always remained quite capable of playing swinging hard bop too. When his period on Blue Note ended in 1967, McLean became involved in jazz education, inspiring many younger saxophonists with his own example. He remains active, never playing an uninspired chorus or a phrase lacking his intense passion.

Lou Donaldson, like McLean, was initially strongly influenced by Charlie Parker, but he created a soulful style that is more blues-based, melodic, and accessible. His records from the second half of the 1950s are bop-oriented, but due to their soulful tone, Donaldson's recordings became particularly popular on jukeboxes. He added a conga player to his band in 1959 and in 1961 replaced his pianist with an organist, making his music lean more towards soul jazz. By 1967 when he recorded *Alligator Boogaloo*, Donaldson's music was emphasizing funky grooves and catchy melodies; subsequent recordings from the 1960s were aimed at the commercial market, filled with weak and basic material in hopes of increasing his record sales. Donaldson also watered down his sound by often playing an electronic baritone sax, which robbed his playing of his individuality. By the early 1980s, the "real" Lou Donaldson returned, and since then he has played the bop, blues, and ballads that he most enjoys.

Phil Woods began with Charlie Parker–style bebop, graduated to hard bop, made a countless number of sessions, and since 1973 has led quintets that have invigorated the bop tradition with fresh material and inspired solos. Charles McPherson has also kept the Charlie Parker sound alive, whether playing with Charles Mingus or his own groups. In contrast Hank Crawford has consistently been one of the leading alto voices in soul jazz and r&b-oriented jazz. Although fully capable of playing hard bop, Crawford prefers to wrap his very distinctive soulful sound around warm melodies. He worked with Ray Charles during 1958 to 1963 and has had a vital solo career on records since 1960, being an influence and an inspiration to such later soulful saxophonists as David Sanborn and Grover Washington Jr.

THE GREAT TENORS

Coleman Hawkins, Lester Young, and Ben Webster, the major tenors of the swing era, were equaled in impact, influence, and innovations by Dexter Gordon during the bop era and John Coltrane and Sonny Rollins in the 1950s. Many other talented tenor players rose to prominence during this period too.

In some ways Hank Mobley was the definitive hard bop tenor saxophonist. Mobley had the right sound, middle-of-the-road rather than harsh or soft. He worked with Max Roach during 1951 to 1953, Dizzy Gillespie in 1954, and was an original member of both the Jazz Messengers and the Horace Silver Quintet. He also had a less happy association with Miles Davis in 1961 and 1962. Although Mobley did not lead any significant groups of his own in clubs, his long series of recordings as both a sideman and a leader, including twenty-five dates that he headed for Blue Note during 1956 to 1970, included quite a few gems and consistently rewarding playing by both the tenor and the many all-star sidemen. Unfortunately the demise of Blue Note and Mobley's own drug addiction ultimately cut short his career. After a recording with pianist Cedar Walton in 1972, Mobley dropped out of the jazz scene and lived in obscurity for the fourteen years until his death in 1986 at age fifty-five.

Benny Golson, a fine tenor saxophonist initially influenced by Don Byas and Lucky Thompson, became most significant as an arranger-composer. He always had the ability to write catchy melodies while utilizing complex chord changes. The results were songs that listeners remembered and that challenged musicians. Among his best-known tunes are "Killer Joe," "Whisper Not," "Blues March," and "I Remember Clifford," a tribute to Clifford Brown. As a player Golson worked with some early r&b groups, Tadd Dameron, Lionel Hampton, and Johnny Hodges before playing with the Dizzy Gillespie big band from 1956 to 1958. He was an important force in helping Art Blakey establish the Jazz Messengers during his period in the band in 1958 and 1959 before co-leading the Jazztet with Art Farmer for four years. Golson worked primarily as an arranger in the studios for fifteen years before re-emerging in the 1980s as a more modern soloist who was still in his musical prime. He has since played with Art Blakey tribute bands, a Jazztet reunion group, and most often as the head of a quartet.

When it came to soul jazz, few tenors were consistently more soulful than Stanley Turrentine, whose tone on tenor was as distinctive as Hank Crawford's on alto, no matter what the setting. "Mr. T." worked early on with r&b groups, gained some recognition for his playing with Max Roach during 1959 and 1960, married organist Shirley Scott, with whom he often worked, and recorded often for Blue Note in the 1960s. Whether gigging with organist Jimmy Smith, jamming with a quartet or being backed by a big band, Turrentine was very consistent, accessible, and creative within the soul jazz idiom. In the early 1970s Turrentine had his greatest success while associated with the CTI label, recording his hit "Sugar" and holding his own with Freddie Hubbard. He remained a popular figure up until the time of his death in 2000 at the age of sixty-six.

Rahsaan Roland Kirk was one of the most amazing musicians of all time. He could play any reed instrument in any style ranging from New Orleans jazz and bop to free-form and soul jazz. Kirk could play three saxophones at once, with two independent lines, functioning as his own horn section. He also mastered circular breathing so he could create a twenty-minute solo in one breath. He had to be seen to be fully believed, and even then much of what he played seemed impossible. Blind from the age of two, Kirk played several instruments before settling on tenor as his main horn, working in r&b bands when he was fifteen. He discovered two ancient instruments, the manzello, which is similar to a soprano sax, and the stritch, a straight alto, learning to play them at the same time as the tenor. In time he added flute, clarinet, reed trumpet, and a variety of other miscellaneous instruments. Kirk first recorded in 1956 and then really started making an impression in the early 1960s. While some critics and musicians wrote him off as being gimmicky, that was because they did not listen closely to what Rahsaan was doing, and they could not deal with the impossible feats he was accomplishing. He could do close impressions of everyone from John Coltrane to clarinetist Barney Bigard while still sounding like himself. A few videos and the double-CD *Bright Moments* show how Rahsaan sounded live in concert while his other recordings focus on various aspects of his artistry. Only a serious stroke in 1976 that resulted in his death the following year stopped this magical musical man.

Of the other tenor saxophonists, Booker Ervin played with intense soul, often in adventurous settings including with Charles Mingus. Eddie "Lockjaw" Davis and Johnny Griffin led a competitive and fiery two-tenor quintet from 1960 to 1962 in addition to having productive solo careers. Jimmy Heath, a survivor of the bebop era, developed not only as a tenor saxophonist but on flute, soprano, and as an arranger, cutting six superior albums for the Riverside label from 1959 to 1964. Yusef Lateef, in addition to his excellent tenor playing, became one of the top flutists in jazz in the 1950s and introduced to jazz such instruments as the oboe and a variation called the shanai, exotic percussion instruments from other countries, and the argol, a double-reed clarinet sounding a bit like a bassoon.

Lateef mastered jazz, a term he never liked, and infused his performances with "World Music" before that idiom had a name. Eddie Harris, who started out as a bop-oriented tenor player, having a hit in the early 1960s with "Exodus," by the late 1960s was playing creatively on an electric saxophone. He composed the standard "Freedom Jazz Dance," cut comedy albums in addition to his soul jazz outings, and was a major, although underrated, player up until the time of his death in 1996.

Joe Henderson was a consistently modern hard bop tenor saxophonist who initially became known during 1962 and 1963 for his association with Kenny Dorham. Henderson could play both inside and outside of the chord changes, ranging from standard hard bop to free jazz while always being instantly recognizable. He was very consistent throughout his career, associated with Horace Silver from 1964 to 1966 and Herbie Hancock in 1969 and 1970, and was rediscovered in 1991 and given a lot of publicity due to his series of inventive tribute albums. Henderson passed away in 2001.

WES MONTGOMERY AND THE GUITARISTS

Although the electric guitar was gaining acceptance as a solo instrument in jazz, to a large extent the jazz guitarists of the 1950s and 1960s were still students of Charlie Christian. Even the biggest name among guitarists of the period, Wes Montgomery, used many of Christian's phrases in his solos.

Wes Montgomery took the innovations of Charlie Christian several steps further in the 1960s, with his octaves becoming his trademark.
Photo courtesy of the Wayne Knight Collection, Star Line Productions.

Wes Montgomery was born in Indianapolis, Indiana, in 1925 and was self-taught on guitar. He used his thumb instead of a pick to play notes, so the quieter sound would not disturb his neighbors. Montgomery toured and recorded with Lionel Hampton during 1948 to 1950 before returning to Indianapolis to raise a family. He spent most of the 1950s working a day job, playing a club gig at night, and sometimes playing at after-hours sessions, rarely getting any sleep. Although this lifestyle ultimately ruined his health, it resulted in Montgomery developing quickly as a guitarist. His fast octave runs became a trademark. His brothers, vibist-pianist Buddy Montgomery and the pioneering electric bassist Monk Montgomery, had success as The Mastersounds, an easy-listening group that sometimes featured Wes as guest.

In 1959, when Wes Montgomery began to record for Riverside, he was discovered and quickly considered a sensation, showing that he could swing as hard, and with as much fluency, as any horn player. Montgomery was mostly heard in bop and hard bop settings during the next few years. After he switched to the Verve label in 1964, his recordings ranged from quartet jams to encounters with big bands and studio orchestras that were purposely concise and a bit commercial. Montgomery's fame began to grow beyond the jazz world. In 1967 and 1968, he switched to the A&M label where the three resulting albums had Wes doing little other than stating the melody of a variety of pop tunes. These were very popular and became staples on AM radio stations. Finally after years of struggle, Wes Montgomery was becoming rich and famous, but sadly his prosperity did not last long. On June 15, 1968, the overworked guitarist suffered a fatal heart attack. He was just forty-three.

Grant Green was in Wes Montgomery's shadow during the 1960s although he was his equal. Green was twenty-nine in 1960 when he moved to New York and caught on, becoming the house guitarist for Blue Note from 1961 to 1965. During this period he led twenty albums of his own and was a sideman on scores of sessions that covered the wide range of hard bop and soul jazz. Green was unusual in that he stuck almost exclusively to single-tone lines, very rarely playing chords. He was less active from 1966 to 1968, and then when he returned to a higher profile in 1969, Green was primarily interested in playing funkier music that displayed his interest in soul and r&b. Although he always played well, the material that he explored during the 1970s was mostly not worthy of his talents, nor did his dates succeed in selling much better than his earlier records. Drug problems helped cut short the life of Grant Green, who died in 1979 at the age of forty-eight.

Other significant guitarists of this period include Kenny Burrell, who sounded at his best when teamed with Jimmy Smith, the Hungarian guitarist Gabor Szabo, who first came to fame with Chico Hamilton, the great bop guitarist Joe Pass, whose extensive set of Pablo recordings from the 1970s show that it is possible to play up-tempo pieces as unaccompanied performances on guitar, and George Benson. The latter first gained recognition while being featured with organist Jack McDuff's band from 1962 to 1965. His early solo records were hard bop oriented, and Benson had strong success with his instrumental CTI albums of the early 1970s, extending the ideas of Charlie Christian and Wes Montgomery. However it was his vocal recording of "Breezin'" in 1976 that made him world famous. Since then Benson has often de-emphasized his guitar playing in favor of his pop singing, but he is still capable of playing swinging and soulful guitar with the best.

THE MANY NEW PIANISTS OF THE HARD BOP ERA

The generation of pianists after Bud Powell utilized Powell's approach of chordal improvisation, where the right hand played rapid single-note lines while the left irregularly stated the chords, but there were an infinite number of variations on how to play within the style. Sonny Clark, who sounded very close to Powell, led six Blue Note albums and one for the Time label in addition to being in demand as a sideman, before drug abuse resulted in his death in 1963 at the age of thirty-one. Kenny Drew, whose son Kenny Drew Jr. became a significant pianist in the 1990s, also was featured on many bop and hard bop dates playing in a Powell-like style before he moved permanently to Copenhagen in 1964. Elmo Hope, a contemporary of Powell and Thelonious Monk, was both an underrated pianist and a skilled composer. However he never gained much fame and died prematurely in 1967.

Phineas Newborn, a virtuoso from Memphis, moved to New York in 1956 and amazed jazz followers with his technique, which was comparable to that of Oscar Peterson, and his ability to sound relaxed at very fast tempos. Unfortunately health problems caused Newborn to be less active after 1962, so the pianist, who died in 1989, a decade after his last recording, is more of an underground legend now than a household name. However he inspired the next generation of talented Memphis pianists, including James Williams, Harold Mabern, Mulgrew Miller, Donald Brown, and Geoff Keezer.

Ahmad Jamal became famous in the 1950s. Jamal, whose original trio during 1951 to 1954 had guitarist Ray Crawford and bassist Eddie Calhoun, became notable for its use of space, his mastery of dynamics, and his very close interaction with his sidemen. Miles Davis listened closely, basing his recordings of "Old Devil Moon," "Will You Still Be Mine," "The Surrey with the Fringe on Top," "A Gal in Calico," and "Billy Boy," which featured his rhythm section, on Jamal's renditions. Most unusual was Jamal's version of "Pavanne," with one section that is similar to Davis' "So What" and a melody statement that is exactly the same as John Coltrane's "Impressions." Both "So What" and "Impressions" would not be "composed" for a few more years. By 1956 Jamal's trio consisted of bassist Israel Crosby and drummer Vernell Fournier, and their version of "Poinciana" was so catchy that it became their trademark. Although evolving during the decades since, Ahmad Jamal has retained the qualities of his earlier trios in his later groups.

Red Garland was the pianist with the Miles Davis Quintet in 1955 and 1956 and for a few months in 1958, displaying original chord voicings while sometimes emulating Jamal, at Davis' urging. Garland recorded no less than twenty-six CDs' worth of material as a leader from 1956 to 1962 before settling in his native Texas where he chose to mostly play locally. He emerged for further recordings in 1971 and from 1977 to 1979 before going back to semi-retirement.

Wynton Kelly, who worked with Miles Davis from 1958 to 1963, Wes Montgomery, and as leader of his trio, had his own soulful style out of the Bud Powell tradition and was greatly in demand as an accompanist for jazz dates. Other significant hard bop pianists developed their own voices: Horace Parlan, who learned to play primarily using his left hand because of contracting polio as a child, Freddie Redd, composer of the music for the play *The Connection*, Duke Pearson, and Cedar Walton, who was with the Jazz Messengers from 1961 to 1964 before leading his own trios.

Several pianists were influenced in their playing by Thelonious Monk. Mal Waldron utilized Monk's use of space and dissonance while having a brooding introverted style of his own. Waldron worked with Charles Mingus from 1954 to 1956, was Billie Holiday's last regular accompanist from 1957 to 1959, was the musical director and chief composer for many Prestige record dates in the 1950s, and moved to Europe in 1965, settling in West Germany. His style was flexible enough to appear in fairly free settings where his distinctive chord voicings were always quite welcome. Randy Weston was also touched by Monk's style although he has a more joyful style than Waldron, being also influenced by calypso music. Weston, who has recorded with trios, has always been very interested in African folk music, and his work with larger groups, often utilizing Melba Liston's arrangements, were among the first jazz pieces to be overtly African oriented. Weston lived and taught in Morocco from 1968 to 1973, becoming a very important educator in Africa while learning about African music. He remains an important force today, and two of his pieces, "Hi-Fly" and "Little Niles," have long been jazz standards.

With the rise of Horace Silver, some other pianists developed funky and bluesy styles that were flexible enough to fit into both hard bop and soul jazz settings. Bobby Timmons was not only an important member of Art Blakey's Jazz Messengers from 1958 to 1961 and the Cannonball Adderley Quintet in 1959 and 1960 but he wrote "Moanin'" for Blakey and "This Here" and "Dat Dere" for Adderley, hit songs that really helped make those two bands into permanent institutions. Les McCann, who was originally a singer, became quite popular in the 1960s for his gospel-flavored trio performances on piano, recording frequently for Pacific Jazz and occasionally taking vocals. His career changed in 1968 with his appearance at the Montreux Jazz Festival. Tenor-saxophonist Eddie Harris and trumpeter Benny Bailey sat in with McCann's trio, and that set, which was filmed and recorded, became the hit of the festival, due to McCann's timely vocal on "Compared to What" and the fireworks on the instrumental "Cold Duck Time." From then on, McCann became as well known as a soulful vocalist as he was for his funky piano playing. Ramsey Lewis, who formed a trio with bassist Eldee Young and drummer Red Holt, was initially a bop pianist but had a knack for playing catchy melodies. In time the Ramsey Lewis Trio became one of the most popular of all piano groups, having hits in the mid-1960s with "The In Crowd," "Love Theme from *Spartacus*," "Hang on Sloopy," "Hi-Heel Sneakers," and "A Hard Day's Night" by the Beatles. Its great commercial success resulted in the group breaking up, with Lewis' sidemen forming the briefly successful Holt-Young Unlimited, but Ramsey Lewis has remained a popular attraction in jazz since then, occasionally exploring electric keyboards and mood music but also returning to straight-ahead jazz on a regular basis.

Arguably the pianist in this section who made the greatest long-term impact was Herbie Hancock. A very open-minded player who, like Miles Davis, has evolved through many styles of music, Hancock was initially influenced by Bill

Evans' chord voicings while also being a soulful player when it fit the music. In 1961 he was a member of the Donald Byrd–Pepper Adams quintet, but he gained his initial fame for his first album as a leader, *Takin' Off* on Blue Note. That record introduced "Watermelon Man," a tune that particularly caught on in the Latin jazz world. Hancock joined the Miles Davis Quintet in 1963 and stayed five years, while continuing to record one significant album after another as a leader for Blue Note. His writing was well showcased on *My Point of View*; *Inventions and Dimensions* is a fairly free quartet outing; *Empyrean Isles* featuring Freddie Hubbard introduced "Cantaloupe Island;" and *Maiden Voyage*, which includes "Dolphin Dance" and "The Eye of the Hurricane," mixes the feel of mid-1960s r&b with adventurous jazz improvising. Hancock, who continued to evolve, would become a major force in fusion and post-bop jazz.

MILT JACKSON AND THE VIBRAPHONISTS

Lionel Hampton and Red Norvo originally set the pace for jazz vibraphonists. Milt Jackson became the dominant influence on vibes after emerging during the bebop era and as the key soloist with the Modern Jazz Quartet (MJQ). Jackson also had a very active solo recording career, often teamed with all-star groups. Through the years he held his own with John Coltrane, Coleman Hawkins, Cannonball Adderley, Oscar Peterson, Wes Montgomery, Freddie Hubbard, and the who's who of straight-ahead jazz. These excursions gave him a change of pace from the tight structures imposed by John Lewis on the music of the Modern Jazz Quartet. Jackson eventually tired of the MJQ and left the band in 1974, causing its demise, but in 1981 he relented and the band became active for a further fifteen years.

Although Jackson was the definitive hard bop vibraphonist, two brilliant new vibists emerged in the 1960s. Gary Burton utilized four mallets that gave him the fluency of a pianist and sometimes made it sound as if he were two players. He started in straight-ahead jazz and country music in the early 1960s and worked with George Shearing and Stan Getz before leading a pioneer fusion group and working in post-bop jazz. Bobby Hutcherson was involved in the more adventurous hard bop sessions of the 1960s, ones influenced by avant-garde jazz. From 1962 to 1967 he recorded on Blue Note with Jackie McLean, Eric Dolphy, Grant Green, Hank Mobley, Herbie Hancock, Andrew Hill, and many others. He co-led a post-bop quintet in the late 1960s with tenor-saxophonist Harold Land. Over time he became more conservative while still being quite virtuosic and individual, remaining a vital force up to the present day.

OTHER HARD BOP AND SOUL JAZZ MUSICIANS AND SINGERS

In addition to the musicians already mentioned, there were many other strong players from this era who are well worth mentioning. Key trombonists who followed J. J. Johnson include Jimmy Cleveland and Curtis Fuller, who played with the Jazztet and Art Blakey. The fluent baritone-saxophonist Pepper Adams was a major contrast to Gerry Mulligan and the "cool school" baritonists, in that he had a deep guttural tone, returning the baritone to its lower notes. He co-led a band with Donald Byrd from 1958 to 1962 and worked with the Thad Jones–Mel Lewis Orchestra. Herbie Mann helped popularize the flute, particularly with his Latin jazz recordings of the 1960s and his later pop-oriented efforts. In the 1970s Hubert Laws showed that classical technique need not restrict a jazz flutist's creative ideas, and his work for CTI ranks with the best recordings of his career. Among the major bassists of the 1950s and 1960s, ones who were inspired by Jimmy Blanton and Oscar Pettiford, were Paul Chambers with Miles Davis and the Wynton Kelly Trio, Sam Jones with Cannonball Adderley, Wilbur Ware, Doug Watkins, and Ron Carter. Significant drummers included Jimmy Cobb who succeeded Jones with Davis, Louis Hayes, veterans Buddy Rich and Louie Bellson, Roy Haynes, Max Roach, Art Blakey, and Philly Joe Jones, particularly when he was with Miles Davis.

Although there were not a lot of singers associated with hard bop or soul jazz, a few new vocalists emerged during this period. Carmen McRae caught on in the mid-1950s. Her behind-the-beat phrasing, ability to improvise, and ironic sense of humor made her a favorite for decades. Abbey Lincoln, an underrated songwriter, was an actress and a strong hard bop singer, as shown on a trio of late 1950s records, before marrying Max Roach and becoming involved in some political civil rights recordings. She has recorded many albums during the past five decades. Shirley Horn, a fine pianist and a masterful interpreter of ballads, made her initial impact in the early 1960s choosing to perform mostly in Washington, DC, for many years while raising her daughter. In the 1980s Horn gained a high profile when she was signed to Verve and traveled throughout the United States. Many younger singers have been influenced by Horn's phrasing. Among male singers, Johnny Hartman became famous for his warm voice and the way he treated ballads. His 1963 album, *John Coltrane and Johnny Hartman*, is considered one of the most romantic jazz recordings.

Of the fulltime groups that caught on in jazz in the 1960s, the Jazz Crusaders made an impact. Originally formed in 1954 as the Swingsters by Houston schoolmates—pianist Joe Sample, tenor-saxophonist Wilton Felder, trombonist Wayne Henderson, drummer Stix Hooper, flutist Hubert Laws, and bassist Henry Wilson—they were soon known as the Modern Jazz Sextet. In 1960 Sample, Felder, Hooper, and Henderson moved to Los Angeles and, using different bassists, adopted the Jazz Crusaders as their new name. They were signed by Pacific Jazz and recorded regularly in the 1960s, performing their own brand of hard bop and soul jazz, music that also included some r&b and Memphis soul. In 1970 they changed the name of the group to the Crusaders, feeling that the word "jazz" limited their commercial potential and their music. Adding several guitars, including Larry Carlton as a soloist, the Crusaders had success for another decade in pop/jazz, even having the hit "Street Life" in 1979 after

Henderson had departed to become a producer. The group broke up in the mid-1980s but has had several reunions since.

THE END OF THE HARD BOP/SOUL JAZZ ERA

During the 1960s hard bop gradually became more complex as many of its soloists showed their awareness of the free jazz movement's developments. Soul jazz, in contrast, often became simpler, focusing on danceable grooves, repetition, and soulful solos.

When Blue Note was sold to Liberty in 1966 and then gradually declined during the next five years, hard bop lost its main outlet. The rise of rock greatly cut into hard bop's record sales, as did the beginnings of fusion. By the early 1970s, hard bop was considered passé, a historical influence but no longer a contemporary style. The same fate hit soul jazz within a few years. Its subtleties were replaced by a more obvious funk beat, as record executives sought to record music that would appeal to a larger dancing audience. By the early 1970s, fusion was overshadowing soul jazz, and by the time disco took over, soul jazz was largely extinct.

Both hard bop and soul jazz made comebacks in the 1980s that have continued. When two brothers, trumpeter Wynton Marsalis and tenor-saxophonist Branford Marsalis, became the unofficial leaders of the Young Lions movement, the music that they and their contemporaries explored was often hard bop of the 1960s, along with the more modern playing of the Miles Davis Quintet of that era. Straight-ahead jazz made a comeback among younger players who sought to follow in the footsteps of such giants as Lee Morgan, Hank Mobley, and Jackie McLean. After a period of being eclipsed by electric keyboards, the organ returned, thanks largely to the rise in prominence of Joey DeFrancesco, a young high-energy player influenced by Jimmy Smith. The rise of rap and the use of sampling revived the careers of some of the soul jazz survivors, since their funky music was considered quite suitable as background music at dance clubs.

Hard bop and soul jazz are again being played on a regular basis by younger musicians, taking their place next to Dixieland, swing, and bop as important early styles well worth exploring.

RECOMMENDED RECORDINGS

Abbey Lincoln. *Abbey Is Blue*. Original Jazz Classics, 205.
Ahmad Jamal. *But Not for Me*. MCA/Chess, 9108.
Art Blakey's Jazz Messengers. *The Big Beat*. Blue Note, 46400.
Art Blakey's Jazz Messengers. *Keystone 3*. Concord, 4196.
Art Blakey's Jazz Messengers. *Moanin'*. Blue Note, 46516.
Art Farmer/Benny Golson Jazztet. *Meet the Jazztet*. MCA/Chess, 91550.
Bill Evans. *Empathy/A Simple Matter of Conviction*. Verve, 837 757.
Bill Evans. *Portraits in Jazz*. Original Jazz Classics, 088.

Blue Mitchell. *The Thing to Do*. Blue Note, 84178.

Bobby Hutcherson. *Components*. Blue Note, 29027.

Cannonball Adderley. *Cannonball Adderley Quintet in San Francisco*. Original Jazz Classics, 035.

Cannonball Adderley. *Dizzy's Business*. Milestone, 47069.

Carmen McRae. *Carmen Sings Monk*. RCA, 63841.

Charles Earland. *Living Black*. Prestige, 24182.

Clifford Brown. *The Beginning and the End*. Columbia/Legacy, 66491.

Clifford Brown/Max Roach Quintet. *At Basin Street*. Emarcy, 814 648.

Donald Byrd. *Free Form*. Blue Note, 84118.

Eddie Harris. *The Electrifying Eddie Harris/Plug Me In*. Rhino, 71516.

Freddie Hubbard. *Ready for Freddie*. Blue Note, 32094.

Freddie Hubbard. *Red Clay*. Epic/Legacy, 85216.

Gary Burton. *Alone at Last*. Collectables, 6360.

George Benson. *The George Benson Cookbook*. Columbia/Legacy, 66054.

Gil Evans. *New Bottle Old Wine*. Blue Note, 46855.

Grant Green. *The Latin Bit*. Blue Note, 37645.

Hank Crawford. *Memphis, Ray and a Touch of Moody*. 32 Jazz, 32054, 2 CDs.

Hank Mobley. *Soul Station*. Blue Note, 46528.

Herbie Hancock. *Maiden Voyage*. Blue Note, 46339.

Herbie Hancock. *Takin' Off*. Blue Note, 46506.

Horace Silver. *And the Jazz Messengers*. Blue Note, 46140.

Horace Silver. *Song for My Father*. Blue Note, 84185.

Jackie McLean. *Let Freedom Ring*. Blue Note, 46527.

Jackie McLean. *One Step Beyond*. Blue Note, 46821.

Jazz Crusaders. *Live at the Lighthouse '66*. Pacific Jazz, 37988.

Jimmy Smith. *Back at the Chicken Shack*. Blue Note, 46402.

Jimmy Smith. *The Sermon*. Blue Note, 24541.

Jimmy Smith/Wes Montgomery. *The Dynamic Duo*. Verve, 521 445.

Joe Henderson. *Page One*. Blue Note, 84140.

Joe Pass. *Virtuoso*. Pablo, 2310-708.

John Coltrane. *Blue Train*. Blue Note, 46095.

John Coltrane. *Giant Steps*. Atlantic, 1311.

Johnny Hartman. *John Coltrane and Johnny Hartman*. Impulse, 157.

Larry Young. *Unity*. Blue Note, 84221.

Lee Morgan. *Candy*. Blue Note, 46508.

Lee Morgan. *The Sidewinder*. Blue Note, 84157.

Les McCann. *Swiss Movement*. Rhino, 72452.

Lou Donaldson. *Blues Walk*. Blue Note, 81593.

Miles Davis. *Kind of Blue*. Columbia/Legacy, 64935.

Miles Davis. *Miles Ahead*. Columbia/Legacy, 65121.

Miles Davis. *'Round about Midnight*. Columbia/Legacy, 85201.

Milt Jackson. *Plenty, Plenty Soul*. Atlantic, 1269.

Oliver Nelson. *The Blues and the Abstract Truth*. Impulse, 154.

Phil Woods. *The Right of Swing*. Candid, 79016.

Phineas Newborn. *Here Is Phineas*. Koch, 8505.

Rahsaan Roland Kirk. *Bright Moments*. Rhino, 71409, 2 CDs.

Ramsey Lewis. *In Person 1960–1967*. GRP/Chess, 814, 2 CDs.
Randy Weston. *Uhuru Africa/Highlife*. Roulette, 94510.
Richard "Groove" Holmes. *Soul Message*. Original Jazz Classics, 329.
Shirley Horn. *Close Enough for Love*. Verve, 837 933.
Shirley Scott. *Queen of the Organ*. Impulse, 123.
Sonny Clark. *Cool Struttin'*. Blue Note, 46513.
Sonny Rollins. *Saxophone Colossus*. Original Jazz Classics, 291.
Sonny Rollins. *Way Out West*. Original Jazz Classics, 337.
Stanley Turrentine. *A Chip off the Old Block*. Blue Note, 84129.
Stanley Turrentine. *Sugar*. Epic/Legacy, 85284.
Wes Montgomery. *Impressions: The Verve Jazz Sessions*. Verve, 521 690, 2 CDs.
Wes Montgomery. *The Incredible Jazz Guitar*. Original Jazz Classics, 036.
Woody Shaw. *The Moontrane*. 32 Jazz, 32019.

9

New York: Free Jazz and the Avant-Garde

In the early days of jazz, the world was a much bigger place. Musical events that took place in New Orleans were not heard in the North until traveling musicians brought the style to different cities. New Orleans jazz developed in isolation for twenty years, and few people outside of the South heard jazz even in its early form until at least 1915.

When jazz began to be recorded, bands that were located in the biggest cities or were lucky enough to be documented by the larger labels during field trips had their music heard all over the country, but it was only a partial picture of the jazz world. Many musicians either did not record or were only caught playing obscure music on tiny, mostly unheard labels. Musicians in different cities came up with different solutions to playing jazz. Jazz in 1924 Chicago was very different than that in New York, which was why Louis Armstrong, relocating from Chicago to New York, made such an impact.

During the Depression, many Americans could not afford to buy records, but radio was free. When the swing era caught on, the top jazz orchestras were heard on the radio constantly, influencing musicians all over the country. Music made in New York was quickly duplicated in Los Angeles, Cleveland, and

Detroit, and regional styles began to be watered down and disappear altogether. To an extent, regionalism returned briefly during the bop years because many radio stations simply refused to play the radical new music. Jazz in New York, where bop was based, was not heard much in Los Angeles, at least until the younger musicians caught on to Charlie Parker and Dizzy Gillespie's work. During the 1950s, West Coast cool jazz was accessible, and there was no real resistance to playing its recordings. Many East Coast musicians, although influenced by cool jazz, preferred to develop their earthier style, hard bop.

With the rise of free jazz in New York in the 1960s, the new music was facing a situation like bebop had two decades before. Very little of the music was considered playable on the radio, so there was a slight delay between when the music was created and when it was heard in other cities. The dramatic growth of the record industry, however, resulted in all of the significant avant-garde players being documented, and adventurous musicians everywhere could hear what was recorded and learn from the leading players. Although some Chicago musicians came up with a slightly different way of playing free jazz and a conservative movement in New Orleans in the 1980s affected the jazz world, regionalism in jazz, at least in the United States, largely ceased to exist in the 1960s.

While each of the major cities have had their own local jazz scenes during the past four decades, other than Chicago and New Orleans, none have made a major impact or differed significantly since the end of the prime years of West Coast cool jazz. If important new music happened in New York, such as the free jazz movement, it was soon heard everywhere.

Throughout jazz history, the most creative musicians have always sought their own individual sounds and styles. The music evolved so fast into the 1960s that jazz over ten years old was often written off by younger musicians as old-fashioned, even though each style was far from exhausted. By 1960 the music of Charlie Parker and Dizzy Gillespie, no longer thought of as radical, was mainstream, and many younger players were looking ahead towards complete musical freedom.

The first free improvisations to be recorded were two brief numbers, "Intuition" and "Digression," by the Lennie Tristano Sextet with Lee Konitz and Warne Marsh in 1949. In 1954 a West Coast session featuring the unusual trio of drummer Shelly Manne, trumpeter Shorty Rogers, and Jimmy Giuffre on reeds with no piano, guitar, or bass, recorded a few free numbers. Those experiments, however, had little influence, and it appeared that the future of jazz would be dominated by "third stream music," attempts to combine cool jazz with classical music.

Although West Coast cool jazz reflected the conservative 1950s, and hard bop in its idealization of "soul" and funky blues looked towards the civil rights movement, free jazz was one of the first major steps in a counterculture that questioned everything about society. Musically speaking, why do instrumentalists have to confine themselves to conventional sounds and tones? Why do improvised ideas have to be placed in a specific structure or based upon chords instead of the musicians simply playing whatever they think of at a particular moment?

Before Ornette Coleman's arrival in New York, there had been hints of a new movement, although it was very much underground. Pianist Cecil Taylor led an adventurous quartet with soprano-saxophonist Steve Lacy that, although featuring a walking bass, became increasingly freer as the late 1950s progressed. Sun Ra's Arkestra in Chicago utilized some unusual harmonies, experimented with electronics, and created otherworldly sounds, inspired by Ra's unusual philosophy. Taylor, who rarely worked in public during this era, and Ra, however, were not noticed much by the jazz world.

Ornette Coleman's situation was different altogether. He had developed his style in Los Angeles where he worked at day jobs and read music theory books. Over time he formed a group of other open-minded improvisers, recording two albums for the Contemporary label. Coleman's brand of free jazz, which did not use chord changes and emphasized improvising new melodies, picked up two important champions in John Lewis, pianist of the Modern Jazz Quartet, and Gunther Schuller, one of the leaders of the third stream movement, leading to a record contract with the Atlantic label.

Early free jazz was partly developed in Chicago with Sun Ra and in Los Angeles, where Ornette Coleman, Don Cherry, altoist Eric Dolphy, and the more adventurous West Coast jazz players were based. New York, however, was where the music received the exposure required to blossom and grow.

Although his music remained controversial, Coleman had a strong effect on the jazz world after he relocated to New York. Horn players loosened up their sounds and became more expressive, while rhythm sections became more interactive. John Coltrane and Jackie McLean were two of the older players who were inspired by Coleman's innovations, leading to a quicker evolution of their styles. Many musicians from the next generation took Coleman and Coltrane's music as a point of departure. By 1965 free jazz was a major force, causing many veteran fans and musicians to be somewhat bewildered by the high-energy, freely improvised jam sessions featuring the likes of tenors Archie Shepp, Pharoah Sanders, and Albert Ayler. In this music, sound explorations often replaced songs and melodic solos. Impulse, John Coltrane's musical home after 1960, and ESP were two of the top labels documenting this innovative if often scary new music.

WHAT IS FREE JAZZ?

Classic jazz, swing, Dixieland, bebop, cool jazz, and hard bop, despite their differences, have chordal improvisation in common, meaning that the soloists base their choice of notes on the chord structure of the song; the majority of the pieces are thirty-two bars or twelve-bar blues. Once a group gets to the end of a chorus, it begins the next chorus. The format is a bit predictable and comfortable, with the creativity expressed in the solos and the jammed ensembles.

It was quite a shock, therefore, when the Ornette Coleman Quartet began playing regularly at New York's Five Spot Cafe in 1959, performing originals that dispensed with chords altogether. Altoist Ornette Coleman and cornetist Don Cherry, with stimulating backup and commentary by bassist Charlie Haden and drummer Billy Higgins, performed a melody in unison just as classic bebop groups had a decade earlier; but when the solos started, the lead player was free to improvise, based on the mood of the song rather than the chords. Haden was possibly the only bassist of that time who could set a feeling of forward momentum, usually stating notes right on the beat, without restricting the soloist to specific chords. While the group often played in a specific key, both Coleman and Cherry soloed in a highly expressive fashion, playing between the standard notes and sounding a bit as if they were talking. The nightly audiences were full of musicians who debated the merits of "the new thing," not just wondering whether it was the future of jazz, but whether it was music at all.

By the mid-1960s the free jazz movement had evolved to the point where the original Ornette Coleman Quartet almost sounded conservative. Many performances were free improvisations altogether, the musicians playing without any preplanned music. Not only were chord structures not being used, but also melody, steady rhythms, and harmonies were abandoned. Musicians were free to play whatever they wished, and the range of emotions utilized by the performers, particularly the horn players, became vast and at times quite violent, breaking the sound barrier. It is not surprising that free jazz became the least commercial and accessible form of improvised music.

One of the breakthroughs in avant-garde jazz of the 1970s and 1980s was the idea that any combination of instruments can potentially result in rewarding music, whether it be the World Saxophone Quartet, unaccompanied Anthony Braxton alto solos, or percussion ensembles. A piano-bass-drums rhythm section was not required for the music to be coherent and viable.

The term "avant-garde jazz" overlaps with free jazz but covers a wider area of ground. While free jazz emphasizes free improvisations, avant-garde jazz, while using fairly free improvising, often contains melodies, harmonies, a steady rhythm, and arrangements, although all of these are much more complex, dissonant, and unpredictable than in standard straight-ahead jazz.

In classic jazz, swing, and Dixieland, some notes were wrong if placed in certain spots, clashing with the chords, whereas in bebop and its direct descendants, any note could fit in any place, if it were resolved. In free improvisations there are no "right" or "wrong" notes, just notes and sounds that are better at a particular moment than others. The way to judge the music is simply to decide if it has an emotional impact and if the musicians' interactions are enjoyable. Are the results colorful or meaningless?

CHARLES MINGUS AND ERIC DOLPHY

Charles Mingus' relationship to the avant-garde was like that of Thelonious Monk to bebop or Duke Ellington to swing. His music was really in its own category, but it helped lead the way toward freer and more emotional approaches to playing jazz.

Born in 1922 Mingus grew up in Los Angeles and had short stints on trombone and cello before switching to bass as a teenager. Influenced initially by the songs he heard in church, Mingus loved the music of Duke Ellington, was intrigued by classical music, and was writing adventurous pieces before he turned twenty. Jimmy Blanton and Oscar Pettiford originally influenced his bass playing, but he was soon displaying his own highly emotional personality. Mingus gained experience playing swing and Dixieland with Barney Bigard in 1942 and the Louis Armstrong big band, led groups in Los Angeles, and toured with the Lionel Hampton Orchestra in 1947 and 1948 and with the Red Norvo Trio in 1950 and 1951, a vibes-guitar-bass combo with guitarist Tal Farlow. Moving to New York, Mingus played with pianists Billy Taylor, Art Tatum, and Bud Powell and had a short stint with Duke Ellington. In 1952 he and drummer Max Roach formed Debut Records, a label that lasted five years. For two years his own projects were classical and third stream oriented, seeking to expand jazz beyond bebop.

Bassist bandleader Charles Mingus always infused his band's adventurous music with his own passionate emotions. *Photo courtesy of the Wayne Knight Collection, Star Line Productions.*

In late 1955 Mingus found his musical voice, shifting away from the potentially cold-sounding third stream music toward a new brand of modern jazz. He mixed his backgrounds in bebop, swing, and Dixieland with church music, modern harmonies, and emotional sound explorations. Mingus began pushing his sidemen to the breaking point, adding group improvising on suite-like structures, often having two or three musicians soloing together. During the next ten years he recorded extensively, created some of his most enduring works, including "Goodbye Pork Pie Hat," "Better Get It in Your Soul," "Fables of Faubus" and the album-long *The Black Saint and the Sinner Lady*, and led a continuous stream of young all-star groups. Among Mingus' sidemen were trumpeters Ted Curson and Lonnie Hillyer, trombonist Jimmy Knepper, altoists Jackie McLean and John Handy, tenor-saxophonist Booker Ervin, pianist Jaki Byard, his longtime drummer Danny Richmond, and Eric Dolphy.

Dolphy was one of the unique jazz musicians to emerge in the 1960s, developing a very distinctive voice on three different instruments. On alto he could play melodies in a conventional fashion, but his solos were percussive, featured wide interval jumps, and were virtually impossible to copy, infused with his own wit and logic. On flute he was inspired by the sound of birds. Dolphy was also the first major jazz soloist on bass clarinet, often playing very high notes full of passion. He grew up in Los Angeles, was a member of Roy Porter's late 1940s bebop big band, worked in obscurity for years, and then gained some recognition as a member of the Chico Hamilton Quintet during 1958 and 1959.

Whether on alto, flute, or bass clarinet, no one sounded like Eric Dolphy.
Photo courtesy of the Wayne Knight Collection, Star Line Productions.

After moving to New York, Dolphy began recording regularly as a leader and working with Mingus. He played with John Coltrane in 1961, was involved in some third stream projects with Gunther Schuller and Orchestra USA, was among the first jazz musicians to play unaccompanied solos, and led a few classic sessions of his own. Unfortunately his life and career did not last long. In 1964 he led his classic Blue Note album *Out to Lunch*, toured Europe with the Charles Mingus Sextet including trumpeter Johnny Coles, tenor-saxophonist Clifford Jordan, Jaki Byard, and Dannie Richmond, and decided to stay overseas for a while. A diabetic, he was rushed to a hospital on June 29 when he suffered an attack, and doctors mistakenly gave him an overdose of insulin, causing his death. Eric Dolphy was just thirty-six.

Back in the United States, Mingus was shocked by Dolphy's death, but continued on. His band was the hit of the 1964 Monterey Jazz Festival. He was frustrated, however, by the lack of lucrative work in the next year and by his own inner demons. Mingus dropped out of music for most of 1966 to 1968. He began making a comeback in 1971 and found a surprisingly large audience for his music. Among the bassist's key sidemen from the early to mid-1970s were trumpeter Jack Walrath, George Adams on tenor, baritonist Hamiet Bluiett, pianist Don Pullen, and the loyal Richmond. Although Mingus had mellowed a bit since his early fiery days, his music remained powerful, and his works were quite ambitious. He was a major musical force until his health began to fail in the fall of 1977; he passed away less than two years later at the age of fifty-seven.

Since Charles Mingus' death, some of his alumni became members of Mingus Dynasty, a band that performed his works. In 1991 his widow Sue Mingus put together the Mingus Big Band, which still plays once a week in New York's Time Café, makes occasional recordings, and tours. This very exciting large ensemble really understands Charles Mingus' music and does it justice. It is the type of orchestra he should have had during his lifetime.

ORNETTE COLEMAN

Free jazz officially arrived in New York with Ornette Coleman in 1959. Unfortunately the altoist did not make his first records until he was twenty-seven, so his early musical growth is very difficult to trace. Born in Fort Worth, Texas, in 1930, Coleman began on alto when he was fourteen, adding tenor two years later. His early influence was Charlie Parker, and he worked mostly in r&b bands throughout the Southwest, but by the early 1950s he was already having difficulty with audiences and other musicians as he sought to form his own style. Coleman moved to Los Angeles in 1953 and was thrown out of a few jam sessions, but he met kindred spirits in trumpeters Don Cherry and Bobby Bradford, bassist Charlie Haden, and drummers Ed Blackwell and Billy Higgins.

In 1958 Coleman made his recording debut with Cherry and Higgins for the Contemporary label. Although pianist Walter Norris and bassist Don Payne set chordal patterns on the initial album, the beginnings of Coleman's free jazz appeared on this date. From the same period, Coleman, Cherry, Higgins, and Haden can be heard on two live sessions with pianist Paul Bley, even doing their interpretations of some standards in addition to Coleman's originals.

In May 1959 Coleman started a series of innovative recordings for Atlantic, after a second album for Contemporary with a pianoless rhythm section that has drummer Shelly Manne and either Percy Heath or Red Mitchell on bass. His records from 1959 to 1961, usually with Haden and

Ornette Coleman showed that it was possible to play jazz without chord changes or predictable structures.
Photo courtesy of the Wayne Knight Collection, Star Line Productions.

either Higgins or Blackwell on drums, sounded quite revolutionary for the time, setting the standard for free jazz and making many musicians question their own styles. Most intriguing among these dates is an album titled *Free Jazz* that utilizes a double quartet comprising Coleman, bass clarinetist Eric Dolphy, Cherry, trumpeter Freddie Hubbard, both Haden and Scott LaFaro on basses, and Blackwell and Higgins on drums. The thirty-seven-minute piece has a quick opening melody and brief, loosely organized parts between the solos but is otherwise a free improvisation, with the other horns being free to comment musically on what the lead voice is creating. Despite some meandering sections, there are plenty of inspired moments, particularly Coleman's rollicking ten-minute solo.

In the summer of 1961 Ornette Coleman made the very surprising decision to retire from active playing because he was frustrated at how little he was being paid by clubs and record companies. Other than a special Town Hall concert in late 1962, Coleman did not play in public again until he returned to the scene in 1965, playing not only alto, but also trumpet and violin. Unlike his much-improved alto playing, Ornette merely used his primitive-sounding trumpet and violin as props, additional sounds that were added to his music. He had a trio with bassist David Izenzon and drummer Charles Moffett, later in the decade adding tenor-saxophonist Dewey Redman, who had a complementary style. Coleman had reunions with virtually all of his alumni on some early 1970s recordings and became involved in writing avant-garde music for classical ensembles; the best known was his complex work *Skies of America*. He developed a theory called "harmolodics" that emphasized the equal importance of melody, rhythms, and harmony. Utilizing that method, in 1975 Coleman formed Prime Time, an ensemble that developed into a new type of double quartet consisting of two guitars, two electric bassists, two drummers, and the leader's alto. The music, which could be called fusion, but was really free funk, emphasized dense and noisy ensembles with Coleman as lead voice in the ensembles. Among the players was Ornette's son Denardo Coleman as one of the drummers.

Since that time, Ornette Coleman has continued appearing occasionally with newer versions of Prime Time, had acoustic reunions with his surviving alumni, and been involved in special projects. He has never compromised his music and remains a highly original innovator.

JOHN COLTRANE IN THE 1960s

While Ornette Coleman appeared fully formed on the jazz scene in 1959, seeming to have come out of nowhere with a radical way of playing jazz, John Coltrane had developed through the ranks. It was much easier for conservative musicians and fans to write off Coleman's playing than to dismiss Coltrane because 'Trane had long since proven himself.

Coltrane had already recorded *Giant Steps* before leaving Miles Davis' group in 1960. A master of chordal improvisation, Coltrane created a masterpiece in *Giant Steps*, which brought that style of improvising to its logical extreme. In forming his own quartet, Coltrane sought to stretch jazz beyond chords. He began doubling on the soprano sax, resulting in that instrument making a comeback, and searched for musicians who could inspire him while leaving the structures open for his lengthy solos. Along the way he used pianist Steve Kuhn, drummer Pete LaRoca, and bassists Steve Davis, Art Davis, and Reggie Workman before settling on the members of what would be known as his classic quartet: pianist McCoy Tyner, bassist Jimmy Garrison, and drummer Elvin Jones.

From 1961 to 1967 John Coltrane was the undisputed leader of jazz. The previous year his initial recording of "My Favorite Things," which was opened up to feature his soprano playing over an endless two-chord vamp, had become popular. Coltrane's recordings for the Impulse label were closely followed by many in the jazz world, as was his personal and musical evolution. In 1961 he added Eric Dolphy to his group for a period; their lengthy and explosive solos during an engagement at New York's Village Vanguard were branded as "anti-jazz" by a couple of critics. As if to answer the writers and fans who felt he had gone off the deep end, Coltrane recorded a trio of melodic albums: *Ballads*, a collaboration with the warm ballad vocalist Johnny Hartman, and *Duke Ellington & John Coltrane*, a quartet set highlighted by "In a Sentimental Mood" and "Take the Coltrane."

The spiritual leader of the avant-garde movement, John Coltrane inspired a countless number of saxophonists to emulate his sound, various styles, and go-for-broke musical philosophy.
Photo courtesy of the Wayne Knight Collection, Star Line Productions.

Coltrane's music became more explorative from 1962 to 1964, resulting in his famous spiritual album *A Love Supreme*, and *Live at Birdland*, which is high-lighted by "Afro Blue" and his long cadenza on "I Want to Talk about You." In 1965 Coltrane's career changed with his playing much freer and more violent, a contrast to his soft-spoken personality, as he continually pushed and stretched himself to create new sounds.

Recorded on June 28, 1965, his album-length piece *Ascension* displayed his approach to free improvisation. Similar in format to Ornette Coleman's *Free Jazz* of five years earlier, *Ascension* was much more intense and passionate. Coltrane used an eleven-piece group with trumpeters Freddie Hubbard and Dewey Johnson, altoists Marion Brown and John Tchicai, tenors Pharoah Sanders and Archie Shepp, McCoy Tyner, Elvin Jones, and both Jimmy Garrison and

Art Davis on basses. Other than a short sketch that the group played at the album's start and between soloists, the music is completely free and atonal. From then on with occasional exceptions, usually opening melody statements, John Coltrane's playing consisted of sound explorations that often overwhelmed audiences, hypnotizing some and repelling others.

As if his playing were not intense enough, Coltrane added Pharoah Sanders to his group later in 1965. After 'Trane had worked his solos to a ferocious level, Sanders built from there, playing shrieks, roars, and squeals that were unthinkable in the 1950s, sometimes shocking listeners. Coltrane also soon added a second drummer, Rashied Ali. By early 1966 both McCoy Tyner, who felt he could no longer hear himself, and Elvin Jones had departed, with the saxophonist's new wife Alice Coltrane taking over on piano in the new quintet; only bassist Jimmy Garrison stayed from the classic quartet. While the pianist and bassist set up drones, Coltrane and Sanders were able to improvise quite freely, interacting with Ali's drums.

How this music would have resolved will never be known. John Coltrane's health began to decline in 1966, and the following year he died from liver ailments at the age of forty. The jazz world was in shock. Coltrane had given no hint to most people that he was ill, and he had mercilessly driven himself, even practicing backstage during breaks between sets. Since his death, Coltrane's sound, style, and approach have inspired many musicians, some of whom have spent virtually their entire careers exploring just one period of John Coltrane's musical life.

ALBERT AYLER

Even more than Ornette Coleman, Albert Ayler and Cecil Taylor were the most controversial of the free jazz musicians. A tenor saxophonist with a large tone and a wide vibrato, Ayler often played pure melodies that were punctuated by screams, honks, and wails. His music looked back toward the early twentieth century in his utilization of simple themes and religious fervor, and his group with his brother trumpeter Donald Ayler often sounded eerily like a runaway New Orleans marching band from 1905.

Ayler, like Coleman, started his career playing with r&b bands. His early alto playing was undocumented but apparently influenced by Charlie Parker. He served in the army during 1958 to 1961, during which he switched to tenor and became a much more explorative player. After his discharge Ayler found it difficult to find any work in the United States, so he spent 1962 and 1963 in Sweden and Denmark where he made his first recordings, playing with rhythm sections that had no idea what he was attempting to create. In 1964 after he returned to New York, Ayler began to work with musicians more in tune with his free-form explorations, including bassists Henry Grimes and Gary Peacock, drummer Sunny Murray, and cornetist Don Cherry. On tunes such as "Holy Holy," "Saints," "Spirits," and his most famous original, "Ghosts," Ayler played with remarkable intensity and fire, creating solos that were sometimes blood-curdling. The following year he formed a quintet with his brother Donald, altoist Charles Tyler, bassist Lewis Worrell, and either Sunny Murray or Beaver Harris on drums that utilized military themes, Scottish jigs, and New Orleans brass band melodies plus some of his earlier themes that served as a contrast to the often riotous solos. Sometimes Michel Sampson, playing his violin as a drone, was added along with other instrumentalists.

When Ayler was signed to the Impulse label in 1967, it seemed for a moment as if his career would gain a higher profile. But his projects for Impulse were erratic with the addition of unsuitable vocalists and some odd commercial material. The group with his brother broke up, and Ayler's career became aimless, for he seemed confused as to what direction to go toward next. It all ended under mysterious circumstances in 1970 when Ayler's body was discovered in New York's East River. It has never been determined if the thirty-four-year-old saxophonist had committed suicide or been murdered. Albert Ayler's legacy, as a musician who always went for broke and was never shy to create new sounds no matter what the risk, is still felt in jazz.

CECIL TAYLOR

Cecil Taylor was among the very first free jazz musicians, and nearly a half century later, he is still arguably the most advanced musician performing jazz. Born in 1929 he started piano lessons when he was six and was classically trained at the New York College of Music and the New England Conservatory. Taylor's early influences were Duke Ellington, Thelonious Monk, and Dave Brubeck. He picked up experience in the early 1950s playing with the groups of Johnny Hodges and Hot Lips Page, but Taylor was quite original by the time he made his recording debut in 1955. He led a quartet at the time that included soprano-saxophonist Steve Lacy, bassist Buell Neidlinger, and drummer Dennis Charles, and although his sidemen were advanced, Taylor was already far ahead of them. His chord voicings were quite dissonant, and though he played some standards through 1960, his improvising was already almost completely free. Not too surprisingly, Taylor found it difficult to get much work in jazz clubs.

During his recordings of 1960 and 1961, Taylor performed standards for the last time, introduced tenor-saxophonist Archie Shepp, and showed that he was the leading voice in avant-garde jazz. By 1962 he was leading a trio with altoist Jimmy Lyons and drummer Sunny Murray, the first "free" drummer; there was no need for a bass. Taylor's improvisations were now completely atonal and full of dense high-energy outbursts of emotion. In the 1960s he recorded two notable group albums for Blue Note and worked in Europe, but otherwise it was a lean decade for Taylor, who was too advanced for even many of the free jazz players. The pianist's career improved greatly in the 1970s when he became active as an educator and was featured at many European jazz festivals, leading to greater recognition in the United States. He has recorded more frequently since then, both as a piano soloist and with his Unit, and his playing became even more relentless than earlier.

Listening to Cecil Taylor is almost like observing a thunderstorm. His music is about waves of sound rather than notes, and to a certain extent he plays the piano as if it were drums, with thunderous rolls and powerful abstract rhythms. Taylor, who turned seventy-five in 2004, has not mellowed with age, still playing with as much passion, energy, and uncompromising creativity as ever.

SUN RA ARKESTRA

Sun Ra was one of the most unusual and eccentric of all jazz musicians. Way ahead of his time in the 1950s and 1960s, Ra was one of the first pianists to explore electric keyboards, hinting at avant-garde jazz with his Arkestra as early as the late 1950s. Because Ra was deeply involved in developing his own inscrutable philosophy of life, he often had his bands dress in outlandish costumes, and he utilized chanting lyrics that combined his interests in ancient Egypt, religion, and science fiction, it was easy to write him off as a joke during much of his career. It didn't help that his ensembles combined superior musicians, especially tenor-saxophonist John Gilmore, altoist Marshall Allen, and baritonist Pat Patrick, with out-of-tune amateurs, and that his countless number of recordings were released in haphazard fashion.

Ra, born Herman Sonny Blount, claimed he was from Saturn, but he was actually born in Birmingham, Alabama, in 1915. He led a band as early as 1934, worked with Fletcher Henderson in 1946 and 1947, and formed his Arkestra in Chicago in 1953. Ra's Arkestra evolved quickly from a hard bop band to one that became increasingly adventurous, experimenting with atonality by the late 1950s. In 1961 Ra and the main members of his ensemble moved to New York where during the next decade much of their music was very avant-garde, using odd electronic instruments, chants led by singer June Tyson, and dense ensemble work. After relocating to Philadelphia in 1970, Ra rediscovered swing and Fletcher Henderson's music, spending the remainder of his career until his death in 1993 alternating between free-form explorations, outer space music, and his own quirky brand of spaced-out swing.

OTHER FREE JAZZ AND AVANT-GARDE MUSICIANS

In addition to the giants already covered in this chapter, there have been countless numbers of significant players who have explored avant-garde jazz during the past four decades. In fact the majority of recordings released these days on small independent labels are by free jazz and avant-garde players.

Don Cherry initially led the way among free jazz trumpeters, playing his pocket cornet as a member of the Ornette Quartet from 1958 to 1961. Cherry teamed up for projects later in the 1960s with Albert Ayler and tenors Gato Barbieri and Pharoah Sanders, sounding mellow and lyrical next to these very passionate saxophonists. After some reunions with Ornette Coleman in the early 1970s, Cherry became a world traveler who played flute, studied world music, and moved away from both free jazz and his cornet, although he returned on an occasional basis.

Bill Dixon, who in October 1964 organized six October Revolution concerts in New York that helped introduce twenty avant-garde jazz groups to the New York press, has mostly specialized in low notes and contrasting sound with silence. Other major avant-garde jazz trumpeters include Kenny Wheeler who often played more structured post-bop music and the versatile Dave Douglas who in the twenty-first century seems to be always involved in at least five major projects.

One of the most expressive of all instruments, the trombone, was inexplicably underutilized in the early days of free jazz, although it quickly caught up. Roswell Rudd had a Dixieland background with Eli's Chosen Six from 1954 to 1959 before jumping all the way to avant-garde jazz, recording with Cecil Taylor in 1960. He was in a quartet with soprano-saxophonist Steve Lacy that stuck exclusively to playing Thelonious Monk songs, co-led the New York Art Quartet during 1964 and 1965 with altoist John Tchicai, worked with Archie Shepp, freelanced, and led his own bands. Grachan Moncur III also played with Shepp during part of the time that Rudd was there, in addition to working with Sonny Rollins for a few months. Moncur led two major sets for Blue Note during 1963 and 1964 with such sidemen as Lee Morgan, Jackie McLean, Bobby Hutcherson, Wayne Shorter, Herbie Hancock, and a teenaged Tony Williams on drums.

Other notable trombonists of the avant-garde include Craig Harris, Ray Anderson, and George Lewis, who is also a composer for electronics. Anderson, whose wild sense of humor is even more broad than Lester Bowie's, greatly stretched the range of the trombone by developing a mastery of extreme high notes.

The horn that developed the most during the early free jazz years and has continued evolving in the decades since is the tenor sax. The playing of such trumpeters as Don Cherry and Dave Douglas can be traced to the hard bop players, but there is a less-obvious connection between the most intense tenor saxophonists and their predecessors. John Coltrane's tone was originally influenced by Dexter Gordon, but he was a true original long before he went over the line into atonal sound explorations in 1965. Although Albert Ayler sounded a little like Sonny Rollins on his earliest recordings, by the time he returned to New York from Europe he sounded unlike any earlier tenor.

Among the other tenor saxophonists to emerge in the mid-1960s, Archie Shepp was unusual because his tone paid allegiance to Ben Webster, even as he greatly extended the Webster vocabulary to include roars, shrieks, and cries of anguish. Pharoah Sanders was the perfect choice for Coltrane's last group because during that era he had the ability to turn up the heat with his tone and range of sounds to an alarming degree. Sanders had a true rarity a few years later, an avant-garde "hit," when he teamed up with singer Leon Thomas, who often yodeled, to record "The Creator Has a Master Plan." Ironically both Shepp and Sanders in later years became traditional players. The former explored early standards in the 1980s in duets with pianist Horace Parlan, and the latter reverted to sounding like late 1950s John Coltrane, sprinkled with occasional shrieks to remind listeners of his stormy musical past.

Other noteworthy avant-garde tenors have included Sam Rivers, Frank Wright, John Gilmore with Sun Ra's Arkestra, Fred Anderson, Rob Brown, David S. Ware, and Dewey Redman, who echoed Ornette Coleman while with his group. One of the present-day giants of the tenor is David Murray, who has shown throughout his career that, although he is an adventurous improviser who often leaps to his extreme upper register, he also has a large tone and the ability to caress melodies.

Among the many other colorful avant-garde altoists have been Jimmy Lyons who played with Cecil Taylor for twenty-six years, Marshall Allen, with Sun Ra's Arkestra for forty-two years, Marion Brown, Ken McIntyre, who also played bass clarinet, flute, oboe, and bassoon, Sonny Simmons, Thomas Chapin, Joe Maneri, and Tim Berne. John Zorn, a leader of cutting-edge projects in New York's Downtown scene during the 1980s and 1990s, and Arthur Blythe, whose soulful tone resembles r&b even though his choice of notes is very advanced, were also major players.

The World Saxophone Quartet started playing regularly in 1976. It consisted originally of David Murray on tenor, baritonist Hamiet Bluiett, and altoists Oliver Lake and Julius Hemphill, who since his death has been replaced by John Purcell. An a cappella saxophone group, the World Saxophone Quartet featured four of the most adventurous saxophonists in an inspired setting without a rhythm section, playing music that ranged from quite esoteric to an occasional standard.

Unlike most other styles of jazz, avant-garde jazz can utilize virtually all instruments if the players have mastered the art of expressing themselves through the instruments. Steve Lacy made the soprano sax an accepted instrument in jazz just prior to John Coltrane and has continued through his scalar improvisations to be a productive giant. Jane Ira Bloom and Lol Coxhill are also major soprano players. Hamiet Bluiett, who anchors the World Saxophone Quartet, has a giant tone on the baritone and the ability to hit notes in the soprano range. The clarinet, largely neglected in jazz since swing, has been utilized by Jimmy Giuffre, John Carter, Perry Robinson, Marty Ehrlich, and the versatile Don Byron. James Newton brought a fresh new voice to the flute, as did Prince Lasha in the late 1960s. When vibraphonists in the 1960s were utilized instead of a piano, Bobby Hutcherson often received the first call. Hutcherson, whose work after 1970 is more in the hard bop vein, during the 1960s showed that he could play in the freest of settings and sound quite natural. Ornette Coleman became one of the first avant-garde violinists when he returned from his sabbatical in 1965, but his playing was rather primitive, using the violin merely as another sound. Other adventurous violinists who had much more technique include Leroy Jenkins, Billy Bang, Mark Feldman, and Mat Maneri.

Cecil Taylor demonstrated one way of playing avant-garde jazz piano. His dense clusters of notes were full of unrelenting energy. To the uninitiated, his solos sound like noise, but to his followers, they are waves of remarkable sounds. Paul Bley, originally a bop-based player, offered an alternative approach. A brief association with Ornette Coleman in 1958 gave him many new ideas. Rather than fill up his solos with sounds, Bley used silence effectively and felt free to utilize melodies, diversity in moods, and even occasional chord structures while improvising quite freely but in a gentle way. Stressing the equality of the piano, bass, and drums, his trios of the 1960s were a step forward from Bill Evans, and he has since recorded extensively, experimented with electronics in the 1970s, being one of the first synthesizer players in jazz, and been a major, if subtle, force in jazz.

Other significant avant-garde pianists include the dramatic Ran Blake, Marilyn Crispell, Matthew Shipp, Don Pullen, Anthony Davis, Amina Claudine Myers, Michele Rosewoman, Jason Moran, and Andrew Hill, whose *Point of Departure* album from 1964 with Eric Dolphy and Joe Henderson is a classic. McCoy Tyner, despite being a member of the classic John Coltrane Quartet of 1960 to 1965 and a very influential force, was more of a post-bop pianist, one with his own sound and tied to chordal patterns, at least in abstract fashion. His successor with Coltrane, Alice Coltrane, primarily set moods and played over one-chord vamps with her husband's group. After his death, she made a few worthy recordings before becoming involved in Eastern religion and retiring from music except for special occasions.

The string bass, formerly tied down to the specific functions of keeping time and stating chord patterns for the other instruments, was freed during the 1960s in avant-garde jazz settings. Charlie Haden with Ornette Coleman's quartet showed how to state a powerful forward momentum while staying free of chords. Scott LaFaro with the Bill Evans Trio and Charles Mingus expanded upon the possibility of bass solos. Jimmy Garrison with John Coltrane played endless variations on two-chord vamps and by 1966 was expert at creating drones. One of the top free jazz bassists, Henry Grimes, disappeared altogether in 1967, only to be rediscovered and make a major comeback in 2003. Other significant bassists in the avant-garde included Buell Neidlinger, Reggie Workman, Gary Peacock, Art Davis, David Izenzon, Dave Holland, Cecil McBee, Fred Hopkins with Air, John Lindberg, Anthony Cox, Mark Dresser, Mark Helias, William Parker, and Matthew Garrison, Jimmy's son. Although each of these bassists was quite capable of swinging in a conventional fashion when hired for more conservative groups, they also possessed the ability to inspire other musicians with their large tones, knack at creating new sounds, and skill at driving an ensemble without limiting the soloists to any preset pattern.

As the 1960s progressed, drummers in free jazz were often called upon to provide color and drive rather than a steady rhythm. Elvin Jones proved to be a master at polyrhythms, playing two or more rhythms at once, even on ballads. His own groups, like McCoy Tyner's, tended to be more hard bop and post-bop than avant-garde, but he became a major influence. Jones' successor with Coltrane, Rashied Ali, is a freer drummer who avoids stating a dominant rhythm altogether, performing waves of sound that perfectly suited Coltrane in 1966. Dennis Charles and Andrew Cyrille with Cecil Taylor made strong impressions, but Sunny Murray has the distinction of being the first completely free drummer. Other important free jazz drummers, some of whom were percussionists as much as drummers, included Ed Blackwell, Barry Altschul, Gerry Hemingway, Milford Graves, Charles Moffett, Paul Motian, Joey Baron, Pheeroan Ak Laff, Beaver Harris, Steve McCall, Matt Wilson, and Hamid Drake.

There was little room for vocalists in the earlier free jazz sessions, though Jeanne Lee fared well on a duet recording with Ran Blake. The first free singer was Patty Waters, who recorded two stirring albums for the ESP label during 1965 and 1966, including a rather scary and lengthy free-form version of "Black Is the Color of My True Love's Hair."

Probably the most significant singer to utilize aspects of the avant-garde in her singing, although her roots were in bebop, was Betty Carter. After making an early impression with her recordings between 1956 and 1964, Carter became a much more daring singer, sliding between notes and taking very spontaneous and abstract solos, often at rapid or very slow tempos. She had to form her own Bet-Car label in order to be documented, but after signing with Verve in the early 1980s, Betty Carter gained long overdue recognition, becoming a very influential force on later generations of jazz singers with her chance-taking improvisations.

MILES DAVIS, 1965 TO 1968

When the free jazz movement hit New York and began to have an impact, Miles Davis at first watched from the sidelines. His quintet of 1961 and 1962 featured hard bop tenor-saxophonist Hank Mobley and the swinging Wynton Kelly Trio, giving Davis an opportunity to show off his bebop chops. He soon hungered to move ahead again. After Mobley and the rhythm section departed in 1963, Davis worked on putting together a new quintet. By the end of the year he was using pianist Herbie Hancock, bassist Ron Carter, and drummer Tony Williams, but was unsure about which tenor saxophonist would fit best. For a time George Coleman worked well; but the rhythm section, particularly Williams, considered Coleman's hard bop style to be too predictable, and Coleman departed by mid-1964. Sam Rivers toured Japan with Davis, but he thought Rivers' avant-garde playing was out of place. The trumpeter had really wanted Wayne Shorter in his group as early as 1962, but Shorter was with Art

Blakey's Jazz Messengers. Finally in September 1964, he joined Davis' highly original band.

Although the second classic Miles Davis Quintet often played standards in concert, usually at much faster tempos than the originals, their studio albums were full of new compositions. Wayne Shorter, whose tenor solos had their own fresh new logic, was also a major composer, and his songs inspired the other members of the quintet to write and develop new ways to improvise. Sometimes the quintet was a little reminiscent of the no-changes approach of the Ornette Coleman Quartet, leaving Hancock to create innovative piano playing to avoid restricting the other musicians, but the interplay between Davis and Shorter had never been heard before. In addition, Tony Williams' approach to drumming was brand new and soon became as influential as that of Elvin Jones. The quintet's recordings, *E. S. P., Miles Smiles, Sorcerer, Nefertiti*, and *Miles in the Sky*, were esoteric and certainly much more subtle and complex than those of the better-publicized, high-energy, free jazz jam sessions of the 1960s, not to mention the albums by the John Coltrane Quartet.

Nothing about the music of the second classic Miles Davis Quintet was obvious or predictable. The music was actually closer much of the time to post-bop, falling between advanced hard bop and the avant-garde, than to free jazz, and despite Davis's celebrity status, it was largely overlooked and overshadowed in the 1960s. In fact, it was not until the rise of Wynton and Branford Marsalis in the 1980s that other musicians began to explore Davis' unusual brand of jazz.

In 1968 both Davis' music and his band began to change. He encouraged Hancock to use electric piano and began to open his music up ever so gradually to the influences of rock and r&b. Soon Chick Corea, mostly on electric keyboards, had succeeded Hancock, and Dave Holland took over for Ron Carter; Filles De Kilimanjaro had recordings by both rhythm sections with Davis, Shorter, and Williams. By the following year, Miles Davis was leading the way in fusion, helping jazz to move into its next phase.

NEW YORK AVANT-GARDE JAZZ TODAY

Avant-garde jazz has remained a major force in improvised music up to the present time, although it never caught on as popular music and by the 1970s was overshadowed by fusion. In the 1970s many musicians in New York became part of the "loft movement." It was a time when some of the players opened up their lofts and rental spaces to adventurous concerts, essentially running their own concert halls rather than always relying on conventional night clubs.

In the 1990s the Knitting Factory in New York became one of the centers of avant-garde jazz, as Minton's Playhouse had helped to spawn bebop in the early 1940s, featuring music that was completely unheard of a decade earlier. Although Cecil Taylor and Ornette Coleman are the acknowledged senior statesmen of free jazz, there have been scores of younger and major free jazz and avant-garde musicians during the past four decades who have enriched the music, recording frequently for independent labels and stretching the boundaries of jazz. Other styles may have generated more headlines since the 1970s, but free jazz and avant-garde jazz have continually enriched improvised music with new ideas and approaches.

RECOMMENDED RECORDINGS

Albert Ayler. *Live at Lorrach: Paris, 1966*. Hatology, 3500.
Andrew Hill. *Point of Departure*. Blue Note, 84167.
Archie Shepp. *Four for Trane*. Impulse, 218.
Arthur Blythe. *Retroflection*. Enja, 8046.
Betty Carter. *Look What I Got*. Verve, 835 661.
Cecil Taylor. *Jazz Advance*. Blue Note, 84462.
Cecil Taylor. *Silent Tongues*. 1201 Music, 9017.
Charles Mingus. *Charles Mingus Presents Charles Mingus*. Candid, 79005.
Charles Mingus. *New Tijuana Moods*. Bluebird, 68591.
Charles Mingus. *Pithecantropus Erectus*. Atlantic, 75357.
Dave Douglas. *Five*. Soul Note, 121276.
David Murray. *Murray's Steps*. Black Saint, 120065.
David S. Ware. *Passage to Music*. Silkheart, 117.
Don Pullen. *Kolo Mou Bana*. Blue Note, 98166.
Eric Dolphy. *Out to Lunch*. Blue Note, 46524.
Eric Dolphy. *Outward Bound*. Original Jazz Classics, 022.
Grachan Moncur III. *Some Other Stuff*. Blue Note, 9548.
Jason Moran. *Modernistic*. Blue Note, 39838.
John Coltrane. *Live at Birdland*. Impulse, 198.
John Coltrane. *A Love Supreme—Deluxe Edition*. Universal/Impulse, 589 945, 2 CDs.
John Coltrane. *Meditations*. Impulse, 199.
John Coltrane. *My Favorite Things*. Atlantic, 1361.
John Zorn. *Naked City*. Elektra/Nonesuch, 79238.
Matthew Shipp. *The Multiplication Table*. Hat Art, 516.
Miles Davis. *Miles Smiles*. Columbia/Legacy, 65682.
Mingus Big Band. *Nostalgia in Times Square*. Dreyfus, 36559.
Ornette Coleman. *Free Jazz*. Rhino/Atlantic, 75208.
Ornette Coleman. *Love Call*. Blue Note, 84356.
Ornette Coleman. *The Shape of Jazz to Come*. Rhino/Atlantic, 19238.
Patty Waters. *Patty Waters Sings*. ESP, 1025.
Paul Bley, *Open for Love*. ECM, 827751.
Pharoah Sanders. *Karma*. Impulse, 153.
Ray Anderson. *Old Bottles, New Wine*. Enja 79628.
Roswell Rudd/Steve Lacy. *Regeneration*. Soul Note, 121054.
Sam Rivers. *Fuschia Swing Song*. Blue Note, 90413.
Sun Ra Arkestra. *Planet Earth/Interstellar Low Ways*. Evidence, 22039.
World Saxophone Quartet. *Steppin With*. Black Saint, 120027.

10

Chicago: The Avant-Garde

A NEW WAY OF THINKING

After free jazz broke the sound barrier in New York and virtually all music rules were considered optional, it was time for a reassessment. Could jazz evolve only by becoming more crowded, dense, and dissonant? Was jazz heading towards a dead end, unable to become freer and more modern without becoming completely unlistenable?

Jazz musicians, who were finding themselves short of work with rock's rise in popularity and clubowners' reluctance to hire more adventurous players, were going to have to take control of their situation. New ideas were needed, ranging from alternative venues to forming artist-owned labels and somehow educating the public about the new music.

A group of musicians in Chicago came up with some possible answers in the 1960s and started a powerful organization.

THE AACM

In 1962 pianist Muhal Richard Abrams formed the Experiment Band in Chicago. Although starting out as a fairly conventional big band, over the next few years it incorporated freer sounds, adventurous arrangements, and innovative improvisations. Unfortunately the group never recorded, but it was influential within Chicago and led to the formation of the Association for the Advancement of Creative Musicians (AACM).

The AACM was formed in 1965 in Chicago. It has had many goals through the years including encouraging young musicians with technical ability and a knowledge of music history to express themselves, coming up with new types of performance spaces rather than the stereotypical smoky nightclub, documenting the music, and creating community outreach programs so the music could reach a larger audience without compromising its ideals. The organization has helped several generations of major improvising musicians through the years.

THE ART ENSEMBLE OF CHICAGO

Among the musicians in Abrams' group was saxophonist Roscoe Mitchell, an early member of the AACM. In 1966 he led the first AACM group to record, resulting in the album *Sound*. His sextet, which included trumpeter Lester Bowie and bassist Malachi Favors, utilized "little instruments," some of which were toys, to add color to the music, hinted at past styles both satirically and with reverence, and contrasted silence with sound rather than sticking exclusively to high-energy ensembles. On December 3, 1966, Mitchell led a quartet at a concert that included Bowie, Favors, and multi-reedist Joseph Jarman. It was billed as the Art Ensemble, with the "of Chicago" added a couple years later. The group became a permanent band, making a strong impact in Chicago before spending 1969 to 1971 in Paris where they added drummer Don Moye.

A very theatrical performance group, the Art Ensemble of Chicago made music more accessible than many avant-garde units, thanks to Bowie's wit, constantly changing instruments and styles, and paying close attention to dynamics and mood variations. Their motto became "Great Black Music—Ancient to the Future." Audiences were never sure what was going to happen onstage next, particularly when scores of instruments were available to be played including all types of reeds and exotic percussion.

The band, which returned to Chicago in 1972, was at its prime during the 1970s and early 1980s. After that the individual musicians, particularly Bowie, spent as much time on their own projects as with the group, and live appearances by the band became rare. Jarman left the Art Ensemble in 1993, and in 1999 Bowie passed away. The Art Ensemble of Chicago regrouped as a trio with Mitchell, Favors, and Moye, and in 2003 Jarman returned. Malachi Favors died in early 2004 making the future of the unique group uncertain after thirty-seven years.

The Art Ensemble of Chicago, and many of the musicians associated with the AACM, showed that space could be used in the music, along with melody, catchy rhythms, and aspects of past styles, while still creating very modern, and sometimes startling, new music. Rather than reject the past, the musicians of the Art Ensemble of Chicago built upon the past innovations while feeling free to break any of the rules they desired.

OTHER AACM MUSICIANS

The AACM started with thirty-six musicians in 1965 and has grown quite a bit since, remaining an important force in the Chicago area. One of the most controversial of the AACM musicians was Anthony Braxton, who early in his career used mathematical symbols and formulas as song titles for his originals and wrote overly complex, barely comprehensible liner notes. A master at most reed instruments, but sounding especially distinctive on alto, Braxton has an original improvising style. He became a member of the AACM in 1966, played with pianist Chick Corea, bassist Dave Holland, and drummer Barry Altschul in Circle during 1970 and 1971. Since then he has recorded extensively in a bewildering variety of settings including unaccompanied solos and encounters with four orchestras at once. Among his finest efforts have been his quartets, particularly when he utilized trombonist George Lewis or pianist Marilyn Crispell.

Leo Smith, an early member of the AACM, was one of the most esoteric of the trumpeters to emerge in the 1960s, one whose brittle tone and adventurous style makes every unpredictable note count. Other major players were trombonist George Lewis, tenor-saxophonist Fred Anderson, drummer Steve McCall, and altoist-composer Henry Threadgill, who led the group Air before beginning his innovative solo career. Groups included Kahil El'Zabar's Ethnic Heritage Ensemble, Ernest Dawkins's New Horizons Ensemble, Malachi Thompson's Africa Brass, and Edward Wilkerson's Eight Bold Souls.

The success of the AACM inspired a similar organization, Black Artists Group, in St. Louis, and adventurous musicians everywhere to play original music that they felt and believed in, despite the obstacles and the potential lack of commercial success and acceptance.

RECOMMENDED RECORDINGS

Air. *Air Lore*. Bluebird, 6578.
Anthony Braxton. *Quartet—Dortmund 1976*. Hat Art, 6075.
The Art Ensemble of Chicago. *Live at Mandel Hall*. Delmark, 432.
Henry Threadgill. *Rag, Bush and All*. Novus, 3052.
Leo Smith. *Rastafari*. Boxholder, 035.
Lester Bowie. *The Great Pretender*. ECM, 829369.
Roscoe Mitchell. *Sound*. Delmark, 408.

11

New Orleans: The Young Lions

LOOKING TO THE PAST FOR INSPIRATION

Throughout jazz history, each new generation comes up with a new way of playing, expanding upon jazz's legacy with new approaches and ideas. After the free jazz movement of the 1960s and the prominence of fusion in the 1970s, a conservative new movement was born, the Young Lions. Led by trumpeter Wynton Marsalis and fueled by pianist Ellis Marsalis, his father who taught many promising young musicians in New Orleans, the movement looked back to 1960s hard bop, Blue Note recordings, and the post-bop music of the Miles Davis Quintet from the mid-1960s. Rather than utilize electronics, the musicians were purely acoustic and even favored older clothing styles: young men wearing suits. In many ways it was a welcome change, an admission that jazz's past styles were not exhausted of possibilities and that bands should not look scruffy in public.

On the plus side, the movement focused a lot of attention on acoustic jazz, inspiring younger musicians to explore jazz rather than focus on more commercial music. On the minus side, however, after a short time the major labels jumped on the bandwagon, signing up every attractive, young acoustic jazz musician they could find, many of whom were not ready to be leaders. It also inspired a backlash from overlooked and more mature musicians in their forties and fifties who were playing at a higher level than many of the Young Lions,

and by avant-gardists who were stung by some of Wynton Marsalis' more outlandish statements about their chosen style.

Leader of the Young Lions movement in the 1980s, Wynton
Marsalis remains one of jazz's top trumpeters.
*Photo courtesy of the Wayne Knight Collection, Star Line
Productions.*

Although much of the music took place
in New York, the concept was largely born
in New Orleans, where many of the top
Young Lions were originally based. Since
twenty-first-century youngsters in New
Orleans, just as in the old days, still hear
brass bands at parades on a regular basis,
the musicians have often found ways to
incorporate parade rhythms in their originals, even when harmonically the style is
light years away from the traditional New
Orleans music. This feature often made
their music sound different than that of the
original hard boppers.

WYNTON MARSALIS

In the early 1980s Wynton Marsalis became the symbol for the revival of
acoustic jazz, and to a certain extent he still is. A New Orleans native, he grew
up surrounded by the sounds of traditional jazz, Dixieland, the small local
modern jazz scene that his father was a part of, New Orleans r&b, and the
funk/pop music of the 1970s. Marsalis began playing when he was six, studied
classical music and jazz, and as a teenager played in both funk groups and
classical orchestras. A brilliant trumpeter from a young age, in time he
gravitated towards straight-ahead jazz. He already had phenomenal technique
when he was eighteen, before attending Julliard and joining Art Blakey's Jazz
Messengers.

Marsalis was on his way to becoming a household name. In addition to starring with Blakey from 1980 to 1982, he toured with Herbie Hancock and started
leading albums of his own for Columbia. Not only was he recording jazz, but
Marsalis also worked on classical projects, winning awards in both areas. He
was also generating a great deal of publicity. During a period when most young
black musicians were drawn toward r&b, rock, pop, funk, or fusion, Marsalis
championed acoustic jazz and helped to revive hard bop. He was unquestion-
ably a remarkable technician, as well as attractive, articulate, and outspoken.
He was frequently quoted criticizing avant-garde jazz and fusion, even making
unfavorable comments about Miles Davis' later musical directions, despite
Davis being a primary influence. Marsalis made headlines, and many younger
musicians noticed.

In 1982 Wynton Marsalis formed a quintet that featured his older brother
Branford Marsalis on tenor and soprano. Branford stayed with the group until
1985 when he departed to tour with rock bassist Sting, leading to a temporary

rift with his brother. The siblings soon made up, and there remains a magical chemistry between them during their rare performances together. Over the past twenty years Marsalis' sidemen have included such major talents as the late pianist Kenny Kirkland, bassists Charnett Moffett and Robert Hurst, drummers Jeff "Tain" Watts and Herlin Riley, and pianists Marcus Roberts and Eric Reed. His strongest band was a septet that included trombonist Wycliffe Gordon, altoist Wes Anderson, and Todd Williams on tenor. Marsalis' own playing has gradually become more individual, moving away from the Miles Davis model by 1990, while his music has grown from its hard bop foundation toward more adventurous improvising, yet retaining a reverence for the music of Louis Armstrong and Duke Ellington, whose music he often plays. He recorded frequently during the 1980s and 1990s and won a Pulitzer Prize, the first for a jazz musician, with his marathon work *Blood on the Fields*.

Having gained early recognition as one of jazz's most important spokesmen, Marsalis has had a very strong impact on younger generations as artistic director of the Lincoln Center Jazz Orchestra and as an important force in the jazz education movement. His statements tend to be conservative and have been controversial, but they have always been sincere and fueled by his experiences.

OTHER MODERN NEW ORLEANS PLAYERS

New Orleans has had three major musical movements. The first was early jazz, followed by a lively r&b scene that was at its prime in the 1950s and 1960s. The most recent movement, the Young Lions, has spawned not only Wynton Marsalis and his brothers, Branford on tenor and soprano, trombonist Delfeayo, and drummer Jason, but also many other talents.

Ellis Marsalis deserves a large part of the credit. A modern jazz pianist starting in the 1950s, Ellis Marsalis played hard bop and post-bop in New Orleans when it was underground music. To earn a living and raise his family, he also played regularly with Dixieland trumpeter Al Hirt's band and was an important teacher. Among his students were pianist-singer Harry Connick Jr., flutist Kent Jordan, altoist Donald Harrison, and trumpeters Terence Blanchard, Nicholas Payton, and Marlon Jordan. All have had significant careers.

The musical role models for most of these players and the Young Lions who came from other cities included trumpeters Miles Davis and Lee Morgan, altoist Jackie McLean, tenors Hank Mobley and Wayne Shorter, and pianists McCoy Tyner, Herbie Hancock, and Bill Evans, not to mention Art Blakey's Jazz Messengers. Some of the Young Lions, particularly Connick, Payton, Harrison, and Wynton Marsalis, occasionally play traditional New Orleans jazz or incorporate aspects of that idiom into their new music, while others barely hint at New Orleans.

Among the other members of the Young Lions movement were trumpeters Roy Hargrove from Texas and Wallace Roney from Philadelphia, tenorsaxophonist Joshua Redman from Berkeley, pianists Benny Green from

New York, and Marcus Roberts from Jacksonville, Florida. They share with the New Orleans–born musicians the desire to learn from the past, basing their early styles players from twenty or thirty years earlier, before in time finding their voice.

The best Young Lions survived both the initial acclaim and the backlash. They have since developed more original styles, sounding much more individual in their thirties than they had a decade earlier. Although they appreciate the accomplishments of their predecessors, they ultimately realized that to add to the legacy of jazz, they have to play themselves and develop fresh new ideas. They found ways of dealing with the jazz tradition rather than merely recreating the past, and now the Young Lions of the 1980s and 1990s are some of the main musical giants of today.

RECOMMENDED RECORDINGS

Benny Green. *These Are Soulful Days*. Blue Note, 99527.
Branford Marsalis. *The Beautyful Ones Are Not Yet Born*. Columbia, 46990.
Joshua Redman. *Beyond*. Warner Bros., 47465.
Nicholas Payton. *Gumbo Nouveau*. Verve, 314 531 199.
Roy Hargrove. *With the Tenors of Our Time*. Verve, 523019.
Terence Blanchard. *The Malcolm X Jazz Suite*. Columbia, 53599.
Wynton Marsalis. *Black Codes from the Underground*. Columbia, 40009.
Wynton Marsalis. *Live at the Village Vanguard*. Columbia, 69876, 7 CDs.

12

Modern Jazz: Fusion and Beyond

BEYOND REGIONALISM

With the end of regional styles, jazz ironically has not become a unified whole, but instead has been evolving in many different directions simultaneously. Fusion, the last dominant style, garnered the most headlines during the 1970s, but jazz musicians have since explored virtually every past style from Dixieland to free jazz. Many have chosen a bit of this and a bit of that to create unusual combinations of idioms and all types of new fusions that have little to do with the rock/jazz style, except in its spirit.

What Is Fusion?

Fusion is a mixture of the rhythms, sounds, and often the instrumentation of rock with jazz improvisation. Prior to 1967 the worlds of jazz and rock and roll rarely overlapped. Occasionally a jazz musician, usually urged on by a record label, would cover a rock song in hopes of increasing sales; but this usually created a dud, both artistically and commercially. Jazz musicians looked on rock and roll of the 1950s as juvenile music, even though some backing players came from the jazz world, and although more impressed in the 1960s by the Beatles, the compositions of Paul McCartney and John Lennon seemed simplistic compared to the legacy of Duke Ellington, Charlie Parker, and John Coltrane. In addition, few of the rock musicians of the early 1960s were sophisticated enough players to stretch out on jazz pieces.

That situation began to change during 1967 and 1968. The rise of the counterculture that attracted many jazz players had been prefigured in the social conditions of the jazz world as early as the 1950s, particularly in the racial integration resulting from the civil rights movement, the recreational use of drugs, and the fight for self-expression as opposed to being part of the dominant conformist culture. Although jazz had always stood for freedom and musically had found it in the avant-garde movement, rock of the late 1960s spoke much more to the new generation than did free jazz.

Rock musicians were generally much better players by 1968 than they had been in 1963, and this growth showed in their compositions and musicianship. While jazz musicians of the early 1960s had grown up on Charlie Parker, the younger ones of the late 1960s had often listened to the early rock-and-roll bands and were intrigued by the Beatles and Jimi Hendrix. In fact, early mixtures of the new style were called jazz/rock or rock/jazz until the fusion term was coined. The electric piano and synthesizers of the 1970s began to be utilized, as was the electric bass, competing favorably with the acoustic piano and string bass in significance at least for a time.

Among the earliest examples of fusion on record are an album by the Free Spirits and the first recordings by Gary Burton's quartet. The Free Spirits, a quintet featuring tenor-saxophonist Jim Pepper and two guitarists including Larry Coryell, only recorded one very obscure record in 1967. Burton, a young vibraphonist who was interested not only in jazz but also in country music and the era's new rock scene, added Coryell to his quartet that same year. Coryell, who came from the world of electric blues and rock, has the distinction of being the first fusion guitarist, and Burton's group, including bassist Steve Swallow and either Roy Haynes or Bob Moses on drums, lasted into mid-1968. Burton's band set a trend in another area. Up until that time, jazz musicians almost always appeared on stage wearing suits or at least ties, but Burton's group dressed much more informally.

During the next few years Gary Burton's groups featured such guitarists as Jerry Hahn, Sam Brown, Mick Goodrick, Pat Metheny, and John Scofield. The vibes never became a major instrument in fusion, and after 1977 Burton's music was much more in the post-bop field, but he and his quartet had blazed an early path for others to follow.

MILES DAVIS: THE FUSION YEARS

Miles Davis, who had already moved through bebop, cool jazz, hard bop, modal jazz, and his own brand of the avant-garde, wanted to continue evolving. The soul and rock music of James Brown, Sly Stone, and Jimi Hendrix interested him, and by 1968 he was opening up his own music to those outside influences. He encouraged Herbie Hancock to play electric piano and Ron Carter to switch to electric bass. Before the end of the year, Hancock had departed to form his own sextet while Carter became a very busy studio musician; they were replaced by keyboardist Chick Corea and bassist Dave Holland. In early 1969 drummer Tony Williams also departed to form his own Lifetime group and was succeeded by Jack DeJohnette. Shortly before Williams left, Miles Davis' ensemble, the quintet augmented by the keyboards of Hancock and Joe Zawinul plus guitarist John McLaughlin, recorded the two lengthy medleys that formed *In a Silent Way*, a moody and groundbreaking electronic album.

In a Silent Way surprised Davis' longtime fans, but many of them were much more disturbed by its follow-up, *Bitches Brew*. This six-song double LP essentially launched the fusion movement. Davis was joined by Wayne Shorter on soprano, Corea, Holland, DeJohnette, Bennie Maupin on bass clarinet, Zawinul, electric bassist Harvey Brooks, percussionists Don Alias and Jumma Santos, plus on a few selections drummer Lenny White and Larry Young on electric piano. Most of the performances are very extended with the emphasis on ensembles, though the trumpeter had some solos, and a rock-like sound. The music is quite unpredictable and very different from the ensemble-solos-ensemble format of straightahead jazz. While some detractors accused Davis of "selling out," in reality his new music was not that easy to comprehend and often featured twenty-minute selections that could never catch on as pop hits. "Selling out" for Davis actually would have involved sticking with his 1950s repertoire and repeating the same ideas throughout his career, instead of constantly forging ahead.

From 1970 to 1975 Davis took his music through a lot of phases, utilizing many different players in his expanded groups. In addition to his alumni, such musicians as keyboardist Keith Jarrett, percussionist Airto, and saxophonists Dave Grossman, Gary Bartz, Dave Liebman, and Sonny Fortune spent periods in his group. Among Davis' recordings of the era were *Miles Davis at Fillmore*, which has Corea and Jarrett constantly banging their keyboards as if they were trying to destroy them; the excellent *Live/Evil*; *A Tribute to Jack Johnson*; *On the Corner*, by which time Davis was completely distorting his own sound with electronics; *Dark Magus*, a 1974 set that has the group utilizing three electric guitars; and *Agharta* and *Pangaea*, a pair of live concerts that were both recorded February 1, 1975.

After having created such challenging approaches to fusion, with overcrowded ensembles, guitarists emulating Jimi Hendrix, and fiery trumpet solos, Davis surprised everyone by dropping out of music completely in mid-1975. In bad health and burnt out, he did not perform in public until 1981 when he began a comeback, taking about two years to gain back all of his trumpet "chops." His older fans were disappointed that he did not return to the music of the 1950s and 1960s that had made him famous, but the trumpeter's music was different in the 1980s than during the first half of the 1970s. The multiple keyboardists were gone, and he only used one guitarist. He no longer distorted his tone, he rediscovered the value of using space, and he showed a greater appreciation for melodies again, even though he looked much more to the pop world than to jazz, with two of his ballad features being Michael Jackson's "Human Nature" and Cyndy Lauper's "Time after Time." In addition, one of the highlights of his sets was when he played a lowdown blues. Although by the late 1980s it seemed like Davis was treading water to an extent, he never played it overly safe.

It could also be said that the trumpeter never looked back, except once. At the 1991 Montreux Jazz Festival, Davis agreed to revisit some of the Gil Evans arrangements written for his *Birth of the Cool*, *Miles Ahead*, *Porgy and Bess*, and *Sketches of Spain*, projects from earlier decades. Although some of the solo space was given to trumpeter Wallace Roney, who closely emulated Davis, and altoist Kenny Garrett, overall Davis did a good job in interpreting this difficult music, just two months before his death at age sixty-five. During his more than four decades in the spotlight, Davis created enough intriguing music and innovations to last several lifetimes.

LIFETIME AND THE MAHAVISHNU ORCHESTRA

Miles Davis not only gave fusion a major boost in its early days, but his alumni were key members of the most important fusion groups of the 1970s. When drummer Tony Williams left Davis' quintet in early 1969, it was to form Lifetime. The explosive trio, featuring the British guitarist John McLaughlin and the innovative Larry Young stretched out on rock structures, but with the sophistication of jazz. Young was notable for being one of the few organists to escape the dominant influence of Jimmy Smith. McLaughlin moved the jazz guitar way beyond the influence of Charlie Christian, with an original sound and approach that mixed aspects of rock guitar innovator Jimi Hendrix's electronic explorations with jazz. Lifetime recorded enough material in 1969 to fill two LPs called *Emergency*. These are full of youthful energy and virtuosity, only disappointing in the surprisingly distorted recording quality. McLaughlin stayed with Lifetime through 1970, recording *Turn It Over* with the rock group Cream's bassist Jack Bruce making the band a quartet, before going out on his own. Williams continued leading Lifetime through two additional phases, with Ted Dunbar on guitar in 1971 and a 1975 and 1976 version with the adventurous rock guitarist Allan Holdsworth.

Tony Williams, who was still only thirty at the end of 1975, broke up Lifetime in 1976 and spent years freelancing and studying music. In 1986 he formed an all-star hard bop quintet with trumpeter Wallace Roney, saxophonist Billy Pierce, pianist Mulgrew Miller, and bassist Charnett Moffett, who was eventually replaced by Ira Coleman, that lasted until his premature death in 1997.

John McLaughlin had already had extensive experience playing in his native England when he was offered a job in 1969 with Lifetime. At the same time Miles Davis also noticed the highly original guitarist and utilized him on several of his recordings, including *In a Silent Way*, *Bitches Brew*, and *Jack Johnson*. A more extroverted guitarist than Larry Coryell, McLaughlin could play with the ferocious power of the most radical rock players, yet his ideas were light years ahead of them. His 1970 album, *My Goals Beyond*, has strong hints of two of his future directions. McLaughlin is heard on eight unaccompanied acoustic guitar solos, mostly modern jazz originals, and also investigating Indian rhythms with a group comprising both American and Indian musicians.

First John McLaughlin explored a completely different style of music. During 1971 and 1972 his Mahavishnu Orchestra was the definitive rock-oriented fusion band. The quintet, including violinist Jerry Goodman, keyboardist Jan Hammer, bassist Rick Laird, and drummer Billy Cobham, was the most powerful of the fusion groups. It could compete with any rock band in volume and intensity, yet was on its own level in creativity and musicianship. Considered at the time to be a rock group, but now thought of as a leader in fusion, the Mahavishnu Orchestra filled stadiums and drew many rock fans into jazz. During its brief period of existence, the Orchestra recorded four albums, one of which was not released until 1999, and set the standard for fusion.

After the Mahavishnu Orchestra broke up, McLaughlin had a new version of the band with violinist Jean-Luc Ponty and singer-keyboardist Gayle Moran, but it made less of an impression. In 1975 McLaughlin switched directions completely, specializing on the acoustic guitar and forming Shakti, a quintet with violinist L. Shankar, Ramnad Raghaven on mridangam, T. S. Vinayakaram on ghatan, and tabla master Zakir Hussain. With this unit that lasted three years, McLaughlin helped pioneer what could be called world fusion, mixing Indian classical music with the improvising of jazz.

Since then, McLaughlin has been involved in many different projects, switching between electric and acoustic guitar, leading a short-lived third version of the Mahavishnu Orchestra, playing with orchestras, and leading a Shakti reunion group called Remembering Shakti. He remains one of the giants of the guitar.

WEATHER REPORT

Wayne Shorter was a member of the Miles Davis Quintet until 1970, leaving to co-lead Weather Report. A very original tenor saxophonist and composer with his own musical logic, Shorter had also carved out a distinctive voice on soprano sax. His co-leader with Weather Report, Joe Zawinul, had been Cannonball Adderley's pianist for years, composed the soulful hit "Mercy, Mercy, Mercy," and was an early pioneer on electric piano and synthesizers, contributing "In a Silent Way" to the Miles Davis album of the same name and guesting on some of Davis' dates.

The original version of Weather Report comprised the co-leaders, electric bassist Miroslav Vitous, drummer Alphonse Mouzon, and percussionist Airto. With the focus on ensemble playing rather than individual solos, everyone and no one was soloing. Zawinul's keyboards were a dominant force, although Shorter's soprano was also a key voice. Initially Weather Report's music was more abstract than that of the other fusion bands, but over time it became funkier and featured catchier melodies along with world music elements. While Zawinul and Shorter were constants, the other spots were soon filled by a variety of top young musicians, including drummers Eric Gravatt and Ndugu Chancler; percussionists Dom Um Romao, Alyrio Lima, and Alex Acuna; and by late 1973 bassist Alphonso Johnson. Johnson helped redefine the role of the electric bassist in the group as a near equal with Zawinul in setting grooves and leading the increasingly infectious rhythms.

In 1976 Jaco Pastorius took Johnson's place. A revolutionary on the electric bass, Pastorius played with the facility of a guitarist. His background was in r&b and rock, but he had also played jazz with multi-instrumentalist Ira Sullivan, pianist Paul Bley, and guitarist Pat Metheny. During his five years with Weather Report, Pastorius became a major influence on other electric bassists, playing with a very distinctive tone, plenty of power, and the ability to both accompany and challenge other soloists. He was a true powerhouse on his instrument, and even after his death, he is still a major force to be reckoned with.

Starting with the 1977 album *Heavy Weather*, which includes the big hit "Birdland," Pastorius' role with Weather Report was so important that he was practically a co-leader with Zawinul. Shorter became more of a special ingredient in the group's sound although not that involved in the group's evolution, while Peter Erskine was stimulating on drums. Weather Report's popularity was at its height after "Birdland" caught on, and Pastorius put in spectacular performances that nearly overshadowed Zawinul at times.

In 1980 Pastorius formed a big band, Word of Mouth, and his solo projects resulted in his leaving Weather Report altogether the following year. Pastorius should have been able to enjoy a busy and lucrative solo career, but he suffered from mental illness, and after 1983 his life was increasingly erratic. Reluctant to take the medication he needed or to seek therapy, Jaco Pastorius was on a downward spiral in his last few years before being beaten to death in 1987 by a bouncer when he tried to break into a Florida nightclub.

By then Weather Report was also a thing of the past. After Pastorius left, his spot was ably taken by bassist Victor Bailey with Omar Hakim succeeding Erskine on drums, but the group had seen its prime. Joe Zawinul's keyboards completely dominated the band's sound with Wayne Shorter becoming much less significant; the balance between the co-leaders was gone. In 1985 after fifteen years, Weather Report broke up. Since then, Zawinul has led a series of groups, first known as Weather Update and then becoming Zawinul Syndicate, that are as much world music as jazz, featuring vocals in various languages interacting with Zawinul's still-innovative work on synthesizers. Shorter had a low profile for years, just making occasional guest appearances, but in the early twenty-first century he emerged with an exciting quartet with pianist Danilo Perez, bassist John Patitucci, and drummer Brian Blade. On both tenor and soprano, Shorter at the age of seventy showed that his highly original post-bop playing was still adventurous and among the freshest voices in jazz.

CHICK COREA AND RETURN TO FOREVER

Although Weather Report lasted fifteen years, its main competitor, Chick Corea's Return to Forever, did not make it to its sixth year—counting three different versions of the group. Corea, a talented pianist, spent important periods playing with the bands of Mongo Santamaria, Willie Bobo, trumpeter Blue Mitchell from 1964 to 1966, Herbie Mann, Stan Getz, and Miles Davis from 1968 to 1970. With Davis he began performing on electric piano and was one of the first keyboardists to develop his own individual sound on this instrument. After leaving the trumpeter, Corea took a detour, playing in the avant-garde quartet Circle with altoist Anthony Braxton in 1971 before deciding that he had a need to communicate to a much wider audience.

Corea formed the original version of Return to Forever in late 1971. It was a quintet featuring singer Flora Purim, Airto on drums and percussion, Joe Farrell on reeds, and bassist Stanley Clarke. Among the songs they popularized were Corea's "Spain," "500 Miles High," "Sometime Ago," "La Fiesta," and "Captain Marvel." Its music was an interesting combination of post-bop jazz and Brazilian fusion, played with a light melodic feel.

In 1973 Purim and Airto went out on their own, and Corea put together his most famous version of Return to Forever. With Clarke returning, and now emphasizing electric bass, the group was filled out by drummer Lenny White and originally Bill Connors on guitar; Al DiMeola took over from Connors after the first album when the latter decided to focus on acoustic guitar in his solo career. This very rock-oriented version of Return to Forever lasted three years, at its best when playing Corea's compositions. It was a perfect setting for Clarke and White in particular, and an excellent training ground for DiMeola who was only nineteen when he joined.

From 1973 to 1976, Return to Forever gave Weather Report a run for its money as the most popular of the fusion band. Its complex rock-oriented performances delighted huge crowds of rock fans, some of whom were inspired to explore Corea's earlier work. Although no loss of enthusiasm can be heard on the band's final album, *Romantic Warrior*, Return to Forever's breakup seemed inevitable, given DiMeola's growing popularity and Clarke's interest in playing funk. By the end of 1976 Corea broke up the band. There was a third version of Return to Forever in 1977, a nine-piece group that included Clarke, Joe Farrell, and singer Gayle Moran, Corea's wife. That small big band hinted at fusion while also being hard bop oriented, but it did not last long.

None of the members of the second version of Return to Forever had difficulty finding work after the group disbanded. Corea worked on a wide variety of short-lived projects for the next decade, including occasional duets with vibraphonist Gary Burton, a two-piano tour with Herbie Hancock, collaborations with tenor-saxophonist Michael Brecker, and recordings with trios and as a solo pianist. In 1986, after years of mostly emphasizing his work on acoustic piano, Corea organized a new fusion group, the Elektric Band. Comprising bassist John Patitucci, drummer Dave Weckl, altoist Eric Marienthal, and guitarist Frank Gambale who replaced Scott Henderson, the Elektric Band lasted for five years. It featured more variety than Return to Forever, with acoustic interludes and some swinging moments in addition to the rock, funk, and electronics. Patitucci proved to be a phenomenal bassist and also played with Corea in his more straight-ahead Akoustic Band, an acoustic trio with Weckl. Corea has since had a reunion tour with the Elektric Band and continued working on acoustic projects too, including the sextet Horizon and trios with bassist Avashi Cohen.

After the end of Return to Forever, Stanley Clarke switched to playing funk in a group with keyboardist George Duke, wrote movie scores, and only occasionally played jazz and fusion. Lenny White became a busy freelancer who was often heard in straight-ahead settings, although his own fusion records failed to catch on. In contrast, Al DiMeola had a major career as a leader. Early on he had the reputation of playing too many notes and relying on speed over substance, but he eventually matured into a versatile player who learned the value of space and dynamics. DiMeola's interest in world music, particularly that of Latin America and Argentina, his ability to be distinctive on both electric and acoustic

Chick Corea and Herbie Hancock are two leaders of fusion who eventually switched back to acoustic pianos and have been involved in a countless number of rewarding projects. *Photo courtesy of the Wayne Knight Collection, Star Line Productions.*

guitars like John McLaughlin, and his brilliant technique have resulted in one stimulating project after another, keeping the legacy of fusion guitar alive.

HERBIE HANCOCK

Herbie Hancock already had a strong name in jazz before he joined Miles Davis in 1963, having composed "Watermelon Man" and recorded his own albums for Blue Note. While with Davis, he continued to grow, finding a role for the piano in the trumpeter's post-bop period and beginning to develop his own voice on electric piano during 1967 and 1968. After leaving Davis, Hancock formed a sextet that lasted until 1972, in its final two years including trumpeter Eddie Henderson, trombonist Julian Priester, Bennie Maupin on reeds, bassist Buster Williams, and drummer Billy Hart. The Herbie Hancock Sextet's music was funky at times and hinted at fusion, but was also avant-garde and quite unpredictable. It remains one of the most underrated bands of the period.

Hancock, however, grew tired of playing for small crowds and constantly scuffling. In 1973 he broke up the sextet and formed the Headhunters, a much more accessible group. The Headhunters flavored their brand of fusion with funk and r&b rather than rock, immediately generating a large audience. Originally consisting of Hancock on electronic keyboards, Maupin, electric bassist Paul Jackson, drummer Harvey Mason, and percussionist Bill Summers, the Headhunters had a big hit with "Chameleon" on their debut recording. They played for dancing audiences who were at least as interested in funk as they were in jazz.

Like Miles Davis and Chick Corea, Hancock never stays in one project for too long. If anything, he has been the most changeable of the three musical giants. After a concert at the 1976 Newport Jazz Festival featured Hancock with the Headhunters, his reunited sextet, and the special V.S.O.P. Quintet of Wayne Shorter, Ron Carter, Tony Williams, and Freddie Hubbard in Miles Davis' place, he toured with the latter group and made some new acoustic recordings, breaking up the Headhunters.

Since then Herbie Hancock alternated between acoustic groups, often with a trio or heading a combo featuring trumpeter Roy Hargrove and tenor-saxophonist Michael Brecker, and electronic projects that sometimes went way beyond jazz, including some disco in the late 1970s, dance music, some African world music, and the use of turntables, such as on the electronic funk hit "Rock It." More than forty years after he arrived on the scene, Herbie Hancock remains a consistently stimulating and continually unpredictable performer.

FREE FUNK AND M-BASE MUSIC

As is true of the most significant jazz groups, the best fusion bands have their own unique personality and sound. Few were as dense, noisy, and adventurous as Ornette Coleman's Prime Time. Altoist Coleman's quartets of 1959 to 1961 paved the way for free jazz and the avant-garde movement of the mid-1960s. In

1976 when fusion was starting to decline, Coleman put together a group called Prime Time that eventually consisted of his own alto and a double rhythm section with two guitars, two electric bassists, and two drummers. The music, sometimes called "free funk," featured funky but utterly unpredictable rhythms from sidemen while Coleman wailed over the top. The performances were supposed to be very democratic with all of the musicians having an equal role, displaying Coleman's "harmelodic" theories, with harmonies, melodies, and rhythms all having equal importance. Due to the sound of the instruments, Coleman always appeared to be leading the heated ensembles. His sidemen at various times have included drummer Ronald Shannon Jackson and bassist Jamaaladeen Tacuma, both leaders of their own important free funk groups. Prime Time continued on a part-time basis. Ronald Shannon Jackson's Decoding Society and Jamaaladeen Tacuma's Spectacle were exciting free funk groups in the 1980s.

In the mid-1980s altoist Steve Coleman became one of the main founders of the M-Base movement, which is slightly related to 1970s fusion in its openness to mixing idioms and approaches. M-Base, or macro-basic array of structured extemporization, was similar in concept to free funk with danceable but unpredictable rhythms, dissonant but ultimately logical solos, crowded ensembles, and a very different way of improvising from bebop. The key innovators in this informal movement, in addition to Steve Coleman, were altoist Greg Osby, tenor-saxophonist Gary Thomas, trumpeter Graham Haynes, trombonist Robin Eubanks, pianist Geri Allen, bassist Lonnie Plaxico, drummer Marvin "Smitty" Smith, and singer Cassandra Wilson. Not all of the M-Base projects were equally rewarding—some of Coleman's recordings in the 1990s allowed rappers to dominate—and the musicians have largely gone their separate ways since then, but their joint projects were always stimulating if abrasive, and their approaches to soloing remain influential.

OTHER FUSION PLAYERS

In addition to the musicians mentioned, there have been other significant fusion players. Violinist Jean-Luc Ponty, a virtuoso from France, led the Jean-Luc Ponty Experience from 1970 to 1972, had stints with rock guitarist-composer Frank Zappa, and the second Mahavishnu Orchestra, and then beginning in 1975, led a series of impressive albums for the Atlantic label. Ponty's band of that era consisted of his violin, guitar, keyboards, electric bass, and drums, a very cohesive unit with all of the instruments at times blending together as one.

Though overshadowed by John McLaughlin and Al DiMeola among guitarists, Larry Coryell, who had preceded both of them, worked steadily after leaving Gary Burton's band in 1968. He led The Eleventh House from 1972 to 1975, a fusion group that also featured drummer Alphonse Mouzon and trumpeter Mike Lawrence, who was preceded by Randy Brecker. Coryell has since explored acoustic guitar, Brazilian jazz, and bebop, having an eclectic and underrated career.

Chick Corea, Herbie Hancock, and Joe Zawinul were among the top electric keyboardists of the 1970s continuing in that role into the twenty-first century. Jaco Pastorius and Stanley Clarke set the standard for fusion bassists, although they were challenged by John Patitucci and Marcus Miller, also a notable producer.

Billy Cobham, the drummer with the original Mahavishnu Orchestra, gained recognition as the premiere fusion drummer of the 1970s, competing favorably with Alphonse Mouzon and Jack DeJohnette. Cobham, yet another alumni of Miles Davis' recording groups who appeared on *Bitches Brew*, *Live-Evil*, and *Jack Johnson*, recorded frequently in a variety of jazz settings. After the Mahavishnu Orchestra broke up, in 1973 he led his own fusion group, Spectrum, utilizing such players as keyboardist Jan Hammer, formerly with Mahavishnu, the Brecker brothers—trumpeter Randy and tenor-saxophonist Michael Brecker—and guitarists John Abercrombie and John Scofield. Cobham has had a lower profile since the 1980s, occasionally coming out of semi-retirement to lead electronic modern fusion bands.

THE DECLINE OF FUSION

During the first half of the 1970s, fusion was everywhere in jazz, and acoustic jazz was being forced underground to a certain extent. The jazz world was split in two by the new style that many on the acoustic side doubted was jazz at all. By 1975 the style was starting to run out of creative gas, and by the early 1980s fusion was considered passé by many.

What happened to fusion? It may have been a victim of its own success. The initial joy of mixing together jazz improvisation with the sound and rhythms of rock had excited many young musicians. As the music became more and more complex, however, it lost some of its charm and much of its initial idealism. The rise of guitarists John McLaughlin and Al DiMeola inspired other guitarists to play faster and louder, and many of the original fusion compositions of the mid-1970s sound almost like exercises.

Competition from disco took away much of the dancing audience, and rock eventually shrank fusion's audience which nevertheless stayed fairly large. When Chick Corea, Herbie Hancock, John McLaughlin, Larry Coryell, and Tony Williams gradually shifed back toward acoustic music, at least part of the time, and with Miles Davis' retiring, fusion lost a lot of its creative giants. The revival of acoustic jazz fueled by the return of Dexter Gordon to the United States, the maturation of swing tenor Scott Hamilton and cornetist Warren Vache, and in the 1980s the prominence of the Young Lions led by Wynton Marsalis, pushed fusion out of the headlines in the jazz world.

Despite it all, fusion is still played today by many local and under-documented groups of creative rock musicians and open-minded jazzers. Probably the best examples are guitarist Scott Henderson's Tribal Tech, some jam bands, and any time such guitar giants as John McLaughlin, Al DiMeola, Hiram Bullock, Mike Stern, and Allan Holdsworth choose to really cut loose.

FROM FUSION TO SMOOTH JAZZ

During the late 1960s and early 1970s, fusion combined aspects of jazz and rock, forging a dynamic and exciting style that drew in many listeners from the rock world. At the same time, other jazz musicians sought to combine their music with elements of pop. Sometimes the result was accessible variations of melodic jazz, but in other instances it was merely pop music with a little bit of jazz for seasoning.

The beginnings of pop/jazz can be found in the 1960s recordings of the Ramsey Lewis Trio and soulful altoist Hank Crawford, in the early 1970s work of the Crusaders, formerly known as the Jazz Crusaders, in the music of tenor-saxophonist John Klemmer, whose 1975 *Touch* album served perfectly as a romantic background, and in the work of flugelhornist Chuck Mangione, particularly his orchestra projects. The music is characterized by an emphasis on long melody statements, a light, groovin' melody, an openness to pop elements, and a general lack of chance-taking during the improvisations.

In the 1970s and 1980s, this form of "lite-jazz" was sometimes called contemporary jazz as a way of distinguishing it from so-called traditional jazz, with the latter utilizing a 4/4 walking bass. The problem with those terms is that it made pop/jazz sound more advanced and adventurous than post-bop or free jazz.

The contemporary jazz movement ran parallel with that of the Young Lions but had different principles and purposes. The emphasis was less on spontaneity than on creating music to please the largest audience possible. Recordings tended to be slick, tightly produced, overly safe, and "perfect," devoid of any mistakes or missteps. Vocalists were as close to r&b and pop as they were to jazz, and instrumentalists sounded lightly soulful without blazing any new musical paths.

Among the more popular artists in the contemporary jazz field have been keyboardist-arrangers Bob James and Dave Grusin, pianist David Benoit, keyboardist Jeff Lorber, altoist David Sanborn, tenor-, alto-, and soprano-saxophonist Grover Washington Jr., tenor-saxophonist Tom Scott, Chuck Mangione, guitarists Lee Ritenour, Larry Carlton, Earl Klugh, and George Benson (after he started emphasizing his singing), singer Al Jarreau, and such groups as Spyro Gyra, the Rippingtons, and the Brecker Brothers. All of these musicians are quite talented but held back during their recordings and many of their performances, playing it safe and sticking close to the themes.

As in any jazz-based style, contemporary jazz has its variations. The term "rhythm and jazz" can be used to describe the musicians who combine r&b rather than pop with jazz, including Grover Washington Jr., David Sanborn, the Yellowjackets, and Fattburger. Grover Washington Jr., the towering giant in this field, was born in 1943 and grew up in Buffalo, New York, but he moved to Philadelphia in 1967 and considered it his real home. He was playing in clubs by the time he was twelve, over time developing distinctive voices on tenor, alto, and soprano. Although his background was in r&b and soul jazz organ combos, Washington was capable of playing stirring straight-ahead jazz. He worked in the late 1960s with organists Charles Earland and Johnny Hammond Smith. In 1971 Washington had his biggest break, filling in at a recording date for altoist Hank Crawford. The album *Inner City Blues* became a big seller and made Grover Washington Jr. famous. A talented player who really knew how to work a crowd, Washington had further hits in 1975 with *Mister Magic* and in 1980 with *Winelight*, which included "Just the Two of Us" and was always quite popular. Although identified with contemporary jazz and its successor smooth jazz, Washington often seemed overqualified for those idioms, taking long solos in concerts and constantly pushing himself. A much-beloved figure in Philadelphia and throughout the world, he was greatly mourned after he died of a heart attack in late 1999.

Another sleepier movement was briefly popular, New Age. Influenced by some of the 1970s recordings on the German ECM label, although those were much more adventurous in general, New Age was a type of mediation music that had musicians staying for a longer-than-usual period on one chord, emphasizing long tones and quiet sounds, while developing their music very slowly, similar to classical music's minimalism movement. The Windham Hill label had strong success with many of their New Age recordings, particularly those of pianist George Winston, guitarist Will Ackerman, trumpeter Mark Isham, and pianist Liz Story. New Age ran out of gas after a few years due to the similarity of its many one-mood recordings and lack of any blues elements.

In the 1990s contemporary jazz was renamed smooth jazz, becoming the basis for an extremely successful radio format. Smooth jazz should more accurately just be called smooth, since its jazz content is often minimal, closer to instrumental pop music, or crossover, than contemporary jazz. One of its main leaders and biggest seller has been soprano-saxophonist Kenny G, whose sound is based in Grover Washington Jr., although his improvising is much more predictable and safe. Kenny G became so popular that, to the anguish of many jazz listeners, he became one of the foremost musicians that the average non-jazz listener named when asked who they liked on today's jazz scene.

Among the bigger names in smooth jazz are trumpeters Rick Braun and Chris Botti, saxophonists Kirk Whalum, Richard Elliot, Dave Koz, Boney James, Candy Dulfer, and Gerald Albright, guitarist-singer Joyce Cooling, the Bob James group Fourplay, and the key survivors from contemporary jazz. David Sanborn and Grover Washington are the dominant influences on commercial saxophonists. Many of the musicians and singers including Norah Jones and Sade actually come from the r&b and pop worlds. Because smooth jazz is as much a radio format as it is a style, the pressures of the commercial marketplace constantly influence it. If radio programmers decide that a particular recording is too adventurous, then it is not considered smooth, such as some of the more recent recordings of David Sanborn, the Yellowjackets, and guitarist Pat Metheny.

It is a unique situation for a jazz-based style to have its definition, boundaries, and future commercial success so dependent on radio programmers. Many in the jazz world, whether from mainstream or the avant-garde, do not consider smooth jazz to be creative jazz. Certainly the main intent behind the music—selling recordings and pleasing a large audience—differs from that of other jazz styles, which emphasize finding one's own voice. On the other hand, it is difficult to argue with smooth jazz's commercial success.

AFTER THE FUSION ERA

Rather than jazz racing towards total freedom, which was reached during the mid- to late 1960s, or evolving in one main direction due to the work of a few individuals, the music since the fusion era has been shooting out in dozens of different places at once. To casual observers, jazz may seem to have stopped evolving altogether, because there are no longer one or two dominating giants, and because the jazz of ten or twenty years ago is no longer considered automatically passé.

The earlier attitude that newer styles of jazz "replace" and are superior to older ones began to change in the 1970s when it was recognized that the ranks of the classic greats were starting to thin and that there were many veteran performers who were still in their musical prime. One of those greats, tenor-saxophonist Dexter Gordon, created a sensation when he returned to the United States in 1976 after more than a decade in Europe. His bop/hard bop music had not changed much since the early 1960s, but it was still viable. Fans who had never seen Gordon waited in long lines outside clubs so they could experience the living legend's music in person. The rise of fusion had not decreased the power of Dexter Gordon's brand of straight-ahead jazz.

In the mid-1970s tenor-saxophonist Scott Hamilton and cornetist Warren Vache, two players in their early twenties, chose to spend their careers not performing fusion, funk, or avant-garde jazz, but mainstream swing instead. There had been revivalists in jazz since at least the early 1940s, but many were either veterans of earlier eras or amateurs. Hamilton and Vache were young world-class players who would have succeeded at any music they chose to explore. Their career choice signaled to many other musicians and listeners that there was nothing wrong with artists defying trends and playing whatever style of jazz they desired, as long as they did it with creativity and individuality.

The developments of the second half of the 1970s cheered listeners who feared that, with the rise of fusion, acoustic jazz was finished. As it turned out, no style of jazz has been exhausted yet. Any doubts to that statement were washed away with the rise of Wynton Marsalis and the Young Lions.

TODAY'S JAZZ SCENE

One of the most common questions about recent jazz is also one of the most difficult to answer. New listeners of current music often ask, What is it called? Although the historic styles have names, a large portion of post-1980 jazz does not fall into any simple category, mixing aspects of several styles with original ideas. What is the music of tenor-saxophonist Joe Lovano, altoist Kenny Garrett, or guitarist Pat Metheny, to name three top artists, called?

One name that fits much of the music is post-bop, jazz that is more advanced in its chords, rhythms, and improvisations than hard bop but is not as free or generally as dissonant as avant-garde. An enormous amount of dissimilar music falls into that wide area so, unlike bebop, the boundaries of post-bop are very fluid. Post-bop can also be thought of as modern jazz that is not fusion, crossover/smooth, avant-garde, or a historic style.

There have been many changes in the jazz scene since the 1950s and 1960s. Racism has greatly declined in American society, illegal rather than institutional policy, and therefore many doors have been opened for black musicians. Whereas in the 1950s, black jazz musicians mostly made their living playing in clubs, now the best ones can, with their white counterparts, also play in the studios and/or teach privately. The music education system once only accepted classical music, and jazz musicians had to sneak in practice time behind their instructors' backs, but jazz has become part of the curricula at many colleges and high schools. Boston's Berklee School of Music is only the best known of the numerous music colleges offering classes and degrees in jazz. Many well-respected jazz musicians work at least part-time as professors and other educators. The IAJE (International Association for Jazz Educators) and its large annual conventions that attract as many as 7,000 educators, students, professional musicians, and fans demonstrate the size and strength of the jazz education movement.

For young musicians, to a large extent their former apprenticeship and training in jam sessions and as members of touring bands headed by veteran jazz greats has been replaced by time spent in classrooms and playing with their peers and under the guidance of teachers. There has been a longstanding debate over whether this is good or not. Music schools tend to graduate students who are technically skilled but not necessarily very unique in their improvising abilities, often sounding like the musical apostles of their teachers. Also, music schools often emphasize work in big bands to serve as many students as possible, so some students graduate with skills that are no longer in great demand, since there are not that many regularly working jazz orchestras. Perhaps the problem is with the perception that students who graduate from music schools are "finished" jazz musicians, when in fact they are just beginning their careers. Most twenty-two year olds cannot be expected to solo with the maturity and creativity of someone who is thirty.

The jazz world is very fragmented, with virtually every jazz style being explored by at least a few very creative musicians. Ragtime, which made a comeback when Scott Joplin's music was used in the movie *The Sting* in the early 1970s, is still being performed today, with new compositions written and added to the repertoire. Dixieland is featured at large classic jazz festivals held nearly every weekend somewhere in the United States, including the world's largest American festival, a gigantic event held in Sacramento, California, each Memorial Day weekend. Other traditional jazz musicians, who look to the 1920s for inspiration, have revived vintage arrangements and frameworks from obscure recordings. A generation of small-group swing players who came up after Scott Hamilton and Warren Vache has made pre-bop combos viable again, keeping alive the music of the 1920s, 1930s, and 1940s, including trombonist Dan Barrett, Ken Peplowski on clarinet and tenor, C-melody saxophonist Dan Levinson, tenorman Harry Allen, trumpeter/cornetists Randy Sandke and Peter Ecklund, guitarist Howard Alden, pianist Judy Carmichael, drummer Hal Smith, and singers Banu Gibson and Rebecca Kilgore.

In the late 1980s a strange new mixture of styles began to be heard, particularly from the Royal Crown Revue. The main forefather to the Retro Swing movement was Louis Prima and his band of the mid- to late 1950s. Prima, who had spent periods playing Dixieland in the 1930s and leading a big band the following decade, had a Las Vegas act in the 1950s that combined his New Orleans trumpet and a swing repertoire with the honking r&b tenor of Sam Butera, the ballad vocals of Keely Smith, a shuffle rhythm, Italian comedy, and a rock-and-roll sensibility. More than thirty years later, the Royal Crown Revue and other bands in the 1990s inspired a large dancing audience by utilizing swing and rock and roll in their music.

Some of the Retro Swing bands were really rock bands with vocalists and horn sections that paid lip service to swing without swinging, but there were exceptions. Big Bad Voodoo Daddy uses humor effectively, has fine musicianship, and has performed some catchy new songs including "You and Me and the Bottle Makes Three." Singer Lavay Smith and her Red Hot Skillet Lickers, which has grown beyond retro swing, are a throwback to Dinah Washington and the jump bands of the mid-1940s, balancing blues, early r&b, and boogie-woogie with heated instrumentals that usually feature three horn players. Also worthwhile are Steve Lucky and the Rhumba Buns, the Magnum Brutes, Mora's Modern Rhythmists, and Ron Sunshine's Full Swing. Of the few big bands that were formed during the era, Bill Elliott's orchestra is the most authentic, sounding like a new swing orchestra from 1940.

While there has not been a major revival of bebop or cool jazz, most straight-ahead musicians play bop standards now and then, while the arranging approaches of cool jazz remain influential on many of today's writers. The hard bop revival that gained momentum with the Young Lions continues, with the

Blue Note recordings of the late 1950s and 1960s still providing inspiration. African Cuban jazz remains very popular, perhaps the most popular overall of current jazz styles, filled with scores of talented players both from Cuba and the United States who perform stirring and danceable music.

Soul jazz made a full comeback. The rise of Joey DeFrancesco in the late 1980s and early 1990s, a young organist with a great deal of energy who sounds close to Jimmy Smith, led to interest in the surviving organists of the 1960s, many of whom had been neglected. In addition, deejays in dance clubs, in their desire to create funky new music out of older recordings, have frequently sampled once-discarded soul jazz albums of the late 1960s. When their concoctions appear on new recordings, using fragments of older records and overdubbing funky contemporary rhythms and sometimes rap, the results have often been unexpectedly generous royalty checks for the original performers, and in some cases, their tickets to the comeback trail. Experiments by rappers who mix their productions with jazz have generally been unsuccessful, at least from the jazz standpoint. As with attempts to mix poetry with jazz in the late 1950s, the music tended to be subservient to the spoken word, adding a little atmosphere but never achieving a true mix of equals.

By the late 1970s, free jazz and the avant-garde seemed to be in decline. John Coltrane and Albert Ayler were long gone, the loft movement in New York had largely ended, and free jazz was no longer generating headlines in the jazz world, being overshadowed by fusion. Avant-garde jazz, however, has always attracted many of the most creative jazz musicians. While the ESP and Impulse labels, which had documented many of the important sessions in the 1960s, were defunct, European labels including Black Saint and Soul Note and a countless number of tiny independent companies, many run by musicians, have filled the gap. In fact, the majority of contemporary independent jazz releases are avant-garde jazz, music that the larger labels are afraid to take a chance on, but that attracts a small and dedicated audience.

In 1987 the Knitting Factory opened in New York, becoming one of the centers of the American avant-garde. Always opening doors to new jazz sounds, avant-rock and experimental styles outside of jazz, the Knitting Factory was the Minton's Playhouse of the 1990s and the twenty-first century. Among the top "Downtown" musicians who have been associated with the Knitting Factory are altoist John Zorn, guitarist Bill Frisell, trumpeter Dave Douglas, and tenor-saxophonist Charles Gayle, plus the who's who of the avant-garde at one time or another.

Although it is beyond the confines of this book, jazz has been an international music since American jazz musicians and their recordings started traveling overseas just prior to the 1920s. With the exception of Django Reinhardt's brand of gypsy jazz in the 1930s, it was not until the rise of avant-garde jazz that Europeans first began to really develop their own styles. Rather than try to come up with something fresh to say in bebop or Dixieland, styles that were fully formed in the United States, Europeans found avant-garde jazz to have more potential for originality. They have been able to mix in their own musical heritage, whether it is classical music, regional folk melodies, or ethnic instruments and rhythms, with the improvisation of jazz to create new and colorful variations of free jazz.

Like the European avant-garde, some Americans have combined their own folk heritage with jazz. A group of Jewish jazz musicians, including John Zorn's Masada, helped to revive klezmer, adding adventurous improvisations and reconstructing the traditional music into a new style and format. Latin, Cuban, and South American musicians have done the same with their own musical heritage. Some Americans who are considered advanced players have utilized aspects of the past in new ways, including New Orleans parade rhythms, swing-era riffing, a modernized vintage repertoire, and funky bass patterns.

In addition to fusion, which still exists although with a much lower profile since the late 1970s, a new variation of rock/jazz has been heard in recent years, the jam bands. The movement, which began in the early 1990s, features rock-oriented bands improvising at great length, influenced at least in their concept by the Grateful Dead and the Allman Brothers. Some of the jam bands also include bluegrass, funk, and electronic sounds in their lengthy improvisations. Thus far the jam band scene and the jazz world have largely stayed separate, with the exception of the participation of guitarist John Scofield and the adventurous organ trio Medeski, Martin, and Wood. Among many other jam bands, String Cheese Incident and Widespread Panic are popular, with Phish gaining the most notoriety before its breakup in 2004.

Historic styles, the Young Lions' brand of hard bop, smooth jazz, and the avant-garde aside, there is a wide range of unclassifiable music performed by today's jazz musicians. With countless ways to play jazz, the best contemporary musicians follow their own instincts rather than worrying about stylistic rules and boundaries. Some of the younger players, who grew up listening to rock rather than jazz, enjoy taking songs from the rock or pop repertoire, or writing originals that have elements of rock, pop, or funk, turning them into creative jazz.

For today's jazz vocalists, finding a fresh repertoire can be one of the biggest dilemmas. The major composers and lyricists of the classic American songbook who flourished in the era between 1915 and 1960, are almost all deceased, and relatively few of the songs written during the past thirty years for pop music, movies, or Broadway shows are easily transferable to jazz. Most jazz originals are instrumentals, and few of today's jazz singers and musicians are major composers, much less skilled lyricists. Jazz singers have three basic choices. They can perform standards from decades ago, doing their best to make the words and sentiments sound relevant. Diana Krall has had great success in reviving swing standards, and in Los Angeles Judy Chamberlain is one of the leading singers performing music from the great American songbook. If they have the talent, the singers can write tunes of their own, though few have the skill of such great wits as Dave Frishberg, Bob Dorough, or Mose Allison, or they can come up with rock, r&b, and pop songs. Usually obscurities that fit their style work best, as Cassandra Wilson has demonstrated. The

Diana Krall, today's best-known jazz singer, usually plays piano but at this concert is accompanied by Benny Green.
Photo courtesy of the Wayne Knight Collection, Star Line Productions.

days of merely performing the latest songs from the Hit Parade, however, are decades in the past.

One of the biggest challenges facing jazz instrumentalists and singers alike is simply getting noticed and making a living. On the one hand, there is an enormous amount of talent in most American cities, with no shortage of worthy players and female singers, though there is a drought when it comes to male jazz vocalists. On the minus side, there are many fewer jazz clubs, other than in the biggest cities, now than there were even twenty years ago. Jazz CD sales, not counting reissues, are low, there are few worthy jazz radio stations, and jazz is rarely mentioned by the mass media. Jazz musicians and singers have to be as creative with managing their careers as they are in performing music. They have more choices, but that is still no guarantee of success.

Most jazz recordings made prior to 1970 are currently available on CD, a real goldmine for collectors who love vintage music and have an unlimited budget. While there are always some rare items that have not been rediscovered yet, there is a remarkable amount of reissues that have been put out on collectors' labels or as imports that can be found in specialty shops, through mail order, or on the Internet.

The situation is a bit different for jazz fans primarily interested in the current scene. There are countless new jazz CDs released each week, but very few are available at chain stores, played on local radio stations, or released by the major record labels. The key to discovering new music is to read the main jazz magazines, *Jazz Times*, *Downbeat*, *Jazziz*, *Cadence*, *Coda*, and the better regional jazz papers, and to search the Internet for opportunities to listen to national jazz radio stations. Use your own ears to decide what you like best, staying open to newer sounds and approaches, and then search the Internet for sources for CDs, including the Web sites of the main jazz artists.

This book is just an introduction to some of the most important historic jazz figures, so I have tried not to burden the reader with an excess of names. There are many more great classic jazz artists and modern jazz musicians to discover. A list of all of the top current players and singers would be enormous. Despite that, some artists are well worth exploring for a start, all superior exponents of modern jazz. The following brief list does not include those artists who are primarily exploring earlier styles of jazz.

Trumpeters: Dave Douglas, Russell Gunn, Roy Hargrove, Tom Harrell, Ingrid Jensen, Brian Lynch, Wynton Marsalis, Nicholas Payton, Hugh Ragin, Arturo Sandoval

Trombonists: Ray Anderson, Robin Eubanks, Conrad Herwig, Steve Turre

Clarinetists: Don Byron, Eddie Daniels

Altoists: Ornette Coleman, Steve Coleman, Paquito D'Rivera, Kenny Garrett, Antonio Hart, Jackie McLean, Greg Osby, Bobby Watson, Phil Woods

Tenors: James Carter, George Garzone, Charles Gayle, Javon Jackson, Joe Lovano, Branford Marsalis, Chris Potter, Joshua Redman, Sonny Rollins, David Sanchez, Wayne Shorter, David Ware

Pianists: Geri Allen, Michel Camilo, Bill Charlap, Cyrus Chestnut, Chick Corea, Kenny Drew Jr., Eliane Elias, Benny Green, Herbie Hancock, Fred Hersch, Keith Jarrett, Adam Makowicz, Brad Mehldau, Jason Moran, Danilo Perez, Eric Reed, Marcus Roberts, Gonzalo Rubalcaba, Matthew Shipp, Cecil

Taylor, Jacky Terrasson, McCoy Tyner, Chucho Valdes, Kenny Werner, Jessica Williams

Guitarists: Howard Alden, Bill Frisell, Scott Henderson, Charlie Hunter, Stanley Jordan, Russell Malone, Pat Metheny, John Scofield

Bassists: Brian Bromberg, Robert Hurst III, Christian McBride, Marcus Miller, Charnett Moffett, John Patitucci

Drummers: Brian Blade, Dennis Chambers, Roy Haynes, Elvin Jones, Ralph Peterson

Vibists: Gary Burton, Terry Gibbs, Stefan Harris, Bobby Hutcherson

Violinist: Regina Carter

Singers: Claudia Acuna, Karrin Allyson, Dee Dee Bridgewater, Harry Connick Jr., Madeline Eastman, Kurt Elling, Nnenna Freelon, Diana Krall, Kitty Margolis, Bobby McFerrin, Jane Monheit, Mark Murphy, Dianne Reeves, Diane Schuur, Cassandra Wilson

Jazz, originally a regional folk music based in the southern United States, has developed into an international art form that influences all other styles of music. It has surmounted many difficulties through the years, from misrepresentation to neglect, and it will continue to thrive as long as creative musicians are continually inspired to express themselves through music and as long as there are enough fans willing to open their minds and experience the exciting and creative music.

RECOMMENDED RECORDINGS

Al DiMeola. *Splendido Hotel*. Columbia, 46117.
Banu Gibson. *You Don't Know My Mind*. Swing Out, 104.
Big Bad Voodoo Daddy. *Big Bad Voodoo Daddy*. EMI-Capitol, 74234-93338.
Bill Frisell. *Have a Little Faith*. Elektra/Nonesuch, 79301.
Billy Cobham. *Spectrum*. Atlantic, 7268.
Brad Mehldau. *The Art of the Trio, Vol. 3: Songs*. Warner Bros., 47051.
Cassandra Wilson. *New Moon Daughter*. Blue Note, 32861.
Chick Corea. *Past, Present & Futures*. Stretch, 9035.
Chick Corea's Elektric Band. *Eye of the Beholder*. GRP, 9564.
Chris Potter. *Gratitude*. Verve, 549433.
Claudia Acuna. *Wind from the South*. Verve, 543 521.
Dan Barrett. *Jubilesta*. Arbors, 19107.
Dan Levinson. *Where the Morning Glories Grow*. Loup-garous, 1002.
Danilo Perez. *Motherland*. Verve, 543 904.
Dave Douglas. *Charms of the Night Sky*. Winter & Winter, 15.
Dave Douglas. *Five*. Soul Note, 121276.
David Sanborn. *Upfront*. Elektra, 61272.
Diana Krall. *All for You*. Impulse, 182.
Diane Schuur. *Love Walked In*. GRP, 9841.

Dianne Reeves. *The Grand Encounter*. Blue Note, 38268.

Don Byron. *No-Vibe Zone: Live at Knitting Factory*. Knitting Factory Works, 191.

Gary Burton. *Duster*. Koch, 7846.

Gary Burton. *Virtuosi*. Concord Jazz, 2105.

Geri Allen. *Some Aspects of Water*. Storyville, 4212.

Greg Osby. *Banned in New York*. Blue Note, 96860.

Grover Washington Jr. *Mister Magic*. MoJazz, 530 103.

Grover Washington Jr. *Winelight*. Elektra, 305.

Herbie Hancock Sextet. *Mwandishi: The Complete Warner Bros. Recordings*. Warner Archives, 45732, 2 CDs.

Herbie Hancock's Headhunters. *Headhunters*. Columbia/Legacy, 65123.

Jacky Terrasson. *Jacky Terrasson*. Blue Note, 29351.

Jaco Pastorius. *Jaco Pastorius*. Epic/Legacy, 64977.

James Carter. *Jurassic Classics*. DIW/Columbia, 67058.

Jason Moran. *Modernistic*. Blue Note, 39838.

Jean-Luc Ponty. *Voyage: The Jean-Luc Ponty Anthology*. Rhino, 72155, 2 CDs.

Joe Lovano. *Rush Hour*. Blue Note, 29269.

Joey DeFrancesco. *Where Were You*. Columbia, 45433.

John Scofield. *A Go Go*. Verve, 314 539 979.

John Zorn. *Masada Live at Tonic, 2001*. Tzadik, 7334, 2 CDs.

Judy Carmichael. *Chops*. C&D, 5.

Karrin Allyson. *Collage*. Concord Jazz, 4709.

Keith Jarrett. *Whisper Not*. ECM, 543816, 2 CDs.

Kenny Garrett. *Triology*. Warner Bros., 45731.

Kitty Margolis. *Heart & Soul: Live in San Francisco*. Mad-Kat, 53.

Kurt Elling. *The Messenger*. Blue Note, 52727.

Larry Coryell. *Introducing the Eleventh House*. Vanguard, 79342.

Lavay Smith and the Red Hot Skillet Lickers. *One Hour Mama*. Fat Note, 0001.

Louis Prima. *Capitol Collectors Series*. Capitol, 94072.

Mahavishnu Orchestra. *Birds of Fire*. Columbia/Legacy, 66081.

Mark Murphy. *Song for the Geese*. RCA, 44865.

Michel Camilo. *Triangulo*. Telarc, 83549.

Miles Davis. *Bitches Brew*. Columbia/Legacy, 65774, 2 CDs.

Miles Davis. *Pangaea*. Columbia/Legacy, 65346, 2 CDs.

Miles Davis. *In a Silent Way*. Columbia/Legacy, 65345.

Ornette Coleman's Prime Time. *Of Human Feelings*. Antilles, 20002.

Pat Metheny. *Speaking of Now*. Warner Bros., 48025.

Ray Anderson. *Where Home Is*. Enja, 9366.

Rebecca Kilgore. *I Saw Stars*. Arbors, 19136.

Regina Carter. *Rhythms of the Heart*. Verve, 547 177.

Return to Forever. *Light as a Feather*. Polydor, 827148.

Return to Forever. *Where Have I Known You Before*. Polydor, 825206.

Ronald Shannon Jackson. *Mandance*. Antilles, 848397.

Scott Hamilton. *Major League*. Concord Jazz, 4305.

Scott Hamilton/Ken Peplowski/Spike Robinson. *Groovin' High*. Concord Jazz, 4509.

Scott Henderson. *Tribal Tech with Gary Willis*. Relativity, 1049.

Stanley Jordan. *Standards Vol. 1*. Blue Note, 46333.

Steve Coleman. *On the Edge of Tomorrow*. Winter & Winter, 919005.
Steve Turre. *In the Spur of the Moment*. Telarc, 83484.
Tony Williams Lifetime. *Spectrum: The Anthology*. Verve, 537075, 2 CDs.
Warren Vache. *Easy Going*. Concord Jazz, 4323.
Weather Report. *Heavy Weather*. Columbia/Legacy, 65108.
Weather Report. *Weather Report*. Columbia, 48824.
Yellowjackets. *Blue Hats*. Warner Bros., 46333.

Biographies of Jazz
Leaders and Legends

The subjects of these thumbnail sketches include many of the innovative giants of the past and some of the great veterans (all of whom are at least sixty) on the current jazz scene. This list could easily be several times longer. Also included are a recommended recording or two for most of the artists, augmenting the ones listed after each chapter.

Abrams, Muhal Richard (1930–). Abrams began his career in the 1950s as a hard bop pianist, but developed into one of the key leaders of the Chicago avant-garde. He led the Experimental Band during 1961–1965, was one of the main founders of the AACM, and has since blossomed as both an avant-garde pianist and composer.
Recordings: Levels and Degrees of Light (Delmark, 413), *Rejoicing with the Light* (Black Saint, 120071)

Adams, Pepper (1930–1986). At first a major part of the Detroit jazz scene, Adams moved to New York in 1958 and became recognized as one of the top baritone saxophonists, a hard bop player with a guttural tone and a passionate swinging style.
Recording: 10 to 4 at the Five Spot (Original Jazz Classics, 31)

Adderley, Cannonball (1928–1975). A highly influential altoist with an exuberant tone and a major bandleader, Adderley was one of the most accessible jazz musicians. His quintet/sextet of 1959–1966 was one of the great bands.

Recordings: Things Are Getting Better (Original Jazz Classics, 032), *Mercy, Mercy, Mercy* (Blue Note/Capitol, 29915)

Adderley, Nat (1931–2000). The brother of Cannonball Adderley played cornet in a style influenced at times by Miles Davis. He was content to be in Cannonball's shadow and proved to be a talented songwriter who wrote "Work Song" and "The Old Country."
Recording: Work Song (Original Jazz Classics, 363)

Akiyoshi, Toshiko (1929–). A Bud Powell–inspired pianist, Akiyoshi has led and arranged for her own big band in Los Angeles (1972–1981) and New York (1981–2003). Her inventive arrangements have also paid tribute to her Asian heritage.
Recording: Carnegie Hall Concert (Columbia, 48805)

Aleman Oscar (1909–1980). Aleman had a sound and style on guitar very similar to that of Django Reinhardt. He played in Paris in the 1930s and his native Argentina after 1941.
Recording: Swing Guitar Masterpieces 1937–1957 (Acoustic Disc, 29)

Alexander, Monty (1944–). A brilliant pianist, Alexander was initially influenced by Oscar Peterson but developed his own style, inspired by both straight-ahead jazz and the music of his native Jamaica.
Recording: Jamboree: Monty Alexander's Ivory and Steel (Concord Jazz, 1024)

Allen, Henry "Red" (1908–1967). One of the last of the major New Orleans trumpeters to emerge during the 1920s, Allen had an advanced style but was mostly heard in swing and trad settings during his long and productive career.
Recording: World on a String (Bluebird, 2497)

Allison, Mose (1927–). A fine pianist and a personable down-home singer influenced by country blues as well as bop, Allison is most renowned for his insightful and often humorous lyrics.
Recording: I Don't Worry about a Thing (Rhino/Atlantic, 71417)

Almeida, Laurindo (1917–1995). Almeida helped introduce the Brazilian guitar to jazz, working with Stan Kenton in the late 1940s, recording with Bud Shank in the 1950s, and having a lengthy solo career.
Recording: Artistry in Rhythm (Concord Jazz, 4238)

Ammons, Albert (1907–1949). One of the major boogie-woogie pianists of the 1930s and 1940s, Ammons was a powerhouse.
Recording: 1936–1939 (Classics, 715)

Ammons, Gene (1925–1974). A highly versatile tenor saxophonist with a huge tone, Ammons (the son of Albert Ammons) could play bebop with Sonny Stitt and caress ballads with soul. He was at his best in the 1950s and early 1960s.
Recording: Boss Tenor (Original Jazz Classics, 297)

Armstrong, Louis (1901–1971). The most beloved of all jazz musicians, both as a trumpeter and as a vocalist, Armstrong permanently changed jazz with his phrasing and ability to "tell a story." Whether with the Hot Fives in the 1920s, his swing-era big band, or his later All-Stars, Satch was the real king of jazz.
Recordings: Vol. 6: St. Louis Blues (Columbia/Legacy, 46996), *Satch Plays Fats* (Columbia/Legacy, 40378)

Art Ensemble of Chicago (1966–2004). Comprised of trumpeter Lester Bowie, saxophonists Roscoe Mitchell and Joseph Jarman, bassist Malachi Favors, and drummer Don Moye, the Art Ensemble of Chicago always seemed to have fun on stage, no matter how forbidding their brand of avant-garde jazz was that year. They returned space and dynamics to free jazz.
Recording: Nice Guys (ECM, 827 876)

Ayler, Albert (1936–1970). One of the most radical of the free jazz players, Ayler had a giant tone on tenor and reached back to the prehistoric era of jazz in his use of simple melodies.
Recording: Spirits Rejoice (ESP, 1020)

Bailey, Derek (1932–). Bailey uses his guitar to make sounds and noise, not bothering with melodies, harmonies, or rhythms. No other guitarist has ever sounded like him.
Recording: Han (Incus, 02)

Bailey, Mildred (1907–1951). One of the top jazz singers of the 1930s, Bailey combined a little girl's voice with a blues feeling and swinging phrasing.
Recording: The Rockin' Chair Lady (GRP/Decca, 644)

Baker, Chet (1929–1988). In the 1950s, Baker was the epitome of cool with his romantic middle-register trumpet solos and vulnerable (if shaky) vocals. His unapologetic abuse of heroin took away his Hollywood looks, but during his last decade, Baker was still capable of playing trumpet at his very best.
Recording: My Favourite Songs Vols. 1–2 (Enja, 79600)

Barretto, Ray (1929–). In the 1950s Ray Barretto was among the first to play conga on straight-ahead jazz dates. His career as a bandleader has included bugalu dance hits, salsa, and top-notch Afro-Cuban jazz.
Recording: My Summertime (Owl, 35830)

Barron, Kenny (1943–). Always underrated, Kenny Barron played with the bands of Dizzy Gillespie, Freddie Hubbard, Yusef Lateef, and Ron Carter, becoming one of the finest modern mainstream pianists in jazz.
Recording: Wanton Spirit (Verve, 314 522 364)

Bartz, Gary (1940–). Ranging in his career from borderline avant-garde jazz to crossover, altoist Bartz sounds at his best when playing advanced straight-ahead jazz. He is one of the underrated greats.
Recording: West 42nd Street (Candid, 79049)

Basie, Count (1904–1984). As a pianist, Basie realigned the function of the rhythm section with his light touch. As a bandleader from 1935 on, he led the definitive swinging institution, an orchestra that still tours the world decades after his death.

Recordings: Count Basie at Newport (Verve, 833 766), *Atomic Mr. Basie* (Roulette, 59025)

Bauza, Mario (1911–1993). The musical director of Machito's orchestra during 1941–1976, Bauza was largely responsible for the mixture of jazz with Afro-Cuban rhythms that resulted in Latin jazz. He also led his own impressive big band during his final decade.

Recording: 944 Columbus (Messidor, 15828)

Bechet, Sidney (1897–1959). The first great horn soloist to emerge on records, Sidney Bechet (originally a clarinetist) played the soprano sax with passion, intensity, and plenty of vibrato in trad settings. In later years he moved to France where he became a national celebrity.

Recording: Paris Jazz Concert (RTE, 1003)

Beiderbecke, Bix (1903–1931). A cornetist with a beautiful tone and a very fertile imagination, Bix Beiderbecke's fortunes rose and fell with the 1920s. Every solo he played during his short career is well worth hearing.

Recording: At the Jazz Band Ball (Columbia, 46175)

Bellson, Louie (1924–). A spectacular drum soloist who is also happy to play quietly in a trio, Bellson was always full of taste and class.

Recording: Live from New York (Telarc, 83334)

Benson, George (1943–). Originally a fiery and soulful guitarist, Benson gained pop fame with his crooning on "This Masquerade" in 1976. He is still capable of playing memorable guitar solos.

Recording: Tenderly (Warner Bros., 25907)

Berigan, Bunny (1908–1942). One of the most colorful of all trumpeters, Berigan took plenty of chances during his solos in the 1930s and usually succeeded. He had a beautiful tone in all ranges of his horn and made "I Can't Get Started" into a standard.

Recording: The Complete Bunny Berigan, Vol. 1 (Bluebird, 5584)

Berry, Chu (1910–1941). One of the up-and-coming tenor saxophonists of the 1930s, Chu Berry was influenced by Coleman Hawkins but developed his own sound with Cab Calloway's band before his premature death.

Recording: 1937–1941 (Classics, 784)

Bigard, Barney (1906–1980). Originally a tenor saxophonist with King Oliver, Bigard developed into a distinctive clarinetist who added a great deal to the bands of Duke Ellington (1927–1942) and Louis Armstrong (1947–1955 and 1960–1961).

Recording: Bucket's Got a Hole in It (Delmark, 211)

Blackwell, Ed (1929–1992). Famous for being one of the drummers (along with Billy Higgins) in the Ornette Coleman Quartet, Blackwell fit in perfectly while never discarding his New Orleans heritage.
Recording: Walls-Bridges (Black Lion, 120153)

Blake, Eubie (1883–1983). An early ragtime pianist-composer who with lyricist-singer Noble Sissle was a pioneering black composer for Broadway shows in the 1920s, Blake survived long enough to make a comeback in his late eighties. He was the last living link to the ragtime era and a delightful entertainer.
Recording: The 86 Years of Eubie Blake (Columbia, 22223, 2 LP set)

Blakey, Art (1919–1990). An explosive drummer from the bebop era, Blakey's prominence as the leader of the Jazz Messengers and his nurturing of younger hard bop musicians became legendary.
Recordings: The Freedom Rider (Blue Note, 21287), *Caravan* (Original Jazz Classics, 038)

Blanton, Jimmy (1918–1942). During his short life, Jimmy Blanton revolutionized the bass in jazz. While with Duke Ellington, Blanton's solos and work behind soloists and ensembles were decades ahead of their time.
Recording: Duke Ellington—Solos, Duets and Trios (Bluebird, 2179)

Bley, Carla (1938–). A pianist/organist, Bley is most significant as an arranger who was not shy to display her broad sense of humor and a big bandleader.
Recording: European Tour (ECM, 831 830)

Bley, Paul (1932–). A subtle but continually creative pianist, Bley explores free jazz quietly, using space and dynamics and offering an alternative approach from Cecil Taylor's constant fire.
Recording: The Nearness of You (Steeplechase, 31246)

Bluiett, Hamiet (1940–). An avant-garde innovator on the baritone sax, Bluiett can screech out high notes with ease, yet his deep, giant tone acts as a perfect anchor for the World Saxophone Quartet.
Recording: Young Warrior, Old Warrior (Mapleshade, 2932)

Blythe, Arthur (1940–). Combining together a soulful sound with an explorative style, altoist Blythe has always been distinctive and constantly willing to stretch himself.
Recording: Illusions (Koch, 7869)

Bolden, Buddy (1877–1931). The symbolic founder of jazz, the unrecorded New Orleans legend led a band as early as 1895 but only had a short reign before insanity led to him being committed in 1906.

Boswell Sisters (1925–1936). One of the great jazz vocal groups, Connie, Helvetia, and Martha Boswell performed sophisticated arrangements in the early 1930s, had wonderful voices, and scatted up a storm.
Recording: The Boswell Sisters Collection, Vol. 2 (Collector's Classics, 3008)

Bowie, Lester (1941–1999). Trumpeter with the Art Ensemble of Chicago, Bowie was also a great humorist who enjoyed poking fun at various musical styles. His Brass Fantasy played jazz versions of unlikely pop and rock songs.
Recording: The Fire This Time (In & Out, 7019)

Braff, Ruby (1927–2003). A major and distinctive cornetist who chose to play small-group swing rather than modern jazz, Braff never played a passionless note. He recorded scores of exciting albums through the years.
Recording: Live at the Regettabar (Arbors, 19131)

Brookmeyer, Bob (1929–). As a cool jazz valve trombonist (along with Gerry Mulligan, Stan Getz, and Clark Terry) and as a composer-arranger for large orchestras, Brookmeyer has always excelled.
Recording: The Dual Role of Bob Brookmeyer (Original Jazz Classics, 1729)

Brotzmann, Peter (1941–). Few tenor saxophonists have ever been as passionate as Brotzmann, a firebrand who plays remarkably intense atonal solos.
Recording: Machine Gun (FMP, 024)

Brown, Clifford (1930–1956). A superb trumpeter with a beautiful tone who never seemed to play an unworthy note, Brownie was one of the all-time greats, despite having a tragically brief life.
Recording: The Best of Max Roach and Clifford Brown in Concert (GNP/Crescendo, 18)

Brown, Lawrence (1907–1988). Duke Ellington's trombonist during 1932–1951 and 1960–1970, Brown had impressive technique, his own sound, and a mastery of the swing vocabulary.
Recording: Slide Trombone (Verve, 314 559 930)

Brown, Oscar, Jr. (1926–). A dramatic singer with a strong expressive voice, Oscar Brown Jr. has also proven to be a genius as a lyricist. His lyrics for "Work Song," "Dat Dere," and "Afro Blue" are only three of his gems.
Recording: Sin & Soul … And Then Some (Columbia/Legacy, 64994)

Brown, Ray (1926–2002). Whether touring with the Oscar Peterson Trio or leading his own combos, Brown defined the sound of the acoustic bass for over five decades.
Recording: Don't Get Sassy (Telarc, 83368)

Brubeck, Dave (1920–). Leader of quartets since the early 1950s (the one with altoist Paul Desmond was most famous) and a master of polyrhythms, polytonality, and playing in different time signatures, Dave Brubeck has been popular for over a half century without ever compromising his music.
Recording: 40th Anniversary Tour of the U.K. (Telarc, 83440)

Burrell, Kenny (1931–). As tasteful a straight-ahead guitarist as one will ever hear, Burrell is at his best when inspired by fiery players, especially Jimmy Smith.
Recording: Midnight Blue (Blue Note, 46399)

Burton, Gary (1943–). A master at utilizing four mallets on the vibes, Burton sometimes sounds like two or three vibraphonists at once. In addition to his work leading groups (including an early fusion band with Larry Coryell), Burton has long been a significant educator at Berklee.
Recording: Dreams So Real (ECM, 833329)

Byas, Don (1912–1972). One of the great tenor saxophonists of the 1940s, Don Byas' decision to move permanently to Europe in 1946 cut short his fame but probably lengthened his life. His knowledge of chords was only second to his idol, Coleman Hawkins.
Recording: 1944–1945 (Classics, 882)

Byrd, Charlie (1925–1999). Byrd's mastery of Brazilian music caused him to stand out from most other guitarists of the 1960s, and his introduction of bossa nova to American audiences with Stan Getz on Jazz Samba made him immortal.
Recording: Latin Byrd (Milestone, 47005)

Byrd, Donald (1932–). An up-and-coming hard bop trumpeter in the 1950s, Byrd was at his prime during the following decade before succumbing to the lure of electronic funk in the 1970s.
Recording: Byrd in Flight (Blue Note, 52435)

Calloway, Cab (1907–1994). Mr. Hi-De-Ho, Calloway became famous for "Minnie the Moocher" in 1931. His exuberant scatting, dancing, and showmanship made him one of the most popular entertainers ever, in addition to being an important bandleader in the 1930s and 1940s.
Recording: Are You Hep to the Jive (Columbia/Legacy, 57645)

Carmichael, Hoagy (1899–1981). Of all of the major songwriters of the 1930s and 1940s, Carmichael had the closest association to jazz, playing jazz piano whenever he had a chance. Among the many standards that he composed are "Star Dust," "Georgia on My Mind," "The Nearness of You," "Lazy River," and "Skylark."
Recording: Stardust and Much More (Bluebird, 8333)

Carney, Harry (1910–1974). Duke Ellington's baritone saxophonist for forty-seven years, Carney virtually introduced the instrument to jazz, and he never declined in importance. Virtually all of his recordings were made with Ellington.

Carter, Benny (1907–2003). As altoist, trumpeter, arranger, composer, and bandleader, Benny Carter was rarely equaled during his seven-decade career. No wonder he was nicknamed "The King."
Recordings: All of Me (Bluebird, 3000), *Cosmopolite: The Oscar Peterson Verve Sessions* (Verve, 521 673)

Carter, Betty (1930–1998). Although a bebopper at heart, Carter's vocals stretched way beyond the style by the 1960s, and she never played it safe. She remains one of the main influences on jazz singers of today.
Recording: I Can't Help It (GRP, 114)

Carter, John (1929–1991). Carter brought the clarinet into the avant-garde, playing free jazz on the swing-oriented instrument. Late in life he created a five-album musical depiction of the story of African Americans in the United States.
Recording: Dauwhe (Black Saint, 120057)

Carter, Ron (1937–). Bassist Carter has performed on a countless number of recordings and settings but will always be best known for his membership in the Miles Davis Quintet of 1964–1968.
Recording: Mr. Bow Tie (Blue Note, 35407)

Chaloff, Serge (1923–1957). Chaloff preceded Gerry Mulligan as a major light-toned baritonist, playing with Woody Herman's Second Herd. Drug problems cut short his life, but he left a few major recordings behind.
Recording: Blue Serge (Blue Note, 94505)

Chambers, Paul (1935–1969). A major bass soloist, Chambers was greatly in demand from the time that he joined the Miles Davis Quintet in 1955. He also worked extensively with the Wynton Kelly Trio and had the song "Mr. P.C." named after him by John Coltrane.
Recording: Bass on Top (Blue Note, 46533)

Cheatham, Doc (1905–1997). After decades of obscure work as a lead trumpeter in big bands and Latin groups, Cheatham emerged as a major swing soloist while in his mid-seventies, still hitting high notes at age ninety-one.
Recording: The Fabulous (Parkwood, 104)

Cherry, Don (1936–1995). Ornette Coleman's pocket cornetist, Cherry developed into a world traveler both geographically and musically, exploring world music during the latter part of his career.
Recording: Art Deco (A&M, 5258)

Christian, Charlie (1916–1942). The first giant of the electric guitar, Christian's phrases on his recordings with the Benny Goodman Sextet became the vocabulary of the jazz guitar for the next twenty-five years.
Recording: Radioland 1939–1941 (Fuel, 2000-061 167)

Christy, June (1925–1990). After coming to fame with Stan Kenton, Christy's string of vocal albums for Capitol in the 1950s (most notably *Something Cool*) made her one of the most popular jazz singers of the era.
Recording: The Misty Miss Christy (Blue Note, 98452)

Clarke, Kenny (1914–1985). Clarke was the first drummer to shift the time-keeping role from the bass drum to the ride cymbal, thereby changing the sound of the rhythm section from the bop era on. He was on many sessions both in the United States and Europe and co-led a notable big band with pianist Francy Boland.
Recording: Handle with Care (Koch, 8534)

Clayton, Buck (1911–1991). A major trumpet soloist with Count Basie's band of 1936–1942, Clayton remained a vital swing player until bad health forced his retirement after 1967. Clayton's string of jam session albums in the 1950s was notable as were his arranging skills, even in the years after he stopped playing.

Recording: Baden, Switzerland 1966 (Sackville, 2028)

Cohn, Al (1925–1988). Cohn was equally skilled as a cool-toned tenor saxophonist and an arranger-composer. He made many recordings and sounded particularly joyful when teamed with Zoot Sims.

Recording: Broadway (Original Jazz Classics, 1812)

Cole, Nat King (1917–1965). Originally one of the major swing pianists and leader of the King Cole Trio, by 1950 Cole was on his way to becoming a very popular crooner who occasionally would remind listeners that he was also a great pianist.

Recording: Jazz Encounters (Capitol, 96693)

Coleman, Ornette (1930–). When altoist Coleman arrived in New York with his quartet in 1959, he caused shock waves throughout the jazz world as musicians found they had to reassess their own playing. Whether as one of the founders of free jazz, playing free funk with Prime Time in the 1970s, Coleman is always a true original.

Recordings: Ornette on Tenor (Rhino, 71455), *New York Is Now* (Blue Note, 84287)

Coltrane, John (1926–1967). Coltrane's accomplishments are so vast (developing a new sound on tenor, reintroducing the soprano sax to jazz, mastering chordal improvisation, playing endlessly over vamps, and exploring passionate new sounds) that it is difficult to believe that his playing prime was less than a dozen years.

Recordings: Lush Life (Original Jazz Classics, 131), *Ole Coltrane* (Rhino/Atlantic, 79965), *Sun Ship* (Impulse, 167)

Condon, Eddie (1905–1973). A propagandist for freewheeling Dixieland, Condon was a creditable rhythm guitarist and a superb bandleader and organizer.

Recording: The Town Hall Concerts, Vol. 2 (Jazzology, 1003/1004)

Corea, Chick (1941–). A master on both acoustic and electric keyboards, Corea has excelled in many different settings through the years ranging from three versions of Return to Forever, the Elektric Band, the Akoustic Band, and all-star groups to working with Miles Davis.

Recordings: My Spanish Heart (Polydor, 543 303), *Three Quartets* (Stretch, 9002)

Coryell, Larry (1943–). The pioneering fusion guitarist, Coryell has also explored bebop, world music, and the acoustic guitar.

Recording: Monk, Trane, Miles & Me (High Note, 7028)

Crawford, Hank (1934–). A soulful altoist, Crawford influenced David Sanborn and the later smooth saxophonists, but he has always retained a closer tie to straight-ahead and soul jazz, making a series of fine records with organist Jimmy McGriff.

Recording: Steppin' Up (Milestone, 9153)

Crosby, Bing (1903–1977). Famous ever since the early 1930s, Crosby brought jazz phrasing into pop music, and his warm baritone voice saved listeners from the deluge of boy tenors. He always loved early jazz and was proud of his association with Paul Whiteman and Bix Beiderbecke.
Recording: And Some Jazz Friends (GRP/Decca, 603)

Dameron, Tadd (1917–1965). One of the top arrangers and composers of the classic bebop era, Dameron was overly modest about his piano playing. Among his compositions were "Hot House," "If You Could See Me Now," "Our Delight," and "Good Bait."
Recording: The Magic Touch of Tadd Dameron (Original Jazz Classics, 143)

Daniels, Eddie (1941–). A very good tenor saxophonist, Eddie Daniels chose to stick exclusively to clarinet for a decade to establish his reputation as the best on that instrument. His recordings show that the clarinet does fit well into modern straight-ahead jazz, at least when he is the clarinetist.
Recording: Under the Influence (GRP, 9716)

Davis, Eddie "Lockjaw" (1922–1986). A tough-toned tenor, Lockjaw was equally effective on roaring up-tempo tunes and on passionate renditions of ballads. He was closely associated with both Count Basie and Harry "Sweets" Edison and co-led a notable two-tenor quintet with Johnny Griffin in the early 1960s.
Recording: Swingin' till the Girls Come Home (Steeplechase, 31058)

Davis, Miles (1926–1991). Whether it was bebop, cool jazz, hard bop, modal music, the avant-garde, fusion, or pop/crossover, no other musician was as prominent in as many different styles as trumpeter Miles Davis. In addition, his abilities as a talent scout ranked with those of Art Blakey.
Recordings: Miles Davis, Vol. 1 (Blue Note, 32611), *Milestones* (Columbia/Legacy, 85203), *E.S.P.* (Columbia/Legacy, 65683)

Davison, Wild Bill (1906–1989). The perfect Dixieland cornetist/trumpeter, Wild Bill Davison's solos were always full of personality, ranging from sarcasm to sentimentality. Whether playing with Eddie Condon in Europe or with his own pickup groups, Davison showed how exciting trad jazz should really sound.
Recording: The Commodore Master Takes (GRP, 405)

DeFranco, Buddy (1923–). The definitive bebop clarinetist, DeFranco made his instrument sound easy to play during encounters with the finest jazz musicians. Until the rise of Eddie Daniels, no post-swing clarinetist was in his league.
Recording: Like Someone in Love (Progressive, 7014)

DeJohnette, Jack (1942–). More than just one of jazz's finest drummers, DeJohnette has led several major post-bop bands and is a fine pianist and composer.
Recording: Special Edition (ECM, 827 694)

Desmond, Paul (1924–1977). Desmond's beautiful floating tone on alto, a contrast to Dave Brubeck's heavy chordings, was always a joy to hear. He was subtle, witty, always distinctive, and a classy player.
Recording: Two of a Mind (RCA, 64019)

Dodds, Baby (1898–1959). An important pioneer in jazz drumming of New Orleans and the 1920s, Dodds could say so much with just a cymbal crash. He can be heard at his best on recordings with Jelly Roll Morton, Louis Armstrong's Hot Seven, and his brother Johnny Dodds.

Dodds, Johnny (1892–1940). Arguably the finest clarinetist of the 1920s, Dodds had a cutting tone, a real feel for the blues, and the ability to hold his own with Louis Armstrong on the classic Hot Five recordings.
Recordings: 1926 (Classics, 589), *1927* (Classics, 603)

Dolphy, Eric (1928–1964). Dolphy had his own very unusual voice on alto sax, bass clarinet (which he introduced to jazz as a solo instrument), and flute, sounding utterly unique. He worked with Charles Mingus and John Coltrane and recorded quite as a bit as a leader from 1960 to 1964 before his early death.
Recordings: Outward Bound (Original Jazz Classics, 22), *Vintage Dolphy* (GM, 3005)

Donaldson, Lou (1926–). Donaldson has always emphasized the blues and soul in his boppish solos. Influenced most by Charlie Parker, Donaldson found his own voice and became a popular figure in soul jazz.
Recording: Birdseed (Milestone, 9198)

Dorough, Bob (1923–). A talented songwriter who wrote "Devil May Care," "I've Got Just about Everything" and the lyrics to Charlie Parker's "Yardbird Suite," Dorough is also a personable singer and a fine pianist.
Recording: Just about Everything (Evidence, 22094)

Dorsey, Jimmy (1904–1957). One of the top altoists and clarinetists of the 1920s, Dorsey became a major big bandleader in the 1930s. His orchestra's most popular records featured singers Helen O'Connell and Bob Eberle in the 1940s, but JD never lost his talents as a soloist.
Recording: Contrasts (GRP/Decca, 626)

Dorsey, Tommy (1905–1956). Jimmy's younger brother, TD was renowned for his pretty tone on trombone and his breath control. His big bands were quite popular from 1935 on, with his sidemen including Bunny Berigan, Ziggy Elman, Buddy DeFranco, and many singers including Frank Sinatra.
Recording: Seventeen Number Ones (RCA, 9973)

Eckstine, Billy (1914–1993). Eckstine's baritone voice was quite influential in the 1940s and 1950s as he became a big success in middle-of-the-road pop music, but he will be always be remembered most fondly as the leader of the first bebop big band, an organization that he kept together as long as possible.
Recording: Basie and Eckstine, Inc. (Blue Note, 28636)

Edison, Harry "Sweets" (1915–1999). Trumpeter Edison, like his longtime employer Count Basie, got the most mileage of one note. His swing style, open to the influence of bop, enlivened a countless number of record sessions in a sixty-year period.

Recording: Edison's Lights (Original Jazz Classics, 804)

Edwards, Teddy (1924–2003). Underrated due to his decision to spend his life living in the Los Angeles area, Edwards was one of the great tenors of the bebop era and the half century that followed.

Recording: Teddy's Ready (Original Jazz Classics, 748)

Eldridge, Roy (1911–1989). One of the most competitive of all jazzmen, Eldridge had a crackling sound on trumpet along with a harmonically advanced swing style that influenced Dizzy Gillespie. Eldridge came of age in the 1930s and made some of his finest recordings in the 1950s, including a set in which he matched wits with Gillespie.

Recording: Montreux 1977 (Original Jazz Classics, 373)

Ellington, Duke (1899–1974). The most productive of all jazz musicians, Duke Ellington would have been very significant if all he had done was lead his orchestra for forty-nine years. Add to that his piano playing (which evolved from stride to quite modern), innovative arrangements, thousands of compositions, and ability to gather individualists and somehow blend them into a recognizable ensemble sound, and one is talking about a genius.

Recordings: Ellington Uptown (Columbia/Legacy, 87066), *The Far East Suite—Special Mix* (Bluebird, 66551)

Evans, Bill (1929–1980). Evans changed the way that the piano sounds in jazz. His chord voicings and the way his trios worked as near equals are still extremely influential.

Recordings: Sunday at the Village Vanguard (Original Jazz Classics, 140), *Paris Concert, Edition One* (Blue Note, 28672)

Evans, Gil (1912–1988). Most famous for his collaborations with Miles Davis (the *Birth of the Cool* Nonet and three classic albums from the late 1950s), Evans also led and arranged quite a few special sessions of his own. Like Ellington, he had the knack for combining together very different tones in a coherent and colorful fashion.

Recording: Gil Evans and Ten (Original Jazz Classics, 346)

Farlow, Tal (1921–1998). One of the hottest bop guitarists of the 1950s, Farlow had huge hands yet a very light touch. He later became a bit of a recluse, resurfacing on the national scene on an irregular basis, but otherwise content to play locally and work as a sign painter.

Recording: The Return of Tal Farlow: 1969 (Original Jazz Classics, 356)

Farmer, Art (1928–1999). The bop-based Farmer had a mellow tone on his flugelhorn along with the ability to make the most complex music sound effortless. The Jazztet that he co-led with Benny Golson may have only lasted three years, but his career lasted fifty.

Recording: Something to Live For (Contemporary, 14029)

Ferguson, Maynard (1928–). One of the great high-note trumpeters, Maynard Ferguson's music ranged over time from a great bop-oriented big band in the late 1950s to more commercial ventures. Somehow he was always able to pop out those stratospheric notes.

Recording: Si! Si!/Maynard '64 (Roulette, 95334)

Fitzgerald, Ella (1917–1996). The much-beloved artist sang lyrics with joy, uplifting everything she interpreted. She could also outscat and outswing anyone, yet appeared modest, as if she did not quite realize how great she was.

Recording: Ella in Rome: The Birthday Concert (Verve, 835 454)

Freeman, Bud (1906–1991). Virtually the only tenor saxophonist from the late 1920s who did not sound like Coleman Hawkins, Freeman went his own way throughout his career. He showed that the sax can indeed be part of a Dixieland band, although he preferred to play superior swing standards.

Recording: 1939–1940 (Classics, 811)

Frishberg, Dave (1933–). One of the wittiest of all lyricists, Frishberg's words are full of both humor and insight. He is also an excellent swing-to-bop pianist and a cheerful if world-weary vocalist.

Recording: Live at Vine Street (Original Jazz Classics, 832)

Garner, Erroll (1921–1977). Garner could not read music and rarely looked at the keyboard when he played, yet he always sounded inspired. Garner could go into a studio, sit at a piano, and emerge three hours later with three complete albums, all full of joy and excitement.

Recording: Dreamstreet & One World Concert (Telarc, 83350)

Gayle, Charles (1939–). A very passionate free jazzer, Gayle screams and screeches on his tenor with religious fervor, starting where Albert Ayler left off.

Recording: Touchin' on Trane (FMP, 48)

Getz, Stan (1927–1991). Producer of one of the most beautiful tenor tones, Getz never relied purely on his sound. His career found him evolving through bop, cool, bossa nova, post-bop and hard bop, always playing with great intelligence.

Recording: Soul Eyes (Concord Jazz, 4783)

Gibbs, Terry (1924–). Gibbs plays vibes even faster than he talks, taking ballads at double or triple time and tearing into up-tempo tunes with ease. He has been one of the unheralded giants of the vibes ever since playing with Woody Herman's Second Herd in the late 1940s.

Recording: Air Mail Special (Contemporary, 14056)

Gillespie, Dizzy (1917–1993). Gillespie not only helped found bebop but was also one of the pioneers of Afro-Cuban jazz. A masterful showman, humorist, and scat-singer, Dizzy was hugely entertaining in addition to being one of the greatest trumpeters ever.

Recordings: The Modern Jazz Sextet (Verve, 1842), *Birk's Works: The Verve Big Band Sessions* (Verve, 527900)

Giuffre, Jimmy (1921–). A cool-toned clarinetist, tenor, and baritonist, Giuffre started in cool jazz (composing "Four Brothers"), led a notable folk jazz trio, and by the early 1960s was playing a quiet brand of avant-garde.

Recording: Conversations with a Goose (Soul Note, 121258)

Golson, Benny (1929–). Golson emerged in the mid-1950s playing tenor with a sound similar to Don Byas and Lucky Thompson. As a songwriter, he has the knack of fusing catchy melodies to complex chord changes, delighting listeners and creative musicians alike.

Recording: New York Scene (Original Jazz Classics, 164)

Goodman, Benny (1909–1986). The King of Swing, Goodman was one of the greatest clarinetists of all time and the leader of the big band that launched the swing era. He rarely changed his style after 1935, yet usually played with enthusiasm, sticking to what he loved best.

Recording: On the Air 1937–1938 (Columbia/Legacy, 48836)

Gordon, Dexter (1923–1990). Long Tall Dexter was the king of bop tenors in the 1940s, a star on the Blue Note label in the 1960s, a celebrity in Europe during his long period overseas, and, in the 1985 *Round Midnight* film, a movie star.

Recording: Stable Mable (Steeplechase, 31040)

Grappelli, Stephane (1908–1997). Violinist with the Hot Club of France next to Django Reinhardt in the 1930s, Grappelli continued playing for six decades afterwards. After he became a world traveler in the 1970s, his fame grew as a masterful swing violinist.

Recording: 1935–1940 (Classics, 708)

Green, Grant (1931–1979). Blue Note's house guitarist during the first half of the 1960s, Green (who stuck to single-note lines) excelled in every setting whether it was post-bop, hard bop, or soul jazz. Later in life he tried the commercial route without much success, but his 1960s work still sounds fresh and classic.

Recording: Matador (Blue Note, 84442)

Griffin, Johnny (1928–). Once billed as the world's fastest tenor saxophonist, Johnny Griffin is coherent and swinging at any speed. On separate encounters, he more than held his own with John Coltrane and Eddie "Lockjaw" Davis.

Recording: The Congregation (Blue Note, 89383)

Gullin, Lars (1928–1976). Sweden's answer to Gerry Mulligan, Gullin was a superior cool jazz baritonist who had his own musical personality.

Recording: 1953–1956: With Chet Baker, Vol. 1 (Dragon, 224)

Haden, Charlie (1937–). One of the very few bassists who could have played with Ornette Coleman in 1959 and contributed a forward momentum without tying Ornette down to following chords, Haden has had a productive solo career since the 1960s.

Recording: Dream Keeper (Blue Note, 95474)

Hall, Edmond (1901–1967). A clarinetist with a cutting tone that could be heard over a brass section, Hall was a swing player who also excelled as a member of the Louis Armstrong All-Stars in the late 1950s.

Recording: Profoundly Blue (Blue Note, 21260)

Hall, Jim (1930–). Harmonically advanced, subtle, and explorative, guitarist Hall started in bop and evolved to post-bop. His playing has inspired Pat Metheny and Bill Frisell.

Recording: Alone Together (Original Jazz Classics, 467)

Hamilton, Chico (1921–). The Chico Hamilton Quintet was a major West Coast jazz group that featured the improvising cellist Fred Katz along with unusual tone colors. Drummer Hamilton has led other intriguing bands since the mid-1950s, and his sidemen have included tenor-saxophonist Charles Lloyd, guitarist Gabor Szabo, and more recently altoist Eric Person.

Recording: My Panamanian Friend (Soul Note, 121265)

Hampton, Lionel (1909–2002). The always exuberant vibraphonist (who introduced his instrument to jazz) grew from being a member of the Benny Goodman Quartet into a leader of his own big bands. Hampton always loved to play "Flying Home" and excite audiences.

Recording: Hamp and Getz (Verve, 831672)

Hancock, Herbie (1940–). From composing "Watermelon Man," finding a role for the piano in the music of Miles Davis' second classic quintet, and leading the funky Headhunters to exploring world music, electric funk, and modern acoustic jazz, pianist/keyboardist Hancock never seems to run out of new projects. He sounds like himself no matter what the setting.

Recording: Speak Like a Child (Blue Note, 46136)

Harris, Eddie (1934–1996). An underrated tenor saxophonist, Harris was particularly inventive on electric sax. He composed "Freedom Jazz Dance," made strong selling recordings, was a good pianist and singer, and even cut comedy albums.

Recording: Exodus to Jazz/Mighty Like a Rose (Vee-Jay, 904)

Harris, Gene (1933–2000). Harris practically defined soul jazz with his 1960s group The Three Sounds, and after some time away, the pianist made a full comeback in the 1980s. His style combined gospel influences with Oscar Peterson's brand of swinging jazz, and he was consistently excellent throughout his career.

Recording: Listen Here (Concord Jazz, 1006)

Hasselgard, Stan (1922–1948). The Swedish-born Hasselgard was such a strong clarinetist that Benny Goodman actually added him to his septet in 1948. Hasselgard might have had luck helping the clarinet get accepted into bebop, but a car accident cut short his life.

Recording: Jammin' at Jubilee (Dragon, 29)

Hawkins, Coleman (1904–1969). The first great tenor saxophonist, Hawkins prided himself on being modern throughout his forty-five-year career, whether playing with Fletcher Henderson, using young beboppers on his sessions in the 1940s, or jamming later on with John Coltrane and Booker Little.

Recording: The Hawk Flies High (Original Jazz Classics, 027)

Haynes, Roy (1926–). From Charlie Parker and Bud Powell to Chick Corea and Pat Metheny, drummer Haynes has always been an asset, one whose mind stays wide open.

Recording: Te Vou (Dreyfus, 36539)

Hemphill, Julius (1940–1995). An avant-garde altoist who was also a major writer, Hemphill was a key force in founding the World Saxophone Quartet and had a strong solo career.

Recording: Fat Man and the Hard Blues (Black Saint, 120152)

Henderson, Fletcher (1897–1952). Most important as the leader of the first great jazz big band (from 1923 on), Henderson was a masterful talent scout, a good pianist, and a significant arranger starting in the early 1930s. His arrangements were used and loved by Benny Goodman.

Recording: 1926–1927 (Classics, 597)

Henderson, Joe (1937–2001). Always distinctive, Joe Henderson was a classic inside/outside tenor saxophonist. Late in his career he gained great commercial success without changing his sound or style one bit.

Recording: So Near So Far (Verve, 517 674)

Hendricks, Jon (1921–). The genius of vocalese, Hendricks is a masterful and productive lyricist in addition to being a fine singer.

Recording: Boppin' at the Blue Note (Telarc, 83320)

Herman, Woody (1913–1987). A pretty good clarinetist, altoist, and singer, Herman is most important for leading a big band on and off for fifty years and for encouraging his younger sidemen to be creative.

Recordings: Blues on Parade (GRP/Decca, 606), *The Raven Speaks* (Original Jazz Classics, 663)29.5

Hill, Andrew (1937–). A highly original pianist and composer, Hill's music falls between hard bop and the avant-garde, quite advanced while following its own logic.

Recording: Verona Rag (Soul Note, 121110)

Hines, Earl (1903–1983). A 1920s pianist with the trickiest left hand in the business who loved to suspend time in death-defying runs, Hines had a big comeback in the 1960s and showed that his style was timeless.

Recording: Tour de Force (1201 Music, 9028)

Hinton, Milt (1910–2000). A lovable figure, bassist Hinton played for years with Cab Calloway and after that period ended worked in the studios and onstage with virtually everyone else. He was also a masterful photographer.
Recording: Old Man Time (Chiaroscuro, 310)

Hodges, Johnny (1907–1970). Altoist Hodges had such a beautiful tone and could sound so sensuous on ballads that his expertise on blues and stomps was sometimes overshadowed. Except for four years in the 1950s, he was Duke Ellington's top soloist from 1928 to 1970.
Recording: Everybody Knows (GRP/Impulse, 116)

Holiday, Billie (1915–1959). Lady Day's expressive behind-the-beat phrasing and tendency to live the words she sang (particularly in later years) was legendary. Her music was mostly jazz oriented in the 1930s, and her voice was at its strongest during the following decade, but some fans prefer her tortured and haunting vocals of the 1950s.
Recording: The Quintessential Billie Holiday, Vol. 8 (Columbia/Legacy, 47030)

Holman, Bill (1927–). One of Stan Kenton's best arrangers in the 1950s, Holman has continued growing through the years and was one of the most inventive arrangers in all of jazz during the 1990s.
Recording: Brilliant Corners (JVC, 2066)

Horn, Shirley (1934–). Though she can sing and play piano on medium-tempo tunes, Horn became famous for her very slow renditions of ballads.
Recording: I Thought about You (Verve, 833 235)

Hubbard, Freddie (1938–). A fiery trumpeter influenced by Clifford Brown and Lee Morgan who became a giant himself by the late 1960s, Hubbard was at his best on his Blue Note and CTI recordings. After the mid-1970s his recordings became erratic (ranging from treasures to trash), and unfortunately he largely lost his trumpet chops after the early 1990s.
Recording: Straight Life (Columbia/CTI, 65125)

Hunter, Alberta (1895–1984). A classic blues singer who first recorded in 1921, Hunter had an episodic career including twenty-one years spent off the music scene as a nurse. In 1977 she enjoyed a memorable musical comeback at the age of eighty-two, still singing double-entendre blues and classic material.
Recording: Chicago: The Living Legends (Original Blues Classics, 510)

Hutcherson, Bobby (1941–). One of the major vibraphonists, Hutcherson in the 1960s often appeared on avant-garde recordings for Blue Note before maturing into an unpredictable hard bop stylist.
Recording: Skyline (Verve, 559 616)

Hyman, Dick (1927–). Able to play in any style, pianist Hyman by the mid-1970s mostly settled on classic 1920s jazz and swing. His technique remains as phenomenal as his huge repertoire.
Recording: In Recital (Reference, 84)

Jackson, Milt (1923–1999). A soulful bebopper, Milt Jackson had the definitive style on vibes. His many years with the Modern Jazz Quartet were balanced out by solo projects that emphasized his love for blues, ballads, and bop.
Recording: Night Mist (Original Jazz Classics, 827)

Jacquet, Illinois (1922–). Jacquet played the famous tenor solo on "Flying Home" with Lionel Hampton that launched rhythm and blues. He also played other romps, remains a warm interpreter of ballads, and has always had a very viable sound that mixed together aspects of Coleman Hawkins and Lester Young.
Recording: Bottoms Up (Original Jazz Classics, 417)

Jamal, Ahmad (1930–). A master at utilizing space and dynamics, pianist Ahmad Jamal has led a series of intriguing and subtle trios for a half century.
Recording: Chicago Revisited: Live at Joe Segal's Jazz Showcase (Telarc, 83327)

James, Harry (1916–1983). A brilliant trumpeter who led the most popular big band in 1942 through 1946, James was a household name for decades. Though he sometimes performed schmaltz and pop music, he could play exciting jazz with the best.
Recording: 1937–1939 (Classics, 903)

Jefferson, Eddie (1918–1979). The founder of vocalese, Jefferson had an average voice but was a very skilled lyricist. He wrote the classic lyrics to "Moody's Mood for Love" and "Body and Soul" (paying tribute to Coleman Hawkins).
Recording: Body and Soul (Original Jazz Classics, 396)

Johnson, Bunk (1889–1949). His supporters considered cornetist Johnson to be the savior of New Orleans jazz when he was rediscovered in the early 1940s, while his detractors thought he was a fraud. Bunk fell somewhere in between, but on his best days could play very good classic jazz.
Recording: Complete Deccas, Victors, V-Discs Alternate Takes (Document, 1001)

Johnson, J. J. (1924–2001). The Charlie Parker of the trombone, J. J. Johnson showed that fast lines were no problem on his potentially awkward instrument. He was also an important composer while maintaining his reputation as jazz's leading trombonist.
Recording: Things Are Getting Better All the Time (Original Jazz Classics, 745)

Johnson, James P. (1894–1955). The father of stride piano, James P. Johnson developed and perfected the style, inspiring Fats Waller. Johnson was also a top songwriter who wrote "The Charleston" and "Old Fashioned Love."
Recording: Snowy Morning Blues (GRP/Decca, 604)

Johnson, Pete (1904–1967). One of the top boogie-woogie pianists of the 1930s and 1940s, Johnson was also a superior blues player who often teamed up with Big Joe Turner.
Recording: 1944–1946 (Classics, 933)

Jones, Elvin (1927–). John Coltrane's drummer from 1960 to 1965, Jones is a master of polyrhythms, even on ballads. He has been an important leader of post-bop combos (the Elvin Jones Jazz Machine) for over three decades.
Recording: It Don't Mean a Thing (Enja, 8066)

Jones, Jo (1911–1985). Jones' light touch on the drums (de-emphasizing the bass drum) while with Count Basie was influential, and he remained one of the top swing drummers into the 1960s.
Recording: The Essential Jo Jones (Vanguard, 101/102)

Jones, Thad (1923–1986). As a cornetist, Jones chose his notes carefully and was quite advanced, even while with Count Basie in the 1950s. He developed into a major arranger-composer (writing "A Child Is Born"), co-leading the Thad Jones/Mel Lewis Orchestra during 1966–1978.
Recording: Consummation (Blue Note, 38266)

Joplin, Scott (1868–1917). The king of ragtime, Joplin largely defined the idiom of classic ragtime, and his "Maple Leaf Rag" remains the style's most popular number. Unfortunately he never recorded.

Jordan, Louis (1908–1975). A fine jump altoist who was a talented and humorous singer, Jordan and his Tympany Five had dozens of hits between 1942–1951, leading the way from swing to r&b.
Recording: 1943–1945 (Classics, 866)

Kenton, Stan (1911–1979). The adventurous arrangements that pianist-arranger Kenton featured with his big band was forceful, sometimes pompous, and almost always risk-taking. His music was worshipped by some (he became a jazz cult figure) and dismissed by others but never ignored.
Recordings: The Innovations Orchestra (Capitol, 59965), *New Concepts of Artistry in Rhythm* (Capitol, 92865)

Keppard, Freddie (1890–1933). The successor to Buddy Bolden and the predecessor of King Oliver, Keppard was considered the top cornetist in New Orleans around 1910. Fortunately he recorded a few sessions in the 1920s that give today's listeners an idea of what his early style sounded like.
Recording: The Complete Freddie Keppard 1923–1927 (King Jazz, 111)

Kirby, John (1908–1952). Bassist Kirby led a unique sextet during the swing era that had cool-toned virtuosos and a repertoire that included some themes from classical music.
Recording: 1939–1941 (Classics, 770)

Kirk, Rahsaan Roland (1936–1977). Kirk frequently did the impossible, whether it was playing three saxophones at once, taking twenty-minute, one-breath solos via circular breathing, or playing credibly in any jazz style on a moment's notice. He had to be experienced live to be fully appreciated.
Recording: Domino (Verve, 833)

Konitz, Lee (1927–). An advanced cool jazz player in the late 1940s who worked with Claude Thornhill, Miles Davis' Nonet, and Lennie Tristano, Konitz has always had a strong musical curiosity. For over fifty-five years, he has consistently pushed himself, performing in a countless number of challenging settings without changing his basic style.

Recording: The Lee Konitz Duets (Original Jazz Classics, 466)

Krupa, Gene (1909–1973). A crowd pleaser who was the first superstar drummer, Gene Krupa may not have been the most subtle drummer, but he was always exciting, whether playing with Benny Goodman or leading his own fine big bands.

Recording: 1935–1938 (Classics, 754)

Lacy, Steve (1934–). Although he started out as a Dixieland clarinetist, by the 1950s Lacy was playing free jazz on soprano sax with Cecil Taylor. He has since become one of the foremost interpreters of Thelonious Monk's music, leader of his own advanced sextet, and a thoughtful but always adventurous scalar improviser.

Recordings: The Straight Horn of Steve Lacy (Candid, 79007), *Live at Sweet Basil* (Novus, 63128)

Lake, Oliver (1942–). A free jazz altoist, Lake's playing experiences range from being a member of the World Saxophone Quartet to leading an avant-garde reggae band.

Recording: Expandable Language (Black Saint, 120074)

Lambert, Hendricks, and Ross (1957–1964). Arguably the finest jazz vocal group of all time, this classic ensemble featured three masters of vocalese in Dave Lambert, Jon Hendricks, and Annie Ross. All of their recordings are memorable.

Recording: Sing a Song of Basie (Verve, 543827)

Lang, Eddie (1902–1933). The first important jazz guitarist, Lang could play single-note blues lines with Lonnie Johnson or the most sophisticated chord voicings of the era. He was in great demand for record dates before his early death and often teamed up with violinist Joe Venuti.

Recording: Pioneers of Jazz Guitar 1927–1938 (Challenge, 79015)

Lewis, George (1900–1968). A primitive but often rewarding New Orleans clarinetist, Lewis first gained attention in the mid-1940s for his playing with Bunk Johnson. In the 1950s he toured the world with his band, becoming quite famous and influential in the trad world.

Recording: In Stockholm 1959 (Dragon, 221)

Lewis, John (1920–2001). The Count Basie of bebop in his use of single-note lines and space, Lewis was the musical director of the Modern Jazz Quartet and loved both classical music and blues.

Recording: Grand Encounter (Pacific Jazz, 46859)

Lewis, Meade Lux (1905–1964). One of the three members of the Boogie Woogie Trio of the late 1930s, Lewis had a long career and stuck throughout to blues and boogie-woogie, occasionally recording on celeste.

Recording: The Blues Piano Artistry of Meade Lux Lewis (Original Blues Classics, 1759)

Lincoln, Abbey (1930–). Like Billie Holiday in her later period, Abbey Lincoln always believed in the words she sang. An underrated lyricist, Lincoln's music ranges from the political to love songs, always sticking to the truth.
   Recordings: Straight Ahead (Candid, 79015), *People in Me* (Polygram, 514626)

Lunceford, Jimmy (1902–1947). A multi-instrumentalist, Lunceford largely gave up playing to lead one of the swing era's most intriguing orchestras. His ensembles featured impeccable musicianship, glee club singing, and concise solos.
   Recording: Lunceford Special (Columbia/Legacy, 65647)

Machito (1912–1984). Leader of the pioneering Afro-Cuban jazz band, Machito sang, played maracas, and was wise enough to have his brother-in-law Mario Bauza be his musical director.
   Recording: Machito at the Crescendo (GNP/Crescendo, 58)

Manne, Shelly (1920–1984). A very versatile drummer based on the West Coast, Manne led jazz groups that were cool in the 1950s and hard bop–oriented during the next decade. He also ran the popular jazz club Shelly's.
   Recording: Manne-Hole. Vol. 4: Swinging Sounds (Original Jazz Classics, 267)

McGhee, Howard (1918–1987). McGhee was influenced by Roy Eldridge and in turn was an inspiration for Fats Navarro. He was one of the top trumpeters of 1945–1950 before drug use slowed him down.
   Recording: Maggie's Back in Town (Original Jazz Classics, 693)

McLaughlin, John (1942–). One of the first jazz guitarists to break away from the Charlie Christian model, the highly original McLaughlin has been a giant in fusion (the Mahavishnu Orchestra), world music (Shakti), and as a soloist on both electric and acoustic guitars.
   Recordings: My Goals Beyond (Knitting Factory Works, 3010), *The Promise* (Verve, 529 828)

McLean, Jackie (1932–). A definitive hard bop altoist in the 1950s, McLean was open to freer sounds in the 1960s. His slightly sharp and intense sound has always been immediately recognizable.
   Recordings: Destination Out (Blue Note, 32087), *Dynasty* (Triloka, 181)

McRae, Carmen (1920–1994). A much-beloved singer ranked just below Ella Fitzgerald and Sarah Vaughan, McRae's ironic interpretations of lyrics and laid-back phrasing have been very influential. She did not record as a leader until she was thirty-four but kept busy for most of the next forty years.
   Recording: For Lady Day (Novus, 63163)

McShann, Jay (1916–). As a big bandleader, McShann will always be remembered for having Charlie Parker as a sideman, but he has also been a top Kansas City swing/blues pianist and vocalist for seventy years.
   Recording: Hootie (Chiaroscuro, 357)

Miley, Bubber (1903–1932). An important force in Duke Ellington's band of 1926–1929, trumpeter Miley's brilliance with mutes was largely responsible for Duke's "Jungle Sound."
Recording: Duke Ellington—The Bubber Miley Era: 1924–1929 (Jazz Giants, 1014)

Miller, Glenn (1904–1944). Leader of the most popular big band of the swing era, Miller started his career as a trombonist but soon de-emphasized playing in favor of his arranging and organizational skills. His orchestra had a remarkable number of hits in 1939 to 1942 before he led the Army Air Force Band while in the military.
Recording: The Chesterfield Broadcasts (BMG Heritage, 54306)

Mingus, Charles (1922–1979). A brilliant bassist and composer, Mingus was highly emotional, driving his sidemen to the breaking point as he got them to play way above their comfort zones for him. The Mingus Big Band today keeps his music very much alive.
Recordings: Blues and Roots (Rhino/Atlantic, 75205), *Mingus at Antibes* (Atlantic, 90532)

Mobley, Hank (1930–1986). A fixture on Blue Note hard bop sessions of the 1950s and 1960s, Mobley may not have been the most innovative tenor saxophonist, but he had the knack for being part of one memorable session after another.
Recording: Roll Call (Blue Note, 9051)

Modern Jazz Quartet (1952–1996). Comprised of pianist John Lewis, vibraphonist Milt Jackson, bassist Percy Heath, and drummer Connie Kay (who replaced Kenny Clarke in 1955), the MJQ had its own delicate sound. They were sometimes involved in over-arranged third stream projects but never gave up playing bop standards and swinging blues.
Recording: For Ellington (East West, 90926)

Monk, Thelonious (1917–1982). Monk was original from the start, as a pianist and a composer. No one sounded like him, so he put in decades of hard work before he was finally treated as a genius and innovator and not merely as an eccentric.
Recordings: Thelonious Monk with John Coltrane (Original Jazz, Classics 39), *Monk's Dream* (Columbia/Legacy, 40786)

Montgomery, Wes (1925–1968). One of the top jazz guitarists of the 1960s, Wes Montgomery made the Charlie Christian style his own, adding his expertise with octaves. Although his last few albums were commercial (allowing him a brief bit of prosperity), his earlier Riverside sessions are permanent proof of his greatness.
Recording: So Much Guitar (Original Jazz Classics, 233)

Moody, James (1925–). Whether on tenor, alto, flute, or singing "Moody's Mood for Love," James Moody is both entertaining and very musical. He came to prominence during the bop era, was closely associated with Dizzy Gillespie, and is still a major force.
Recording: Moody's Mood for Blues (Original Jazz Classics, 1837)

Morgan, Lee (1938–1972). A major trumpeter from the time he turned eighteen, Lee Morgan built on the style of Clifford Brown and became a giant of hard bop. He recorded many rewarding sessions as a leader (including his catchy hit "The Sidewinder"), with Art Blakey's Jazz Messengers, and with his contemporaries.
Recording: The Gigolo (Blue Note, 84212)

Morton, Jelly Roll (1890–1941). One of the pioneers of jazz, Morton was one of the first great pianists and arranger-composers. His work with his Red Hot Peppers of 1926–1928 ranks with the finest jazz recordings.
Recording: Last Sessions: The Complete General Recordings (GRP, 403)

Mulligan, Gerry (1927–1996). The leading baritone saxophonist of the 1950s and a talented arranger and songwriter, Mulligan came to fame leading a piano-less quartet with Chet Baker. His witty style and light sound made him a popular figure for decades.
Recording: Gerry Mulligan in Paris, Vol. 1 (Vogue, 68211)

Murphy, Mark (1932–). An adventurous jazz singer, Murphy alternates between his eccentric falsetto and baritone voice, improvising with the spirit of a bebopper while breaking down new vocal boundaries.
Recording: Stolen … and Other Moments (32 Jazz, 32036)

Nance, Ray (1913–1976). An important member of Duke Ellington's orchestra during the years from 1940 to 1963, Nance was a fine cornetist who succeeded Cootie Williams as a plunger mute specialist. In addition he was an excellent violinist and an entertaining singer. Nance made virtually all of his most significant recordings with Ellington.

Nanton, Tricky Sam (1904–1946). Sitting next to Bubber Miley, Cootie Williams, and Ray Nance with Duke Ellington's band from 1926 to 1946, Tricky Sam played other worldly sounds on trombone that have rarely been duplicated. Despite his talents, Nanton never led his own record date.

Navarro, Fats (1923–1950). A major bop trumpeter during the years from 1945 to 1949, Navarro later influenced Clifford Brown who influenced virtually all the trumpeters to follow. Navarro was a strong contender for Dizzy Gillespie's throne, but heroin and tuberculosis cut short his life.
Recording: Featured with the Tadd Dameron Band (Milestone, 47041)

New Orleans Rhythm Kings (1922–1925). The top jazz band on record in 1922, the NORK extended the legacy of the Original Dixieland Jazz Band by balancing ensembles with short solos, including most notably from clarinetist Leon Roppolo.
Recording: New Orleans Rhythm Kings and Jelly Roll Morton (Milestone, 47020)

Noone, Jimmie (1895–1944). A major clarinetist during the 1920s, Noone had a smooth style that influenced Benny Goodman. His work with the Apex Club Orchestra (starting in 1928) generally had Noone playing over his altoist who purposely stuck to the melody, which created an unusual ensemble sound.
Recording: 1930–1934 (Classics, 641)

Norvo, Red (1908–1999). In the 1930s Norvo was the only xylophonist to lead a big band. He had a distinctive style, even after switching to vibes in 1943, and in the early 1950s led a modern trio with guitarist Tal Farlow and bassist Charles Mingus.

Recording: Dance of the Octopus (Hep, 1044)

O'Day, Anita (1919–). O'Day came to fame singing with Gene Krupa's band ("Let Me Off Uptown"), and after a stint with Stan Kenton, she was at her best on her solo records for Verve during the 1950s. She made a colorful and well-publicized comeback from heroin addiction in the 1970s.

Recording: All the Sad Young Men (Verve, 517065)

O'Farrill, Chico (1921–2001). One of the unsung heroes of Afro-Cuban jazz, O'Farrill's arrangements for Machito, Dizzy Gillespie, Stan Kenton, and his own bands defined the idiom and provided Latin jazz with some of its most stirring moments.

Recording: Carambola (Milestone, 938)

Oliver, King (1885–1938). Considered the top cornetist in New Orleans in 1915, Joe "King" Oliver led the Creole Jazz Band in Chicago from 1922 to 1924 (which featured his protégé Louis Armstrong), the Dixie Syncopators in 1926, and a fine hot dance band in New York in the late 1920s before his failing teeth and bad luck caused his demise in the 1930s.

Recording: King Oliver (RCA, 42411)

Original Dixieland Jazz Band (1917–1923). The first jazz band to record, the ODJB was the pacesetter (at least on records) from 1917 to 1921, sounding absolutely barbaric compared to the polite recordings that were typical of 1915.

Recording: 1917–1923 (EPM Musique, 15849)

Ory, Kid (1886–1973). A pioneering New Orleans trombonist who in the 1920s recorded with Louis Armstrong's Hot Five and Jelly Roll Morton, Ory made a comeback in the 1940s and led one of the top New Orleans jazz bands of the 1950s.

Recording: This Kid's the Greatest (Good Time Jazz, 12045)

Palmieri, Eddie (1936–). In addition to leading top-notch Afro-Cuban jazz bands since the early 1960s, Palmieri is significant as a pianist, updating the style by infusing the influence of McCoy Tyner, Herbie Hancock, and Chick Corea into Latin jazz.

Recording: El Rumbero del Piano (RMM, 82197)

Parker, Charlie (1920–1955). One of the most remarkable saxophonists of all time, Parker's ability to play perfect coherent solos at ridiculously fast tempos, his knack at coming up with new phrases that would be adopted by later generations, and his brilliance at negotiating chord changes are still wondrous. One could not imagine bebop and post-1945 jazz without him.

Recording: Complete Verve Master Takes (Verve, 65597)

Pass, Joe (1929–1994). A very talented bop guitarist in the 1960s, Pass found immortality in the 1970s when he showed that he could play unaccompanied solos on up-tempo bop tunes such as "Cherokee" and "How High the Moon," supplying the melody, harmonies, chords, and bass lines simultaneously.
Recordings: For Django (BGO, 430), *Virtuoso #2* (Pablo, 2310-788)

Pastorius, Jaco (1951–1987). The first truly distinctive electric bassist, Pastorius starred with Weather Report and his own Word of Mouth big band. He showed that the electric bass could be a lead instrument, and he led the way for virtually everyone on his instrument.
Recording: Invitation (Warner Bros., 16662)

Pepper, Art (1925–1982). A superb altoist in the 1950s whose musical consistency contrasted with his very erratic lifestyle, Pepper made a remarkable comeback in the mid-1970s that found him fighting his way back up to the top.
Recordings: Gettin' Together (Original Jazz Classics, 169), *Straight Life* (Original Jazz Classics, 475)

Peterson, Oscar (1925–). Peterson has displayed more technique on piano than any jazz player other than Art Tatum, and his ability to outswing everyone has made him a major attraction for over five decades. Whether with his trios or on unaccompanied solos, Peterson ranked near the top at least until an early 1990s stroke weakened his playing.
Recordings: My Favorite Instrument (Verve, 821 843), *The Trio* (Pablo, 2310-701)

Pettiford, Oscar (1922–1960). The most significant bassist to emerge right after the death of Jimmy Blanton, Pettiford was greatly respected by bop and swing players alike. He was a strong soloist on bass and (with Harry Babasin) a pioneering jazz cellist.
Recording: First Bass (IAJRC, 1010)

Pleasure, King (1922–1981). King Pleasure had the best voice of the voca-lese singers and made "Moody's Mood for Love" and "Parker's Mood" into jazz hits in the 1950s.
Recording: Golden Days (Original Jazz Classics, 1772)

Ponty, Jean-Luc (1942–). The master of fusion violin, Ponty made contri-butions to the bands of John McLaughlin (the second Mahavishnu Orchestra) and Frank Zappa but was at his best on his string of albums for the Atlantic label.
Recording: Live at Donte's (Blue Note, 35635)

Powell, Bud (1924–1966). Powell largely invented bebop piano and the next two generations followed in his giant footsteps.
Recording: Bud Plays Bird (Roulette, 37137)

Pozo, Chano (1915–1948). When percussionist-singer Pozo joined Dizzy Gillespie's big band in 1947, the exciting mix of styles resulted in Afro-Cuban jazz.
Recording: Legendary Sessions (Tumbau, 017)

Puente, Tito (1923–2000). "El Rey" was the best known of the Latin jazz bandleaders and the most durable. His playing of timbales and vibes was impressive, but it was his joyful spirit that was particularly memorable.
Recording: The Mambo King: His 100th Album (RMM, 80680)

Ra, Sun (1914–1993). A true eccentric, Ra was also a visionary who played electric keyboards as early as the 1950s, led the first avant-garde big band, and mixed together ancient Egypt and science fiction both in his philosophy and his Arkestra's outfits.
Recordings: Jazz in Silhouette (Evidence, 22012), *Space Is the Place* (GRP/Impulse, 249)

Redman, Don (1900–1964). One of jazz's first great arrangers, Redman wrote the influential charts for the Fletcher Henderson Orchestra of 1923 to 1927. He also led McKinney's Cotton Pickers and his own swing-era big band, played alto and clarinet, and sang philosophical lyrics in a conversational style.
Recording: 1931–1933 (Classics, 543)

Reinhardt, Django (1910–1953). One of the most remarkable guitarists of all time, Django Reinhardt had no competitors in the 1930s on acoustic guitar. By the late 1940s he had conquered both bebop and the electric guitar.
Recording: Peche a la Mouche (Verve, 835 418)

Rich, Buddy (1917–1970). An incredible drummer, Buddy Rich propelled several swing-era bands (including Artie Shaw and Tommy Dorsey), was featured with Jazz at the Philharmonic in the 1950s, and had his own big band starting in 1966. No drummer was faster or more virtuosic.
Recording: Mercy, Mercy (Blue Note, 54331)

Roach, Max (1924–). The definitive bop drummer, Roach took solos that made one think he was a master architect. Always modern, he led bands from the mid-1950s on, with Clifford Brown, Sonny Rollins, Booker Little, Stanley Turrentine, and Freddie Hubbard, headed the all-percussion group M'Boom, and played duets with avant-gardists.
Recording: Easy Winners (Soul Note, 121 109)

Rogers, Shorty (1924–1994). A solid trumpeter, Rogers was most significant as a West Coast arranger, composer, and organizer of record and studio sessions. He kept everyone working.
Recording: Swings (Bluebird, 3012)

Rollins, Sonny (1930–). One of the giants of the tenor, Rollins had his own sound by the early 1950s. On a remarkable number of important albums, he has always displayed the ability to take continually interesting solos laced with witty and fresh ideas.
Recordings: The Bridge (Bluebird, 52472), *Next Album* (Original Jazz Classics, 312)

Rushing, Jimmy (1903–1972). The best of the male band singers, Rushing ("Mr. Five by Five") sang the blues with Count Basie for over a dozen years and had a solid solo career in the 1950s.
Recording: The Essential Jimmy Rushing (Vanguard, 66)

Russell, Pee Wee (1906–1969). A very original clarinetist who took wild chances in his solos, Russell spent much of his career in Dixieland settings but was really in his own musical world.
Recording: Ask Me Now (Verve, 755 742)

Santamaria, Mongo (1922–2003). The masterful percussionist played congas with Tito Puente and Cal Tjader before leading his own popular groups, having several catchy hits along the way including "Watermelon Man."
Recording: Skin on Skin: The Mongo Santamaria Anthology (Rhino, 75689)

Shavers, Charlie (1917–1971). A brilliant trumpeter from the swing era, Shavers was the star of the John Kirby Sextet, was featured in Tommy Dorsey's band, and battled Roy Eldridge successfully at Jazz at the Philharmonic concerts.
Recording: 1944–1945 (Classics, 944)

Shaw, Artie (1910–2004). Leader of five major big bands during the swing era and one of the finest clarinetists of all time, Shaw did his best to run away from success. Despite that, he had million sellers in "Begin the Beguine," "Frenesi," "Star Dust," and "Summit Ridge Drive."
Recording: The Complete Gramercy Five Sessions (Bluebird, 7637)

Shaw, Woody (1944–1989). A major trumpeter of the late 1960s, 1970s, and 1980s, Shaw had a tone similar to Freddie Hubbard's but a more advanced post-bop style.
Recording: Little Red's Fantasy (32 Jazz, 32126)

Shearing, George (1919–). A top swing pianist by the late 1930s, Shearing embraced bop and made it palatable to the masses with his popular quintet of 1949 to 1970. Since that group's breakup, he has continued touring the world with his duo, always happy to play his "Lullaby of Birdland" as an encore.
Recording: On a Clear Day (Concord, Jazz 4132)

Shorter, Wayne (1933–). A true original as a tenor saxophonist, soprano saxophonist, and composer, Shorter was a major asset to Art Blakey's Jazz Messengers, the second classic Miles Davis Quintet, and Weather Report. In recent times he has shown that in his seventies he is still very much in his musical prime.
Recording: Footprints Live! (Verve, 589 679)

Silver, Horace (1928–). Silver has been very significant as a highly influential funky soul jazz pianist, a bandleader who headed several major quintets, and as a songwriter (including "Señor Blues" and "Song for My Father").
Recording: Finger Poppin' with the Horace Silver Quintet (Blue Note, 42304)

Sims, Zoot (1925–1985). Famous for always swinging, tenor-saxophonist Zoot Sims emerged from Woody Herman's Second Herd to be the star of a countless number of straight-ahead combo albums and sessions.
Recording: Warm Tenor (Pablo, 2310-831)

Smith, Bessie (1894–1937). The Empress of the Blues was arguably the top singer on records of the 1920s, a powerful force whose performances still resonate with today's listeners.
Recording: The Complete Recordings, Vol. 3 (Columbia/Legacy, 47474)

Smith, Jimmy (1925–). Smith burst upon the national scene in 1956, showing that the Hammond B-3 organ was a very viable jazz instrument. His series of jam session records for Blue Note are still the highpoint of his lengthy career.
Recording: Cool Blues (Blue Note, 84441)

Smith, Stuff (1909–1967). The hardest swinging of all jazz violinists, Smith's work with his Onyx Club Boys of the 1930s are some of the most enjoyable and hottest performances of the era.
Recording: Live at the Montmartre (Storyville, 4142)

Stitt, Sonny (1924–1982). Stitt, who was equally talented on alto and tenor sax, breathed bebop and was never shy about taking on all potential competitors.
Recording: Salt and Pepper (GRP/Impulse, 210)

Strayhorn, Billy (1915–1967). Duke Ellington's right-hand man, Strayhorn was a skilled composer, a complementary arranger, and an underrated pianist. Among his compositions are "Take the 'A' Train" and "Lush Life."
Recording: The Peaceful Side (Blue Note, 52563)

Tabackin, Lew (1940–). A high-powered tenor saxophonist inspired by Sonny Rollins and Ben Webster, Tabackin is also a flutist influenced by Asian classical music. In addition to his combo work, he is often featured with his wife Toshiko Akiyoshi's big band.
Recording: Desert Lady (Concord Jazz, 4411)

Tatum, Art (1909–1956). An incredible pianist with remarkable technique and a style thirty years ahead of its time harmonically, Tatum could play blinding runs that amazed even the top classical pianists.
Recording: Piano Starts Here (Columbia/Legacy, 64690)

Taylor, Cecil (1929–). The most radical of all jazz improvisers, Taylor's piano solos are thunderous, dense, and unremittingly atonal yet quite purposeful.
Recording: Unit Structures (Blue Note, 84237)

Teagarden, Jack (1905–1964). Among the first truly fluent trombone soloists, Teagarden was also an excellent singer. He was always a happy presence to have around, mostly appearing in Dixieland and swing settings.
Recording: 1941–1943 (Classics, 874)

Terry, Clark (1920–). Terry has always had an exuberant and joyful sound on flugelhorn and a style full of happiness. He was one of the stars with Duke Ellington in the 1950s and has led his own combos ever since.
Recording: Portraits (Chesky, 267)

Tjader, Cal (1925–1982). Tjader may have been Swedish, but the vibraphonist became one of the most important players and leaders in Afro-Cuban jazz. His bands were always popular and influential.
Recording: Night at the Black Hawk (Original Jazz Classics, 278)

Torme, Mel (1925–1999). Although he spent periods singing pop, Torme was always a jazz singer who loved swing standards. His 1950s work with the Marty Paich Dek-tette and his Concord recordings of the 1980s and 1990s are his prime; few could scat with his sincerity and creativity.
Recording: Fujitsu-Concord Festival (Concord Jazz, 481)

Tristano, Lennie (1919–1978). The pianist-teacher came up with a cool version of bebop in the mid-1940s, one that featured stunning unisons, constant melodic creativity over common chord changes, and quiet timekeeping rhythm sections.
Recording: Lennie Tristano/Thve New Tristano (Rhino, 71595)

Tyner, McCoy (1938–). Famous as John Coltrane's pianist from 1960 through 1965, Tyner has remained a powerful and influential force ever since. His percussive style and chord voicings have been emulated by most modern jazz pianists.
Recording: Enlightenment (Milestone, 55001)

Valdes, Chucho (1941–). The Art Tatum of Cuba, Valdes has remarkable technique and is a true master of complex polyrhythms. He was the leader of Irakere for years and is the son of the notable pianist Bebo Valdes.
Recording: Live at the Village Vanguard (Blue Note, 20730)

Vaughan, Sarah (1924–1990). Vaughan had a wondrous voice with an opera singer's range, and enough endurance to be one of the major jazz singers for forty-five years.
Recording: Crazy and Mixed Up (Pablo, 2312-137)

Venuti, Joe (1903–1978). Jazz's first great violinist, Venuti often teamed up with guitarist Eddie Lang in the 1920s. After decades out of the spotlight, he was very busy during his final years, showing that his brand of classic jazz violin is timeless.
Recording: Joe and Zoot (Chiaroscuro, 128)

Waller, Fats (1904–1943). As a stride pianist, organist (jazz's first), singer, songwriter, and frequently hilarious personality, Thomas "Fats" Waller was brilliant, very musical, and always entertaining.
Recording: Fats Waller and His Buddies (Bluebird, 61005)

Washington, Dinah (1924–1963). Washington was always proud of her ability to sing everything. She was best at blues, swinging jazz, and ballads, and had few competitors in the 1950s.
Recording: Mellow Mama (Delmark, 451)

Washington, Grover, Jr. (1943–1999). On tenor, alto, soprano, and even baritone, Grover Washington Jr.'s playing was full of soul and individuality. He was the top performer in rhythm and jazz and a real crowd pleaser.
Recording: Inner City Blues (Motown Jazz, 530577)

Weather Report (1970–1985). One of the premier fusion bands, Weather Report was Joe Zawinul's brainchild and along the way starred co-leader Wayne Shorter and, for a few glorious years, Jaco Pastorius.
Recording: Black Market (Columbia, 65169)

Webster, Ben (1909–1973). One of the major swing-era tenors, Webster could roar like a lion or purr on ballads like a pussycat. Though famous for his three years with Duke Ellington, Webster had a long solo career afterwards, always playing with a great deal of feeling.
Recording: Music for Loving (Verve, 527 774)

Williams, Cootie (1910–1985). Bubber Miley's replacement with Duke Ellington, Williams not only was a master with plunger mutes but also played very good open trumpet too. After starring with Duke from 1929 to 1940, he took a twenty-one-year "vacation," returning for 1961 to 1974.

Williams, Joe (1918–1999). Williams came to prominence with Count Basie in the 1950s, singing such blues as "Everyday I Have the Blues" and "Going to Chicago." He actually preferred to perform ballads and standards, and, truth be told, he excelled at everything he sang.
Recording: Every Night: Live at Vine Street (Verve, 833 236)

Williams, Mary Lou (1910–1981). She started out as a stride pianist and arranger for Andy Kirk's orchestra, but Williams developed into a much more modern pianist and an inventive composer in her later years.
Recording: 1927–1940 (Classics, 630)

Wilson, Teddy (1912–1986). The definitive swing pianist, Wilson came to fame with Benny Goodman and led trios for decades afterwards, always sounding as if it were still 1935.
Recording: With Billie in Mind (Chiaroscuro, 111)

Woods, Phil (1931–). A major bebop altoist for fifty years, Woods has kept the music fresh by performing newer compositions and leading a regular quartet/quintet since the 1970s.
Recording: Bop Stew (Concord Jazz, 345)

Young, Lester (1909–1959). Young's soft quiet tone on the tenor was innovative in the 1930s, and he was always a true original. Whether with Count Basie or on his own postwar dates, Young was the epitome of cool.
Recording: With the Oscar Peterson Trio (Verve, 521 451)

Zawinul, Joe (1932–). Originally a funky pianist with Cannonball Adderley who composed "Mercy, Mercy, Mercy," Zawinul switched to keyboards and became the creative brains behind Weather Report. His work on synthesizer is still the pacesetter among keyboardists.
Recording: The Rise & Fall of the Third Stream/Money in the Pocket (Rhino, 71675)

Bibliography

Albertson, Chris. *Bessie*. Briarcliff Manor, NY: Stein and Day, 1982.

Badger, Reid. *James Reese Europe—A Life in Ragtime*. New York: Oxford University Press, 1995.

Balliett, Whitney. *American Musicians*. New York: Oxford University Press, 1986.

Berlin Edward A. *King of Ragtime*. New York: Oxford University Press, 1994.

Blesh, Rudi, and Harriet Janis. *They All Played Ragtime*. New York: Oak Publications, 1971.

Chambers, Jack. *Milestones 1*. New York: Beech Tree Books, 1983.

———. *Milestones 2*. New York: Beech Tree Books, 1985.

Charters, Samuel B. *The Country Blues*. New York: Da Capo Press, 1975.

Charters, Samuel B., and Leonard Kunstadt. *Jazz—A History of the New York Scene*. New York: Da Capo Press, 1962.

Chilton, John. *Let the Good Times Roll—The Story of Louis Jordan*. Ann Arbor, MI: University Of Michigan Press, 1992.

———. *Sidney Bechet—The Wizard of Jazz*. New York: Oxford University Press, 1987.

Clarke, Donald. *Wishing on the Moon*. New York: Viking, 1994.

Condon, Eddie, and Thomas Sugrue. *We Called It Music*. New York: Da Capo Press, 1947.

Deffaa, Chip. *In the Mainstream*. Metuchen, NJ: Scarecrow Press, 1992.

————. *Swing Legacy*. Metuchen, NJ: Scarecrow Press, 1989.

————. *Voices of the Jazz Age*. Chicago: University Of Illinois Press, 1990.

Feather, Leonard, and Ira Gitler. *The Biographical Encyclopedia of Jazz*. New York: Oxford University Press, 1999.

Friedwald, Will. *Jazz Singing*. New York: Charles Scribner & Sons, 1990.

Fukioka, Yasubiro, Lewis Porter, and Yoh-Ichi Hamada. *John Coltrane—A Discography and Musical Biography*. Metuchen, NJ: Scarecrow Press, 1995.

Giddons, Gary. *Celebrating Bird*. New York: Beechtree Books, 1987.

————. *Satchmo*. New York: Anchor Books, 1988.

Gioia, Ted. *The History of Jazz*. New York: Oxford University Press, 1997.

Gitler, Ira. *Swing to Bop*. New York: Oxford University Press, 1985.

Gronow, Pekka, and Ilpo Saunio. *An International History of the Recording Industry*. New York: Cassell, 1999.

Handy, W. C. *Father of the Blues*. New York: Da Capo Press, 1941.

Haskins, James, and Kathleen Benson. *Scott Joplin*. Garden City, NY: Doubleday & Company, 1978.

Hentoff, Nat. *The Jazz Life*. New York: Da Capo Press, 1961.

Hinton, Milt, and David Berger. *Bass Line*. Philadelphia: Temple University Press, 1988.

Korall, Burt. *Drummin' Man*. New York: Schirmer Books, 1990.

Litweiler, John. *The Freedom Principle—Jazz after 1958*. New York: Da Capo Press, 1984.

Lomax, Alan. *Mister Jelly Roll*. New York: Pantheon Books, 1950.

Marquis, Donald. *In Search of Buddy Bolden*. New York: Da Capo Press, 1978.

Milkowski, Bill. *Jaco*. San Francisco: Miller Freeman Books, 1995.

Nicholson, Stuart. *Jazz—The 1980s Resurgence*. New York: Da Capo Press, 1990.

Reisner, Robert, ed. *Bird—The Legend of Charlie Parker*. New York: Da Capo Press, 1962.

Rosenthal, David. *Hard Bop*. New York: Oxford University Press, 1992.

Russell, Ross. *Jazz Styles in Kansas City and the Southwest*. New York: Da Capo Press, 1997.

Schuller, Gunther. *Early Jazz*. New York: Oxford University Press, 1988.

————. *The Swing Era*. New York: Oxford University Press, 1989.

Shaw, Arnold. *52nd Street*. New York: Da Capo Press, 1971.

Silvester, Peter J. *A Left Hand Like God*. New York: Da Capo Press, 1988.

Simon, George T. *The Big Bands*. New York: Collier Books Editions, 1974.

————. *Glenn Miller & His Orchestra*. New York: Da Capo Press, 1974.

Spellman, A.B. *Four Lives in the Bebop Business*. New York: Limelight, 1966.

Stearns, Marshall W. *The Story of Jazz*. New York: Oxford University Press, 1977.

Sudhalter, Richard, Philip Evans, and William Dean Myatt. *Bix—Man and Legend*. New York: Schirmer Books, 1974.

Tucker, Mark, ed. *The Duke Ellington Reader*. New York: Oxford University Press, 1993.

Waldo, Terry. *This Is Ragtime*. New York: Da Capo Press, 1976.

Yanow, Scott. *Jazz on Record—The First Sixty Years*. San Francisco: Backbeat Books, 2003.

Yanow, Scott, Michael Erlewine, Vladimir Bogdanov, and Chris Woodstra, eds. *All Music Guide to Jazz*. San Francisco: Backbeat Books, 1998.

Index

About the Author

SCOTT YANOW has written several books on jazz, including *Jazz on Record: The First Sixty Years* and *Jazz on Film.*